Reading
Sedgwick

identity
Boren: as geometry
Hamilton: atmosphere
Hitchcock: composition

of identification (in focus for introspection), Moda as object of active desire: she wished...

identity determined by what is available for identification

cross-identification that uses the other as a conduit for transforming (understanding of) the self. This is different from identification as mimicry, reflection: by offering a particular scene for cross identification, art "changes one."

A series edited by
Lauren Berlant and
Lee Edelman

Reading
Sedgwick

LAUREN BERLANT, EDITOR

DUKE UNIVERSITY PRESS · DURHAM AND LONDON · 2019

Designed by Amy Ruth Buchanan
Typeset in Arno Pro by Westchester
Publishing Services

Library of Congress Cataloging-in-
Publication Data
Names: Berlant, Lauren Gail, [date] editor.
Title: Reading Sedgwick / Lauren Berlant, ed.
Description: Durham : Duke University Press,
2019. | Series: Theory Q |
Includes bibliographical references and index.
Identifiers: LCCN 2019002425 (print) |
LCCN 2019009531 (ebook)
ISBN 9781478005339 (ebook)
ISBN 9781478005001 (hardcover : alk. paper)
ISBN 9781478006312 (pbk. : alk. paper)
Subjects: LCSH: Sedgwick, Eve Kosofsky—
Criticism and interpretation. |
Homosexuality and literature—History—
20th century. | Gays' writings—History and
criticism—Theory, etc.
Classification: LCC PS3569.E316 (ebook) |
LCC PS3569.E316 Z943 2019 (print) |
DDC 818/.5409—dc23
LC record available at
https://lccn.loc.gov/2019002425

"Eve's Triangles, or Queer Studies
beside Itself," was originally published
in *differences* 26, no. 1, pp. 48–73.
© 2015, Brown University and *differences:
A Journal of Feminist Cultural Studies*,
published by Duke University Press.

"Race, Sex, and the Incommensurate,"
by José Esteban Muñoz, was originally
published in *Queer Futures: Reconsidering Ethics, Activism, and the Political*,
edited by Elahe Haschemi Yekani,
Eveline Kilian, and Beatrice Michaelis.
© 2013, Routledge, reproduced by
permission of Taylor and Francis
Books UK.

WE GRATEFULLY ACKNOWLEDGE
THE SUPPORT OF THE SEDGWICK
FOUNDATION IN MAKING THIS
PROJECT POSSIBLE.

Cover art: Eve Kosofsky Sedgwick,
*Tender winds above the snow melt many
kinds of suffering*, ca. 2002. Cyanotype,
stencil, rubber stamp, and sumanigashi
on silk. Photograph by Kevin Ryan.
Collection of Eve Kosofsky Sedgwick
Foundation. © Eve Kosofsky Sedgwick
Foundation.

Contents

Reading Sedgwick, Then and Now

THEN

This book calls up multiple pasts that are not past. Originally, the independent scholar Michael O'Rourke solicited many of these essays for a volume that was going to bear the title *Reading Eve Kosofsky Sedgwick: Gender, Sexuality, Embodiment*. Most of them were first presented as talks at conference memorials to Sedgwick's person, art, and work, providing fresh critical and intimate reflections on the relation among her modes of being herself for her friends, students, colleagues, and for criticism, which meant taking on and addressing her style, her concepts, her fierce and creative modes of political resistance, her intricate, explosive readings, and her strong pedagogies.

As the essays in what is now *Reading Sedgwick* have gone through their final revisions, they honor the occasion of Eve's life and work by moving the status of "occasional writing" to something worthy of a queer respect. Sedgwick herself exemplified how all situational writing from specific historical moments—that might have felt more personal, as in "White Glasses," or collectively held, as in "Interlude, Pedagogic"—insisted on a slowed-down and amplifying attention.[1] The very wobble among styles that the chapters in this volume perform is itself a pedagogy of openness to the possibility that one might learn as much or more from the loose as from the tight, the sparely referential to the meticulously researched piece. Authors have made individual decisions about retaining and erasing traces of their origins as talks, or as memorials. But the presence of their situatedness adds up, making them more striking with the vibrancy and variety of their use of reenactment, repetition, copying, echoing, mirroring, projecting, and imitating something to be found in or around Eve. She emanates a unique and powerful affective-critical compositional charisma. Critics turn to modes of memoir, reading, re-theorizing, and generative conceptualization. That is, if many of the essays in this volume display a strong mimetic drive to be with Eve by being like Eve, "being like" has come to mean a variety of things to a variety of thinkers, and what follows in this volume demonstrates a significant formal and epistemological heterogeneity. These essays are at once personal and attentive to the world, paying homage and queering homage, extending Eve's implication into places Eve can't be. From the start, the volume promised to amplify the impacts of Eve's work but always, inevitably, "she" appears in facets—one might even say taxonomically—through the quirky transference of her reader-heirs. This means that there's a style of being on the page and being with concepts that comes to resonate across many chapters as the many phases of Eve.

Eventually, Michael O'Rourke handed this project to me as an editor of Theory Q, and Lee Edelman and I are delighted to bring it forward in tribute to his hard work and to the legacy of Series Q, which preceded us in time and alphabet. Editing, along with her writing and teaching, also provided a major part of Eve's literary, historical, and theoretical impact, as any readers of her anthology *Novel Gazing* would attest.[2] So many kinds of collaboration were generated by Eve—but I would like to emphasize here the world-shifting impact of her collaborative work with her other editors, Michele Barale, Jonathan Goldberg, and Michael Moon, in Series Q. What a thrill it was to be included in their vision of what queer scholarship could do.

Which remains a centrally queer question. As Ramzi Fawaz's introduction makes clear, the issue of attachment to someone known only through her writing poses different problems and makes possible different modes of reading from those available to those of us for whom Eve was a living presence at very specific historical conjunctures. How can Eve live for a generation of scholars who can assume queerness, paradoxically, as a theoretical field from the beginning of their careers?

For those of us who were Eve's contemporaries, the questions are different. How do we make our attachment to a quality or practice in Eve available to a public that wasn't there at the time? What story do we tell to make the project and her specific angles on it vibrate in unpredicted or alien worlds? Or when we are querying what it was that pulled us into the perceptual universe of Eve's work, how do we continue the project of coming to terms with what we can't specifically have asked for, the shocking impact of the radical reframing, stylistic challenge, theoretical elaboration, historical materialism, mode of focus and attention, and genre lability that mark what it meant, and still means, to be writing with Eve not just on, but in, our minds?

In her introduction to *Tendencies*, Sedgwick calls out the murderousness of the Reaganite neoconservative consensus that made indifference and demonization the twin engines of a politics that brought open expression of genocidal antigay fantasies into mainstream discourse.[3] She tracks the logic by which appeals to a widespread popular homophobia, which would work in conjunction with a pervasive white supremacy and antifeminism, emerged in the 1980s as the weapon of choice to fan the flames of a culture war. The culture war was, of course, never only about "lifestyles" and hierarchies of social belonging. It also was a weapon and smokescreen to allow for and distract from the ultimate goal of dismantling civil rights and the Great Society, among other US systems with tendencies toward progressive taxation, economic equality, and social opportunity.

Especially in the case of those populations metonymically linked to AIDS, the rapidity and nakedness of the slippage from a routinized homophobic aversion to a viscerally enjoyable, and strategically valuable, incitement to violence and hatred lent renewed urgency to the epistemological questions that Eve had examined in *Between Men* and *The Epistemology of the Closet*.[4] But it also alerted her to the necessity of engaging the affective consequences of cultural abjection, humiliation, illness, and political hopelessness. Toting up the numerous ways in which government action and inaction alike seemed focused on the self-destruction of queer youth, she aligned her project in *Tendencies* with the opening of alternative, queer-empowering worlds through modes of thought intended not simply to encourage, but also to enact, political resistance.

When Eve died in April 2009, Barack Obama was in the White House, and many in America wanted to imagine that more than just the tide had turned: perhaps a few pages had been turned, as well. There was the ludicrous millisecond of the postracism fantasy. Then *Bowers v. Hardwick*, the US Supreme Court decision about which Sedgwick wrote so acerbically in *Epistemology of the Closet*, was reversed by *Lawrence v. Texas* in 2003; in the following year, gay marriage, the unexpected wedge issue in the normalization of gay and lesbian life, was legalized in Massachusetts, and the push elsewhere to enshrine the marital privilege of heterosexuals in state constitutions would work, paradoxically, to nationalize that issue and lead to the Supreme Court's affirmation of the right to marriage as a question of "dignity" for lesbians and gay men. At the same time, and without necessarily thinking that the antihomophobic project of Sedgwick's work was superseded, US academics turned their attention to other aspects of Eve: in particular, to the reparative aspiration expressed by her interest in affect—in Silvan Tomkins and Melanie Klein—and to the Buddhist metempsychoses of her later years.[5]

The introduction of "reparativity" as the name for a new critical attitude has been variously traced through the present moment of "post-critique," but clearly the essay "Paranoid Reading and Reparative Reading; or, You're So Paranoid, You Probably Think This Introduction Is about You," from *Novel Gazing*, was its splashiest referent.[6] Much that follows in this volume turns from the need to fine-tune, intensify, and elaborate the negativity of queer critique toward the ethical pressure to figure out repair in the face of intensifying world disrepair. I won't rehearse those arguments here; I will just note that the political moment of the Reaganite culture wars, with the intimate public of white patriarchy claiming its exposure to vulnerability as a traumatic injury, returns with a vengeance now. The undisguised homo-hatred endorsed in the '80s, in political rhetoric as well as in regulatory and funding decisions, now expands into explicit neo-Nazi and white-supremacist pronouncements from the White House itself. The non-mattering of black lives no longer hides its death-driven carceral lens under white liberal sentimental veneers; nor does hatred of nonmarital sexuality and non-normative genders. Official policy on immigration is determined by a president who can declare that all Haitian immigrants have AIDS. The contemporary state not only enjoys but explicitly promotes discrimination—not only as policy but as a constitutional and affective right.

This current iteration of the reactionary turn puts renewed pressure on the tools of our critical analyses and disturbs the textures of our objects. And it makes the Eve who diagnosed the "then" even more newly necessary in the emerging and solidifying "now." The essays that follow were not shaped by the scene of accelerated austerity, populist racism, and xenophobia from within which I now write. But they model how to use an object—Eve Sedgwick's life, work, friendship, style, concepts—to counter the aggressively bad lifeworld contexts infusing our own, to build alternative attachments within them, to resist the redefinition manias of hegemonic power that destabilize our emerging alliances, and to revitalize political and epistemological struggle. We turn to reinterpret, once again, "the personal is political." In constructing a legacy in the wake of loss and in conceptualizing the work of appreciation and grief and what can follow from their bond, these essays offer ways to occupy these dark times not only with anger, depression, and exhaustion, but also with inventiveness, reimagined collectivity, intellectual energy, persistent curiosity, and fierce—the warmest and fiercest; the Sedgwickiest—attention.

NOTES

1 Eve Kosofsky Sedgwick, "White Glasses," in Eve Kosofsky Sedgwick, *Tendencies* (Durham, NC: Duke University Press, 1993), 252–66; Eve Kosofsky Sedgwick, "Interlude, Pedagogic," in Eve Kosofsky Sedgwick, *Touching Feeling: Affect, Pedagogy, Performativity* (Durham, NC: Duke University Press, 2003), 27–34.

2 Eve Kosofsky Sedgwick, "Paranoid Reading and Reparative Reading; or, You're So Paranoid You Probably Think This Introduction Is about You," in *Novel Gazing: Queer Readings in Fiction*, ed. Eve Kosofsky Sedgwick (Durham, NC: Duke University Press, 1997), 1–37.

3 Sedgwick, *Tendencies*.

4 Eve Kosofsky Sedgwick, *Between Men: English Literature and Male Homosocial Desire* (New York: Columbia University Press, [1985] 1993); Eve Kosofsky Sedgwick, *Epistemology of the Closet* (Berkeley: University of California Press, 2008).

5 Eve Kosofsky Sedgwick and Adam Frank, "Shame in the Cybernetic Fold: Reading Silvan Tomkins," *Critical Inquiry* 21, no. 2 (Winter 1995): 496–522; Sedgwick, "Paranoid Reading and Reparative Reading"; Eve Kosofsky Sedgwick, "Melanie Klein and the Difference Affect Makes," *South Atlantic Quarterly* 106, no. 3 (Summer 2007): 624–42.

6 Sedgwick, "Paranoid Reading and Reparative Reading."

"An Open Mesh of Possibilities"
The Necessity of Eve Sedgwick in Dark Times

I think everyone who does queer studies considers Eve Sedgwick one of the, if not *the*, most important theorists of heterogeneity in the twentieth and twenty-first centuries. Across the arc of her prodigious and ceaselessly fruitful oeuvre, Sedgwick obsessively pursued a project of generating rich accounts and interpretations of *human multiplicity*. While she was famous for her axiomatic pronouncement, "People are different from each other,"[1] this statement simply articulated a base-level condition of possibility for her much larger critical aim: to understand at the most expansive conceptual scale how our exceptionally diverse range of affective and material responses to one another's differences constantly run up against culture-wide ways of knowing (or willful *unknowing*) the self and others that, sometimes banally but oftentimes murderously, reduce the complexity of those differences and foreclose countless other ways to apprehend and negotiate them. Early in her field-defining monograph *Epistemology of the Closet*, she would enumerate precisely this problematic:

> Historically, the framing of *Epistemology of the Closet* begins with a puzzle. It is a rather amazing fact that, of the very many dimensions along which the genital activity of one person can be differentiated from that of another (dimensions that include preference for certain acts, certain zones or sensations, certain physical types, a certain frequency, certain symbolic investments, certain relations of age or power, a certain species . . . etc. etc. etc.) precisely one, the gender of object choice, emerged from the turn of the century, and has remained, as *the* dimension denoted by the now ubiquitous category of "sexual orientation."[2]

While in Sedgwick's most virtuosic early publications she precisely identified and schematized cultural logics (most notably, "the closet") that flatten, simplify, ossify, or refuse outright to deal with human differences, in her methods of analysis, her stylistic approach to writing (commonly associated with some of the most breathtakingly superlative yet incandescent prose in modern critical and cultural theory), and her affective orientation to her objects of study, she modeled ways to revivify the reality of heterogeneity not merely as the fact that "people are different from each other," but as a study of what people *do* with those differences. Her work achieves its most stunning heights of intellectual and political force in those moments when she quite literally clears space on the page for transparently naming, playfully taxonomizing, cognitively conceiving, imaginatively rearranging, identifying across, and theorizing the relationship between a seemingly endless range of differences and the identities they underwrite—not only those of race, class, sexuality, and gender ("only four?!" she might say) but also of temperament, body shape, intellectual skill or aptitude, age, life experience, political investment, nationality, spiritual worldview, etc. etc. etc. In *Epistemology*, she would state with exasperation: "It is astonishing how few respectable conceptual tools we have for dealing with [the] self-evident fact" that there are many kinds of people in the world.[3]

Sedgwick sought to grasp how the multiplicity of differentials in embodiment and identity that distinguish any two people also paradoxically provide the ground for, while also being an effect of, the equally multiplicitous attachments we develop with other bodies, objects, affects, experiences, ideas, textures, and particular kinds of erotic and social relationships. She found it endlessly fascinating and exhilarating how the seemingly infinite array of differences between any two people, or *many different kinds* of people, neither diminished the capacity, or potential desire, for relations of exchange and attachment across those differences nor mitigate even slightly the equally manifold ways that people are also very much alike. In other words, as the title of one her most beloved volumes attests, she was a theorist of *tendencies*, of the ways in which *what* we tend toward, invest in, feel affinity with, obsess over, attach ourselves to, and help nourish shapes and reshapes not only our sense of self but our ethical relationship to the world at large.

It is perhaps no surprise that this particular cluster of questions was for Sedgwick not merely an arena of disinterested intellectual inquiry or cool philosophical contemplation but, rather, the very ground for elaborating an explicitly politicized ethical stance toward the experience of *tending* toward, where tending captures the double sense of leaning or reaching toward something while cultivating and helping it thrive. In that collection of essays, she would write: "I think that for many of us in childhood the ability to attach intently to a few cultural objects, objects of high or popular culture or both, objects whose meanings seemed mysterious, excessive, or oblique in relation to the codes most readily available to us, became a prime resource for survival. We needed for there to be sites where the meanings didn't line up tidily with each other, and we learned to invest those sites with fascination and love."[4] Sedgwick repeatedly enjoins us to acknowledge that if we tend toward something, if we feel affinity to it, if we wish to help it flourish, then this relation of tending is itself something of ethical value that should be not only studied but actively developed as an affective orientation or stance for future contacts.

This is perhaps why she was so deeply drawn to the emergent field of queer studies, as it was arguably the first arena of humanistic inquiry to take seriously the public and political dimensions of erotic and affective desire, intimacy, attachment, and kinship; it is a theory, in short, of what we tend toward. Sedgwick pursued and honed methods of analysis that passionately make room for cultivating those forms of tending (such as same-sex desire and familial bonds outside blood relations) that are most devalued and violently prohibited in our culture while at every turn working to jam up, denature, unhinge, or unravel the very logics of prohibition, devaluation, and unknowing that so powerfully direct us all to *tend in the same way*.

Despite the fact that Sedgwick spent most of her career exfoliating the erotic, emotional, gendered, relational, and political logics of a very particular, often canonical (some might even say rarefied) set of late nineteenth-century Euro-American texts, among which the work of Henry James and Marcel Proust stand paramount (with occasional forays into Jane Austen, Willa Cather, Buddhism, Silvan Tomkins, and Shakespeare, to name a few), she masterfully used this set of works to make vast, compelling, transformative claims about the nature of affinities across difference in Western culture. In her commitment to these texts, she acknowledged, both explicitly and implicitly, her own tendencies toward the particular kinds of narratives, social types, relational conflicts and arrangements, and affective projects that drew her back, over and over, to certain objects, questions, and cultural patterns. She was obsessed with the literary production and biographies of a small cadre of (very) queer white male authors of the Euro-American nineteenth century; she cross-identified as a gay man, often through her self-proclaimed embodied experiences as a Jewish, fat, woman intellectual; and as part of this identification, she claimed intense, abiding love relationships with a range of gay male colleagues and friends. She was fascinated by vulnerability of many sorts—by the way people are made vulnerable to one another through physical illness and aging, desire (requited or not), loneliness and emotional need—and by our various modes of identifying, which make us susceptible to a range of intensely volatile emotions, from the pain of rejection and loss to the overwhelming deluge of love and infatuation; and she really, really, *really* didn't like those sites in our culture where meanings are supposed to "line up perfectly with each other" or "everything" is supposed to "mean the same thing!"[5] For a scholar who often presented her arguments in a linguistic and conceptual architecture so stunningly rigorous that it could appear like the Eiffel Tower of critical scholarship, she is a surprisingly open book: read her essays, and you get what she's all about. She is, in this way, a scholar of her own tendencies who brings us into contact with her highly particular psychic and intellectual attachments not so that we may leave knowing more about her (although we certainly do, sometimes uncomfortably so), but so we may have cognitive tools for grappling with the very discursive conditions that enable or foreclose our own ways of tending toward some things and not others. She wants us to leave her writing understanding that what we tend toward may also be an avenue to a vast range of questions, potential relationships, or ways of knowing and being we have yet to fully grasp but still might, with world-transformative results.

If it is difficult to describe Sedgwick's theoretical legacy in a svelte or pithy formulation, it is perhaps because, unlike the many iconic theorists with whom she engaged as beloved and sometimes agonistic interlocutors (Michel Foucault, Sigmund Freud, Jacques Derrida, Melanie Klein, Silvan Tomkins, and Barbara Johnson, to name a few), Sedgwick claimed no steadfast allegiance to any single theoretical lineage or method (moving with dazzling alacrity among deconstructive, Foucauldian, feminist, psychoanalytic, and queer theoretical formulations, depending on the breadth of their explanatory force in any given query) and consistently produced critical interpretations of culture that refuse to congeal into a once-and-for-all, transhistorical explanation for any given aesthetic, social, or political phenomenon or text. If there is a broad trend (or, more appropriately, *tendency*) that one might track across the arc of her writing, it may be a general move from an exploration of the structuring logics of same-sex desire—captured in the elegant polygons of the homosocial triangles of *Between Men*,[6] as well as in the four-square double bind of the minoritizing/universalizing—gender transitive/gender separatist logics of homo/hetero definition mapped so magisterially in *Epistemology of the Closet*—to an abiding interest in theories of affective multiplicity, such as Silvan Tomkins's affect system or Buddhism's nondualistic approach to knowing, that can account for a vastly expanded set of relationships, identities, feelings, and desires that fall outside the stultifying logics she traces in her earlier writing. This shift is not, as it might appear at first glance, a simple reversal of priorities or interests. It is not so much that Sedgwick begins as a structuralist and ends as a poststructuralist (in fact, she does not have any truck with adjudicating the "rightness" of either of these well-worn theoretical lineages, instead showing far more keenness for their distinct utility as explanatory heuristics in particular instances). Rather, she begins by studying the logics that contain or delimit the variability and unpredictability of meaning that can attach to erotic and social relations (and the numerous anxieties that attend the discursive failure to do so) and moves increasingly toward a fascination for, and desire to expand, the many theories that name and encourage the *proliferation* of meanings and attachments that can never quite adequately be contained, fixed, delimited, or once and for all snuffed out by any structure, any logic, any prohibition. In both inquiries, her adherence to the *value* of multiplicity, regardless of whether it is under duress or made to flourish, is the same.

Sedgwick, then, does not confer on us a fully formed theory of her own but a theoretical *position*, stance, or orientation from which to conduct inquiry. I like to think of it, using her classic term, as an axiom or cluster of axioms: in place of a universal theory, structure, or model for analysis, Sedgwick offers us operating procedures to think with and live by. One effect of her orientation is a promiscuous attachment to many theories, and many identities, in the formulation of one's queries of the world and of how one goes about answering the questions that keep one up at night. "As a general principal," she would claim, "I don't like the idea of 'applying' theoretical models to particular situations or texts—it's always more interesting when the pressure of application goes in both directions."[7] The world, she suggests, is full of compelling theories, and more can and should be produced. What it is deficient in are the ethical, affective, and political orientations required to make those theories have a palpable, materially nourishing, or transformative effect on our daily lives.

In this introduction, I aim to render a picture—sharp in its contours yet expansive and open-ended in its concept and content—of Sedgwick's intellectual legacy as a conferral of a particular kind of orientation or mode of approach to the world that she transmits to her readers through the very particularity of her own intellectual and affective tendencies. In other words, I want to give shape to Sedgwick as a particular kind of formation—like a snowflake (aren't we all now?) whose utter distinctness still tells us something about the nature of all other snowflakes, even if it is only that they are all distinct—that has bestowed critical tools, which we might still access, and ones that frankly we *need more than ever* to survive and thrive amid the social and political realities of our time. My main headings are:

Sedgwick is a *particularist with a heart for the universal.*
Sedgwick is a theorist of *multiplicity.*
Sedgwick is a proponent of *cross-identification.*
Sedgwick is a *stylist.*
Sedgwick is an *affective curator.*

SEDGWICK IS A PARTICULARIST WITH A HEART FOR THE UNIVERSAL

Sedgwick's oeuvre is enchanting, or elicits wonder, in part, because of the breathtaking specificity, nuance, detail, precision, and pointedness of her analytical capacities. But even more so because of the way she can, in one magnificent phrase or conceptual leap, scale upward from the stultifying ideological grind of a well-worn binarism in Melville, or the affective work of a particular character type in the work of Henry James, or the recurrent juxtaposition of a particular set of terms in the work of Judith Butler to the most pressing, wide-reaching, world-significant questions or problems of our time. She is a theorist of the particular par excellence. Her work grounds us repeatedly in the specificities of her identity and her historical moment; the influence of the institutions at which she teaches and conducts research; the specificity of distinct texts, characters, or turns of phrase as they appear across time; the fine nuances among varied arguments, positions, or ideologies; and, most pressingly, the particularities of embodied and cultural differences.

Yet if there is any recurrent pattern in Sedgwick's argumentative logic, it is her oscillation between the highly specifying gesture—often accomplished in her naming a fine distinction, homing in on a particular rhetorical gambit, or providing an anecdote of a personal experience—and the sweeping universalizing gesture by which she hypothesizes a large-scale phenomenon as either causally or simply significantly linked to the pointed detail to which she has brought our attention. Consider the epic conclusion to her spellbinding reading of Melville's novella *Billy Budd.* Analyzing this very particular early twentieth-century text, which closes with the ignominious deaths of three implicitly queer men, she radically scales upward from the specificity of this plot trajectory to claim:

> In our culture as in *Billy Budd*, the phobic narrative trajectory toward imagining a time after the homosexual is finally inseparable from that toward imagining a time after the human; in the wake of the homosexual, the wake incessantly produced since first there were homosexuals, every human relation is pulled into its shining representational furrow. . . . One of the many dangerous ways that AIDS discourse seems to ratify and amplify pre-inscribed homophobic mythologies is in its pseudo-evolutionary presentation of male homosexuality as a stage doomed to extinction (read, a phase the species is going through) on the enormous scale of whole populations.[8]

Here, as in all her work, Sedgwick demands that we read the particularity of any given text in relation to large-scale, seemingly universal phenomena and ideological formations—for, after all, the plots of our dearest fictions are *of the world*, not outside or beyond it. A plot that concludes with the eradication of every visibly queer life given shape in the previous narrative, she argues, cannot but materialize an extant fantasy of "a world after the homosexual" and, by extension, of humanity itself, since the society recurrently presumes that anyone and everyone could potentially be secretly, terribly gay.

One effect of this rhetorical and conceptual practice is to make visible the stakes of even the most seemingly aesthetically rarefied rhetorical gestures, accepted modes of argumentation, or taken-for-granted theoretical assumptions we hold so dear: it is in these specific formulations of canonical literary productions, Sedgwick would have us realize, that some of the farthest-reaching structures of Western civilization are played out, given particularity, and made to infiltrate our imagination. But rather than pitting the particular and universal against each other or seeing one as a conceptual starting point that leads to the other, she simply sees both as ways to understand the world, ways to know, that grant insights as much as occlude them. We should inhabit, and see from, both positions, Sedgwick tells us, not only because it is a more generous way to open oneself up to multiple ways of knowing, but because, in truth, we cannot do anything else, since our very sense of self depends on our ability to scale constantly between our individual selves and the collective reality of inhabiting a world with others that is far wider in scope than the limits of our skin.

As she movingly states, "As gay community and the solidarity and visibility of gays as a minority population are being consolidated and tempered in the forge of this specularized terror and suffering, how can it fail to be all the more necessary that the avenues of recognition, desire, and thought between minority potentials and universalizing ones be opened and opened and opened?"[9] In other words, in a world that wants us dead, should we not develop as many stories as possible about our identities as queers to flood the world with our existence? Shouldn't we embrace narratives about our particularity, individuality, and specificity as much as stories about what we essentially share with all human beings (and many others)? Neither kind of story has to be "true" in an unequivocal sense; rather, they can sit productively "beside" each other as different ways of knowing and being queer.

Among Sedgwick's favorite universalizing claims: "I think everyone who does gay and lesbian studies is haunted by the suicides of adolescents"; "I think that for many of us in childhood the ability to attach intently to a few cultural objects . . . became a prime resource for survival"; "Something about queer is inextinguishable"; "A hypothesis worth making explicit: there are important senses in which 'queer' can signify *only when attached to the first person*"; and, perhaps most famous, "This book will argue that an understanding of virtually any aspect of modern Western culture must be, not merely incomplete, but damaged in its central substance to the degree that it does not incorporate a critical analysis of modern homo/heterosexual definition."[10] I say that Sedgwick *has a heart* for the universal, then, because she sees it is a contingent and hence intellectually imaginative space where, even if for a moment, we posit something widely shared among us so that we can create a sense of collective reality and belonging, and where we might offer alternative universals to the existing ones proffered by liberal society that delimit our capacity to be otherwise.

Because of this, and as some of the preceding examples explicitly indicate, for Sedgwick the universal is primarily a space for hypothesizing, for making conjectures about what is going on around us, what is tending to happen, despite our many differences. Precisely because we are all so different from one another, Sedgwick repeatedly suggests, we can never know in advance just how widely certain commonalities, shared experiences, or frames of reference might extend across and between individuals, communities, or perhaps even the entirety of the human race. Remaining agnostic about such a question allows Sedgwick to reach for the universal in her own argumentation and analyze various instances of its deployment (both pernicious and benevolent) in our culture, without delimiting in advance what we might learn from it. When she opens *Epistemology of the Closet* with the line, "[I] am trying to make the strongest possible introductory case for a hypothesis about the centrality of

this nominally marginal, conceptually intractable set of [homo/hetero] definitional issues to the important knowledges and understandings of twentieth-
century Western culture as a whole," she is (1) performatively bringing into
being the very centrality of such questions "to Western culture as a whole,"
and by extension humanistic inquiry, simply by naming them as such; (2) offering a logical supposition about just how far such issues might reach into
a culture that attaches, as a dictum, one form of homo/hetero identity onto
every single subject in existence; and (3) inviting others to expand, contest,
specify, query, or confirm that claim.

To hypothesize or articulate a universal claim is to invite, almost instan-
taneously, criticism of its limitations, attempts to fine-tune its suppositions,
or projects to abolish it altogether (or replace it with another universal).
Sedgwick aims to elicit such responses, particularly from other scholars who
might help her to further define what a field such as queer theory might have
to say about literature, politics, human relationships, community formation,
the state, imperialism, or whatever. Her work is always inviting a counterresponse, a particular, *other* claim to specify her grand sweeping one, rather
than defensively shoring up any given position she herself chooses to take.
"The meaning, the legitimacy, and in many ways even the possibility for good
faith of the positings this book makes," she states in *Epistemology of the Closet*,
"depend radically on the production, by *other* antihomophobic readers who
may be very differently situated, of the widest possible range of *other* and even
contradictory availabilities."[11] We might say that rather than producing fixed
universals, Sedgwick liked to think "universal-*ly*"; to include as much of the
world, or a given "social ecology," as she could in any single claim, without
losing its coherence or meaning, while making that structure of thought available for others to reconstruct in new and unexpected ways. Consider that the
introduction to her single most famous and widely taught monograph, *Epistemology of the Closet*, is titled "Axiomatic." If an axiom offers up a moral dictum,
law, or rule of thumb—a statement about universal operating principles—to
be *axiomatic* is to take an orientation or position willing to entertain universals, or wide-reaching procedures of thought and action, but only in spirit and
not necessarily always in one way.

SEDGWICK IS A THEORIST OF MULTIPLICITY

Under the rule that privileges the most obvious: Sedgwick loves to "pluralize
and specify"; to "make certain specific kinds of readings and interrogations . . .

available in heuristically powerful . . . forms for other readers"; to "keep our understandings of gay origins . . . plural [and] multi-capillaried"; to think in ways that tend "across genders, across sexualities, across genres, across 'perversions'"; to think in "multiply transitive ways"; "to disarticulate" seemingly fixed hierarchies of relationality (the family for instance) or desire; to "invoke the art of *loosing*" or releasing our firm grip on "life, loves, and ideas" so that they may "sit freely in the palm of our open hand"; to think "beside" and to "include, include" wherever possible; alternatively, she hates when everything comes to seem as though it "means the same thing!"[12] Despite its own multiplicity and range, Sedgwick's oeuvre can be understood collectively to forward a sustained project of mapping, and making room for grappling with, multiplicities—of human bodies and identities, of affective orientations and desires, of ideas and methods of analysis, of meanings and practices—and their infinite combinations.

This is gorgeously rendered in her expansive definition of the most central term of queer studies:

> What's striking is the number and difference of the dimensions that "sexual identity" is supposed to organize into a seamless and univocal whole. And if it doesn't? That's one of the things that "queer" can refer to: the open mesh of possibilities, gaps, overlaps, dissonances and resonances, lapses and excesses of meaning when the constituent elements of anyone's gender, of anyone's sexuality aren't made (or can't be made) to signify monolithically. The experimental, linguistic, epistemological, representational, political adventures attaching to the very many of us who may at times be moved to describe ourselves as (among many other possibilities) pushy femmes, radical faeries, fantacists, drags, clones, leather folk, ladies in tuxedoes, feminist women or feminist men, masturbators, bulldaggers, divas, Snap! Queens, butch bottoms, storytellers, transsexuals, aunties, wannabes, lesbian identified men or lesbians who sleep with men, or . . . people able to relish, learn from, or identify with such.[13]

I have written elsewhere about this passage that "Sedgwick's understanding of queerness is expansive and elastic, an orientation from which to articulate multiplicitous identities and desires that do not fit into the schema of heterosexual normativity; yet it is also committed to endless specificity and distinction within a broad frame of reference, attending to the fact 'that people are different from each other.'"[14] At first glance, Sedgwick's reference to an open mesh of possibilities may strike one as odd, if not wholly oxymoronic:

if a mesh describes a tightly bound weave, how can it be open? It is this very formulation—whereby an interconnected network of relations is also understood as expansive and elastic—that defines Sedgwick's canny framing of human multiplicity as that which binds us together while also distinguishing us and requiring affective openness to that "self-evident" fact. For us to be bound together by difference does not necessitate that those differences, or that experience of being linked, must mean or signify in the same way.

As the passage quoted earlier attests, one of the most visible and beloved practices for "cherishing" multiplicity that Sedgwick has in her rhetorical arsenal is *the list*. Listing is a common practice in Sedgwick's work, whether as a nonce-taxonomy that specifies particulars within a broader overarching category; a naming of various elements that make up a single idea, concept, or ideology; or a numerical breakdown of the multiple meanings that spin off from a single phrase or rhetorical gesture. As I discuss later, Sedgwick is also enamored of long chains of adjectives and adverbs that function *as* lists, that modify, complicate, extend, "deform," resignify, or sharpen terms that have come to be taken for granted. This is one of the senses in which I will later describe her a stylist: she fundamentally believes that the formal arrangement of language can stylistically model, and sometimes performatively bring into being or affectively invest, the reality of human multiplicity.

It is rare to come across a page in any Sedgwick essay that does not have one or another form of a list, as an open-ended sequential format (one might venture to say, an "open mesh of possibilities") for expanding or extending a series of ideas. Most often, Sedgwick produces a list to take a seemingly solid, univocal, or monolithically understood concept, term, or operating principle (e.g., the family, sexual identity, the closet) and explicitly reassert its underlying plurality. Consider, for instance, her tour de force deconstruction of "Christmas Effects," a phrase she uses in her introduction to *Tendencies* to describe that season of the year when "[t]hey all—religion, state, capital, ideology, domesticity, the discourses of power and legitimacy—line up with each other so neatly" to impose a grid of family-oriented consumerism and worship on nearly everyone.[15] Here, she brilliantly fragments that seemingly unified monolith of "the family" by providing a list of all of the unruly things that the term attempts to contain: "a surname, a sexual dyad, a legal unit based on state-regulated marriage, a circuit of blood relations, a system of companionship and succor, a building . . . , an economic unit of earning and taxation . . . , a mechanism to produce, care for, and acculturate children . . . and of course the list could go on."[16] The list functions not only to disperse or fragment the very notion of the family but also, in its formal multiplicity, to remind us of plurality *as such*—that is, as a fundamental fact of human existence. It is so easy to forget this fact, Sedgwick suggests, that lists can shake us out of our complacency, reminding us that most things are, in fact, *many things*. One consequence of this move is that Sedgwick's list makes it easier to "disarticulate . . . the bonds of blood, of law, of habitation, of privacy, of companionship and succor . . . from the lockstep of their unanimity in the system called 'family.'"[17]

Fittingly for a scholar whose career-long interest in performative acts shaped nearly every research question she pursued, lists function for Sedgwick precisely performatively: in its literal elaboration on the page a list rhetorically and formally brings into being the very idea of multiplicity that Sedgwick is aiming to capture. Under Sedgwick's deft rendering, lists (1) account for multiple things (ideas, positions, desires, categories, objects, meanings); (2) acknowledge the existence of that which is listed (for instance, Sedgwick repeatedly uses lists to elaborate or give name to desires, pleasures, and fantasies that commonly go unrecognized or wholly ignored by dominant regimes of sexuality); (3) encourage potential addition and hence carry a spirit of inclusion (they are, after all, serial in nature and practically beg for further elaboration—who can read that sexy, ribald list of queer figures, among whom are leather folk, Snap! Queens, butch bottoms, divas, and masturbators, and not want to name and include themselves or their friends?); (4) encourage comparison (each time we read a list related to identity or desire, for example, we are moved to ask, "Do I see myself in this list? How would my inclusion shift the terms, add something, or rearrange the organization?"); and (5) elicit the deployment of multiple frames of reference to comprehend and do something with the items enumerated. Every list, after all, produces a series of objects or ideas that demand more than one way to comprehend them, and in this way a list not only catalogues the actual material fact of multiplicity but elicits multiplicitous reading practices.

On a more immediately visceral level, Sedgwick's lists are a way to do justice to the dead and counter the culture's genocidal "desire that gay people *not be.*"[18] Lists like the one quoted earlier, which fabulously unfolds the manifold styles and sexual and erotic identities of queer culture, also implicitly reference the countless queer lives lost to AIDS. As Sedgwick makes clear in her introduction to *Epistemology of the Closet*, to account for fine human distinctions and multiplicitous identifications is not only a universally ethical project, but for those living through the AIDS epidemic, it is an urgent psychic necessity to keep the specificity of particular friends, lovers, family members, artists, companions, and neighbors vividly alive even past their literal deaths.[19] For Sedgwick, then, lists are one way to reparatively confer plenitude on an event of mass diminishment: they have the potential to revivify the complexity and richness of queer life in the face of the flattening abyss that mainstream culture simply calls "AIDS deaths."

SEDGWICK IS A PROPONENT OF CROSS-IDENTIFICATION

Perhaps no form of multiplicity captivated Sedgwick's imagination, and efforts to grasp, more than the promiscuousness of identification. Across the arc of her work, Sedgwick devoted an extraordinary amount of intellectual energy to understanding the modes, mechanisms, and consequences of people's highly refined ways of knowing, identifying with, relating to, and touching others (both figuratively and literally), despite—or, perhaps, precisely because of—their differences. It is now nearly a cliché to recount that Sedgwick herself promiscuously identified with gay male identity, going so far as to mark herself *as* a gay man and narrating a number of deeply intimate, psychically charged investments in gay male friends who were often also her colleagues and students. This social reality mirrored her intellectual fascination with the discursive production of gay male subjectivity in late nineteenth- and twentieth-century Anglo-American culture, which she often described as an ongoing intellectual and political project to forward an explicitly antihomophobic theory.

Put bluntly, Sedgwick often perceived her work as an attempt to bring into being the very kinds of antihomophobic sentiments that might make the lives of her closest friends more livable and humane. Consequently, we can see that Sedgwick perceived cross-identification as both an inevitable fact of coming into contact with other human beings with whom one might share any number of meaningful experiences and a necessary and ongoing practice of ethical caring for others. This is bracingly evident in her essay "White Glasses," in which she explores the generative, even if sometimes eerie, consequences of her identification with her friend and colleague Michael Lynch:

> From Michael I also seem always to hear the injunction . . . "Include, include": to entrust as many people as one possibly can with one's actual body and its needs, one's stories about its fate, one's dreams and one's sources of information or hypothesis about disease, cure, consolation,

denial, and the state or institutional violence that are also invested in one's illness. It's as though there were transformative political work to be done just *by being available to be identified with* in the very grain of one's illness (which is to say, the grain of one's own intellectual, emotional bodily self as refracted through illness and as resistant to it)—*being available for identification* to friends, but as well to people who don't love one; even to people who may not like one at all or even wish one well.[20]

"Being available to be identified with" functions for Sedgwick as a potentially politically transformative and highly ethical affective orientation to others. It is a description of the very condition for friendship, which requires a bond of trust developed through mutual vulnerability and provides one highly potent basis for long-term associations across difference. In our terrifying contemporary political terrain, in which basic human variety is ever more spectacularly villainized, denigrated, flattened, and murderously prosecuted, and the forces working against such processes are frantically and valiantly struggling to protect, nourish, and sustain the communities most intensely crushed beneath the weight of this society-wide mandate to eradicate difference, it would seem that Sedgwick's particular brand of theorizing multiplicity and encouraging cross-identification would be of utmost utility. And yet, her name and thought are nary spoken of outside the pages of queer and literary studies. My wager is that this is precisely because Sedgwick had little interest in protecting, preserving, conserving, or maintaining the integrity of cultural and political identities. She wanted instead to make all identities as such *available for identification.*

Sedgwick's work is ironically perfectly fit for our times but also runs counter to much of what counts as common sense in the academic and activist left. In the generative intellectual and political scenes of these latter formations, we have seen the elaboration of an entire host of precise terms for identifying pernicious acts of cultural appropriation, exploitation, commodification, violence, microaggression, and all-out theft directed at a vast range of minoritized subjects. According to Sedgwick's oeuvre, however, what we have far fewer terms to describe are the equally multiplicitous, generative, generous, loving, self-critical, and sometimes simply brazen, forms of identification whose ordinary or quotidian expressions go by the names of sharing, learning, growing, nourishing, exchanging, repairing, embracing, loving, caring, inhabiting, modeling, and playfully performing. These are terms of loving relationality, certainly fraught and risky, but for Sedgwick absolutely worth the risk—how will we know if we have appropriated or overstepped if we do not risk the adventure of encounter, identification, and engagement in the first place? More to the point, perhaps, Sedgwick asserts over and over (echoing the classic deconstructive adage, though in queer garb) that we are never identical to ourselves, never one thing internally, just as much as we are not the same with others: "Realistically, what brings me to this work can hardly be that I am *a* woman, or *a* feminist, but that I am this particular one. . . . [I]t is not only identifications across definitional lines that can evoke or support or even require complex and particular narrative explanation; rather, the same is equally true of any person's identification with her or his 'own' gender, class, race, sexuality, nation."[21] Sedgwick's identity politics, then, are precisely a politics of *cross-identification*. At her most forceful, Sedgwick posits cross-identification as having life-or-death implications: in the absence of the ability to identify with others, we become incapable of grasping or wholly insensible to the fact of human multiplicity and consequently lose any ethical ground on which to construct a mutual sense of care, investment, and love, even for ourselves. It is this reality that makes dehumanization and genocidal violence all too possible.

Ultimately, Sedgwick reminds us that our ability to identify across genders, sexualities, classes, ethnoracial formations, temperaments, abilities, nationalities, and family ties is one of our greatest tools for working against the forces of consolidation that seek to make these identities or orientations *mean* monolithically—when people cross-identify, they multiply or complicate the very possibilities and meanings of their own identities simply by stepping out of their most normative, assumed, or habitual workings. Sedgwick understands the process of identifying (which we commonly, and mistakenly, view as a practice of "making same" or identical) as one way that we make explicit, and grapple with, difference broadly construed: to identify is to negotiate the apparent gaps that distinguish people on the basis of their distinctions and to produce new identities from that negotiation, perhaps ones that are better equipped affectively to engage, think through, and do something productive with the fact of human variation.

SEDGWICK IS A STYLIST

To say that Sedgwick is a stylist is by now practically a tautology. Perhaps no one who has ever written explicitly about her does not write paeans to her virtuosic, nearly transcendent command of language; her breathtaking turns of phrase; her epic, multi-claused sentences; and her shriek-inducing wit and humor. She is a theorist's theorist in part because through her language she is constantly performing a meta-critique of the very epistemological foundations on which she makes her most original claims. I often think of her essays as dodecahedrons, each paragraph producing a new dimension or surface of argumentation that complicates and expands but gives further shape and stability to the last until the multisided structure is complete, at which point we realize she has given us the very tools to take that same structure apart, keep what works for our own inquiries, discard other dimensions, or reconstruct a wholly different shape. She makes this explicitly clear when she states in the introduction to *Epistemology of the Closet*: "If the book were able to fulfill its most expansive ambitions, it would make certain specific kinds of readings and interrogations, perhaps new, available in a heuristically powerful, productive, and significant form for other readers to perform on literary and social texts with, ideally, other results."[22] Her writing, as she constantly reminds us, is made to be portable, transposable, disarticulated, and reassembled, depending on the needs of a particular inquiry. It is fundamentally generous and attuned to producing a multiplicity of interpretative possibilities.

Sedgwick's most common writerly qualities include her encyclopedic vocabulary (I confess that even on my fifth reading of *Epistemology of the Closet*, my smartphone sits open on my desk ready to help me locate definitions of such terms as "ukase," "otiose," "omnicide," "pellucid," "lambency," "ramified," and "hypostatized," to name just a few); sentences that compact six, seven, eight clauses to exfoliate the full dimensions of an idea or phenomenon, or else qualify a single subject with a kaleidoscopic range of adjectives and adverbs to allow us to perceive its many modalities; dramatic shifts in tone, whereby the focused analysis of a single rhetorical turn of phrase or plot point in a work of literature gives way to a searing pronouncement about the larger political implications of said work, and said interpretation; and quite simply, a damn-near unparalleled skill at simply telling it like it is: "Has there ever been a gay Socrates? Has there ever been a gay Shakespeare? Has there ever been a gay Proust? Does the Pope wear a dress? If these questions startle, it is not least as tautologies. A short answer, though a very incomplete one, might be that not only have there been a gay Socrates, Shakespeare, and Proust but that their names are Socrates, Shakespeare, and Proust."[23] (I cannot help but read lines such as these in Sedgwick's work and want to shriek, "Yaaaaas Mama!")

Often the diamond-like precision of her prose, not to mention her internally complex organization of ideas, which laminate and interconnect multiple layers of argumentation of the highest caliber, have the tendency to inspire stunned and awestruck reverie or complete repulsion and bewilderment. Despite a general sense of being mind-blown by their first encounter with her work, there are always one or two among my graduate students who grumpily groan, "Why would *anyone* write like this if they wanted people to understand them?" These diametrically opposed responses oddly produce the same intellectual result: we generally remain at a loss to understand what, exactly, she is doing with her distinctive style of writing, even if we adore it (or else turn a sour lip in annoyance). In my discussion of Sedgwick's exploration of multiplicity, I suggested that her virtuosic use of language often has the effect of performatively modeling the value of heterogeneity. This is the case not only in the sheer diversity of her vocabulary and rhetorical formulations, but also, even more substantively, in her constant attempts to spin off ever more expansive, multiplicitous, and capacious meanings from the phenomena and texts on which she sets her gaze. If Sedgwick is so virulently against societal processes, institutions, and discourses that "make everything mean the same thing," then her linguistic gymnastics are no frivolous or showy fare but active attempts to make everything mean a lot of things.

I would say, however, that the most potent and lasting effect of Sedgwick's writing, a legacy she bequeaths us but that many writers assiduously avoid today (perhaps from fear of the effects that might reverberate from any bombastic intellectual gesture, including argumentative or critical counterresponse), is to construct a writing style that functions not merely to transmit ideas but also to pass along, invoke, or generate the very kinds of affects required to understand and grapple with them. In her introduction to *Touching Feeling*, Sedgwick laments,

> A lot of voices tell us to think nondualistically, and even what to think in that fashion. Fewer are able to transmit how to go about it, the cognitive and even affective habits and practices involved, which are less than amenable to being couched in prescriptive forms. At best, I'd hope for this book to prompt recognition in some of the many people who successfully work in such ways; and where some approaches may be new or unarticulated, a sense of possibility. The ideal I'm envisioning here is a mind receptive to thoughts, able to nurture and connect them, and susceptible to happiness in their entertainment.[24]

Sedgwick never assumes that a sentence can adequately convey its meaning if it does not articulate that meaning as also affectively laden—it is not so much that she thinks emotions and feelings should be smuggled into a sentence to make it more exciting but that ideas themselves are, for all intents and purposes, affective states, or at the very least can only precisely arrive at their conceptual destination by virtue of a reading subject *affectively capable of receiving them*. Her sentences are Trojan horses that get under our skin because they use language or turns of phrase that upend what we thought we knew, that make us viscerally uncomfortable or, alternatively, exhilarated, thereby altering our sensorium, or at least leveraging it just slightly open, perhaps enough to change our perception, our investments, or our assumptions so that we may actually be convinced by one or another of her claims.

As with her commitment to cross-identification, Sedgwick's virtuosic style is both perfectly fit for our political moment and often overlooked by contemporary leftist analysis as rarefied, convoluted, or, perhaps worst of all, "flowery" when the demand of the day calls for clarity and simplicity of language in articulating fixed truths lobbied at the litany of falsehoods spun by our unraveling yet seemingly politically invulnerable government. Dare I conjecture, invoking her spirit in the abstract, that Sedgwick would cringe at this near religiously orthodox obsession with truth and fact across the spectrum of leftist politics and intellectual life. Sedgwick's work evinces a consistent suspicion (despite her most reparative impulses) of the attempt to seek out singular truths, not because facts and reality do not matter to her (she masterfully deploys sociological data like statistics in her most famous essays) but because framing them in the language of unequivocal truth simply models the same form of consolidation, convergence, and narrowing of meaning making that the most conservative political orientations covet and promulgate: What does it matter, she repeatedly queries, if being gay is a question of nature or culture, if the fundamental belief structure of our society is that gay people should simply not exist? Rather than adjudicating the truth value of such narrowly constructed binary logics, Sedgwick is interested in the conditions by which certain kinds of truths, or ways of knowing oneself and one's relationship to the world, can become widely shared and recognized or can induce curiosity, even care, in those who might normally wish you harm. In a world where queer life is devalued, she vociferously argues, "We have all the more reason . . . to keep our understandings of gay origin, of gay cultural and material reproduction, plural, multi-capillaried, argus-eyed, respectful, and endlessly cherished."[25] She proposes that such open-ended conditions for knowing are often made possible when the style in which a particular truth is named and delivered—from the form of the claim, to its vocal or textual tonality, to its affective force—hits a viewer or reader in unexpected but potentially radically unsettling or transformative ways.

We need look no farther than Sedgwick's analysis of her own writing to fully grasp the affective impact of her style: "Many people doing all kinds of work are able to take pleasure in aspects of their work; but something different happens when the pleasure is not only taken but openly displayed. I like to make that different thing happen. Some readers identify strongly with the possibility of a pleasure so displayed; others disidentify from it with violent repudiations; still others find themselves occupying less stable positions in the circuit of contagion, fun, voyeurism, envy, participation, and stimulation."[26] I tend to believe that Sedgwick wrote precisely for that third kind of reader who might come to "[occupy] less stable positions in the circuit of contagion, fun, voyeurism, envy, participation, and stimulation." Her style aimed to produce that kind of generative instability, one that induces not alienation, fragmentation, or bewildering vertigo but a potentially exciting, if unnerving, sense that things might not all line up as "tidily" as you might think. It is her investment in "making that different thing happen" that is at the heart of the affective project of her prose: to produce language that performatively affects others.

SEDGWICK IS AN AFFECTIVE CURATOR

Finally, I wish to stake a claim that one of Sedgwick's most potent legacies lies in her studied curation of affective states—most vividly, those of surprise, wonder, passion, and agnostic openness to ideas. She not only identifies and analyzes such states throughout her oeuvre but repeatedly performs them in her pursuit of particular intellectual queries and in the structure of her writing. In her early writings, she is committed to the idea that an antihomophobic criticism remains open to the surprise of encountering queerness in numerous forms across time and space; later in her career she enjoins that very same mode of criticism (and its practitioners) to be open to the surprise of seeing queerness not only and ever caught in the crosshair of homophobia but also in those places where it unexpectedly appears to flourish.

Elsewhere I have theorized the concept of "affective curation" as a pedagogical model for the queer studies classroom that "centralizes the value of intentionally eliciting, or 'triggering,' uncomfortable affective responses from students that then become the object of discussion . . . in order to develop new strategies for retuning, rerouting, or altogether altering their sense perceptions of the world."[27] From the many descriptions she provides of her queerly inflected pedagogy, to her own fascination with the unpredictability, variability, and mutability of affective states (a reality to which she increasingly came to devote much of her intellectual energies later in her career), to the sheer abundance of affectively forceful linguistic formulations that her writing provides, Sedgwick created public intellectual space for feelings to be experienced, named, argued over, and rerouted.

This is frequently on display in Sedgwick's recurrent references to the quotidian or everyday as the site from which affective attachments to particular ideas, theories, research questions, and modes of analysis come to be nourished and grow in intensity. The protracted illnesses of members of her chosen family (among them colleagues and students), her own bodily transformations in relation to an early breast cancer diagnosis, her attendance at activist meetings and rallies, and her negotiations with students in the classroom during the height of the AIDS epidemic all become occasions for her to think through questions of vast theoretical scope. She is no stranger to the anecdote, which, in the mode of Jane Gallop's "anecdotal theory," she consistently uses to encapsulate a problem or question that haunts her and that she wishes to encourage her readers to be equally invested in puzzling over. Like clockwork, these anecdotes or references to personal idiosyncrasy almost always begin with the activation of an affective, sensory, or felt experience that jolts Sedgwick into cognitive action. Take a few scattered examples (the emphasis is mine):

> Probably my most formative influence from a quite early age has been a *viscerally intense*, highly speculative (not to say inventive) cross-identification with gay men and gay male cultures as I inferred, imagined, and later came to know them. It wouldn't have required quite so overdetermined a trajectory, though, for almost any forty year old facing a protracted, life-threatening illness in 1991 to realize that the people with whom she had perhaps most in common, and from whom she might well have most to learn, are people living with AIDS, AIDS activists, and others whose lives had been profoundly reorganized by AIDS in the course of the 1980s.[28]

> I'm *fond* of observing how *obsession* is the most durable form of intellectual capital.[29]

> Patton's comment suggests that for someone to have an unmystified, *angry* view of large and genuinely systemic oppressions does not intrinsically or necessarily enjoin that person to any specific train of epistemological or

narrative consequences. To know that the origin or spread of HIV realistically might have resulted from a state-assisted conspiracy—such knowledge is, it turns out, separable from the question of whether the energies of a given AIDS activist intellectual or group might best be used in the tracing and exposure of such a possible plot. They might, but then again, they might not.[30]

In these and countless other instances, Sedgwick describes a circuit of affective exchange from an intensely felt initial sensation (here, a visceral identification as a child, an intellectual obsession as a scholar, anger and rage as an activist) that occasions an array of other interested affects and practices: the wonder of inventing new forms of cross-identification, the fondness of valuing obsession as a form of intellectual capital, the ability of an outside point of view to reroute one's anger into hope, or simply to allow anger to reside alongside hope and possibility.

Like her feminist forebears, then, Sedgwick sees feelings as genuine sources of knowledge, as places where we might intuit something about ourselves and the world in which we live that traditional modes of humanistic inquiry would ignore or overlook as mere subjective experience. Her deep fascination with the realm of the affective and textural in her later writing, most beautifully condensed in the collection *Touching Feeling*, had much to do with her increasing sense that the study of affect held out one of the supplest models for accounting for the sheer heterogeneity of human sensory experience and, by extension, our ability to invest a nearly infinite number of affective states in our various identities, relationships, desires, and aspirations. In her turn to a largely ignored or overlooked psychoanalytic theorist of affect such as Silvan Tomkins, she quite literally curates her readers' encounter with a theory of affects that she feels positively electrified by, one that, to its core, promulgates the notion that "affects can be, and are, attached to things, people, ideas, sensations, relations, activities, ambitions, institutions, and any number of other things, including other affect."[31]

It makes sense, then, that Sedgwick's most widely circulated, cited, and debated essay, "Paranoid Reading and Reparative Reading," offered a fully formed affective theory of reading, perhaps the closest that Sedgwick ever got to articulating a complete analytical model of interpretation. Describing the mode of interpretation she would famously dub "reparative," she claimed:

> The desire of a reparative impulse . . . is additive and accretive. Its fear, a realistic one, is that the culture surrounding it is inadequate or inimical

to its nurture; it wants to assemble and confer plenitude on an object that will then have resources to offer to an inchoate self. . . . No less acute than a paranoid position, no less realistic, no less attached to a project of survival, and neither less nor more delusional or fantasmatic, the reparative reading position undertakes a different range of affects, ambitions, and risks. What we can best learn from such practices are, perhaps, the many ways selves and communities succeed in extracting sustenance from the objects of a culture—even of a culture whose avowed desire has often been not to sustain them.[32]

Here, Sedgwick appears to anthropomorphize a mode of interpretation as something that itself has feelings such as fear and hope; in so doing, she forces us to see that any mode of analysis is ultimately an expression or extension of human impulses, motives, and desires to make meaning in a particular way in the hope of producing particular effects. She encourages us to loosen our commitments to any singular program of analysis and ask ourselves instead how our own desires, aspirations, fears, and anxieties might provide a key to new ways to read the culture we make and that, in turn, makes us.

And, of course, the list could go on. I have attempted here, however schematically, to map the kind of position, or intellectual orientation, that Eve Sedgwick carved out for those who might follow her. Her work was always aspirational and anticipatory, less in the paranoid frame she so famously enumerated, but more in the sense of a hopeful desire to spin outward analytical possibilities that might help "confer plenitude on an object that will then have resources to offer to an inchoate self."[33] One way to reread this oft-cited line reparatively is to suggest that, for Sedgwick, the object that she sought to confer plenitude on was the field of critical thought itself, while the inchoate self she sought to provide resources to is *all of us*, who trained and came of age in the era of queer theory.

My aim has been to show that Sedgwick's deepest legacy lies not in any single body of knowledge she produced or illuminated—though her contributions to *what* and *how* we know in the vast field of humanistic inquiry are astonishing—but, rather, in her construction and performance of a particular *way of knowing* that at its core is attuned to seeing, valuing, and negotiating multiplicity. I can only ever grasp Sedgwick this way because I never "met" her except in and through her textual performances, which have enjoined me, wherever possible, to scatter, fragment, disarticulate, proliferate, branch outward, or unstitch the lineaments of my most sacred intellectual models and scholarly objects so I can see what they are truly capable of, not simply what I want them to be. In the process, I usually discover they do far more than I could ever have dreamed.

My encounter with Sedgwick, then, has always been with the conceptual tools that she so generously spun outward to those of us who might take her hypotheses seriously, even if we disagreed with her. Perhaps most shocking to those of us trained in the extraordinarily precarious academic climate of the post-poststructuralist era—when jockeying for intellectual capital has become a particularly fraught and fine-grained practice that regularly includes intellectual takedowns, cross-generational infighting and moralism, accusatory pronouncements, and the narcissism of small differences—Sedgwick never made claims that necessarily foreclosed any intellectual position except those that would reinforce heterosexist, misogynist, racist, or other phobic frameworks for apprehending the world. There is nothing in Sedgwick's oeuvre that forecloses its possible uses for the study of race, or the study of gender transitivity, or the study of disability, or the study of a vast range of embodied and cultural differences; as she might say, there is no way to know the extent to which her own theoretical insights might extend to these arenas unless one makes the attempt to deploy them and ceaselessly test them against the limits of any particular query. I remain endlessly surprised, for instance, that Sedgwick has not been placed more often in direct dialogue with the foundational work of black feminist thought. If, as Roderick Ferguson and Grace Hong have so pointedly elaborated, "the definition of difference for women of color feminism . . . [was] not a multiculturalist celebration [or] an excuse for presuming a commonality among all racialized peoples, but a cleareyed appraisal of the dividing line between valued and devalued, which can cut within, as well as across, racial groupings," and if the critique of that mode of political thought is "fundamentally organized around difference, the difference between and within racialized, gendered, sexualized collectivities," then Sedgwick's exceptionally fine-grained attention to "differences within differences" could be read as an indirect descendant of—or, more aptly, queer kin to—black feminist analysis.[34]

In her writings about Tomkins, Sedgwick repeatedly suggests that her fascination with his work has something to do with the way that his theory of affect, what he called "the affect system," essentially modeled her own default orientation toward critical thought: just as she takes as bedrock the operating principle that *everything means a lot of things*, so, too, does Tomkins develop a theory of emotions that claims that *any affect can attach to anything*. She is drawn, in other words, not only to the content of Tomkins's theory, but also to the very logic that underwrites it, a logic of proliferation, dispersal, and multiplicity that is itself affectively generous. Similarly, my attachment to Sedgwick has always been about a visceral sense that she thinks the way that I think—not in a kind of symmetrical identity or in a way that might lead me to reproduce the same analytical conclusions but, rather, in the orientation of our thought; in our commitment to the formulation *both/and*; in our default assumption that a theory that seeks to "include, include" is more valuable than one that forecloses possibilities; in our commitment to the reparative impulse; in our sense that field-wide debates should produce many intellectual positions and possibilities rather than a few; in our promiscuous attachment to many theoretical models and tools; in our irreverence toward moralism of all kinds and the taken-for-granted doxa of any disciplinary formation. And so, I cross-identify with Sedgwick not as a gay, male, Lebanese American immigrant who spent his formative years reading comics and now teaches literature and writes about queer and feminist cultural production, but as someone who is all these things, *as well as* a particular kind of scholar whose thought moves in a particular kind of way.

I can conjure few thinkers whom we have more need of invoking, grappling with, and making use of than Eve Sedgwick at the present time. In the field of queer studies, we have become just as extraordinarily skilled at producing the most elegant ideological readings of our culture as we have at producing a reparative reconstruction of that same culture, often in the same breath. As Tyler Bradway has compelling argued, we have been less successful at taking up Sedgwick's actual call to proliferate numerous analytical positions and perspectives that far exceed even the binary calculus of the paranoid and the reparative.[35] We have been less successful in being generous to one another's intellectual lineages, objects of interest, and theoretical insights. As a consequence, we become members of embattled encampments (commonly known as "subfields") that can be safely neutralized or easily encapsulated in something as innocuous as a graduate seminar title: queer affect studies, queer-of-color critique, queer disability studies, queer Marxism, queer ecologies, queer posthumanism. These labels are by no means pernicious or wrong, but they are too easy to list off as transparently obvious units of knowledge, as though each was not totally and utterly dependent on and interconnected with the others.

Where our field's range of concern has expanded—now taking as its purview the geographical span of the globe, the institutional range of neoliberal capital, even the entire gamut of nonhuman life—I would venture to say that the *affective* range of our arguments and internal conflicts has remained surprisingly narrow: to be social or antisocial, to be normative or antinormative, to think queer or trans, to think sexuality or race, to be Marxist or Foucauldian, to be a decolonizer or an agent of homonationalism, to believe in surface or depth, to study rarefied Literature or neoliberal capital etc. etc. etc. (dare I say, blah blah blah?). The very same binarisms that Sedgwick spent the bulk of *Epistemology of the Closet* deconstructing, and working through, perhaps unsurprisingly (but to my eyes, oftentimes depressingly) shape a large swath of our internal conflicts in the field of queer studies, conflicts that often seem more like interpersonal clashes than substantial axes of conceptual or theoretical differences. These binarisms become so rote, so often repeated and taken up in the structure and modes of our argumentation, that they come to seem like unequivocal truths that actually say something about the theorists who are seen to occupy these various positions; moreover, these truths are often laden with moralizing claims on both sides about who is or is not analytically or historically rigorous enough; who adequately attends to race or gender transitivity and who doesn't; who appropriately cites particular authors and who elides those citations (and what such elisions *say* about said thinker); who adequately "cares" about actual living human beings and who merely makes abstraction of them for their own intellectual gain.

These questions are ethically indispensable, but the dualistic and moralizing frames within which they are repeatedly invoked or articulated most often reproduce knowledge that isn't in the least surprising or useful, for to limn Sedgwick herself, it simply confirms the very suspicions that lead us to ask the questions in the first place rather than giving us another vantage point from which to view the terrain. Speaking through and revising Sedgwick, and without seeking to flatten or reduce the genuine stakes of these disciplinary conflicts, I would still implore us to consider that, regardless of whether you take on the position of the social or the antisocial, the humanist or the posthumanist, the antinormative or the postnormative, "[U]nder the overarching, relatively unchallenged aegis of a culture's desire that [queer studies scholars] *not be*, there is no unthreatened, unthreatening conceptual home for a concept of [a uniformly radical queer theory]. We have all the more reason, then, to keep our understandings of [queer theory], of gay cultural and material reproduction, plural, multi-capillaried, argus-eyed, respectful, and endlessly cherished."[36]

In the rare instances I have ever been explicitly asked to position myself on either side of our field's most recurrent and entrenched conflicts, I simply abjure the request because my work in queer theory, while deeply informed, influenced, and in dialogue with these various formulations, ultimately has no truck with almost any of them. I address antinormativity because it appears everywhere in the cultural texts I analyze (superheroes are non-normative weirdos, in case you didn't know). I take up the antisocial thesis when the objects I study model forms of radical refusal that willfully sever ties to normative social relations. I work with intersectional theories of race because texts and readers I investigate attest to the existence of, and seek to support, multiply marginalized subjectivities. I turn to affect theory to help me explain why reading stories about monstrous superhuman power or viewing art about movements for women's and gay liberation might be exhilarating, bewildering, terrifying, confusing, or just plain fun. I believe in depth reading not because texts are defined by either surfaces or conceptual depth, but because I understand that human beings impute complex and multivalent meaning to the objects they live with and love. None of this means that I forsake the value of certain norms, or have no investment in queer sociality, or do not understand that not all identities are operating simultaneously in the same way at all times.

Rather, my objects of study force me to see terms traditionally opposed within the disciplinary boundaries of our field as productively co-extensive, so that my own positions are endlessly subject to change. It is the precise agonisms of our collective queer theoretical arguments, seemingly so clearly demarcated, colliding with the world's messiness that electrified Sedgwick's thought.

Sedgwick ceaselessly reminded her readers that we need not see queer theory's various frames of reference as a fixed set of assumptions that predetermine what we can think about a given cultural text or phenomenon. She enjoined us to engage in a circuit of exchange between our own intellectual values (grounded in the commitment to attending to multiplicity), the objects we aim to illuminate (the contexts of their making alongside their creative content), the theories that help us name the phenomenon we are seeing, and the insights of our colleagues, who are passionate readers and viewers themselves, whatever theoretical training or commitments they hold. For Sedgwick, "The only imperative [she treated] as categorical is the very broad one of pursuing an antihomophobic inquiry."[37] That inquiry necessitates the embrace of multiplicity not only as a reality of the world, but also as a scholarly orientation to ideas and their co-mingling.

I conclude by asking a question that Sedgwick might have: How can queer studies identify and cultivate the thought of those scholars for whom the current shape of the field seems unresponsive to their interests, attachments, or needs? One answer is simply that we must entertain more than one solution to a given problem and that doing so includes granting scholars the space where they need not align themselves with one or the other of the various positions that have polarized queer studies. This task should not be difficult, considering we claim a field whose mission is to study and cultivate alternative erotic, social, and aesthetic desires, especially those anathema to the broader culture. Over and over, Sedgwick teaches us that the infinitely generative field of erotic possibilities we call *desire* might not be so far from the quotidian ways we obsess over and attach to ideas, methods, terms, and bodies of thought. To realize that might involve respecting desires and methods not our own, valuing answers that do not accord with our initial aspirations, and turning to one another to learn something (dare I say surprising!?) about how our colleagues' investments, even those that rub us the wrong way (perhaps especially those), might have something to teach us through that very irritation. This might look like what Audre Lorde calls "the uses of the erotic," or what Linda Zerilli identifies as feminism's "radical imagination," or what Janet Halley dubs the practice of "splitting decisions," or finally what Sedgwick simply enacted in her life and her writing: in other words, everything she "endlessly cherished" under the term *queer*. I don't believe one has to maintain fixed allegiances to any one of the proliferating strands of queer thought for us to remain ethical, vigilant, politically effective, and intellectually generous. And neither did Sedgwick. We might simply need to learn how to better tend to one other.

NOTES

1 Eve Kosofsky Sedgwick, *Epistemology of the Closet* (Berkeley: University of California Press, 1991), 22.
2 Sedgwick, *Epistemology of the Closet*, 8.
3 Sedgwick, *Epistemology of the Closet*, 22.
4 Eve Kosofsky Sedgwick, *Tendencies* (Durham, NC: Duke University Press, 1993), 3.
5 Sedgwick, *Tendencies*, 6, 20.
6 Eve Kosofsky Sedgwick, *Between Men: English Literature and Male Homosocial Desire* (New York: Columbia University Press, 1985).

7 Sedgwick, *Tendencies*, 12.

8 Sedgwick, *Epistemology of the Closet*, 129.

9 Sedgwick, *Epistemology of the Closet*, 130.

10 Sedgwick, *Tendencies*, 1, 3, xii, 9; Sedgwick, *Epistemology of the Closet*,

11 Sedgwick, *Epistemology of the Closet*, 14, emphasis added.

12 Sedgwick, *Epistemology of the Closet*, 8, 14, 44; Sedgwick, *Tendencies*, xi
    261; Eve Kosofsky Sedgwick, *Touching Feeling: Affect, Pedagogy, Performativity*
    (Durham, NC: Duke University Press, 2003), 8.

13 Sedgwick, *Epistemology of the Closet*, 8.

14 Ramzi Fawaz, *The New Mutants: Superheroes and the Radical Imagination of
    American Comics* (New York: New York University Press, 2016), 32.

15 Sedgwick, *Tendencies*, 6.

16 Sedgwick, *Tendencies*, 6.

17 Sedgwick, *Tendencies*, 6.

18 Sedgwick, *Epistemology of the Closet*, 14.

19 Sedgwick, *Epistemology of the Closet*, 23.

20 Sedgwick, *Touching Feeling*, 261, emphasis added.

21 Sedgwick, *Epistemology of the Closet*, 59–61.

22 Sedgwick, *Epistemology of the Closet*, 14.

23 Sedgwick, *Epistemology of the Closet*, 52.

24 Sedgwick, *Touching Feeling*, 1.

25 Sedgwick, *Epistemology of the Closet*, 43.

26 Sedgwick, *Tendencies*, 19.

27 Ramzi Fawaz, "How to Make a Queer Scene, or Notes toward a Practice of
    Affective Curation," *Feminist Studies* 42, no. 3 (2016): 760.

28 Sedgwick, *Tendencies*, 14.

29 Sedgwick, *Touching Feeling*, 2.

30 Sedgwick, *Touching Feeling*, 124.

31 Sedgwick, *Tendencies*, 19.

32 Sedgwick, *Touching Feeling*, 149–51.

33 Sedgwick, *Touching Feeling*, 149.

34 Grace Kyungwon Hong and Roderick A. Ferguson, eds., *Strange Affinities: The
    Gender and Sexual Politics of Comparative Racialization*, Perverse Modernities
    (Durham, NC: Duke University Press, 2011), 9, 11.

35 Tyler Bradway, "Bad Reading: The Affective Relations of Queer Experimental
    Literature after AIDS," *GLQ* 24, nos. 2–3 (2018): 189–212.

36 Sedgwick, *Epistemology of the Closet*, 43.

37 Sedgwick, *Epistemology of the Closet*, 14.

From H. A. Sedgwick

In October 2005, Eve and I traveled to Dublin at the invitation of Noreen Giffney and Michael O'Rourke. Eve gave a talk at University College Dublin and had informal discussions with Noreen, Michael, and the others in their group. The enthusiasm and vibrancy of that group was impressive. It was clear that they had accomplished a great deal through their creative energy, strong sense of mission, and sheer hard work in an environment that was often less than enthusiastic in its support of queer scholarship.

Michael's and Noreen's commitment to Eve and her work was evident again in the intensive one-day seminar at Independent Colleges, Dublin, that they organized to commemorate her after her death in 2009. At about the same time, Michael began the long process of organizing this book. I am honored to write this brief note and happy to have this chance to express my deep appreciation to him and to everyone else who has worked on this project.

An extended consideration of Eve's work, consisting of three linked panels of papers, took place at the convention of the Modern Language Association (MLA) in January 2011. The panels were spread over three days of the convention, one each afternoon, and the cumulative effect was, for me at least, very powerful. The nine papers that were presented were very different from one another in style, in approach, and in the aspects of Eve's work that they addressed, yet together they evoked a strong vision of the depth, the power, and the underlying coherence of her work. I'm very happy that all nine of those MLA papers, some in expanded form, are now included in this book. The other papers included here add an even greater variety of approaches and contribute to an even more complex vision of Eve's work.

Surely, much of the diversity of all of these contributions is due to the individuality and creativity of their authors—an impressive indication of the talented friends, students, and colleagues whom Eve attracted, or sought out, over the years. But the range and variety of the contributions also resonates with the range of Eve's work and the variety of ways that it touches people.

This book's emphasis is on the best-known portions of Eve's work, drawing largely on the middle period of her career, with only a few of the book's essays exploring her earlier or her later work. Most of Eve's work from the last decade or so of her life was in the form of talks that were unpublished when she died and may not have been known to some of the present authors at the time when their papers were written. Much of this work is now available in a collection titled *The Weather in Proust*, edited by Jonathan Goldberg and published in 2011 by Duke University Press.

Understandably, Eve's early writing—from graduate school, from college, and from even earlier—is not much referenced here, most of it being available, until quite recently, only in her archives. Much of her most intense creative energies during that time were devoted to her poetry, which was already highly accomplished, and strikingly queer, when she was thirteen or fourteen. Eve published only one collection of her poetry, *Fat Art, Thin Art* (1994).[1] In 2014, the twentieth anniversary of that book's publication, Jason Edwards organized a conference on Eve's poetry at the University of York, and then in 2017, he published a collection of essays from that conference. The collection, *Bathroom Songs: Eve Kosofsky Sedgwick as a Poet*, also includes a substantial selection of Eve's previously uncollected poetry, thus making widely available a crucial portion of her work written before *Between Men* (1985).[2]

Eve's earliest attempt at publication that I know of was a letter (now lost) that she wrote to the *Washington Post* when she was twelve protesting the firing of her French teacher for homosexuality. (He was entrapped in a public restroom.) That letter went unpublished because the *Post*'s letters editor called to consult her mother, who denied permission to publish it. Melissa Solomon, in her essay here, suggests that even that denial of publication may have had a profound effect. Addressing herself to Eve, Solomon writes about a conversation that she had, after Eve's death, with Eve's mother:

> At the time, she understood herself to be rightfully protective of you, still a child, who would be caught in the middle of public debate if such a letter were to be published. Now, she worries that she picked the wrong side of right, especially given your career path and your own intellectual, emotional, and political interests. I suggested the possibility that her prohibition was a kind of foundational turning point without which your future might not have progressed in the direction it did. Did you promise yourself

something in childhood that you made come true in adulthood? Would we have *Epistemology of the Closet* if you had not?

Eve's first successful attempt at publication, as far as I know, was an omnibus book review for *Seventeen* magazine, written about a year later. That review was only rediscovered quite recently; it created a flurry of activity as notice of it circulated around the internet. Whatever spurred Eve's development as a writer, her writing at thirteen is already notably mature. Eve's friend Josh Wilner remarks, "What I enjoy most is the way Eve figures out exactly what the features of a chatty sophisticated literary-review for *Seventeen* are—and nails it."[3]

It is my hope that over time more of Eve's writing—unpublished, obscurely published, or created for specific occasions, such as lecture or course handouts—will find its way into her archive and onto her website at EveKosofskySedgwick.net.

Thus, this book, as many of its authors are quick to acknowledge, surely will not be the final word on Eve and her work. But it is a splendid and very welcome contribution, and I have no doubt that it contains the beginnings of much more that will develop from it.

H. A. Sedgwick
New York City, 2013, revised 2019

NOTES

1 Eve Kosofsky Sedgwick, *Fat Art, Thin Art* (Durham, NC: Duke University Press, 1994).
2 Jason Edwards, ed., *Bathroom Songs: Eve Kosofsky Sedgwick as a Poet* (New York: Punctum, 2017); Eve Kosofsky Sedgwick, *Between Men: English Literature and Male Homosocial Desire* (New York: Columbia University Press, 1985).
3 Personal communication with author. Originally published in "Eve's First Publication?," *Eve Kosofsky Sedgwick* (blog), 2012, http://evekosofskysedgwick.net /blog/page5/.

What Survives

"Sex without Optimism" was written for a conference celebrating Gayle Rubin's "Thinking Sex." There we asked what survives the encounter with the scene of sex once it's separated out from the dominant framework of optimism. What survived was being open to or game for the encounter and all that might be unbearable about it. At issue was whether the queer adorable made possible our being in proximity to the unbearable or whether it was a way of aestheticizing and attempting to sublimate or deny it. This chapter returns to the question of survival—sadly, in more ways than one. Eve Kosofsky Sedgwick was too ill to attend the event in honor of Rubin, where she, too, had been scheduled to speak. In a cruel sequel, we first presented this talk on a panel commemorating Eve's life and work nine months after her death.

FAILURE

Lauren Berlant: Lee and I muddled for months over how to structure this— but what is it we offer? A talk, an elegy, a conversation, a literature review, a tribute, a convoluted apostrophe. While unable to figure out a genre in relation to our friend who continues to be absent, we managed to write an abstract that we believed we intended. But it was nonetheless just a placeholder, like all of our objects, like any object; an abstract is but an ambition, after all, an often hastily condensed fantasy decked out as a project, which is the primary academic genre of futurity—and in this case it additionally had to capture the emotion of a nonencounter with Eve through a reencounter with her work. Our abstract promised to consider reparativity, even in the face of the irreparable and the irreversible. But to convert the abstract into an extended piece of writing did not come easily. We recorded our phone calls after note-taking failed, reread our notes after our memories failed, talked for hours while our intentions failed.

Lee Edelman: Fail: from the Latin *fallire*, "to be wanting, to be defective." As if wanting as such were a defect; as if not to want were success. As if loss were a version of failure and failure a lack of aesthetic coherence, a condition of brokenness or incompletion. In such a linguistic context I must respond to this claim of our failure, our repetitive failure, by saying "No." Something important is wanting in describing as wanting those various practices, those tentative approaches to shaping the sundered moment we live as this dialogue's "now" and so in evoking as failure the want, the wanting, that relation presupposes: the rupture across which it takes its shape, the break—perhaps the lucky break—that alone enables its bond.

In the thinking we did together and tried, in the ways Lauren notes, to preserve, Eve held the place of loss as such, the place of what is "wanting" in calling our repetitive practices "failed." We returned to her writings as we did to each other, anticipating, but only nominally, a moment to come when those various returns would have turned into this text. But that anticipation was only nominal; our enjoyment was in those "failures" themselves as we tossed our rough-hewn thoughts in the air without knowing whether or where they would land, what they might or could become, or if they would come to naught. It wasn't the moving forward but the coming back that made our work possible, the joy of a repetition that didn't defer its end but performed it in a space without guarantee. What's missing in calling this "failure," then, is the joy of "no guarantee," the enjoyment of building without blueprint, of conjuring something out of nothing more reliable than the space, the divide, that provokes it.

If I call that space between us, that gap of our want, the place of the no, it's not just to make another pitch for the primacy of negativity but also to attend to the space in which such negativity always takes place, the space that, in our conversations, in our improvised dialogue unmoored by anything that promised to sustain it, allowed a provisional being-together across various sorts of divisions. Our repeated engagements thus spoke to the persistence, the survival of our common failure such that failure became the condition for the survival of relation. It bound us to the multiple iterations of "us" performed in proximity to Eve, whose loss was condensed in our meditations on rupture and repair—or, rather, in our common questions about the insistence of that pair and the seeming necessity of that pairing. What if we chose to demur from the ideological imperative to repair them? What if we attempted—deliberately, even perversely—to hold them apart? What if their very relation depended on the rupture of any such pairing—a rupture that enabled the repetition that "repair," as its prefix suggests, demands?

LB: Not feeling the failure as a happy confrontation with the rupture within reencounter, my mind turned away both from Eve and Lee toward collecting materials about loneliness, a kind of relation to a world whose only predictable is in the persistence of inaccessible love. Eve might have called the affect that I was seeking to document "shame," as she located shame in the experience of interest that a person holds toward an object after it turns its face away. But she might not have called it that—nor would I. Eve developed many ways to gesture toward the space of inexistent relationality and one-sided attachment; not all of those ways denote shame, just as the return to relation does not require revisiting failure insofar as it gestures toward the absolute. Incompletion is another thing, a set that has many members. My focus is to elaborate these zones made by the failure to resolve, repair, or achieve relation. In this chapter I want to expand for us all, beyond shame and love, the referential shorthand implied by the couplet Sedgwick/affect.

Many works auditioned for the loneliness archive. First came Tom Dumm's *Loneliness as a Way of Life*, Claudia Rankine's *Don't Let Me Be Lonely*, and Rae Armantrout's *Versed*.[1] These are documentary works of a sort, addressing the world as seen by one life moving through collectively sensed devastation toward the ongoing state called survival. To document this funneling of a world into a life, the texts engage catastrophic episodes whose becoming-event draws on the experience of other devastations. The clutter of materials we find there points to the lost anchoring thing or things—a person, a world, and confidence in the persistence of a healthy life. The authors' pursuit of a shape for the clutter does not deny its disorganization in search of better working genres for endurance, relationality, and world remagnetizing but becomes a practice of living on, of life itself.

Dumm's theoretical book gathers up solitude's affective history by way of ordinary language philosophy, trauma narrative, and the story of living with the dying of his wife. His aim is to teach not how to flourish in loneliness but how not to. Citing Emerson, Dumm writes, "I grieve that grief can teach me nothing."[2] This nothing is not an absence, though.

As the books of poetry also ask, genuinely and with significant degrees of hesitation: Is it worth, after all, fleeing the shadows of the nothing that comes after a great loss? To what life, after all, is one recommitting, once the thing that stood in for a life worth attaching to no longer obtains? Why bother beginning again to be ordinary? "Why bother" is one phrase that marks a great loss. Bother, from *bodhairim*, "I deafen": After the world has withdrawn from my confidence in it, why should I turn my hearing back on fully to engage with its noise? These works seek not to return to the prior state, though. Nor are they looking for a transformative, confirming event or substitute anchor. Gestural, curious, verbose, and disconnected, they make an aesthetic to focus on this: that what survives loss are so many decisions to patch up, or not.

Doubts about how nextness will persist, then, persist as life goes on. Having looked around to discover a trust in the ongoingness of things shoplifted and noting that aloneness has come to buffer their loneliness, the poets bespeak a live blankness in the ear and eye, an apprehensiveness in all the senses. Rankine: "Define loneliness? Yes. / It's what we can't do for each other."[3] Armantrout: "Objects are silly. / Lonesome / as the word "Ow!" / is."[4] Prehending, grasping at the hurt air around the bruise of loneliness that comes from running into the nonsolidity of the objects that organize your world, you discover that you were merely you all along, dangling in the air. "You know how fantasy works," Eve writes. "It's like a closed room with all the air sucked out of it—hence, no gravity, and just a few, diverse objects tumbling around together. And the objects could be anything; they're all in different registers. . . . words and phrases, some of them acts, organs, angles . . . and what makes them add up to 'fantasy' is that there isn't a stable context for them, or a stable place to identify, or anything."[5]

Fantasy tethers you to a possible world but makes you passive too, she suggests, "waiting—waiting with dread" to discover what you already know: that the shoe of realism will drop.[6] In one version of Eve's project, the subject of this unbearable knowledge shuttles between the paranoid rupture and the depressive position's compulsion to repair the attachment tear that she feels too intimately. In another version, though, in the space of dread and hesitation, there is no agency-generating project, not even a welcome mat. Dread's hesitation might be consumed in a flash, endure a long stretch, or become a state of withheld relaxation that spans an entire life's existence. Dread gives a fundamentally queer shape to life, multiplying a cacophony of futures and attachments. This is a relational style made stark, and collective, by illness. "Dread, intense dread, both focused and diffuse . . . [was] the dominant tonality of" the first phase of AIDS consciousness, she writes, "for queer people, at least for those who survived."[7]

Dread maps out what's weak in reparative desire; in Eve's work, its power is in the tableau of ambivalence it produces, in contrast to shame's familiar contrapuntal dynamic of cloaking, exposing, and desperate attaching, or paranoia's rhythm of projection, attack, and vulnerability. Dread raises uncomfortable questions about repair, the unclarity of what repair would fix, how it would feel as process and telos, and whether it would be possible, desirable, or worth risking. As we will see, the work of dread in Eve's oeuvre points in many directions, and indeed that is its clarifying power. Dread slices between noticing the mood made by the abrasion of loneliness and the discovery that nothing at the moment compels the drives or action toward cultivating anything, or even pretending to: this aggressive passivity is where fantasy offers consolation for living on while failing to provide a reliable cushion. *A Dialogue on Love* demonstrates prolifically the irreparable problem/scene made by dread, staging the interregnum that paces, dilutes, and sometimes abandons the fantasy of repair. At one point, Eve borrows Mark Seltzer's phrase the "melodrama of uncertain agency" to describe this fantasmatic space of flailing or animated suspension.[8]

The impasse not yet or perhaps never caught up in the drama of repair is neither life existentially nor life post-traumatically but existence, revealed in the stunned encounter: with the contingencies of structuring fantasy; in what one loves in one's own incoherence; and in the bruise of significant contact, with people and with words. Eve dreads, for example, what she calls "the zinger."[9] A zinger is a phrase that makes you rear back on impact, rattling your pleasure with the force of its sure verbal aggression; you have no choice but to take the zinger's hit, and then you're dazed and alone with it, even if the aim wasn't to take you down. Even then your buckled footing is collateral damage but damage nonetheless, a lonely "ow." The resulting loneliness cannot be compartmentalized and is not over there, waiting for you to turn your attention to its repair; it has run into the store for cigarettes and never returned, leaving you in the idling car.

Eve, quite a wit herself, writes about fearing zingers that would "decathect me [from an attachment] . . . suddenly, hard, and completely," slicing with a bullying rationality through what fantasy had been holding out against loss.[10] At times life itself becomes zinged, as in the cruel joke that history plays on the joyous subject in the form of accident or catastrophe—a cancer diagnosis, say—or in the betrayal of a friend, a harsh judgment against someone she loves, or a reencounter with homophobia. Then there is the zinger of discovering that she has been trying, all of her life, to seduce intermittent love into becoming a permanent and unconditional flow. Her devastating and constant rediscovery of the eternal task of holding up the world by herself might be why the word "loneliness" appears only once or twice in her writing, and not interestingly: it is too lonely. Her word for this situation of disrepair is abandonment. Abandonment presumes a prior attachment, but there's also something settled about it: not a death sentence but a fact about the riveting state of loss.

Yet at the same time as the outrage of discovery sends Eve into a compulsive formalism, she finds that her abandonment brings optimism with it:

> Yet my fear of the coming operation, if it was fear, didn't register as fear, but as a disconsolate sense that I already had been *abandoned*. And that
>
>> I *was* abandoned
>> in the sense that there was no
>> controlling that grief,
>
> that outrage. A crazy regression, an infantile compulsion. But maybe an alternative to looking forward with dread?[11]

Affect management is always belated. Abandonment is when, in the scene of looking backward, one discovers that the end of sociality has come already and that there is nothing left to fear or constrain—as long as one is not caught up in the depressive position's nostalgia work of reseduction, the repair that is never completed. The abandoned one can be a pillar of salt that is freed to be infinitely salty. The recognition is not a solution, though. The relation of abandonment to dread, of productive pasts to horrible futures, of recognition of the intractable, is a complex one in the Sedgwickian oeuvre: not convertible to a gesture, a politics, or emotional comfort but habitable only on the condition that it is not repaired.

LE: "Paranoid Reading and Reparative Reading," Eve's introduction to *Novel Gazing*, was later republished as the penultimate chapter of *Touching Feeling: Affect, Pedagogy, Performativity*. As she unambiguously defines it there, reparativity is "frankly ameliorative."[12] Fearing the failure, the unsustainability of its relation to the world—fearing, indeed, that the world "is inadequate or inimical to its nurture"—the subject of the reparative impulse attempts a "project of survival."[13] For reparativity, associated with the depressive position in Eve's reading of Melanie Klein (how accurate such a reading of Klein may be is another question entirely), is "an anxiety-mitigating achievement" that responds to and attempts to overcome the paranoiac's "terrible alertness to the dangers posed by . . . hateful and envious part-objects"; the reparative, by contrast, strives "to assemble and confer plenitude on an object" in the hope that the object "will then have the resources to offer to an inchoate self"—resources providing the "sustenance" that subsequently enables the self to survive.[14] Assembling, conferring plenitude, giving the inchoate a sustaining form: the work of reparativity grounds itself in a notion of aesthetic coherence that opposes the incompletion, division, and defectiveness of failure. The paranoid position, Eve argues, stands condemned as "self-defeating"[15]—defeated, that is, in attempting to defend against an anticipated external threat precisely insofar as the paranoid position is itself the *source* of that threat. Associating reality with the relentless danger of impingement from without and initiating, in consequence, a primal separation of the self from the world that would harm it, the paranoid position makes rupture a value in response to the anxiety occasioned by the vengeful part-objects it locates outside.

Reparativity, however, in the face of a threat to its objects posed by the *self*, extends, in Eve's view, some protection to *them* against the self and its paranoid practices. Aesthetic unity and amelioration are indistinguishable in this context. Making the part-object whole protects the object not for its own sake but, rather, for the sake of the self that such an object is intended to sustain. Reparativity becomes a "care of the self," a spiritual and aesthetic practice aspiring "to provide the self with pleasure and nourishment in an environment that is perceived as not particularly offering them."[16]

The self-defeat of paranoia, on the one hand, and the nourishment of the self, on the other: one could be forgiven for thinking, despite Eve's frequent and frequently emphatic denials, that we are caught in the dualistic thinking she associates with paranoia. Eve apprehends such dualism as central to the functioning of closed systems and so to the logic of digitality, with its rigidly binary, on-off schema, in contrast to analog representation and its multiple positionalities. Reiterating the continuity of paranoia and the digital with defectiveness and the condition of wanting—in other words, with failure or defeat—while reinforcing the reparative position's claim to realized form and aesthetic coherence, Eve quotes with approval from Anthony Wilden's work on system analysis: "Digital distinctions introduce gaps into continuums . . . whereas analog differences . . . fill continuums."[17] Put otherwise, the digital will always divide what the analog makes replete, and such repletion depends, as Eve makes clear by quoting Wilden once more, on the analog's characteristic incapacity for negation: "The analog does not possess the syntax necessary to say 'No.'"

By contrast, the paranoid position, which displays what Eve calls a "rigorous exclusiveness," insists above all on saying "No"—saying "No" in particular to whatever threatens to humiliate the subject or destroy it.[18] But in doing so, according to Eve, the paranoid subject calls forth the very part-objects it will then perceive as threats by splitting "both its objects and itself" into elements "exclusively . . . good or bad."[19] The paranoid subject, in other words, preemptively (if self-defeatingly) breaks from the brokenness of the part-objects it sees as threatening to break it in turn. But the reparative subject, by repairing *them*, by turning "part-objects into something like a whole," may reduce, if only briefly, the anxiety of an imminent break in relation and so establish the conditions that secure its "nourishment and comfort."[20]

Where the stakes in the paranoid-reparative difference are so stark and so highly fraught, where the wager of each, and in more than just figure, appears to pit life against death, survival against defeat, nourishment against destructiveness, we seem to be caught in a feedback loop, a trope Eve often made use of in her discussions of paranoid thought. But *this* feedback loop leads reparativity and its project of survival back into the paranoid or digital practice of rupture and division. For the reparative aesthetic emerges by breaking from the breaking characteristic of paranoia. "Paranoid Reading and Reparative Reading": if we read Eve's title (though would this be to read it reparatively or paranoiacally?) as an instance of hendiadys, then the *and* that binds its terms must also separate them as well, making difference out of sameness by naming as two what amounts to one in order to figure, albeit paradoxically, that underlying unity. In doing so the *and* displaces the digitalizing *or*, which then gets banished into the subtitle, or rather into the undefined space between title and subtitle that indicates their relation: "Paranoid Reading and Reparative Reading; or, You're So Paranoid, You Probably Think This Introduction Is about You." But what is the relation between the two? If the *or* suggests an alternative, it's an alternative that seems to lay equal claim to the place of the title itself. Instead of one title, then, we have two: a relation of *and*, not *or*—or one in which, rather than being two, *and* and *or* are one.

Surely no reader has ever missed the aggression of the subtitle's joke (who could, when it interpellates so pointedly everyone who reads it?). But who has observed its redoubling of the binary logic of the title itself—or rather, of the ambiguity as to whether it binarizes or unifies? On the face of it, *and* completes and binds, bringing disparate things together. If that disparity arises only by virtue of the *and* in the first place, however, if the "reading" at issue is not the distinction between paranoid and reparative modes but rather the reading that is paranoid and reparative at once, then *and*, in the guise of conjoining these modes, reifies their difference. Precisely by serving as a trope for *or*—for the twoness of separation and division—the title's *and* effects a literal displacement of that *or*. At the same time, however, the *or* that introduces what we understand as the subtitle begins to play the role of an *and* by identifying what could also properly be thought to title the essay. If the *and* of reparativity tropes the paranoiac *or* precisely by insisting on the distance, the division between paranoia and repair, and so on their distinct modes of reading (reparativity allegedly making whole what paranoia splits), then only in splitting from paranoia by functioning as an *or* can the title's *and* become, paradoxically, an *and* of conjunction once more. One can only conjoin or repair what bears the mark of separation already. *And* and *or* conjoin as conjunctions in their equal commitment to the splitting by which they separate from each other and come together at once. Reparativity similarly repeats the schizoid practice it claims to depart from; but precisely by virtue of proclaiming its essential division from paranoia, and thereby erasing the division between paranoia's division and its own repair, it is able, ironically, to *enact* "repair": the repair that undoes what we now can call *reparativity's* murderous division—and that undoes it by way of its own implication in the negativity it seems to negate.

But "Paranoid Reading and Reparative Reading," when reprinted in *Touching Feeling,* was followed, tellingly, by another essay, "The Pedagogy of Buddhism." After tracing the transformation of Buddhist concepts as they entered Euro-American culture, this essay concludes by discussing the emergence, particularly in the United States after World War II, of an interest in what Eve refers to as "the Buddhist pedagogy of nonself" and further describes as "the vibrant realms of 'no' in Buddhist thought."[21] Identifying herself with those whose medical status has made them vividly conscious of the distance "between [the] knowledge and [the] realization"[22] of death, she rejects the well-meaning assertion with regard to those confronting illness "that we are the last people who should be allowed to lapse from an unremitting regimen of positive thinking."[23] Though wary of a muscular appeal to the negative as an exercise of "sheer will power,"[24] Eve makes space for the negativity that informs those "vibrant realms of 'no,'" making them inextricable from "being and learning to unbe a self."[25]

The place of this "no" must be placed alongside Eve's readings of reparativity in order to see the unstable place of the reparative in her own thought, a place by no means final from the perspective of her critical *performance,* however frequently it may be vaunted as her ultimate critical *statement.* Can anyone attentive to Eve's career misrecognize her own distinctive gestures of negation and repudiation, of moving beyond and turning against the formulations, the versions of her own critical self, for which she had come to be known? Famous for declaring the cultural centrality of the hetero-homo distinction, she later had occasion to rethink that claim and dispute the importance she herself had placed on matters of sexuality. Similar acts of self-negation inform her changing attitudes toward shame, paranoia, epistemology, sexual difference, and even Foucault. The critical desire to stabilize reparativity as Eve's last (and lasting) bequest, as the wisdom surviving her loss—and by which we ourselves survive losing her—may serve, in this case, to simplify what her pedagogy enacts, to bury what only loss as such might serve to keep alive: the rupture to which repair is bound, the persistent place of the "No." Against what she saw as the paranoid position's association with "bad karma," Eve affirms, in what seems an unmistakable instance of paranoid splitting, the reparative position's commitment to turning "bad karma into good."[26] But in a deliberate echo of *Oedipus at Colonus,* an echo heard too in *A Dialogue on Love* when she describes herself as "convinced, with the ancients, that it would be best not to be born,"[27] Eve follows this distinction between bad and good karma, between the paranoid and the reparative, with something different from either: "The best thing of all . . . is to have no karma."[28]

LB: To have no karma is to discover oneself not dropped or abandoned tragically but occupying a separateness from the circuit of attachment and repair. So what survives here, across our readings, are multiple paradigms of Sedgwickian relationality: the clashing quasi-antithetical formalisms of which Lee just spoke and also the sideways zones of suspension that allow for the circulation of multiple affects. Eve hopes for something other than drama that feels dramatic and threatening to the possibility of staying attached to life. She figures this potential more than theorizes it; in relation to the care style of her therapist, Shannon, for example, she describes a foundationless life of watery buoyancy so that she can float careless in the good sense, without a care.[29]

Then there's the revelation Klein provides that is so stunning that Eve keeps forgetting and having to remember it:

> The sense that power is a form of relationality that deals in, for example, negotiations (including win-win negotiations), the exchange of affect, and other small differentials, the middle ranges of agency—the notion that you can be relatively empowered or disempowered without annihilating someone else or being annihilated, or even castrating or being castrated—is a great mitigation of that endogenous anxiety, although it is also a fragile achievement that requires to be discovered over and over.[30]

Add to this list the patient that Shannon recalls to Eve, in whom "the parts . . . were only barely holding hands."[31] This, too, describes the relief that acknowledgment, detachment, and even dissociation can provide, suggesting that a mode of existence can be forged in which the subject lives with an open vulnerability without compulsively inducing a saturating defense that attempts to disavow the noise of abandonment and dread.

WHAT'S LOST

LE: Loss is what, in the object relation, it's impossible to lose; it's what you're left with when an object changes its place or changes its state.

Even change for the better, even gain, involves such loss, where loss is not merely an emptiness but something more dimensional, something that fills the vacated space that's left by what used to be there. Loss, in such a context, may be a name for what survives. In the place of what one had before, loss remains to measure the space or distance relation requires. As relationality's constant, then, loss preserves relation in the absence of its object, affirming the object's contingency, from which relation first takes its sting, even if or when the object is mourned as irreplaceable. Maybe that's one of the motives for Eve's engagement with reincarnation, with the thought of surviving in and as this very loss of self, of *becoming* that loss and maintaining thereby a relation that overcomes it.

At the end of "The Weather in Proust" for example, she quotes this sentence from an account of Plotinus's thought on reincarnation: "When it passes from one inner level to another, the self always has the impression that it is losing itself."[32] But implicit here is a counter-assertion: that such an impression of the loss of self is something the self can *have*. Indeed, that very impression may be what *constitutes* the self. Such a self would emerge from the outset, through its experience of threatened loss, in the paranoid position associated with what I've been calling the place of the "No." What Eve evokes as the reparative position, anxiously responding in its own, distinct way to the anxiety of the paranoid, would trope on this stance of negation by presenting the threat as aimed at the object now instead of at the self, as emanating, in fact, from within that self whose power—that is, whose destructive power—fills the self with dread but in doing so *fills the self nonetheless.*

Protecting, holding, pitying: the reparative process, as Eve asserts, may possess (unlike the schizoid position, with its murderous assertiveness) a "mature, ethical dimension."[33] "Among Klein's names for the reparative process," she tells us elsewhere, "is love."[34] But that doesn't preclude reparativity's implication in violence, aggression, and destruction or exempt it from the consequences of its defensive deployment by a self whose dread of its powers nonetheless enlarges both them and it—and never more successfully than when that self would restrain or renounce them. This is the paradox of the reparative position and also, perhaps, of the mysticism Eve associates with reincarnation. For if mysticism in "The Weather in Proust" is, in Eve's words, "all but defined by its defiance of the closed system of either/or," then we might well ask, as the aural slippage between signifiers here suggests, if such defiance actually *defies* or *defines* what closes the system.[35] Doesn't the act of defiance perform the closed system's distinctive "no" and so reproduce the "either/or" it's intended to defy?

Closed or open? That is the question Eve's essay will force us to ask: "The important question in Proust [is] how open systems relate to closed ones, or perhaps better put, . . . how systems themselves move between functioning as open and closed."[36] The "better" formulation's betterness, of course, depends on the greater openness seen in its invocation of *and*, but even that openness cannot close off the closed system's "either/or." We may now be asking how systems move "between functioning as open and closed," but the functions themselves, as "between" makes clear, remain resolutely digital, where the digital pertains to the paranoid position's insistence on saying "no." While that "no" by no means discredits mysticism's claims to potential openness (any more than the *and* as trope for *or* discredits reparativity), it betrays the negativity indissociable from every gesture of repair: the disjunction or "no" that registers loss as the medium of, the precondition for, and the spur to relationality.

LB: I don't know if loss is the best name for what survives, or what relation it has to your similar observation about failure. But I agree that what we're facing is a spectacle of an unspectacular space in Eve's work, of the subject's own capacity not to be caught up in the tangle of her own circuits of abjection, grandiosity, and aggression. What does it mean to be in them without being torn up by them? What is the relation of narrative contingency to her stated desire to be held, not through the will but by unconditional love? What does it mean to want to write relationality into the unconditional? More and more potential orientations toward the object proliferate. It is as though her pedagogical compulsion to make people smarter translates, after a while, into making them merely proximate, as in the intimate pedagogy she frames so magnificently in "White Glasses," where intimacy is about co-spatiality and not predictability, recognition, or exchange. The unpredictable structure of the later work does not incite mourning in me or a desire to seduce the text toward repair but a curiosity about what's on offer in that space, a Bollasian attentiveness to the possibility of a loving deflation and a stretching out to figure things out, like a cat waking up in the sun. Perhaps the displacements she narrates are not always about loss and repair but a departure from the vanity of achieving perfect form and the risk of unlearning an attachment to the potential for drama to prove that we are really living.

This leads us back to dread: the dread of admitting knowing what brokenness is while managing the rage to repair. This living place of a knowing dread is a hard thing to talk about, much harder than the subject's tenderness, injury, and projected aggression. In some late-career moods, Eve writes not in the emotional vernacular of empathy but with realism about how destructive pure being is:

> The Kleinian infant experiences a greed whose aggressive and envious component is already perceived as posing a terrible threat both to her desired objects and to herself. The resulting primary anxiety is an affect so toxic that it probably ought to be called, not anxiety, but dread. It is against this endogenous dread that the primary defense mechanisms are first mobilized—the splitting, the omnipotence, the violent projection and introjection. These defenses, in turn, which may be mitigated but never go away, can impress their shape on the internal experience of repression as well as the social experience of suffering from, enforcing, or resisting repression.[37]

In this model, the subject who dreads is not successful at disavowal but spends her time encountering the impossible-to-distinguish relation between attaching and destroying and between building a world and annihilating what's inconvenient to it, including herself. Dread marks the core power of this version of the subject, no longer seen as protected by care and the compulsion to repair but as vulnerable to all acts, even acts of love, whose internal relation of violence to preservation is completely cloaked by the ambitions of personality to appear blameless.

LE: Taking in this powerful reading, Lauren, I'm conscious of the implicit drama you trace in the difficult gambit associated with Eve's "spectacle of [the] unspectacular"—a gambit perfectly captured when you write, "Perhaps the displacements [Eve] narrates are not always about loss and repair but [about] . . . the risk of unlearning an attachment to the potential for drama to prove that we are really living." That the real need not be situated in the inflated extremes of "drama" is surely a lesson that Eve learns through Klein (and through her therapist, Shannon, as well). But narratives evoking the "risk of unlearning" such histrionic attachments reenact them through the excitations called forth by the figure of "risk." Drama, like negativity, may be harder to escape than we think. Even the trope of "escaping" drama covertly resurrects it in the same way that self-enlargement may inhere in the effort to make the self minimal, to turn it from actor to witness, or to make such "witness" into something more companionate, more relational, more like withness.

A middle child, as she lets us know in *A Dialogue on Love*, Eve bluntly acknowledges her profound distrust of melodramatic extremes, but she admits that the "middle ranges of agency" that allow for "negotiations" represent, at best, a "fragile achievement," always on the verge of coming undone and so bound up with dramatic suspense no less than with suspensions of drama. Eve, after all, loved the novel; she began her career with a book on the Gothic, and melodramatic extremes were sites of intense erotic potential. Yet she invests much in this space of detachment from the melodramatics of selfhood—invests, that is, in a holding environment as sustaining to us as air, as ubiquitous as weather: a space beyond grandiosity, splitting, anxiety, or dread; a space she lovingly specifies as "quotidian, unspecial, reality-grounded."[38] But what relation obtains between such a space and the intensities of sex or the pressures of drives and desires that make that dread-free space so desirable?

Sometimes Eve posits that space of detachment as a vast circuit of interrelation. In *A Dialogue on Love* she describes it as "big / enough that you could never / even *know* whether // the system was closed, finally, or open."[39] But if the openness of the system is open to doubt, the psychic affordance of this figure for interconnectedness is not. "Picturing this new kind of circuitry was a vital *self-protective* step," she writes.[40] Although for Eve the very point of this circuit "could only // lie in valuing / all the transformations and / transitivities // in all directions / *for* their difference,"[41] that openness to transformation remains in the service of "self-protect[ion]," conserving what is, forestalling loss, and so precluding *her* transformation beyond a recognizable self insofar as she remains what sees and values the transformations around her. That is what becoming witness means here ("picturing this new kind of circuitry") and why witness, which Eve calls "reality-grounded," may not be so different from fantasy. Both rely on a loss of self through identification with the mise-en-scène in order to see what happens in what one imagines as one's absence. Eve distinguishes this open circuitry of what she calls "post-Proustian love" from the circulation of erotic desire in closed or triangular structures—structures in which

you would
eventually

get back all of the
erotic energy you'd
sent around it (so

that the point of this
fantasy was *nothing is ever really lost*).⁴²

But that fantasy continues to animate her thinking about reincarnation
and mysticism. That, I think, is why Eve insists, by the time of "The
Weather in Proust," that even a figure for reincarnation like the fountain of the Prince de Guermantes remains bound to the drama of a linear narrative, to a "conservation of matter and energy" that "might be
called strictly karmic."⁴³ And yet, as she notes, something other than the
logic of karma is at play, too, something that keeps the circuitry open to
prevent the possibility that transformation, that novelty, might get lost.
Observing how the fountain's elegant jets unexpectedly douse Madame
d'Arpajon when a sudden gust of wind diverts them, Eve writes, "Sometimes things that come around don't go around, and vice versa."⁴⁴

Beyond the cycles of karma, then, whether that karma turns out to be
good or bad, reparative or paranoid, lies the space of "no karma" that every
attempt to approach pushes farther away (just as seeking the space beyond drama, aspiring to inhabit its "beyond," already entails the *heroics*
of drama in trying to supersede it). "It seems inevitable for us karmic
individuals," Eve admits at the end of "Melanie Klein and the Difference Affect Makes," that "even the invocation of nonkarmic possibility
will be karmically overdetermined. . . . It can function as an evasion."⁴⁵
An evasion of the desire that attaches us to the vision of freedom from
desire itself? An evasion of the historicity of our own relation to the
"nonkarmic"? An evasion of the ways the nonkarmic may carry, as its
very prefix suggests, the "no" that marks its connection to the splitting
evinced by the schizoid position? Eve ends that essay without specifying just what the nonkarmic would evade, affirming instead that, at least
for her, the "vision of nonkarmic possibility . . . also illuminates some
possibilities of opening out new relations to the depressive position."⁴⁶

Whatever this means, and I think Eve deliberately refuses to give
us its meaning in any propositional form, it strikes the chord of a set

of values to which the whole of her later work vibrates. "Possibilities," "opening out," "new relations": these sound the base tone of those values and they anticipate her explicit summation of them near the end of "The Weather in Proust": "That the universe along with the things in it are alive and therefore good: here I think is a crux of Proust's mysticism. Moreover, the formulation does not record a certainty or a belief but an orientation, the structure of a need, and a mode of perception. It is possible for the universe to be dead and worthless; but if it does not live, neither do the things in it, including oneself and one's own contents."[47] The universe must live, and in living be good, these sentences seem to suggest, either *because* I am living myself or *in order that I may continue to do so.* Just before she makes this claim, Eve talks about viewing the universe as "instinct with value and vitality."[48] Here, in a parallel epithet, though one chiastically inverted, she recoils from seeing it as "dead and worthless." It's not just vitality that she values here but value that proves to be vital: the *valuing* of the universe that sees it as good is precisely what keeps it alive.

The nonkarmic alternative to self-inflation brings us back to a self apparently charged with maintaining and supporting the universe *so that it can hold the self in turn.* As Eve muses in *A Dialogue on Love,* "Without magical thinking I imagine the world would be gray, no colors, air pushed out of it."[49] This world without sequins, deprived of attachment, is the one and only thing, Eve tells us, she truly dreads for herself: "For me, dread only // I may stop knowing / how to like and desire / the world around me."[50] But the dread here attaches less to the prospect of detachment from the world, less to the specific thought of her neither liking nor desiring it, than to the competence-humbling confrontation with not "knowing how" to do so. An affective blockage gets processed as dread when its form is epistemological. Or else, as a defense against dread itself, epistemology here trumps affect. Of course, the tension between these two projects (epistemology and affect) names a rupture in Eve's career even as it names two competing ways in which she encounters Proust. Against what she acknowledges, but devalues, as his "demystifying, propositional level of knowingness and lack," she mobilizes the nonkarmic alternative: "the non-propositional, environmental order of Proust's reality-orientation, which coincides with his mysticism."[51] Between epistemology and object-relations, between the order of propositions and the environment they take place in, we encounter once more the place of the "no," the space of discontinuity, where knowingness, with its endless retinue of erotic potentiality bound up with the limit or lack that's always encountered in the "no," is deposed in favor of an ethical vitalization of the universe.

LB: I am not sure that being erotically knowing, in Eve's work, is trumped by a vitalizing ethical sanitation of the inconvenience and messiness of attachment. Is trumping the only relation we can see when divergent models line up next to each other? Are managerial impulses really, in the end, impulses toward mastery? These are not rhetorical questions, but I'm not saying yes or no. The transferential situation lets us encounter where we don't make sense without being defeated by it. I recognize that I read for what Eve makes possible, for her belief in the work of concepts to make the unbearable livable and the nonrelational part of intimacy a part of what's potentially sustaining in attachment. People often encounter their own dramas undramatically, with not much more than a nod and sometimes comic shrugging. Let me focus on a few related problems emerging in our analysis.

For Eve, dread opens up the possibility of seeing that one's own dramas are murderous and that this knowledge does not make them less murderous. What its acknowledgment does—and this is different from what knowledge does—is to specify those impulses as one mode of action among many. I could destroy the world in my dreaded desire for it—or not, and in the not, be rocked by things without being defeated by it. So at stake in the confrontation with the impulse to use knowledge and writing to repair a relationality constitutively broken while remaining relational is not to note that epistemology trumps affect, or vice versa, but to address how to proceed when one's epistemological and affective dressage no longer provides knowledge, pleasure, or even effective affect management. This is the conceptual rhetorical work of Eve's late ficto-criticism, as well as the motive for therapy. The crisis is of what to do when one's long habit of doing the work of being oneself no longer works, not even in a fake or fantasmatic way: one needs all of one's resources for improvisation, new affective rhythms, better conceptualizations of what the subject is capable of that will always coexist with the aspect of the subject stuck in drama. Likewise, therefore, the problem in Eve's work of risking unlearning the association of life with a dramatics of living is not necessarily a fantasy of escape from drama but a fantasy of making room for the openness imminent to acknowledgment without destroying that space with the dreaded histrionics of one's greedy mastery demands.

Judging what is necessarily or not necessarily the case is a central trope throughout her work, and a trope is not necessarily a drama. It might involve feeling out a territory like a hand skipping over sand in the dark. When she says something "must necessarily" refer—as in "the nation must necessarily refer to sexuality"—it is to insist on the connectedness of things that claim to be separate, and it is always political.[52] But when the "not necessarily related" kind of phrase appears, it ratchets down the melodrama of attachment: "After this, in fact, I get very charmed and relaxed by everything that looks like non-necessity. I've started noticing that lots of Shannon's best comments—the ones that change the aspect of things for me—amount to nothing more profound than 'It ain't necessarily so.'"[53] One could call the discovery of the non-necessity of things, a non- that's predicted by the spontaneity of the Sedgwickian nonce, a moment of heightening that also marks the difference between affect and emotion as vectors of analysis.

In the way she represents her relation to Shannon, Eve does sometimes wish for something simple, an emotional monotone that rules over the affectively inconvenient noise. This is because the noise of affect is inconvenient. But Eve was trying for something else in the work too: not a simple symptom simply calling out to be cured but a messier room. Symptoms overorganize a process into a representation. They seem literal: one problem, one presenting and representing problem. But before something becomes the lie that is a symptom, a fetish, or a fact invested with desire, it is a dispersed environment of causes and pulses. The unconscious is not where she looks to be able to bear this. She looks to her complex world made up of affective extensions. She calls Shannon, her friends, and the authors in whose work she is deeply invested forces that change the aspect of life, etymologically the arrangement of the planets, and she hopes that changing the aspect can change the expect. The question is whether the wish to provide a rearrangement is a defense against the loss of everything or a wish for the unbearable to become the habitable in a way that actually risks changing something. My gamble is that the encounter with her unconditional negativity, the misalignment of her internal planets, is not the same thing as merely a fantasy of being both oneself and otherwise. It matters to say "maybe."

This takes me directly to sex. *A Dialogue on Love* narrates the loss of a life-long masturbatory practice and its refinding as erotic energy both in the transferential therapeutic scene and outside the office as well: just as the "dialogue" on love is not a dialogue but many genres of call and response, so too she finds sex again in anything that can stand as a syncopated relation. Syncopation includes syncope, a fainting feeling. She finds it all, the recession and the return, in caring for the other, in being cared for, in allowing the other to push her body into a new aspect and make it feel solid and liquid; in the concept of a being-with that includes all of what's unshared and discarded in the penumbra of the promise to show up again for more talk; and in the revelation that there was never a singular break to be repaired but tears within a membrane that can take the shock in some spots better than others without being annihilated by it.

In this way, out-of-syncness is not only a drama of negativity but also sociality's great promise and a way to maintain an affective mess for which most people do not have the skill or the trust in the world's, or other people's, patience. Eve never wrote an essay called "Pedagogy of Sex." There are many reasons for this, no doubt, and "A Poem Is Being Written" comes close. There, the main thing is that sex is not a thing of truth but a scene where one discovers potentiality in the abandon that's on the other side of abandonment. She wanted sex at once to expand and become specific by multiplying the range of its potential scenarios and relational rhythms so that her readers, her intimates, could achieve different kinds of aspect-altering acknowledgment of sexuality's genuinely wild object inducements, from the biggest love to something as minimal as a "gay-affirmative detachment."[54]

So I am not saying to you, "Stop with all the drama, already!" Sometimes Eve said things like that, but it was just one of her many wishes. Others were to acknowledge the subject's internal chaos in relation to the chaos of the world; to admit the relief of being managed and managing the situation of attachment without repairing it, were repairing to mean disavowal; and to imagine that different tones could induce unpredicted infrastructures for relationality in the world. Above all, to respect the impact of the concept a wish makes to reroute the effects, and the affects.

LE: I'm glad you're not saying, "Stop with all the drama, already!" since such a self-deconstructing imperative would be a showstopper in spite of itself. We could hardly stop the drama, after all, and still produce a dialogue. Whether delivering this talk at the MLA in a give-and-take always alive to the fear of annihilation through a "zinger," intended as such or not, or here in the space of the printed page where our separate but interwoven words still function contrapuntally, we're mired to our eyeballs in drama—the drama we've known since Plato inheres in encountering an idea but that also inheres, as we've known since Sigmund Freud, in the negativity of relation. The question is how we stage that drama, both for others and for ourselves, and how it stages us.

Together and separate, Lauren and Lee: bound by the dialogic structure that also distinguishes our voices, we're certain to be staged, whether we like it or not, as instantiating the hendiadic logic of "Paranoid Reading and Reparative Reading." Not that you and I occupy, as if we were allegorical figures, the reparative and paranoid positions, respectively (or as if those positions themselves, as I've been arguing, are ever as clear-cut as they seem), but we're certainly susceptible to misrecognition in those binarizing terms. Though we share, that is, a resistance to the pastoral affirmation of cohesiveness, though we both see Eve herself as producing something beyond the repair that endlessly animates rupture's "no," we nonetheless—and, perhaps, unavoidably, given the form in which we're working—subject ourselves to the risk of construction in allegorical terms. Viewed through the distortion of such a lens, I would embody the negativity Eve distrusts in paranoia, the negativity she associates with the demystifications practiced by the "Yale school," whose "masculine" regime of epistemological power she, herself a Yale Ph.D., opposes to "vitality and value" and so to the prospect of aesthetic coherence imagined as "weather" or "environment."

That same false optic would identify you with the affect theory through which Eve envisions an access to immediacy, to the plenitude of possibility, to a less anxious relation to the body, and to a nondestructive, nondualistic ability to be with what is. As understood in this way by Eve, affect theory permits movement beyond the ruptures resurrected by repair, even if only in ways that one—or, at least, the allegorical other one who figures paranoid reading—might describe as largely enacting a fantasmatic repair of repair. Affect theory, as Eve conceives it, which is not, as we know, how you do, envisions the possibility of a universe of good: a holding environment that opens a space beyond histrionic extremes and the lethal conflicts of either/or. That version of affect theory, by holding on to the possibility of the subject's being held (hence, neither abandoned nor allowed to drop), occupies the fantasmatic place of the good, or the good enough, mother for Eve, whether that mother be identified with Shannon or with the text of *À la recherche*. And though such a version of affect theory differs markedly from yours, our audience, Lauren, may align you too with Eve's conflation of affect theory and a sustaining maternal hold, not because you believe in that hold as what affect theory offers, but because Eve, in enlisting affect to affirm the prospect of repaired relation, of the openness of and to "being with," employs your language to imagine a dread-free coexistence with mess. She reads the potentiality inherent in weather—in a quotidian, "reality-grounded" environment—as what holds us by holding out to us the promise of "value and vitality," of the universe as a livable space.

If you face allegorical inscription, though, in the place of the good-enough mother, then I, like the paranoid practices of deconstructive knowingness, am likely to be cast, and no less falsely (at least from my point of view), as theory's equivalent of Darth Vader, a form of the father we love to hate: withholding, histrionic, life-negating, and full of inhuman enjoyment. In such an allegorical setup, though, where both of us get set up (and not by reason of gender alone, although gender will play a role), I'm made to figure something Eve resolutely sought to project, while you figure something Eve equally resolutely wanted to incorporate. And just as neither you nor I conforms to these allegorical images (though saying so won't forestall in the least our assimilation to them), so Eve, or the Eve that survives as her texts, is distinct from the self that such acts of projection and incorporation would induce. Her texts show those acts—or perhaps we should define them as tendencies instead—to be wishes, desires, karmic strivings bound up with the drama of trying to overcome her own intractable resistance. You write, and for me quite movingly, "I read for what Eve makes possible"; I, on the other hand, read in Eve's text what makes its coherence impossible. You resonate to what you call Eve's "belief in the work of concepts to make the unbearable livable and the nonrelational part of intimacy a part of what's potentially sustaining in attachment," while I respond to her text's incapacity to resolve into such propositional utterances without, in the end, repudiating the very privilege of propositional thought.

I view as serious reflections on the different ways we read the series of questions you generate in response to my take on Eve's work: "Is trumping the only relation we can see when divergent models line up next to each other? Are managerial impulses really, in the end, impulses toward mastery?" No doubt there are other models than trumping for thinking what happens when antithetical constructs appear beside each other. But as the contexts of our readings must count for something, so must the language Eve uses. When *A Dialogue on Love* first broaches dread, the book's most troubling affect (and most troubling precisely insofar as it springs from the prospect of love's undoing), she locates it, where dread *for herself* is concerned, *uniquely* in a failure of *knowing*—specifically, a failure of knowing how to mobilize attachment to the world. In that sense, the failure of knowledge, I argued, might be the form, however displaced, that affective blockage takes. Or it might, alternatively, function defensively to trump the incursion of affect. For me, then, the question is not whether trumping is "the only relation we can see when antithetical models line up," but why *in this instance*, when she first explores dread, Eve focuses explicitly on epistemological failure; why the impulse to affect that's figured by dread of a lost attachment to the world takes the form of what affect in Eve would displace: the insistence of epistemological mastery. I'm not interested in globalizing this particular move and making such mastery the secret desire of Eve's writings, both early and late. I want to focus instead on the negativity inseparable from her career-long pursuit of a survivable self—the negativity implicit in her trying and failing to cast out paranoia while also trying and failing to incorporate what affect theory might promise. But "failing," in Eve's case as much as in ours, fails as a name for this practice; for her, too, the want that compels repetition is just what relation most wants.

This repetition has much to do with both survival and affect management. Wanting to allow for what you hail as "sociality's great promise," wanting to provide a space for what you describe as "affective mess," and so for living with an incoherence that needn't prove to be murderous, you ask if "managerial impulses" must, in the end, aspire to mastery. But precisely as an effort to evade the murderousness of paranoid-schizoid splitting, affect management, at least in Eve's work, does aim to master a threat. And that threat is itself an affect: the dread Eve traces to a failure of knowledge.

To make a very long argument short, the discourse of affect management for Eve seems to function like, but as an alternative to, the Freudian reality principle. Hence, she characterizes affect theory as thoroughly grounded in reality. She writes, for example:

[Melanie Klein's] work has a reassuring groundedness, a sense of reality. I realize that this remark may sound implausible to anyone willing to sail through sentences about the cannibalistic defense of the good partial breast against the devouring invasion of the feces. But . . . I feel enabled by the way that even abstruse Kleinian work remains so susceptible to a gut check. It may not be grounded in common sense, but it is phenomenologically grounded to a remarkable degree. A lot of this quality is owing to the fact that Klein's psychoanalysis, by contrast to Freud's, is based in affect.[55]

The capacity to tolerate disturbance, to put up with frustration undramatically, to be with and amid contradiction without resorting to murderous violence: that's what the reality principle affords, and that's why, for Freud, the reality principle and the pleasure principle aren't antithetical. Instead, the former temporalizes the latter in the service of survival. In this nonopposition, the reality principle registers and manages affect by binding the mobile energy of the primary process. This reality-based affect management aims for an overall feeling of evenness as a version of pleasure that's more stable, modulated, and controlled than the primary process's. This may explain why Eve takes great pains to link affect theory's grounding in "reality," and hence its attention to the possibilities for "respond[ing] to environmental (e.g., political) change," with the reparative's investment in pleasure (as opposed to paranoia's investment in knowledge): "Reparative motives, once they become explicit, are inadmissible in paranoid theory both because they are about pleasure . . . and because they are frankly ameliorative."[56] Her recourse to a version of affect theory thus brings reality and pleasure together, and this pairing sketches the outlines of a nonkarmic alternative to paranoia.

But beyond the reality and pleasure principles lie the death drive's repetitions—the pressure of a negativity that insists as a surplus of form over content, of structure over statement, of performance over meaning. Though Eve wanted something other than the death drive's otherness to life, that wanting preserved the place in which its otherness survived. What her work, with its restless intelligence and unyielding commitment, asks of us, and what we, in being true to it, have been asking of each other is whether the *and* can embrace the *or* without, in the process, repeating *or*'s own otherness to *and*. Does such an embrace, in other words, depend on the distance it would abrogate and the negativity it would deny? Which also may be a way of asking: In such an embrace, what survives?

LB: We converge in seeing that reparativity, in Eve's work, marks the and/or in an insuperable negativity that induces nonetheless a wish for relief in repair, which may mean something as minor but major as a shift in attachment styles. But at the same time, I would argue that the very shifting of the subject in response to its own threat to its self-attachment can be the source of an affective creativity that is not just a fantasmatic toupée, but also the possibility of a recalibrated sensorium, as when a comic orientation toward aggression and pleasure produces new capacities for bearing, and not repairing, ambivalence. Eve's work is a training in being in the room with that ambivalence, which she also called unbearable, in its revelation that having and losing are indistinguishable, although sometimes— for example, while one is mourning—it does not feel that way.

NOTES

1   Tom Dumm, *Loneliness as a Way of Life* (Cambridge, MA: Harvard University Press, 2008); Claudia Rankine, *Don't Let Me Be Lonely: An American Lyric* (Minneapolis: Greywolf, 2004); Rae Armantrout, *Versed* (Middletown, CT: Wesleyan University Press, 2010).

2   Dumm, *Loneliness as a Way of Life*, 151–52.

3   Rankine, *Don't Let Me Be Lonely*, 62.

4   Armantrout, *Versed*, 17.

5   Eve Kosofsky Sedgwick, *A Dialogue on Love* (Boston: Beacon, 2000), 171–72.

6   Sedgwick, *A Dialogue on Love*, 172.

7   Eve Kosofsky Sedgwick, *The Weather in Proust*, ed. Jonathan Goldberg (Durham, NC: Duke University Press, 2011), 138.

8   Sedgwick, *A Dialogue on Love*, 157. Mark Seltzer first uses the phrase "melodramas of uncertain agency" in *Serial Killers: Death and Life in America's Wound Culture* (New York: Routledge, 1998), 77.

9   Sedgwick, *A Dialogue on Love*, 142.

10 Sedgwick, *A Dialogue on Love*, 142.

11 Sedgwick, *A Dialogue on Love*, 88–89.

12 Eve Kosofsky Sedgwick, *Touching Feeling: Affect, Pedagogy, Performativity* (Durham, NC: Duke University Press, 2003), 144.

13 Sedgwick, *Touching Feeling*, 149–50.

14 Sedgwick, *Touching Feeling*, 128, 149–50.

15 Sedgwick, *Touching Feeling*, 137.

16 Sedgwick, *Touching Feeling*, 137.

17 Sedgwick, *Touching Feeling*, 121.

18 Sedgwick, *Touching Feeling*, 135.

19 Eve Kosofsky Sedgwick, "Melanie Klein and the Difference Affect Makes," *South Atlantic Quarterly* 106, no. 3 (2007): 633.

20 Sedgwick, *Touching Feeling*, 128.

21 Sedgwick, *Touching Feeling*, 173.

22 Sedgwick, *Touching Feeling*, 173.

23 Sedgwick, *Touching Feeling*, 173.

24 Sedgwick, *Touching Feeling*, 173.

25 Sedgwick, *Touching Feeling*, 179.

26 Sedgwick, "Melanie Klein and the Difference Affect Makes," 641.

27 Sedgwick, *A Dialogue on Love*, 111.

28 Sedgwick, "Melanie Klein and the Difference Affect Makes," 641.

29 Sedgwick, *A Dialogue on Love*, 139.

30 Sedgwick, *The Weather in Proust*, 130.

31 Sedgwick, *A Dialogue on Love*, 111.

32 Sedgwick, *The Weather in Proust*, 34.

33 Sedgwick, "Melanie Klein and the Difference Affect Makes," 638.

34 Sedgwick, *Touching Feeling*, 128.

35 Sedgwick, *The Weather in Proust*, 5.

36 Sedgwick, *The Weather in Proust*, 3.

37 Sedgwick, "Melanie Klein and the Difference Affect Makes," 633–34.

38 Sedgwick, *The Weather in Proust*, 4.

39 Sedgwick, *A Dialogue on Love*, 114.

40 Sedgwick, *A Dialogue on Love*, 115.

41 Sedgwick, *A Dialogue on Love*, 114.

42 Sedgwick, *A Dialogue on Love*, 114.

43 Sedgwick, *The Weather in Proust*, 3.

44 Sedgwick, *The Weather in Proust*, 3.

45 Sedgwick, "Melanie Klein and the Difference Affect Makes," 641–42.

46 Sedgwick, "Melanie Klein and the Difference Affect Makes," 642.

47 Sedgwick, *The Weather in Proust*, 32.

48 Sedgwick, *The Weather in Proust*, 32.

49 Sedgwick, *A Dialogue on Love*, 111.

50 Sedgwick, *A Dialogue on Love*, 4.

51 Sedgwick, *A Dialogue on Love*, 6; Sedgwick, *The Weather in Proust*, 4.

52 Eve Kosofsky Sedgwick, "White Glasses," in Eve Kosofsky Sedgwick, *Tendencies* (Durham, NC: Duke University Press, 1993), 147.

53 Sedgwick, *A Dialogue on Love*, 112.

54 Sedgwick, "White Glasses," 169.

55 Sedgwick, "Melanie Klein and the Difference Affect Makes," 628.

56 Sedgwick, *Touching Feeling*, 144.

Proust at the End

A change in weather is sufficient to recreate the world and ourselves.
–Marcel Proust, *The Guermantes Way*

I am honored to think with Eve Kosofsky Sedgwick once again on the occasion of memorializing her. She taught me about memory, and teaches me still. She argued with me productively, and I keep those conversations alive. Memory was indeed one of the issues about which she thought most attentively in the years before we lost her, or so it would seem on the basis of her work on Proust.[1] It strikes me as important that both Eve and Barbara Johnson were reading Proust in the years before they died, and I wondered whether one could find a point of convergence between these two readings. Barbara Johnson always wanted to know what Eve was working on, and she made sure, despite increasing physical challenges in 2005, to find her way to Harvard Law School in 2005 to hear Eve's paper, "The Weather in Proust." In that piece, Sedgwick cites Johnson explicitly, which should come as no surprise, since they wrote in each other's orbit. Indeed, Eve was known to pose that unforgettable question, "Who among us is *not* in love with Barbara Johnson?" It was a question that rhetorically suspended and crossed gender and sexual orientation in a way that was, and is, infamously Sedgwick. What Eve perhaps did not quite consider is that a similar question circulates about her: Who among us has not had our breath taken away by Eve Sedgwick—only to have it blown back in radically surprising ways?

My reference to breath is not casual. What seemed to claim Eve's attention in Proust's work was the constant evocation of climate, the way the narrator notices the shifts in temperature, wind, and light, and how the narrator functions as what Proust called an "animated barometer." Indeed, one expects Proust's narrator to be living for love, for consummation, for the possession of the lover and the vanquishing of any possible rival. But another economy emerges that decenters the first, focusing instead on the changes in climate to which one wakes in the morning, taking in the world in a new way, the sudden surprise that any shift in the weather brings. At stake is not just a preference for one mode of attending the world over another, but a basic reordering of how we understand what is most fundamental to being a body in the world. Sedgwick wrote,

> The lacerating quality of Proust's narrator's inability to sleep in an unfamiliar space—as though the environment threatened not his desires but his life—feels less like the fear of having to share someone's love than like the asthmatic's fear of being unable to breathe. I would argue that even the mortal dread he feels, in childhood, at having to go to bed without his mother's kiss derives its quality and rhythm much more from a threatened existential function, such as breathing, than from a frustrated second-order drive, such as libido.[2]

Here as elsewhere, Sedgwick asks us to reconsider the theory of the drives, since one of the most fundamental biological strivings is, indeed, to breathe, and to continue to breathe. And one of the most profound panics possible is induced by any obstruction to breathing. To breathe requires a conducive world, a world of air, and in this way we are bound to our environments, to shifts in climate, in ways that bear consequences for bodily survival. For this reason, among others, Sedgwick turns to the psychoanalytic work of Michael Balint, who steers a course away from Oedipal logics that end up stoking desires for possession that can only and always end in defeat. Over and against this tragic drama of omnipotence, Balint suggests that there are modes of transferring to the ambient environment. Sedgwick makes clear that this functions as an important alternative modality within psychoanalysis, one that links it with other important religious and philosophical traditions, from Plotinus to Buddhism. In her view, the Oedipal presumption presupposes that desire strives infinitely and vainly for omnipotence and exclusivity and so is perpetually vanquished by jealousy and defeat. Sedgwick emphasizes another modality of desire that seeks instead what is adequate and that forms itself around the very material and ecological conditions of support, sustenance, and persistence. This brings her to a reconsideration of basic drives, but also to breathing and the circumambient world in which that is possible.

Here Sedgwick links Balint's perspective to Barbara Johnson's essay, "Using People: Kant with Winnicott," published most recently in *Persons and Things*.[3] Sedgwick writes that the more benign form of transference, which attaches to the environment itself, "requires from its object . . . a mode of being, specifically a mode of being that characterizes the natural elements."[4] She then cites in succession Balint and Johnson. Balint refers to a mode of transference within psychoanalysis that

> presupposes an environment that accepts and consents to sustain and carry the patient like the earth or the water sustains and carries a man who entrusts his weight to them. In contrast to ordinary objects, especially to ordinary human objects, no action is expected from these primary objects or substances; yet they must be there and must—tacitly or explicitly—consent to be used, otherwise the patient cannot achieve any change: without water it is impossible to swim, without earth impossible to move on.[5]

It is interesting here that nature or the environment is personified as "giving consent" to those who breathe its air and move upon its earth with the presumption of gravity. Its mode of consent is not precisely contractual or legal, and there is no speech act that articulates this mode of giving consent. It gives, lends itself out, offers itself to be used, and trusts that it will survive being used. Sedgwick then turns to Johnson's paraphrase of Winnicott: "The object becomes real because it survives, because it is outside the subject's range of omnipotent control."[6] In Johnson's reading of Winnicott's analysis of the transferential object, the desire for the object is a desire to mangle and maul it, to use it, even to use it up, on the condition that the object survive all that use. Indeed, the point that became crucial for Melanie Klein, a figure who binds Sedgwick and Johnson, is that the desirous child needs to know that its efforts to master, devour, and abuse the object, understood broadly but not exclusively as the maternal, will be survived by the mother, or indeed, by any animate or inanimate object who serves that primary function. In other words, the object-world must remain intact not only to support and sustain the life of the child whose dependency on that world is a matter of life and death, but because the child cannot live with too much power. Indeed, if the object survives its use, the child proves not to be as omnipotent as she feared she was. For both Johnson and Sedgwick, the animated and surviving object and object-world mark the limits of human omnipotence. The survival of the object is also my own survival. This is why, for Sedgwick, breathing is more primary than libido, and it is why, for Johnson, the object must survive its use, marking the limit of human destructiveness.

There is another dimension to the analysis here: guilt is also a second-order phenomenon for Klein, since whatever check we impose on our own destructiveness emerges from the implicit understanding that our survival depends on the survival of the object—indeed, the object-world, or the ambient environment. If we succeed in toxifying the air, we will not survive, and if we destroy our lover for having shared his or her love, we will lose our lover and our loving. Thus, for Klein, guilt is a way of managing destructiveness in order to survive, and in that way guilt, rather than the paradigmatically moral disposition that distinguishes humans from animals, is a second-order permutation of the desire to persist, linking us with animals, both human and nonhuman.

So what, if anything, does this excursus on an expanded account of object-relations have to do with reading Proust? The wager here is that both Sedgwick and Johnson were reading Proust at the end, perhaps because he offered a way to counter omnipotence even as he recruits us into its most maddening vicissitudes. Although I read in both English and French (learned my French in graduate school by reading Proust), in preparing to write this essay I spent some weeks rereading Proust in English, appreciating how Johnson accepted the gift of the English translation, since translations are gifts, to be sure. Toward the end of her life she requested to listen to Proust on tape and rejected the English version I once sent her. "Moncrieff?" she asked, incredulously. Later I learned that she had requested that a French friend come weekly to read from Proust, and she did. I asked that friend whether Barbara spoke at all about what she heard, and the answer was "not a word." She was taking it in; perhaps we could say, with Eve: she was breathing Proust in.

Sedgwick's reading of Proust has done something brilliant. Among the many astonishing characteristics of the opening third of *Remembrance of Things Past* is the extraordinary length of time that Proust dwells on Swann's love for Odette, his mad and inventive jealousy, his repeated and retractable realization that her love has gone elsewhere, and his conviction that he himself has become odious in her eyes. Only after several hundred pages of attentive detail, culminating with the recognition that he has suffered so terribly for a woman who, in the end, is "not even his type," we receive the report from our young narrator not only that Swann did marry her, but that he did so for the purpose of presenting her in social company to a certain Duchesse de Guermantes. Although there is already a Madame Swann remarked on by the narrator in earlier passages, the entirety of Swann's relation to Odette is narrated without any explicit reference to marriage, past, present, or future. Matters become more confusing when Swann marries Odette and she turns out to be the Madame Swann so firmly and explicitly backgrounded in the first five hundred pages of the text.

Of course, the marriage plot would have us expect something else. Odette is Swann's mistress and therefore *not* his wife. Or Swann marries Odette at the height of their love, and she happily becomes Madame Swann. But in this text, it is only when the love is wrecked and the striving for possession has failed that marriage becomes a distinct narrative possibility. Only when Odette proves to be unequivocally elusive in the face of various forms of abject pleading and accusation does marriage enter the story. We appear to witness what seems to be a final break or the death of love, the cessation of a long story in which Swann's love and jealousy seem mainly derived from his own inventive powers. The marriage of the next chapter emerges on the condition of the death of love, perhaps as its ratification. When we come to the end of "Swann in Love," and Odette escapes a party with one provisionally named Napoleon III, with whom a furtive arrangement apparently has been made, and Swann "felt that he really hated Odette," we are given to assume that the chapter's end is the end of that love. We expect the pain to be redoubled when a painter, described as a strange young man, burst into tears, announcing that he was also Odette's lover. It is Swann, then, apparently calm, who comforts the young man, remarking that "he was obviously the man to understand her."[7] What follows is the relapse of the second character into the first. Proust writes, "So Swann reasoned with himself, for the young man whom he had failed at first to identify was himself too; like certain novelists, he had distributed his own personality between two characters, the one who was dreaming the dream, and another whom he saw in front of him sporting a fez."[8] Indeed, the narrator of the story is a young man who is following the life of Swann, so we are no longer certain at such a moment whether there is a stable distinction between narrator and character. Indeed, it seems that Swann is also narrating, since he gave the name "Napoleon III" to Forcheville, precisely the man to whom he riveted his jealous attentions for some hundred pages at least.

In "Madame Swann at Home" we learn that many people are surprised by the marriage, we finally learn something about Odette's class-based conviction that Swann would never marry her, and it is speculated that she suffers from shame and humiliation. Swann resolves to marry her only after a series of painful realizations become unbearable. Proust writes, "A new regimen, that of matrimony, would put an end with almost magical swiftness to those painful incidents." The narrator explains that this follows from "the purely subjective nature of the phenomenon that we call love, or how it creates, so to speak, a supplementary person, distinct from the person whom the world knows by the same name, a person most of whose constituent elements are derived from ourselves."⁹ Thus, the act of falling in love seems to participate in that same distribution of personality that describes the narrator's relation to his character. Swann is narrating, but he is also dreaming, and in his dreams he takes great pleasure in the "creative power by which he was able to reproduce himself by a simple act of division."¹⁰

His marriage was then part of the making of a supplementary person, but what name does that person have? Odette, Swann himself? It is not, though, in his own eyes that this supplementary person must appear. It is in the eyes of yet some third person, the one whose social opinion he values most highly and who credibly represents that social power. An impossible figure, since such a one would never offer the recognition he sought. We are told that he dies with the certainty that the Duchesse will never have known the two of them, and this deprivation is final, if not fatal.

Many Sedgwickian themes proliferate here. Hilarious and shocking as the sequences may be, the death of love leads to marriage, and marriage becomes bound up with the desire for an impossible recognition that works its fatality on Swann himself. He no longer quite loves his Odette, was arguably not even attracted to her at the beginning, but some other desire takes its place or was working as its substitute from the start. What he seeks is precisely what the narrator calls "a posthumous love," one that requires the death of both love and life.

At such a moment we see perhaps a certain transition in Proust that we also find in Sedgwick. Her early work on triangularity exposed not only the way that homosociality streaks through heterosexuality, but also how the dyad is never quite as closed as it may appear. Even then, however, Sedgwick sought to offer a way to think about triangulation that did not rigidify laws of exclusion, possession, and displacement, those that characterize the most orthodox version of the Oedipal scenario. Desire was more multiple and circuitous, but also more interesting, than the Oedipal version could narrate. With the help of Sedgwick's reading, we might now identify a certain Buddhist turn in Proust. Here is the passage that Paul de Man used to teach many years ago. I offer it here because I think it can be read in a new way with Sedgwick's inflection. It reflects on the improbable event of Swann's marriage:

> The laborious process of causation which sooner or later will bring about every possible effect, including, consequently, those which one had believed to be least possible, naturally slow at times, is rendered slower still by our desire (which in seeking to accelerate only obstructs it) by our very

existence, and comes to fruition only when we have ceased to desire—have ceased, possibly, to live.[11]

Interestingly enough, it is not the vanquishing of desire that leads to the expansion of possible effects, but its *deceleration*. What world of possibility opens here? It is as if on the flip side of the map of jealousy is the grid that tracks interrelated connections among humans and things that belong to an expanding network or horizon. For Proust, love always involves a certain proliferation of character. One becomes another self, and one's lover does, as well, and it is always either under the gaze of another that love becomes real or, indeed, in a mad effort to escape the gaze, which keeps that third equally indispensable. If an acceptance of this proliferated and interrelated mapping becomes possible, it is on the condition of a decelerated desire, precisely not the frantic effort to secure and vanquish, one that lets go of a strictly egoistic position. There is some invariable displacement that articulates this relationality, which is why displacement is not the same as being simply negated. It is about being determined in relation to others and to an ambient world. In this sense, what started as a maddening triangle becomes the very basis of relationality, the counterpoint that object-relations is to Freudian orthodoxy, and the freeing of the ego from its madness. Swann is no model, to be sure, but we are left wondering about this "posthumous love" toward which he is said to strive, since that is also the question that so many ask now: What is one to do with one's love for Eve Sedgwick? Swann's love for Odette now belongs to "eternity," but what about ours?

To fathom this, we have to return to breathing—and, in fact, we have to return there in any case. It is not precisely a matter of our will but the condition of any possible willing. It is a prerequisite of our somatic life, and it is, for Sedgwick, prior to libido. It takes some deceleration of desire to notice one's breathing and to discern there precisely the drive that links us to other biological beings who strive, prior to any cognition and volition, to survive. And yet breathing crosses both sexual and nonsexual embodiment—that we breathe in ways that we do not ordinarily do when we are sexually passionate, and that we also have to breathe (are often, in fact, told to breathe) to divest from whatever sexual passion may be driving us mad. This is clearly a tenet of Yoga and its Hindu basis, but it is also a tenet of Buddhism more generally: to notice what happens in the mind without judgment. For Proust, the object of love never stays the same, so duplication happens as a matter of course. The hallucinatory pain that rivets jealous consciousness is clearly also something that is countered, when it is, by refusing to become so fully self-enclosed. What gives relief is precisely what takes one out of oneself, what is unanticipated, what arrives as a surprise that one finds oneself taking in, as if the world itself supplied an unexpected nourishment. There is not only a shifting and remarkable world outside oneself, but one is, in spite of oneself, still open to it, and must be, to ingest, to inhale, and so to survive.

This opens up the question of how we might with Buddhist assistance re-read Freud himself. The Fort-Da game depends on some mother or supporting person having to leave the room, going elsewhere, driven by a desire that does not have us at the center. In the same way, our lovers are always going somewhere else; they come from somewhere else, they live somewhere else, they have histories of elsewhere that arrive with them and never leave. And most emphatically in the case when the lover represents "somewhere else" for the mind, as is so often the case for Swann or the narrator, there is a "somewhere else" for that lover that disrupts the mental or phantasmatic idea, the one that relies on the absence it seeks to vanquish.

So enough already with vanquishing! We are left to ponder what the narrator might have meant by Swann's effort to achieve a "posthumous happiness" with Odette through his marriage. I confess to gaining a posthumous happiness with Eve Sedgwick by reading Proust with her reading . . . and by bringing that reading together with Barbara Johnson's writing, if only briefly. The point is not that she "would have loved that" but that something about this other way of loving is what is happening still, in her name, with her text. As we breathe still, or even as we sometimes find it difficult to breathe, we are in some ways helpless and striving, a duality that drives us. And it seems to me that we read as we do only because we took her in, and breathe her in still, with surprise, and with gratitude.

NOTES

Epigraph: Marcel Proust, The Guermantes Way, trans. C. K. Scott Moncrieff and Terence Kilmartin (New York: Random House, 1981), 358.

1 Eve Kosofsky Sedgwick, The Weather in Proust, ed. Jonathan Goldberg (Durham, NC: Duke University Press, 2011).
2 Sedgwick, The Weather in Proust, 8.
3 Barbara Johnson, Persons and Things (Cambridge, MA: Harvard University Press, 2008), 94–108.
4 Sedgwick, The Weather in Proust, 8.

5   Michael Balint, *The Basic Fault: Therapeutic Aspects of Regression* (Evanston, IL: Northwestern University Press, 1992), 145, quoted in Sedgwick, *The Weather in Proust*, 8.

6   Barbara Johnson, "Using People: Kant with Winnicott," in *The Turn to Ethics*, ed. Marjorie Garber, Beatrice Hanssen, and Rebecca L. Walkowitz (New York: Routledge, 2000), 27, quoted in Sedgwick, *The Weather in Proust*, 8.

7   Marcel Proust, *Remembrance of Things Past: Swann's Way and Within a Budding Grove*, trans. C. K. Scott Moncrieff and Terence Kilmartin (New York: Random House, 1981), 412.

8   Proust, *Remembrance of Things Past: Swann's Way*, 412–13.

9   Proust, *Remembrance of Things Past: Swann's Way*, 505.

10 Proust, *Remembrance of Things Past: Swann's Way*, 413.

11 Proust, *Remembrance of Things Past: Swann's Way*, 508.

For Beauty Is a Series of Hypotheses?
Sedgwick as Fiber Artist

FAT ART, THIN ART

To date, Eve Kosofsky Sedgwick is, perhaps, best known as the author of a number of paradigmatic queer and affect theoretical texts. She was also a passionate fiber and book artist, whose exhibitions included "Floating Columns" at the Cedar Creek Gallery (1998), "In the Bardo" at the City and State Universities of New York (1999–2000), "Works in Fiber, Paper and Proust" at Harvard University (2005), and the show I focus on in this essay, "Bodhisattva Fractal World" at Dartmouth and Johns Hopkins (2002–2003). With these exhibitions in mind, I want to emphasize, for the first time, in this introduction, Sedgwick's art historical rather than literary interests. On Sedgwick's dustjackets we encounter Giovanni Battista Piranesi, Édouard Manet, Baron de Meyer, Clementina Hawarden, Ken Brown, and Judith Scott, as well as snapshots of Sedgwick herself. While underneath the covers, Sedgwick's visual repertoire ranged from the San Marco horses through Michelangelo, Bronzino, and Rubens to paintings of the Madonna and Venetian art. Sedgwick also referred to a veiled Medicean Venus, waxwork memento mori figures, Grecian portals, and rococo and Victorian stucco. She discussed Piranesi's prisonscapes; Claude Martin's as well as John Martin's landscapes; the nineteenth-century American sculptor Hiram Powers; and the eminent Victorian artists John Ruskin, Dante Gabriel Rossetti, and Julia Margaret Cameron, not to mention Paul Cézanne, Georges Rouault, Egon Schiele, Cubism, and David Hockney. In addition, Sedgwick contemplated tapestries, jewelry, and Dust Bowl photography, miniature painting, stained glass, and the Staffordshire potteries, as well as Warhol's whiteness, Joan Walsh Anglund illustrations, and Javanese bamboo mats, bronze jars, and pots. Fuller inventories would include Greek marbles and Chinese, Egyptian, and Eskimo *objects*.

Three topics stand out among Sedgwick's art historical interests: visual epistemologies; discourses on the sublime; and the phenomenologies of photography, sculpture, and the graphic arts. For instance, Sedgwick was predictably interested in point-of-view effects; in light and focal length as constitutive components of vision; in Paul de Man's meditations on blindness and insight, and in Michael Fried's theorizations of theatricality and absorption, as well as realism, writing, and disfiguration.[1] When it came to photography, Victorian pictorialists predominated, in the form of Hawarden, Cameron, and Beatrix Protheroe, the fictional landscape photographer in "The Warm Decembers."[2] But Sedgwick also considered the broader history of photography, from the camera obscura through the flashbulb to one-hour snapshots, while *Tendencies* and *Fat Art, Thin Art* include, respectively, examples of her photomontage and photographs scanned and printed on textiles.

Sedgwick's interest in the graphic arts was similarly wide-ranging. Her writings differentiate "drypoint-stroke[s]," "chalk-faced *plage*[s]," "pen-scratches," "etchy lids" and "pencilled lowland[s]."[3] She was also interested in the different textural states of Piranesi's plates and the way in which washy, painterly effects might "brush over . . . etched lines," a concern with the detail and patch that proves central to much of her fiber art, as we shall see.[4]

While ranging widely across Asian and Western canons, monochrome and painted, Sedgwick's writings were not especially enamored with sculpture. Indeed, she repeatedly characterized the supposedly monolithic medium as insensate, inanimate, isolated, affectless, lumpish, and recalcitrant. Following Adrian Stokes, Sedgwick differentiated carving and modeling and characteristically plumped for clay over bronze or marble, perhaps unsurprisingly, given the supposed masculine heroics of carving, which she identified with struggle, exhaustion, and pain, and her assimilative techniques as an artist.

For example, one of Sedgwick's alphabet cards features a photograph of a panda she modeled in a coat of many colors (plate 1), while the poem "One of Us Falls Asleep on the Other's Shoulder" contains a touching tableau of an ear pressed gently into the plasticine-like "fat of a shoulder."[5] Indeed, if one's thinking had to be modeled on something sculptural, Sedgwick repeatedly suggested, it should be on the differentiated, patterned level of a stone's grain. Better still, however, it should be modeled on the complex texture of a material.

When Sedgwick talked about her textiles in her texts, she often downplayed their potential significance for scholars, their formal and intellectual complexity, and the continuities between her texts and textiles.[6] But textile vocabularies and imagery constituted the warp and weft of Sedgwick's texts from the start, especially when considering the *structure* of anything, and within this richly embroidered linguistic fabric, certain motifs predominated. Metaphors of covering, discovering, and recovering, as well as weaving, webs, and silk loom predictably large within the context of the hermeneutics of depth and suspicion, and perhaps in the latter cases because of the queerly evocative way in which spiders and mulberry worms spin silk from their bowels and bodies.[7] In what may be her clearest account of queerness, in *Tendencies*, Sedgwick pointed to the weaving-like "open mesh of possibilities, gaps, overlaps, dissonances and resonances, lapses and excesses of meaning when the constituent elements . . . aren't made (or *can't be* made) to signify monolithically."[8] She also documented that she was already in the habit of "hurling [her] energies outward to inhabit the very farthest of the loose ends where representation, identity, gender, sexuality and the body" couldn't be "made to line up neatly together."[9] And am I the only one hearing, braided into the word "weave," Eve's name, the French word for "yes," a euphemism for urinating, and the abbreviated, collaborative form of "we have"—all characteristic Sedgwick topoi?[10]

THE QUEER SCARF SUTRA

With weaving in mind, let's consider a scarf Sedgwick made in the mid-1990s (plates 2 and 3). Now sometimes, of course, a scarf is just a scarf, and while some of the patterns articulated by her textiles, and genres of fiber art she employed, might be perceived as simply decorative, there may be a *queer* logic to the way in which Sedgwick characteristically did not bind up the loose ends of her kimono scraps here and to the "seamy," rather than seamless, character of many of her textiles. For example, given what Sedgwick described as the "weaving of intertextual discourse," we might want to think about the relationship between her warp and weft in relation to the eroticized version of *enjambment* she was partial to, with its idioms of "*straddling . . . together*" and "pushing *apart*" in relation to a "finger's-breadth by finger's-breadth" dilation,[11] or in terms of the stripes left on flagellated bodies, another characteristic Sedgwick scene.[12]

The scarf might also articulate a conceptually productive, unresolved tension between the relatively closed system of warp and weft and the openness of the tassels at each end. In addition, we might compare the architecturally stable and clean-cut edges of Sedgwick's published pages, whose uniformity encourage a centripetal orientation in toward the words, especially in *Fat Art, Thin Art,* with the more worldly, centrifugal orientation of the scarf's characteristically fraying, free-fiber edges, which recall the ragged right margins of her poems more than the justified visual character of most of her prose.

It might also be worth noticing the coincidence, in Sedgwick's biography, among the return of her poetic muse, her emergence as a fiber artist, and her diagnosis with metastatic cancer. Keeping this in mind, we might understand the scarf as reflecting a period of Sedgwick's life in which she felt her nerves or edges fraying, a relative untetheredness and sense of feeling sad and ragged, especially since she used rags from old kimonos as a key ingredient in her weaving. The scarf's loose ends might also, though, suggest that Sedgwick's synapses were newly snapping, the newly growing edges of her experience, and the sense that hope could feel equally fraying.[13] Alternatively, we might characterize the tassels as a form of shy flirtation. After all, in one of her poems—"In Dreams on Which Decades of Marriage Haven't"—Sedgwick described the "upthrown lashes" of a girl in an airport seeking an audience, which "entangle[d] with, or tease[d], the long/fringe of her bangs." She also described how, beginning a book for the first time, "your fate and preoccupations, / hundreds of things, ... / flirt[ed] with what seem" the "knowing, solicitous," "thousand tendrils, all / responsiveness" of the text.[14] To think about some further *queer* resonances of Sedgwick's textiles in this period, this time in terms of her iconography rather than methodology, the next section considers her bodhisattva imagery.

QUEER LITTLE GODS? "BODHISATTVA FRACTAL WORLD"
AS A SECOND DOSSIER ON DIVINITY

As an exhibition, "Bodhisattva Fractal World" is characterized by a number of indigo-dyed, cyanotype textiles incorporating images of Chinese bronze sculptures of Guan Yin, the bodhisattva of compassion, dating from the late Tang and Sung dynasties, which is to say, from around the turn of the last but one millennium (plate 4). For the uninitiated, bodhisattvas are a kind of Buddhist semi-divinity who defer entering nirvana so they can re-enter the stream of samsara to help other living creatures escape the cycles of reincarnation.[15] Inspired by the title of Sedgwick's 2007 Harvard talk, "Cavafy, Proust, and the Queer Little Gods," I want, in this section, to look at her depicted bodhisattvas with a queer eye.[16] This seems appropriate, since Sedgwick's earlier textual divinities had never been especially normative. For example, Michael Moon and Sedgwick's dossier on divinity compares John Waters's character Francine wielding a deodorant or aerosol cleaner to "an eight-armed divinity,"[17] while "Trace at 46" describes an "anomalous," "grace-less," "dwarfish" and "incontinent," "aubergine-shaped" class of "unaffected" Javanese "clownish-servants"-cum-divinities called *punåkawan*, who are "dis-tinguished . . . by being always addressed/or referred to in the plural number." Indeed, keeping the *punåkawan* in mind, with their "distended breasts," "ex-pectant gibbous" bellies, and "wildly salient" asses, as well as their make-up, jewelry, and men's clothing, "if any," we might notice that bodhisattvas were not the first of Sedgwick's queer little gods who "plait[ed] together . . . lines female," "male[,] and divine."[18] And although earlier Sedgwick had been wary of naive, utopian imaginations of an "apparent 'androgyny'" that, "while . . . pretending to share equally in the qualities of two symmetrically opposite groups, really manipulated the *asymmetry* of their status for personal ad-vancement,"[19] Guan Yin's trans-, non-, or variously gendered status was cer-tainly part of the divinity's appeal to Sedgwick, whose thought and hope was that many of these highly sensuous, loved, and regal figures had not been shaped or perceived through the lens of gender.[20]

We might also, however, note the bodhisattvas' characteristically extended right forearms as part of a larger, condensed image cluster in Sedgwick's writ-ings, one that emphasizes the diverse tactile address of her corpus (plate 5). For example, like the paired manicules that open all but the introductory chap-ter of *Touching Feeling*,[21] the iconography of the bodhisattvas' arms exist in pa-limpsestic relation to Michelangelo's laconic, limp-wristed creation of Adam in the Sistine ceiling; to what Sedgwick described as the exquisitely masoch-istic and sadistic repertoire of *port de bras* ballet moves;[22] to Gary Fisher's ele-gant dancing hands in "A Vigil";[23] to the boy's arm that, in "Trace at 46," Cissy sees making floaty gestures above his male lover's shoulders in the back of a pickup truck;[24] to the Buddhist pedagogies of the sniffed finger, open hand, and pointing at the moon;[25] to the Gothic warning of Catherine's "bloody hand plunging through the broken window" in Emily Brontë's *Wuthering Heights* (1847);[26] to the twist of a policeman's wrist at a protest in "Interlude, Peda-gogic";[27] to the rhythmically spanking hand; to Humby's "leathery obstetric hand" extended in Chinese White's delighted direction in "The Warm Decembers";[28] and, perhaps most persistently, to the thrice-returned-to scene of Henry James's fisted golden bowels, which Sedgwick described as a "virtually absolute symbol of imaginative value."[29]

Then there is the suggestive iconographic overlap among the bodhisattvas' seated poses, the queer and bookish, force-field-creating attitude of reading, and shame's classically downcast head and averted eyes.[30] And that is without touching on the powerfully queer epistemological and ontological challenges the bodhisattvas pose as they embody and represent the kaleidoscopic slippage between male and female, passive and active, Occidental and Oriental; diffuse and focused, ascetic and theatrical; transcendent and powerless; confident and modest; concentrating and free-associating. But as the next section demonstrates, Sedgwick's textiles pose such difficult questions all the time and at every level.

TWO ARTS, FAT AND THIN: FROM TEXT TO TEXTILE AND BACK AGAIN

At first glance, and following Sedgwick's lead, we might be tempted to emphasize the differences between her texts and textiles and to understand her drift toward fiber art as a deliberate move away from the smooth, clear-cut, bright, "thin," white, monolithic, and flat aesthetics of printed rectangular paper of a uniform thickness, weight, and texture, in portrait orientation, to the variously colored, textured, weighted, folded, ragged, collaged, patched and stitched, elastic, and "fat" materiality of landscape-oriented fibers. But there are obvious problems in characterizing, in more or less neutral terms, the white paper of Sedgwick's books, even if her published works do tend to be composed in mostly black font whose relation to the mostly white supporting paper is binary—in the relation of foreground to background, a digitally minimal relief of imaginatively raised letters on white support. This is to say, at the risk of universalizing, that when reading Sedgwick, readers are usually able to presume on and forget the binary relation between the figure of the crystalized, clear, black, graphic text, in standard fonts, and the stable, apparently neutral ground of the page, and an overall, rather than a differential, change in font style or color would make little difference to the sense.[31] Readers are also characteristically used to holding Sedgwick's books in their hands so they can maintain a consistent focal length and parallel or perpendicular relation to the text. In so doing, they probably deemphasize their tactile relation to the books in favor of a visual, or even apparently unmediated, epistemological relation.[32]

With Sedgwick's textiles, by contrast, seeing, touching, and our over-all corporeal orientations are not as stable or predictable, and the material ground is not an invisible given. As a result, there is perhaps more possibility for cognitive confusion and transformation, as well as less potential for sensory deprivation. For example, in Sedgwick's textiles, the colors and styles of her fonts and the shapes, colors, and textures of her material grounds are more various; they exist in a less obvious figure-ground relation, and the colors chosen may not simply be read as ornamental or optional. Instead, we are encouraged to understand meaning as colorable and color as meaningful, as representing both the product and generator of affect, given Sedgwick and Adam Frank's characterization of different affective possibilities as "a color wheel of different risks."[33]

In addition, when dealing with Sedgwick's textiles, we are very often in the domain of the leaky, creased, and fuzzy, compared with the clear-cut character of her writings' printed fonts. Indeed, we might characterize Sedgwick's textiles as "fat" and "loose" in a number of senses: because of the way they emphasize and aestheticize elastic creases and folds of skin-like fabric when compared with paper's uniform thinness and flatness; the way Sedgwick described the rather sluttish, excitingly amateurish, and certainly "fat, buttery condensations and inky dribbles of the mind's laden brush" when it came to her textile language and imagery;[34] and because of her move from her texts' clean type to her textiles' characteristic metonymy and spread.

We might also think about some of the differences between reading Sedgwick or hearing her give papers and looking at, but also (imaginatively) touching, her textiles. Now, as I have already briefly suggested, it might be a mistake to imagine that Sedgwick's readers do not experience a subtle, powerful, and varied tactile relation to her books. She invited us to imagine the feel of a "cheek on cool notebook," after all,[35] and like all texts, Sedgwick's are eminently manipulable. At the risk of being heavy-handed, or of this metaphor getting out of hand, the manicules that recur throughout *Touching Feeling* do not just deictically break the text into manageable sections. They conjure the handwritten scene of manuscripts, the finger-wagging reproach that characterizes much contemporary criticism, and childlike scenes of reading with our fingers, the words on the tips of our tongues. In addition, these manicules may point to the fragilities of our never less than embodied epistemologies and to our fear of losing sight of, or touch with, Sedgwick's oeuvre. But where the pages of Sedgwick's codex books are bound together along a single spine and characterized by their sequential recto-verso relations between and under their covers, her textiles characteristically inhabit low-relief, collage, and patchwork's two-and-a-half dimensions. Keeping this in mind, we might briefly consider the differences made by encountering Sedgwick's ideas in collaged fibers rather than on mass-produced paper (plate 6).

For example, Sedgwick's early kimono patchworks provide a rich resource for thinking about her characteristic epistemologies and performativities. We might see parallels between such collages and Sedgwick's pleasure in co-authorship and in dossiers as a genre.[36] Compared with her relatively flat works on paper, Sedgwick's "fat" collages deepen and thicken our sense of meaning, offering a more elastic understanding of the complex, juxtaposed layers of cognition and affect. They remind us to be alert to the feedback loops among, and systemic interrelation of, three epistemological axes—horizontal-vertical, temporal-spatial, and profound-superficial—as connected by her rarely less than decorative and always more than functional embroidery. And keeping this in mind, it seems crucial that Sedgwick mostly stitched rather than glued her fabric collages, despite the potentially rich, queer metaphorics of adhesiveness in the extended Whitman circle.

We might also think about the fragmented, discontinuously connected way in which Sedgwick reproduced her sculptural images, interrupted, over-laid and underpinned by decorative stitches, patches, and apparently less re-lated materials (see plate 5) as pointing to the blockages in thought, as well as the unexpectedly idiomatic trains and angles of free association. Alternatively, from a Kleinian perspective, we might register the endless volleys between the paranoid-schizoid work of destroying the object and reparative attempts to reconstitute it.[37] Then there are the queer, paranoid, and cosmopolitan pleasures we might take in packing and unpacking these various levels.

In addition, we might think about the relationship between the distributive syntactic pressure of Sedgwick's collages and the related pleasures of her hy-potactic sentences; the different, hierarchical registers of closeted, concealed, and sublimated knowledge; the supposedly transcendent nature of reading and spectatorship; the impoverishment of the horizontal ties of collaboration in favor of an ethics and aesthetics of criticism and competition;[38] and the relations among literal, figural, and structural—metonymy and synecdoche, fragmentation and integration, submergence and emergence, successiveness and stratification, suppression and expression, and reproduction and distri-bution; as well as Sedgwick's breathtaking skill in manipulating the overlap of contradictory and fractured ideologies. There is also something epidermal about these layers, and we might consider, too, the affective and structural semiotics of *relief* and the suppositional, hypothetical grammar of "it seems," as suggestively articulated within the fraying seams.

From another angle, however, when compared with the "fatness" of Sedgwick's characteristic, major-phase sentences, with their complex syntax and semantic suspension, the phrases she employs in her textiles, when not from Marcel Proust, are often rather ascetic.[39] They are rarely more than a haiku, and more like eventually, intuitively grasped mantras than complex arguments that persuade by clauses.[40] However, while the two-part, binary imagery of haiku might initially encourage readers to think about Sedgwick's artworks in digital terms, in the context of the visual and material qualities of the pieces as a whole, beholders seem to be in a more analog, spectral, fractal world, as the title of her second show indicates. I say "fractal" because, at least compared with the stable and corporeal, if not cognitive and affective, point of view readers might adopt in relation to Sedgwick's texts, her textiles invite a more self-conscious and various set of "micro-orientations."

For example, beholders could walk around Sedgwick's suspended figures during the "In the Bardo" show, could crouch under or look down on them, from a number of angles and focal lengths (plate 7). Beholders could also enjoy the fantasy of hugging, pushing up against, or rotating Sedgwick's precisely Sedgwick-scaled forms, as if they were parents, partners, punching bags, or piñatas. Indeed, with this in mind, we might understand Sedgwick's textiles, in comparison with her texts, as not just a "queer enough aesthetic," but as her most queer aesthetic, if queerness is understood to dramatize "locutionary position itself."[41] After all, and as the next section makes clearer, Sedgwick's textiles repeatedly, surprisingly, and euphorically dramatize shifts in interpretive perspective by employing Rorschach techniques and the kinds of optical illusions that characterized Gestalt psychology, in conjunction with the intuitive, rather than argued-for, interrelation of the two parts of a haiku.

REALITY IS FLOWERLIKE

Consider this early collage, with its haiku-like translation of a Japanese death poem: "Reality is flowerlike; cold clouds sinking through the dusk." Note the way in which the collage compares reality to both a flower and cold clouds (plate 8). Consider the amount of explanatory work done and elided by the semicolon. Think about the implied relation and not quite equivalence between those two things; the way in which reality is minimally metamorphic, first one thing, flowerlike, and then like cold clouds. At least on first reading, the relationship between those two comparisons is sequential, although once you have the poem in mind, the relations become less temporally syntactic. In the first case, the flowerlike reality might be short-lived but, as a static image, can be quickly grasped. In the second, reality is more cinematic and durational: it takes time for clouds to sink into the dusk.

Sedgwick's layout of the text is also important. After all, she was a scholar who was unusually alive to the tableau of lyric poetry.[42] Sedgwick organizes the poem diagonally, emphasizing the assonance between "like" and "sink." The single first line of the text harmonizes with its simple present tense, supporting our earlier perception that there is something straightforwardly declarative and static about the flowerlike reality. The more temporally sustained cloudlike reality, by contrast, sinks toward the ground, apparently blown one way, then the other, by winds at different atmospheric heights.

Sedgwick distributes nine more-or-less intact, five-petal, blue- and rainbow-colored flowers across the piece, interspersed with what appear to be three light-green leaves and one similarly colored flower. If we imagine looking down at this textile from above, the flowers seem to be floating on the surface of some murky water, perhaps Proustian Japanese paper flowers unfolded in lost time. If we encountered the piece on a gallery wall, however, the flowers would appear to be blowing in a similar breeze to that affecting the text below. But we might also read those flowers as cloudlike or alluding to the water cycle. After all, they rise up, rainbow-colored, from the left-hand side and evaporate to become blue, like the sky, and then slowly condense and sink down again toward the middle and, in so doing, take on the rainbow colors of the dusk, before evaporating up again, once more blue toward the top right. Only it is not that simple. At the point of the fifth of the flowers from the left, viewers can follow the rising diagonal floral path up to the top right-hand corner or drop down into the blue flower in the bottom right-hand corner, perhaps encouraged by the snow that appears to be falling in the background of the right-hand side of the collage, only to rise almost immediately up again into the rainbow flower immediately above it to the right, and then continue the path up to the top right, or reverse the left-to-right direction of the sequence in the gravitational pull of the undulating wave back toward the bottom center.

But other representational systems are at work here, as well as the word-image parallel. For instance, Sedgwick seems to offer us, if not quite a Rorschach test, then a textile version of the game of finding images in the cumulus such that we recognize that clouds are flowerlike, and vice versa. It might be worth recalling, here, her earlier description, in "The Warm Decembers," of "inexpressive, overprecise clouds / that could not change in shape."[43] In addition, toward the top right corner, at least my attention volleys, in a sublime gestalt-like effect, between the sense of a green leaf, half-rainbow-colored flower, and full-five-petal blue flower, and my re-cognition of it as a green moth or butterfly and a rainbow-colored bumble bee chasing each other up toward the five-petal blue flower at the top right. This perception is encouraged by the caterpillar-like form, juxtaposed with flowers, in the horizontal gray panel in the middle left. In short, Sedgwick keeps my synapses snapping, but once these possibilities have flickered into intelligibility, they flicker in a dynamic relationship.

In this piece, then, reality may be flower- and cloudlike, but viewers are also invited to think about the radical metamorphosis among these and other perceptions and life-forms. As such, reality seems Buddhist, if we recall that, in certain, stereotypical forms of Buddhist pedagogy, "solidity is an illusion of the senses,"[44] and that seeing and understanding are processes that can take seconds or lifetimes. But reality is also Proustian, if we recall Sedgwick's artist's statement for her last show, which described a sustained mysticism in À la recherche that relied not "on the esoteric or occult, but on simple material metamorphoses as they are emulsified with meaning and language."[45] In addition, reality seems "cybernetic" here, given the way in which Sedgwick derives a considerable aesthetic and conceptual value and complexity by layering digital and analog representational models.[46]

All of this, of course, takes time to recognize and realize, particularly since, whereas the printed texts in Sedgwick's books are comparatively stable and long-lasting, the inks she used for the texts in her textiles appear to be bleeding, leaking, and fading fast.[47] Four further examples of Sedgwick's deployment of text in "Bodhisattva Fractal World" help explain why this is significant. In the first, one of the title pieces from the show, the majority of the stenciled white letters seem to be not just floating on but dissolving into the watery, suminagashi ground[48]—an example of melting ice capitals, if you will, or of the fractal dimension among words, images, and patterns (plate 9). In the second example, the Is resemble columns seen in elevation and the Ss and the Os resemble snakes and coiled-up cats, respectively, offering a more gestalt-like experience of word-image relations (plate 10). In the third example, Sedgwick again arranges the words pictorially, as if alluding to a snowfall. She also again positions the words to emphasize the end rhymes of "day" with "today" and "then" with "melting" and "snowman," among diamond-shape *shibori* patterns that volley between snowflakes and barnacles, while the individual letters, constituting a layer of white overlaid on brown ink on an indigo ground, suggest the watery cycle from snow through slush to water (plate 11).[49]

In addition to taking part in Sedgwick's visual-textile exploration of the fractal dimensions among word, image, and pattern; foreground and background; figure and ground; detailed, blurry, washy, and sketchy; and lapses and wellings up of meaning, the next section examines some of the more embodied implications of the way in which Sedgwick's textile letters bleed into one another.

X MARKS THE SPOT

As originally exhibited, the "Bodhisattva Fractal World" collages were pinned to a wall and sealed, like specimens of lepidopterology within glass cases, perhaps appropriately, given that many of them are made of silk. In addition, the shibori method by which Sedgwick fashioned many of the pieces involved tying and pinning before dyeing and unfolding them, processes that leave visible pinholes (plate 12). Now, pins and needles were a corporeal and neurological, rather than neutral, topic for Sedgwick in her late life, in terms of the paresthesia from which she suffered in her feet and the many painful injections she underwent.[50] And it is, perhaps, partly in relation to such topoi that we should contextualize such pinpricks and Sedgwick's decorative and structural needlework while remaining mindful of her descriptions of the tremendous energies Michael Lynch made available to "inject into" her and the way in which painful hospital scenes were subsequently woven into her s/m fantasy life.[51]

In this medical-aesthetic context, we might also consider the relationship among many of the "Bodhisattva Fractal World" patchworks and bandages, gauzes, and sanitary napkins used for absorbing blood and other bodily fluids, while other pieces bring to mind differently unstanchable flows, particularly Sedgwick's interest in urethral eroticism and in other things that come "out the wazoo" (plate 13).[52] For example, consider the way in which the J. M. W. Turner–like, gold-on-blue inks of one of Sedgwick's "aired and inky" silk sheets featuring the sentence, "I borrow moonlight for this journey of a million miles," twines together with two related scenes from "The Warm Decembers."[53] The first focuses on an unidentified child who repeatedly wets its bed, with violent consequences, but ultimately survives and "finds somewhere an art" (plate 14). The second concerns the similarly "sloppy landscape" in which Beatrix Protheroe, caught unbearably short on a moonlit flit to London and surrounded by "sea" and "fresh water," squats down to take a leak, the "moon behind her / inking the sandy road ahead."[54]

Keeping these uncomfortably corporeal and poetic contexts in mind, we might also hear in the title "Bodhisattva Fractal World" the sotto voce phrase "Bodhisattva fracture ward," especially given Sedgwick's penchant for homophonic puns and the way in which three of the patchworks incorporate X-rays of the fractured arms of a sculptured image of Guan Yin (plate 15).[55] There is also, perhaps, something more Kleinian about a closely related, early piece of Sedgwick's. This patchworked together four kinds of images: an X-ray bone scan of her trunk; photographs of abandoned and plundered Buddhist stupas at Ayutthaya;[56] a depiction of a dragonfly as it moves on a stream; and two strings of more abstractly patterned fabric—an evocative juxtaposition that seems to condense various theoretical, image, and idiom clusters. For example, the X-ray images bring to mind Sedgwick's powerful reflections on reparative and paranoid reading positions.[57] They do so by articulating both the paranoid fear of one's own transparency and the related, diagnostic hermeneutics of depth and detection within the broader context of the reparative aesthetics of a laboriously and idiomatically pieced-together collage. Like W. B. Yeats's poem "Long-Legged Fly" (1937–38), which compares the long-lasting achievements, but brief lives, of Caesar and Michelangelo with the shorter life span, but greater evolutionary longevity, of a daddy longlegs, Sedgwick's collage invites us to fix our eyes "upon nothing" and to contrast the different life spans, vulnerabilities, and metamorphoses of a dragonfly, diseased human spine, and the "topless towers" of the Buddhist stupas in their "lonely place[s]."[58] In so doing, the collage reminds us that, as in Proust, if nothing lasts for long in the same form, nothing is entirely lost. Cities are abandoned to tourists and mice; Buddhas are vandalized; and bodies are transformed by tumors, but, like dragonflies, which represent the final, short-lived incarnations in a quite various tripartite life cycle, new varieties of beauty and spiritual, aesthetic, and cultural opportunity emerge.

Before concluding this essay, two last images suggest themselves—this time in the queer context of thinking about similarity, difference, and the "homo."[59] It is worth finally pausing over these pieces because they provide good visual examples that might help us to reinhabit more fully the now apparently evacuated conceptual space between two and infinity that was so close to Sedgwick's heart in Touching Feeling.[60]

In an untitled piece (plate 16), Sedgwick depicts a more or less mirrored image of another bodhisattva sculpture, but the figures, steeped in blue dye, also bring to mind identical, intrauterine twins. As a result, Sedgwick encourages us to think simultaneously about the pair's genetic identity and possible pre- and postnatal differences. Our twins, however, may be drowning, not floating in their aqueous indigo holding environment. If so, what seems to be occurring to them, five fathoms down, is a *Tempest*-like "sea-change into something rich and strange."[61] Given that the pair are bodhisattvas, the piece invites us to consider the diverse range of possible incarnations that next await them.

At the center of our penultimate collage, meanwhile, Sedgwick juxtaposes with another bodhisattva and the text—"Tender winds above the snow melt many kinds of suffering"—rubber-stamped images of three carp swimming in a sumanigashi textile (plate 17). The koi usefully remind us of sumanigashi's aqueous origins, as a practice in which ink is floated on the surface of water, and, at the risk of being punny, they perhaps encourage us to hear the word "whorled" within "Bodhisattva Fractal World." The piece also perhaps helps explain why silk was such an overdetermined material for Sedgwick, one that raised issues of mortality, since it relied on silkworms' being boiled alive and to death to unravel the threads of their cocoons, as well as incontinent infancy, since it reminded her of her baby brother "drooling" and "making fishes" on his pillow. Given the way in which carp both drink from and excrete in their aqueous environment, the panel might also help explain why "silk and shit" went together for Sedgwick.[62] With this in mind, we might also notice how the carp seem to swim through, and meet in the bowels of, the meditative figure and recall both Sedgwick's repeated exploration of James's golden bowel, from which he "fished out" the various elements of his novels,[63] and the "appetites," "lusts," and "desire" of the creatures that James Merrill described in his poem "Carp" (1988), a text whose alchemical preoccupation with "glittery nerves" and "fresh lapses into gold" finds echoes here in the fraying gold threads binding the collage together.[64] Then again, that same gold embroidery, braided with the stitched-epidermal patches' possible pun on silk-skin, might subtly allude to Sedgwick's therapist Shannon Van Wey, since he was a person she characterized as resembling Rumpelstiltskin, a figure famous for "spinning straw into gold."[65]

This chapter has been, perhaps, unusually speculative; it is full of hypotheses, and, in concluding with this final collage (plate 18), I want to emphasize the Proustian idea that "beauty is a series of hypotheses," not because I think that beauty is merely hypothetical. As Sedgwick's gorgeous work everywhere makes clear, beauty is anything but.[66] Rather, I want to suggest that there might be something potentially *beautiful*, in the Edmund Burkean sense of a kind of energizing and inspiring but unaggressive rhetorical or aesthetic effect, about Sedgwick's "late" work and about the making and sharing of hypotheses, rather than the picking and unpicking of arguments.[67] I want to make this claim because it seems increasingly obvious to me, as it was to Sedgwick, that there is something ugly, if often comprehensible and vital, about the way in which a few eminently teachable critical axioms are routinely used to short-circuit, cut short, or cut off a whole range of other potential responses to art objects, as if these were always somehow naive. Thus, it seems to me that trying out a range of hypotheses, rather than rehearsing the standard critical tropes that we have inherited as more or less professionalized and theorized folks in the humanities, *may*—and Sedgwick notes that "may" may be one of her and Silvan Tomkins's "least dispensable locution[s]"[68]—enable us to imaginatively sidestep, without disrespecting the power of, increasingly reflex critiques, such as those that might point to Sedgwick's aesthetic Orientalism.[69]

But the real—indeed, perhaps most exciting and characteristic—Sedgwickian pedagogy, involving two sets of related questions, remains to be done. First, how do my various hypotheses interrelate? And second, how have you been feeling while you have been reading this chapter? What did you, and might you, make of the ideas and images? And how can we develop, among ourselves, the least painful and most surprising, skillful, and productive means of moving things along?

> To everyone who joined Hal, Sarah,
> Wabi-Sabi, and I for that wonderful, week-long seminar,
> on Eve's art,
> seven years ago, now, in September.

NOTES

1   For more, see Paul de Man, *Blindness and Insight: Essays in the Rhetoric of Contemporary Criticism* (London: Routledge, 1989); Michael Fried, *Absorption and*

Theatricality: Painting and Beholder in the Age of Diderot (Chicago: University of Chicago Press, 1980); Michael Fried, *Realism, Writing, and Disfiguration: On Thomas Eakins and Stephen Crane* (Chicago: University of Chicago Press, 1987).

2   Eve Kosofsky Sedgwick, "The Warm Decembers," in Eve Kosofsky Sedgwick, *Fat Art, Thin Art* (Durham, NC: Duke University Press, 1994), 89–160.

3   Sedgwick, *Fat Art, Thin Art*, 50, 54, 116, 133.

4   Sedgwick, *Fat Art, Thin Art*, 56. For more, see Georges Didi-Huberman, "The Art of Not Describing: Vermeer—The Detail and the Patch," *History of the Human Sciences* 2, no. 2 (1989): 135–69.

5   Sedgwick, *Fat Art, Thin Art*, 35.

6   Eve Kosofsky Sedgwick, *A Dialogue on Love* (Boston: Beacon, 1999), 206–7.

7   See Eve Kosofsky Sedgwick, *Touching Feeling: Affect, Pedagogy, Performativity* (Durham, NC: Duke University Press, 2003), 123–53. For more on the queerness of silk, see Jacques Derrida, "A Silkworm of One's Own (Points of View Stitched on the Other Veil)," *Oxford Literary Review* 18, no. 1 (1996): 3–66.

8   Eve Kosofsky Sedgwick, *Tendencies* (Durham, NC: Duke University Press, 1993), 8.

9   Sedgwick, *Tendencies*, 13.

10 On Sedgwick's love for the "we," see Sedgwick, *A Dialogue on Love*, 106. On her urethral poetics, see Jason Edwards, "Bathroom Songs: Eve Kosofsky Sedgwick as a Poet," in *Bathroom Songs: Eve Kosofsky Sedgwick as a Poet*, ed. Jason Edwards (New York: Punctum, 2017), 29–35.

11 Sedgwick, *Touching Feeling*, 140; Sedgwick, *Tendencies*, 185; Sedgwick, *Fat Art, Thin Art*, 149. Italics original.

12 See, e.g., the poems "Lost Letter" and "The Palimpsest" in Edwards, *Bathroom Songs*, 225–34.

13 For a sense of the fraying character of hope, see Sedgwick, *Touching Feeling*, 151.

14 Sedgwick, *Fat Art, Thin Art*, 39.

15 Sedgwick, *Touching Feeling*, 160–61. For more, see John Blofeld, *Bodhisattva of Compassion: The Mystical Tradition of Kuan Yin* (Boston: Shambala, 2009); Sandy Boucher, *Discovering Kwan Yin: Buddhist Goddess of Compassion: A Woman's Book of Ruminations, Meditations, Prayers, and Chants* (Boston: Beacon, 1999); Stephen Karcher, *The Kuan Yin Oracle: The Voice of the Goddess of Compassion* (London: Piatkus, 2001); Martin Palmer and Jay Ramsay, with Man-Ho Kwok, *The Kuan Yin Chronicles: The Myths and Prophecies of the Chinese Goddess of Compassion* (Charlottesville, VA: Hampton Roads, [1995] 2009); and esp. Chun-Fang Yu, *Kuan-yin: The Chinese Transformation of Avalokitesvara* (New York: Columbia University Press, 2001).

16 The essay was posthumously collected in Eve Kosofsky Sedgwick, *The Weather in Proust*, ed. Jonathan Goldberg (Durham, NC: Duke University Press, 2011), 42–68.

17 Sedgwick, *Tendencies*, 245.

18 Sedgwick, *Fat Art, Thin Art*, 67–68. For more, see Benedict Anderson, *Mythology and the Tolerance of the Javanese* (Jakarta: Equinox, [1965] 2009).

19 Eve Kosofsky Sedgwick, *Between Men: English Literature and Male Homosocial Desire* (New York: Columbia University Press, 1985), 197.

20 In the published version of the essay, Sedgwick expressed her "thought and hope" that "even in the expression of a strong sensuality, many of these regal and loved divinities may not have been shaped or perceived through the eyes of gender at all—not male, not female, not both male and female, and not neither male nor female": Sedgwick, *The Weather in Proust*, 105.

21 For more on the longer history of the manicule, see William H. Sherman, "Toward a History of the Manicule," accessed July 13, 2006, http.www .livesandletters.ac.uk/papers/FOR_2005_04_001.pdf.

22 Sedgwick, *Fat Art, Thin Art*, 155.

23 Sedgwick, *Fat Art, Thin Art*, 13–14. For more on Fisher, see Gary Fisher, *Gary in Your Pocket: Stories and Notebooks of Gary Fisher*, ed. Eve Kosofsky Sedgwick (Durham, NC: Duke University Press, 1996). For critical discussion of Sedgwick and Fisher, see José Esteban Muñoz, "Race, Sex, and the Incommensurate: Gary Fisher with Eve Kosofsky Sedgwick," in *Queer Futures: Reconsidering Ethics, Activism, and the Political*, ed. Elahe Yekani, Eveline Killian, and Beatrice Michaelis (Aldershot, UK: Ashgate, 2013), 103–15; Ellis Hanson, "The Future's Eve: Reparative Readings after Sedgwick," *South Atlantic Quarterly* 110, no. 1 (Winter 2011): 101–19.

24 Sedgwick, *Fat Art, Thin Art*, 60.

25 For more, see Sedgwick, *Touching Feeling*, 153–83. See also Lauren Berlant, "The Pedagogies of Pedagogy of Buddhism," Supervalent Thought (blog), 2010, accessed July 13, 2016, https://supervalentthought.com/2010/03/18/after-eve-in -honor-of-eve-kosofsky-sedgwick.

26 Eve Kosofsky Sedgwick, *The Coherence of Gothic Conventions* (London: Methuen, 1985), 118.

27 Sedgwick, *Touching Feeling*, 27–34.

28 Sedgwick, *Fat Art, Thin Art*, 202.

29 Sedgwick, *Touching Feeling*, 48. For James and fisting, see Eve Kosofsky Sedgwick, *Epistemology of the Closet* (Berkeley: University of California Press, 1991), 182–213; Sedgwick, *Tendencies*, 73–103; Sedgwick, *Touching Feeling*, 35–66.

30 For more on shame, see Eve Kosofsky Sedgwick and Adam Frank, eds., *Shame and Its Sisters* (Durham, NC: Duke University Press, 1995), esp. 1–29, 133–78.

31 For helpful context, see Andrew Crompton, "How to Look at a Reading Font," *Word and Image* 30, no. 2 (2014): 79–89.

32 For a bravura account of how to "Look with Your Hands" at Sedgwick, see Angus Connell Brown's essay with that title in Edwards, *Bathroom Songs*, 75–84.

33 Sedgwick and Frank, *Shame and Its Sisters*, 20.

34 Sedgwick, *A Dialogue on Love*, 194.

35 Sedgwick, *Fat Art, Thin Art*, 63.

36 For examples, and in addition to those already mentioned, see Eve Kosofsky Sedgwick and Andrew Parker, eds., *Performativity and Performance* (London: Routledge, 1995); Eve Kosofsky Sedgwick, Michael Moon, Benjamin Gianni, and Scott Weir, "Queers in (Single Family) Space," *Assemblage* 24 (August 1994): 30–37; Eve Kosofsky Sedgwick, Michael Moon, Benjamin Gianni, and Scott Weir, "Queers in (Single Family) Space," in *The Design Culture Reader*, ed. Ben Highmore (New York: Routledge, 2009), 40–49; Eve Kosofsky Sedgwick and Michael Moon, "Confusion of Tongues," in *Breaking Bounds: Whitman and American Cultural Studies*, ed. Betsy Erkkila and Jay Grossman (New York: Oxford University Press, 1996), 23–29; Eve Kosofsky Sedgwick and Michael D. Snediker, "Queer Little Gods: A Conversation," *Massachusetts Review* 49, nos. 1–2 (2008): 194–218.

37 For more on Sedgwick's relation to Klein, see Sedgwick, *The Weather in Proust*, 123–24; Eve Kosofsky Sedgwick, "Teaching/Depression," *Scholar and Feminist Online* 4, no. 2 (Spring 2006), accessed March 11, 2006, http://www.barnard.columbia.edu/sfonline/heilbrun/conference.htm.

38 For more on "Beyond, Beneath, and Beside," see Sedgwick, *Touching Feeling*, 8–9.

39 For more on Sedgwick's relation to Proust, see Sedgwick, *Epistemology of the Closet*, 213–51; Sedgwick, *The Weather in Proust*, 1–166. See also Joseph Litvak, "Review of *The Weather in Proust*," *Modernism/Modernity* 19, no. 4 (November 2012): 805–7. For Litvak's sustained engagement with Proust, see Joseph Litvak, *Strange Gourmet: Sophistication, Theory, and the Novel* (Durham, NC: Duke University Press, 1997).

40 For the majority of Sedgwick's non-Proustian sources, see Yoel Hoffmann, ed., *Japanese Death Poems Written by Zen Monks and Haiku Poets on the Verge of Death* (Boston: Tuttle, 1986).

41 Sedgwick, *Tendencies*, 9.

42 For the locus classicus on this topic, see Sedgwick, *Tendencies*, 177–214.

43 Sedgwick, *Fat Art, Thin Art*, 111. For more on clouds and representation, see Hubert Damisch, *A Theory of Cloud: Toward a History of Painting* (Stanford, CA: Stanford University Press, 2002), a book in Sedgwick's library.

44 Sedgwick, *Touching Feeling*, 169.

45 Quotation from artist's statement written for the "Works in Fiber, Paper and Proust" exhibition at Harvard University in 2005. I am eternally grateful to Hal A. Sedgwick and Sarah McCarry for giving me such sustained access to Sedgwick's archive.

46 For more, see Sedgwick, *Touching Feeling*, 101.

47 On the distinction between "Reality and Realization," see Sedgwick, *The Weather in Proust*, 206–16.

48 For more on suminagashi, see Anne Chambers, *Suminagashi: The Japanese Art of Marbling—A Practical Guide* (London: Thames and Hudson, 1991).

49 For more on shibori, see Yoshiko Iwamoto Wada, *Memory on Cloth: Shibori Now* (Tokyo: Kodansha, 2002); Yoshiko Iwamoto Wada, Mary Kellogg Rice, and Jane Barton, *Shibori: The Inventive Art of Japanese Shaped Resist Dyeing* (Tokyo: Kodansha, [1983] 1999).

50 See, e.g., Sedgwick, *Fat Art, Thin Art*, 29.

51 Sedgwick, *Tendencies*, 260.

52 Sedgwick, *Fat Art, Thin Art*, 5.

53 Sedgwick, *Tendencies*, 213.

54 Sedgwick, *Fat Art, Thin Art*, 109–11, 147.

55 For more, see Sedgwick, *Tendencies*, 176.

56 For more, see Silpa Birasri, *Thai Buddhist Sculpture* (Bangkok: National Culture Institute, 1956); Dorothy H. Fickle, *Images of the Buddha in Thailand* (Oxford: Oxford University Press, 1989).

57 For more, see Sedgwick, *Touching Feeling*, 123–53. For more, in general, on X-rays and other medical imaging systems, see Jose van Dijck, *The Transparent Body: A Cultural Analysis of Medical Imaging* (Seattle: University of Washington Press, 2005).

58 The quotations all derive from Yeats's poem.

59 Sedgwick, *Epistemology of the Closet*, 1, 22–27. My thinking in the following section is indebted to very many conversations with Ben Nichols. For more on queer sameness, see Ben Nichols, "Reductive: John Rechy, Queer Theory, and the Idea of Limitation," GLQ 22, no. 3 (June 2016): 409–35; Jonathan Flatley, "Like: Collecting and Collectivity," *October* 132 (Spring 2010): 71–98; Madhavi Menon, *Indifference to Difference: On Queer Universalism* (Minneapolis: University of Minnesota Press, 2015).

60 Sedgwick, *Touching Feeling*, 108.

61 Sedgwick, *Touching Feeling*, 48.

62 Sedgwick, *A Dialogue on Love*, 206.

63 Sedgwick, *Touching Feeling*, 58.

64 James Merrill, "Carp," in *Collected Poems*, ed. J. D. McClatchy and Stephen Yenser (New York: Alfred A. Knopf, 2002), 531. For more on Sedgwick's relation to Merrill, see Eve Kosofsky Sedgwick, "The 1001 Seances," GLQ 17, no. 4 (2001): 457–517; as well as the rest of the special issue on this topic. See also Edwards, *Bathroom Songs*, 40–51.

65 Sedgwick, *A Dialogue on Love*, 206.

66 For brilliant accounts of why beauty matters, see Elizabeth Prettejohn, *Art for Art's Sake: Aestheticism in Victorian Painting* (New Haven, CT: Yale University Press, 2007); Elizabeth Prettejohn, *Beauty and Art 1750–2000* (Oxford: Oxford University Press, 2005).

67 For more, see Edmund Burke, *A Philosophical Inquiry into the Origin of Our Ideas of the Sublime and Beautiful* (Oxford: Oxford University Press, [1757] 1990).

68 Sedgwick, *Touching Feeling*, 99–100.

69 The locus classicus is obviously Edward W. Said, *Orientalism* (London: Penguin, [1978] 2003). A bracing alternative is John M. Mackenzie, *Orientalism: History, Theory and the Arts* (Manchester: Manchester University Press, 1995). That none of this was news to Sedgwick should be apparent, although it often has not been to at least my audiences, from "The Pedagogy of Buddhism" (Sedgwick, *Touching Feeling*, 153–82) and "Reality and Realization" (Sedgwick, *The Weather in Proust*, 206–16).

In

The rumor might be dead in the world, but in him it had come alive.
—John Updike, "The Rumor"

It would seem, then, that the function of a judgment is to convert an ambiguous decision into a decidable one. But it does so by converting a difference *within* (Billy as divided between conscious and submissiveness and unconscious hostility, Vere as divided between understanding father and military authority) into a difference *between* (between Claggart and Billy, between Nature and the King, between authority and criminality). A difference *between* opposing forces presupposes that the entities in conflict be knowable. A difference *within* one of the entities in question is precisely what problematizes the very *idea* of an entity in the first place, rendering the "legal point of view" inapplicable.
—Barbara Johnson, "Melville's Fist: The Execution of Billy Budd"

Eve Kosofsky Sedgwick's death in 2009 was one of five for me. This particular quintet consisted of John Updike, who died on January 27; Sedgwick herself, who died on April 12; Barbara Johnson, who died on August 27; my own father, Denis Kevin Flannery, who died on September 21; and last, my mother, Josephine Flannery, née Cahill, who died on December 30. What the members of this unlikely and potentially far from harmonious ensemble have in common is that each one of them made me fall in love with writing. And in that process, each one (re)sparked the energy of my own ontology and provided me with models of the future.

They all did this through specific moments, texts, scenes. For Updike it was the reading, when I was seventeen years old, of his collection of short stories *Pigeon Feathers* (1962), carried out primarily in the spaces of the adolescent bedroom and the upper deck of a smoke-filled CIE Dublin bus as it rumblingly propelled me from home to school and back in the rainy autumn of 1979. With Sedgwick's work, it was my electrifying, insight-laden, "coarsely energizing," as she herself would say, encounter, at a desk in the study of the New College house where I was living in Oxford in February 1991, of *Epistemology of the Closet*.[1] For Johnson, it was the reading, in the sitting room of my parents' house, of her "Melville's Fist" essay, one that demonstrated both exemplary rigor and exemplary tenderness, in the autumn of 1984. With my father, the scenes are, of course, multiple but would consist mostly of memories of the time between 2006 and 2009, when he and I worked together on a collaborative memoir of his childhood. With my mother, it is all more primal. I was able to read, she told me, long before I ever went to school. Using ads, she taught me on Dublin buses as they rumbled into town in the 1960s. When all of these people died, it felt for a while as if the worlds they had opened up to me and the powers they had passed on might vanish too. Now, I know, those powers are newly (and sometimes falteringly) released.

It seems right to begin a reflection on the preposition "in" as it manifests itself in Sedgwick's work on Henry James's *The Wings of the Dove*, and in critique more broadly, with quotations from Updike and from Johnson. They emphasize the problematic attraction of this word, as well as its related sacerdotal and fantasy-laden qualities.

"The rumor might be dead in the world," concludes John Updike's queer short story from 1994, "but in him it had come alive."[2] This story's hero, the married Frank Whittier, a New York gallery owner, is the object of a rumor that he has left his wife, Sharon, "for a young homosexual with whom he was having an affair."[3] The rumor that, "like a vaporous presence,"[4] circulates about Whittier is laid to rest by Updike's brief and elegant text as a "factual" entity but it comes to persist uncannily as a mode of possibility and as an attractive escape from the bounds of actuality by the story's end, where, in a tellingly fragmented mode, Updike's writing enacts the magnetism for his hero of actually embracing the dismissed rumor's queer truth.

Concluding with the sentence I quote (which is also an entire paragraph), Updike uses, with some repetitive flourish, the preposition "in" as a location of new aliveness. The phrase "in him it had come alive" emphasizes subjectivity as an *interior* location and marks, as the text comes to a close above nearly a whole side of blank paper, the switch from untruth to truth. That terse monosyllable "in," marking a transition from confused speculation to untried, liberating possibility, makes the story's rumor far less "vaporous," giving it an undeniable rhetorical punch.

In Johnson's reading of a story *about* a punch, Herman Melville's "Billy Budd," the monosyllable "in," stitched into the word "within," has a certain delicacy and power. To convert a difference *within* into a difference *between*, as Captain Vere finds himself obliged to do, is to violate a certain, perhaps difficult to comprehend but nonetheless powerfully apprehensible, internal division within Billy, or Vere. It is to convert an elusive but unmistakable sign of life—a division that is also an interiority—into a manageable but weakened and thereby fragile object of lethal legal attention. For Updike, the word "in," and subjectivity considered as inwardness, give words themselves the power to come newly alive and thereby to reform both inwardness and future realities. For Johnson, the "difference within" is, similarly, the location of aliveness. And the inward location of that difference enables, as it does for Updike, a certain power, both epistemological—problematizing "the very idea of an entity in the first place"—and ultimately political. For Johnson, a difference within doesn't so much challenge legal perspective as, to an extent, neutralize it, making it "inapplicable."

Literary critics and students of literature are fond of using the word "in" as part of their work. In the course of working on this essay, I went to a talk by my colleague Matthew Treherne entitled "Pain, Beauty and Incarnation in Dante's *Commedia*." As critics and students reconsider and nuance their work, that word "in" can meet with different fates. Another colleague, David Fairer, told me that he has changed the title of an essay on which he is currently working from "Shakespeare and Eighteenth-Century Poetry" to "Shakespeare in Eighteenth-Century Poetry." Yet another colleague, Laurence Publicover, emailed me to let me know that a talk he gave entitled "'We Are of the Sea!': Transformation and Identity in Early Modern 'Mediterranean Drama'" would be altered, once his talk becomes an article, to "Drowning Consideration: Shakespeare, the Sea, the Self." Three of the nine articles in an issue of the *Irish University Review* published in 2010 contain the word "in" as an intrinsic part of their titles: Yu-chen Lin's "The *Unheimliche* in Brian Friel's *Faith Healer*: Memory, Aesthetics, Ethics"; Michael Pierse's "Reconsidering Dermot Bolger's Grotesquery: Class and Sexuality in *The Journey Home*"; and Mark O'Connell's "The Weight of Emptiness: Narcissism and the Search for the Missing Twin in John Banville's *Birchwood* and *Mefisto*."[5] The first article I ever published was titled, "The Bench and Desolation: Law Judgment and Revenge in Henry James."

With the Dante example, we have three of the mightiest categories imaginable ("pain, beauty and incarnation") "in" the mightiest of texts. Shakespeare's relationship to eighteenth-century poetry is first considered as a relation of addition and proximity but is reworked from "and" to "in" as Shakespeare is imagined occupying the mighty body of eighteenth-century verse. We also, in this list, have a psychoanalytic category (the uncanny) "in" a play from the 1970s, two key categories of cultural analysis, sentience, and self-understanding (class and sexuality) "in" a novel by Dermot Bolger, another psychoanalytic category (narcissism) and the search for an archetypal sibling "in" John Banville's fiction. In the small example of my 1992 article on James's story "The Bench of Desolation," we have three modes of politico-cultural procedure and emotive-ethical condition "in" James's work, although the title as written doesn't suppress the possibility that those procedures and conditions inhabit James's own mighty body.

It is hard to know whether to be stunned by the capacity of writers and texts to contain overwhelming categories, to wonder whether or not "in" might be the right word or begin to think a little about the work this word might do as it helps mold the genre of the critical essay. This work would include connotatively affiliating critical articles with other genres as it helps mold the image of the critic. I've become convinced that "in" makes of the critic someone a bit more searching, brave, experimental, insightful. If I can claim that feature x is "in" text y, then reading my reflections on it can take on, I might hope, the air of an encounter between a heroic travel writer and a new phenomenon. "In" is, after all, a favorite preposition of travel writing, particularly in the nineteenth century but also beyond. We might think of James's own *A Little Tour in France* and, more recently, Bruce Chatwin's *In Patagonia* or Amitav Ghosh's *Dancing in Cambodia and At Large in Burma*.[6] Then there is the "in" of ghost stories. A model for the telling of such tales invoked at the start of James's "The Turn of the Screw" would be Charles Dickens's *The Haunted House*, a text with contributions by, among others, Elizabeth Gaskell, Wilkie Collins, and Anne Procter, and a text for which haunting consists of the occupancy, by ghosts, of different domestic interiors: "The Ghost in the Garden Room" (Gaskell), "The Ghost in the Cupboard Room" (Collins), "The Ghost in the Picture Room" (Procter).[7] Both of these modes—nineteenth-century travel writing and the Victorian ghost story—feed into the famous, though surprisingly rare, "in"s of James's own fiction: "The Figure in the Carpet," "In the Cage," "The Beast in the Jungle," "The Story in It."[8] "In" can affiliate critical work with mystery, travel, sensation, heroic enterprises, and creative literary production on all levels.

With so much to be, not always justly, gained from the employment of this little word for literary criticism across a range of modes, it's not surprising that

Sedgwick employed it, and not just because she was—among other things—a literary critic. Sedgwick was, after all, writing at a time that, as part of the AIDS crisis, the capacity of the anus to be a location of sexual pleasure and to act as an entryway of HIV infection into the body, into the bloodstream, and thereby into layer after layer of baroque corporeal interiority, became the stuff of sensational news and acknowledged common ground. Furthermore, she had an impassioned interest in the closet as a literary-cultural and world-making phenomenon. So for her, the word "in" was going to resonate even louder.[9]

Sedgwick's own career isn't exactly sprinkled with "ins," but they turn up nonetheless. The concluding chapter of *The Coherence of Gothic Conventions* is titled, "The Character of the Veil: Imagery of the Surface in the Gothic Novel," a formulation that establishes a tension among the "character" of a garment, a sometimes diaphanous piece of material, surfaces, and the Gothic novel regarded as an entity with an inwardness. It's easy to forget that Sedgwick wrote only four pieces that were explicitly on James; of them, two—"The Beast in the Closet: James and the Writing of Homosexual Panic" and "Is the Rectum Straight? Identification and Identity in *The Wings of the Dove*"—deploy this preposition in different ways. The first plays with the title of James's powerful story "The Beast in the Jungle" (1903). The substitution of "closet" for "jungle" in Sedgwick's title pivots for its shock/comic effect on the word "in." The aura of the manly Victorian adventure tale becomes, by this rhetorical move, uncanny and Gothic. Kipling becomes Wilde; the imperial becomes domestic. The word "in" here is the rhetorical switch that produces the spark of Sedgwick's effect. The title's second part doesn't locate something called "homosexual panic" *in* Henry James; that would make the essay a depressingly diagnostic exercise in biographical criticism. Sedgwick's reading of James is much more historically rich, emotionally and rhetorically sensitive. But it may be worth considering the suitability of that preposition as applied to "Identity and Identification" with regard to *The Wings of the Dove*. Can it be said that identity might be projected onto James's novel in response to what Elaine Scarry might call instructions from James as a writer?[10] If identifications are taking place between readers and characters, aren't they taking place between *The Wings of the Dove* and its readers? If identifications are taking place between characters, aren't they perhaps taking place *across The Wings of the Dove*? And doesn't Sedgwick's own reading of the pairing of Lionel Croy and Milly Theale almost insist on, and enact, this? In 1995, Sedgwick published the poem "Pandas in Trees," described by Jason Edwards as "the best queer bedtime story ever written."[11] In 1999–2000, there was an exhibition of her fiber art titled "Floating Columns/In the Bardo." As her career went on, Sedgwick returned to "in," writing a chapter published in *Touching Feeling* titled "Around the Performative: Periperformative Vicinities in Nineteenth-Century Narrative." In 2005, she gave a talk at Harvard entitled "The Weather in Proust." Again, it is worth considering how the space around certain kinds of utterance (my understanding of peri-performative vicinities) can be "in" Dickens's *Dombey and Son* or "in" nineteenth-century slave narratives. It is also worth wondering how the weather, the outer possibility of all that can be in anything, at least on this planet, can be found "in" Proust.

Edwards describes hearing "Is the Rectum Straight?" as a student at Cambridge in 1992, referring to it as "the *then* rather scandalous paper."[12] My own experience of teaching a master's seminar on *The Wings of the Dove* at Leeds in recent years, one in which we spent a two-hour class reading "Is the Rectum Straight?" alongside some other criticism by, say, David Kurnick, is that Edwards's "then" is not quite the right word. Over the years, students became more, not less, scandalized by Sedgwick's essay, willing to utter any words at all other than "rectum" or "anus" and increasingly insistent that the only lines of erotic possibility in James's novel are heterosexual ones and that Lionel Croy, as I was told, "could not possibly be a homosexual." The emotive and bodily forces that provoked both "Is the Rectum Straight?" and Leo Bersani's "Is the Rectum a Grave?" (1988), to which Sedgwick's piece is, in her words, a "little *homage*," may have altered (and not gone away), but the power of the former to provoke sometimes—quite deafening—outrage has not necessarily decreased.[13] For this reason, as well as for its virtues of intellectual daring, stubbornly lucid connective reading, and emotionally cognizant tenderness, "Is the Rectum Straight?" seems to me to be the perfect locale to help us think about that hardworking preposition and the extent to which we all might be, as James himself would put it in *The Wings of the Dove*, "worked" by it.[14]

As I've said, Sedgwick's piece is a tribute to Bersani's "Is the Rectum a Grave?" When one rereads both pieces, it's hard not to see a kind of queer leonine axis between the Leo who is the object of Sedgwick's tribute and the Lionel (Croy) who in many ways is that tribute's hero. What is a grave if not something whose funerary function and cultural power rely, like the titles of much academic work, on that preposition "in"? And how do Sedgwick and Bersani figure the rectum if not as something into which entities—phalluses, fingers, liquids, coins, and fists—can go *in*, from which they can emerge and, in that process, be a part of what Sedgwick sees as the world-making action of queer people? "I have focused on queer 'parents,'" Sedgwick writes, "rather than queer 'children' because I see an urgency in understanding queer people as not only *what the world makes* but *what makes the world*."[15] Sedgwick's essay implies that the erotic energy of the rectum is one major source of that world-making power.

The preposition "in" permeates her work on *The Wings of the Dove*. It sits— rather inelegantly, I've always felt—in the essay's subtitle. It pops up when Sedgwick writes, "It seems worth hypothesizing that the danger the book treats as implicit in Kate's spring, and in the spring that uncoils between her and Milly, is the danger of a clitoral eroticism (read as mechanical, fatal, like the loaded gun *in* Emily Dickinson) that can be read as conferring an ironic, enabling, by some accounts chilling distance from the heterosexual impera-tive."[16] Why, we might wonder, is that loaded gun *in* Emily Dickinson and not, say, something that resonates *with* Dickinson's famous poem? Why, in creating an allusive flirt between her own critical prose and Dickinson's poetry, does Sedgwick put a thing into a person (the loaded gun in Emily Dickinson) and not map a network of allusion between James's prose, her own critique, and "My Life Had Stood—a Loaded Gun"?

"In" is used about texts ("in a 1988 essay"; "in *The Wings of the Dove*"; "in the completed novel"; "in the Preface"; "in the second half of the novel").[17] It is used about textual effects and contexts ("in the rhyme that isn't a rhyme," "in the context of *The Dunciad*").[18] It is used colloquially ("in turn"; "in the course of nature"; "in an important sense"; "in a hurry").[19] It is used about emotional and sexual states and possibilities ("in a gender"; "in a contagious sexual aes-thetic"; "in anal positionalities"; "in the thematics and aesthetics of anality"; "in the abeyance of any homosexual labeling process").[20] Obviously, it is used about places. The phrase "in Venice" turns up about four times.[21] Curiously, though, Sedgwick doesn't use the phrase "in London," even though that city is the primary locale of *The Wings of the Dove* and its point of return. It is used about characters ("in Kate's vicinity"; "Milly Theale who sees in Kate"; "in Milly").[22] Lionel Croy, the character on whom Sedgwick's argument pivots, is described as "the character in *The Wings of the Dove* whom it would safest to call a homosexual."[23] Yet the phrase "in Lionel" never appears in Sedgwick's essay, despite the fact that she objects, with a compassionate eloquence, to the way in which the text deprives him of the dignity of any actual desires (and thereby any interiority) even as it makes him the queer source of his daughter's gendering, desiring self and thereby of the tight and tangled emotive plot of James's novel.

To provide a more concrete instance of how "in" works in Sedgwick's reading of *The Wings of the Dove*, let's consider the following passage:

> For all the demeaning flatness of the register of language that defines him, however, the "unspeakable" Lionel Croy is at the very source of the novel's energies. Comparing his fragmentary, framing presence in the completed novel with the "poor beautiful dazzling apparition that he was to have been," James in the 1907 Preface to the New York Edition says that in his original plans for *The Wings of the Dove*, "the image of [Kate's] so compromised and compromising father was all effectively to have pervaded her life, was in a certain particular way to have tampered with her spring."[24] James writes as if the novel as written didn't convey exactly this, but I think it does. Kate herself asks, "How can such a thing as that not be the great thing in one's life?"[25] It seems to be so in hers, but seeing how depends also on seeing how Kate in turn, however "tampered with," or indeed because she has been "tampered with," remains the "spring" of the novel as a whole. Kate Croy's construction as a woman, her sexing and gendering, have her father's homosexual disgrace installed as their very core. That is to say, they have installed at their core the irresolvable compound of a homophobic prohibition with a nascent homosexual identity, both in a gender not her own. They are also intimately structured by an economic poverty that may or may not be the result of her father's homosexual disgrace. In turn, Kate's way of being sexed and gendered seems to be, in an important sense, what propagates gender and sexuality across the novel and across its characters.[26]

Sedgwick's first gesture is to place Lionel in a place of containment that is also a place of creative power. In this her use of "in" has much in common with Updike's and Johnson's use of "in"; it is a location of new vitalities. For Sedgwick, Lionel is "at the very source of the novel's energies." Lionel, in this image, can be read as the nearly secreted point of origin for *The Wings of the Dove*'s spectacular aesthetic effects. But also, through a punning sense of the word "source" in French (i.e., a spring, as in a spring of water), he is also close to the word "spring" in the sense of generous, inspiring flow as well as "spring" in a more eroto-mechanical sense. James's preface to the novel is also made, by "in," a container, something that *holds* retrospective comments and announcements of failed intentions. That holding holds another. James's preface makes comments and concentrates on plans in which other things were to happen. But the purported emptiness of those plans in James's account is turned into a fullness by Sedgwick's. "James," she comments, "writes as if the novel as written didn't convey exactly this [i.e., the pervasive damage Lionel's image does to Kate's life], but I think it does." So at this point, *The Wings of the Dove* is not, as it is figured elsewhere in Sedgwick's essay, a container-like structure. It is more like a telegraph. Things aren't simply in it (or not). Rather, more like mercury than a magical well, it transmits things.

That is how Sedgwick uses the word "in" for the James she paraphrases and narrates. For the James she quotes, however, "in" is both much more indirect and, unsurprisingly, a question of style: "The image of [Kate's] so compromised and compromising father was all effectively to have pervaded her life, was *in a certain particular way* to have tampered with her spring."[27] So for James, it is not so much Lionel's impact as his "image," something that ties in with his bemoaned status as a lost apparition, that pervades (something that is spread throughout, both all over and in) Kate's life. This image does this work "in a certain particular way," and that work is connected with James's tight but wide-ranging metaphor of the spring. Lionel's image will therefore, in this certain particular way, do this tampering, which can be read as mischievously altering a mechanism or perhaps poisoning (putting a dangerous and unwelcome substance into) a well. James's prose and Sedgwick's then go on to echo each other. Sedgwick quotes a pretty crucial line of dialogue between Kate and Densher—"How can such a thing as that not be the great thing in one's life?"—and immediately, in a call-and-response fashion, echoes James's employment of this preposition: "It seems to be so in hers."[28] As the passage moves, we have an instance of the colloquial use of the word "in": "seeing how depends also on seeing how Kate in turn . . . remains the spring of the novel as a whole." We also have an instance of "in" being used about emotional and sexual states and possibilities. Kate's gendering, for Sedgwick, has a combined homophobic prohibition combined with a nascent homosexual identity, both "in a gender not her own." And the colloquial usage of "in" is the last to occur in this passage: "In turn, Kate's way of being sexed and gendered seems to be, in an important sense, what propagates gender and sexuality across the novel and across its characters." For this sentence, *The Wings of the Dove* becomes not a container with containers that themselves contain (a novel in which things can happen, with a preface in which comments can be made about original plans in which certain outcomes were to have been achieved). Rather, the novel becomes a surface across the remnant of which Kate's sexing and gendering can be propagated.

This active though unformulated tension between, on the one hand, a text as a container and, on the other, a surface was to become a major, explicit interest in 1997, when Sedgwick first published "Paranoid Reading and Reparative Reading." A sense that topics are in texts would seem to be a key indicative mode for paranoid criticism. A sense of texts as surfaces with uncertain boundaries and of a not always predictable expanse would have far less use for this busy preposition. As I've been suggesting, the "in" of the closet and of the anus had particular (and by no means undiminished) rhetorical charge in the late 1980s and early 1990s. In our own time, as Stephen Best and Sharon Marcus have argued, a paranoid reading position automatically connected to a sense of the inward and concealed can seem a little redundant. "Those of us," they write, "who cut our intellectual teeth on deconstruction, ideology, critique, and the hermeneutics of suspicion have often found those demystifying protocols superfluous in an era when images of torture at Abu Ghraib and elsewhere were immediately circulated on the internet; the real time coverage of Hurricane Katrina showed in ways that required little explication the state's abandonment of its African American citizens; and many people instantly recorded as lies political statements such as 'mission accomplished.'"[29] These two forms of tension between paranoid reading and reparative reading, between a hermeneutics of suspicion and its superfluity in the face of early twenty-first-century historical injustice, get played out in the bodily configuration of the human behind as, in Edwards's account, Sedgwick encourages us "to think of the arse as a composite muscle, surface *and* hole."[30] The preposition "in" encourages us to think, for all of its heroics, of texts as holes, while their own workings—and, indeed, the way they are read, even when those readings are heavily "in"-debted—might encourage a differently spatialized, and certainly less heroic, readerly relationship.

The preposition "in" recurs, and recurs, in the amazing passage from James's Notebooks that Sedgwick quotes toward her essay's end:

I sit here, after long weeks, at any rate in front of my arrears, with an inward accumulation of material of which I feel the wealth, and as to which I can only invoke my familiar demon of patience, who always comes, doesn't he?, when I call. He is here with me in front of this cool green Pacific—he sits close and I feel his soft breath, which cools and steadies and inspires, on my cheek. Everything sinks in: nothing is lost; everything abides and fertilizes and renews its golden promise, making me think with closed eyes of deep and grateful longing when, in the full summer days of L[amb] H[ouse], my long dusty adventure over, I shall be able to [plunge] my hand, my arm, *in* deep and far, up to the shoulder—into the heavy bag of remembrance—of suggestion—of imagination—of art—and fish out every little figure and felicity, every little fact and fancy that can be to my purpose. These things are all packed away, now, thicker than I can penetrate, deeper than I can fathom, and there let them rest for the present, in their sacred cool darkness, till I shall let in upon them the mild still light of dear old L[amb] H[ouse]—in which they will begin to gleam and glitter and take form like the gold and jewels of a mine.[31]

The word "in" occurs about eight times in this passage as an independent preposition. And "in" features four times as part of a compound word ("inward," "invoke," "inspires," "into"). Its first compound usage occurs when James writes about his "inward accumulation of material," of which he feels the wealth. In its compound state, "in" is intensified here, first as repetitive variant of the word's first usage ("I sit here . . . in front of my arrears" being the first). James writes about being "in front" of that which constitutes his behindedness. Then, with the compound usage of "inward," he sentiently, perhaps relishingly, feels the wealth of "this inward accumulation of material," which I read as in part constituting a pleasurable anticipation of creation. Sedgwick, I think rightly, reads this as a happy sense of eroticized fullness. "Inward," as with Updike's rumor and Johnson's Melvillean differences, stands here for the most treasured sense of being "in." And if "in" becomes "inward" in this first sentence, then that prized sense of contained, perhaps painful, eroticized possession turns into a form of compulsive action when James writes that he can "*only* invoke" his own familiar, increasingly sexy demon of patience.

A little after she quotes this passage, Sedgwick writes: "Part of what is so productive about the fisting image as a sexual phantasmatic is that it can offer a switchpoint not only between homo- and heteroeroticism, but also between allo- and autoeroticism (after all, James in the *Notebooks* passage is imagining fisting *himself*) and between the polarities that a phallic economy defines as active and passive."[32] This is where I disagree somewhat with her. It makes pretty sensational—and convincing—rhetorical sense to talk about fisting as *écriture*. And the pleasures of the erotic manual access to something possibly forbidden, patient, living, inviting—all aspects of the pleasures of anal sex, between men and between others, manual and otherwise—certainly seem to be around here. If Sedgwick is keen to link her reading of Bob Dylan's "You're Gonna Make Me Lonesome When You Go" (1975) with that song's invocation of "Verlaine and Rimbaud," then it is more than justified to assert that the collaborative "sonnet du Trou du Cul" (1870) by those French poets is a formative presence in her reading of James's note. A linkage of taboo and wonderment seems absolutely part of what James finds so creative and enabling here. But I read the temporality, the localities—and the sociabilities—of this passage differently.

Sedgwick seems keen to have James fisting himself in California, a memorable—if perhaps lonely—scenario. But what about that Demon of Patience, invoked so memorably by James, perhaps rising, almost Venus-like, from the sea? Not only is the Demon simply there in this fantasy, making it something much less solipsistic than Sedgwick claims, but he is also—for a Demon—amazingly reliable in his persistence. James refers to him as "my familiar demon of patience, who always comes, doesn't he?, when I call." That amazing persistence can also be read as matched by an equally amazing orgasmic reliability: James's Demon "always comes," we are told, in response to his Master's voice. And if Sedgwick is right to hear an echo of Shakespeare's *The Tempest* and the song "Full Fathom Five" in this passage, then James's use of the word "familiar" makes of him perhaps something like a witch? Perhaps a witch like Sycorax? Is James positing himself as a witch-mother here?

The bodily positioning of James and his familiar Demon in this passage is worth considering: "He is here with me in front of this cool green Pacific—he sits close and I feel his soft breath, which cools and steadies and inspires, on my cheek." Like James himself, the Demon is in front of the ocean's expanse. He sits "with" James in the fantasy, and we could, of course, read that as the Demon sitting next to him. Such a position would certainly allow James to "feel" that breath in all of its cooling, steadying, and inspiring force on his cheek. We can admit that possibility at the same time that we can recognize that this note doesn't rule out the possibility that the Demon is perhaps sitting *behind* James. The Demon's breath might be said to cool and steady and inspire James as he ministers to the Master possibly, in this fantasy, from behind. Whatever the literal placement (if we can talk of having literal placements in fantasy), the Demon's presence amounts to an absorption or a push—an absorption or a push *into* James, and one that he relishes for its possibilities of preservation and retention. "Everything sinks in," he writes; "nothing is lost."

This closing over, this retention, which can certainly be read in terms of anal control, or capacity, or human attention (or all three), provokes other interpretive possibilities. First, it can be read as James being fisted by his Demon or as James being fucked or, if we consider the semantic extension and vagueness of the word "cheek" (potentially extending to the cheek of the buttock[s], as opposed to the cheek of the face), the possibility of James being rimmed by this Demon does not seem so off the scale of likelihood. No one of these possibilities rules out the other, but it's certain that, for the James of this note, any one or more of these things bring about a transformation.[33]

First, they bring about the closing of James's eyes. James's reference to his "closed eyes of deep and grateful longing" is readable in anal-erotic terms, particularly when we remember the opening line of the Rimbaud-Verlaine sonnet: "Obscur et froncé comme un *oeillet* violet."[34] Jeremy Harding translates this line as, "Dark and puckered like a purple carnation."[35] But *oeillet* contains the French noun *oeil*, and a secondary meaning of *oeillet* is an eyelet—as in a little hole. A little later in the same sonnet, the anus is compared to "a wild wet eye's edge, a nest for my tears."[36]

Sedgwick doesn't emphasize this note's two temporal levels—and its two locations. There is a "present," California, and there is a "future," Lamb House. The switch between the one and the other occurs in the middle of that sentence, which reads:

> Everything sinks in: nothing is lost; everything abides and fertilizes and renews its golden promise, making me think with closed eyes of deep and grateful longing when, in the full summer days of L [amb] H[ouse], my long dusty adventure over, I shall be able to [plunge] my hand, my arm, *in* deep and far, up to the shoulder—into the heavy bag of remembrance—of suggestion—of imagination—of art—and fish out every little figure and felicity, every little fact and fancy that can be to my purpose.

It is only when James writes about the anticipation of closing his eyes and of their own powers of longing that the word "in" really begins to increase its rhetorical energy. That energy is provoked by the phrase "everything sinks in." The comfort of that inwardness, the sense of breathy relief and joy that permeates the sentence, really follow on from that phrase "everything sinks in." And in the mode of relief, it envisages a time of creative possibility "in the full summer days" of James's beloved home. But two things have happened. In the fantasy, the sense of exposure to the sea gives over to a sense of enclosed, cool interiority as a form of relief. The inward movement of the Demon of Patience's effect moves from a pleasurable incorporation (by James of the Demon) to a pleasurable occupation (by James of his own home). The word "in" has an important temporal aspect here. The phrase "in the full summer days of L. H." indicates a time other than the present but a time that Sedgwick's reading doesn't take into account. Sedgwick's exploration of this passage connects fisting as écriture, wealth, and parturition, but her promptness to move on to these more "productive" realms, along with her insistence on James as engaging in a solitary act here, leave out the possibilities that James in this note is recounting a scenario of being inspired by his Demon of Patience, who, though clearly a projection, is also conceived of as another being—one with the capacity to inspire and to confer inspiration in a way that makes James the passive recipient of his cool, tender attention. That coolness links the Demon with the Pacific in this note. (James goes from the "cool, green Pacific" to the Demon's cooling breath.) It also links the Demon with the interior of Lamb House. Endowed with the menacing, calming property of ocean and Demon, the cool interior of James's house enables him to take a powerfully active role in relation to his memory—"the heavy bag of remembrance." That remembrance obviously has as its range of possible objects anything that happened during James's US stay, including his encounter with his Demon of Patience.[37] And his move of plunging and reaching his hand in can therefore be seen as an anticipated reciprocation of the cool inspiration, where everything sank in, ministered by his California Demon of Patience. It can be said that there may well be two Demons in this note: that of Patience is explicitly allegorized here, and that of Remembrance can be said to participate in an allegorical structure. The note's concluding sentence reinforces its temporal shift. "These things are all packed away now," James writes, "and there let them rest for the moment." When he does envisage finally gaining access to these things, their inward milieu is the body neither as a metaphor for patience nor as a vehicle for embodied, erotic pleasure in its own anality. Rather, we are in the realm of light. "I shall let *in* upon them the mild, still light," James writes, "*in* which they will begin to gleam and glitter."[38] Sedgwick is more than justified to read this passage in terms of fisting, and James's note insists on a connection between homoerotic, manual anality and James's own sense of creative possibility. I see it as fisting certainly, but differently. For me, the James of this passage—and the word "in" is crucial to this—is all too joyously readable as being the object of a number of attentions from another male figure. Halfway through the passage, albeit in the same sentence, the change in location and the anticipated change in time brings about a switch for James, too, where *he* is fisting his "heavy bag of remembrance," readable as himself, perhaps, but also readable as a return (or a passing on) of the attentions paid to him by his Pacific Demon. The word "in" moves from positioning to absorption, to temporality, to manual penetration, to anticipated illumination. The other "in"s—related compound words of this passage ("inward," "invoke," "inspire," "into")—enable this narrative of enlightenment.

I'd like to conclude by turning again to Lionel Croy as James writes about him in *The Wings of the Dove* and to do so in the light of an exchange that takes place between Michael Snediker and Sedgwick in their interview titled "Queer Little Gods":

MDS: I love that in Catholicism you can bury your little gods and it's a totally nonfunerary version of burial, it's less that they've died because they're little gods but it's as though they have to do their work underground for some reason. I've never quite understood that. The underground St. Anthony versus the Anthony venerated on an altar.

EKS: I haven't run into that.

MDS: I think St. Anthony is the saint one buries if one is trying to sell one's house, and he'll only work if you bury him. You need to bury him in your yard and it will somehow attract buyers. But it's as though the powers get released in the burial.

EKS: That's great.[39]

Sedgwick's great gesture in "Is the Rectum Straight?" is to take Lionel Croy seriously, to empathize with James's anxieties about his inadequate representation at the same time that she doesn't quite buy into James's frantic articulations of his failures in the preface to the New York Edition. Taking Lionel Croy seriously as a source for the queer energies of James's impassioned novel means that, for Sedgwick, Lionel Croy, and Milly Theale, who in the novel's realistic register never "meet," become very much partners in crime. I use this phrase quite advisedly. For Sedgwick, Lionel, and Milly almost allegorize two modes in which the nineteenth century envisioned homosexuality. "A turn away from the criminal model of homosexuality in this period," Sedgwick writes, "seemed as if inevitably to involve a turn toward the medical model: from Lionel to Milly."[40] A little earlier she claims that "one of the most astounding effects in *The Wings of the Dove* is the way Milly's relation to her illness winds up, rhetorically, as an echo precisely of Lionel Croy's homosexual disgrace."[41] And she emphasizes how James "framed the two characters in this revisionary relation to one another."[42] Despite this emphasis, Sedgwick gives no attention to the Lionel Croy who doesn't exactly appear but is nonetheless mentioned toward the novel's end, in the glowering aftermath of Milly Theale's death.

Lionel's presence in the house of Marian Condrip, Kate's sister, is recounted by Kate as the novel ends, with considerable emphasis on the preposition I've been contemplating in this essay. Kate tells Densher that Lionel has been in her sister's house for three days, having arrived there suddenly "in a state which made it impossible not to take him in."[43] They talk about Lionel a little longer:

> Densher hesitated. "Do you mean in such want—?"
>
> "No, not of food, of necessary things—not even, so far as his appearance went, of money. He looked as wonderful as ever. But he was—well, in terror."
>
> "In terror of what?"
>
> "I don't know. Of somebody—of something. He wants, he says, to be quiet. But his quietness is awful."
>
> She suffered but he couldn't not question. "What does he do?"
>
> It made Kate herself hesitate. "He cries."
>
> Again, for a moment he hung fire, but he risked it. "What *has* he done?"
>
> It made her slowly rise, and they were once more fully face to face. Her eyes held his own and she was paler than she had been. "If you love me—now—don't ask about father."[44]

There are several connections among these two exchanges (Sedgwick's and Snediker's, Kate's and Densher's), Sedgwick's reading of the pairing of Lionel and Milly, and the preposition "in." First, although "in" as a preposition of occupancy is used here when Kate talks about Marian having to take Lionel in, most of the time it is used to refer to an aberrational state—"in terror." So for Snediker, certain kinds of "powers get released in the burial," but Lionel is described as in the grip of a terrible power. For all that, Lionel, sequestered, Christlike, for three days is far from ineffectual. "Father's never ill. He's a marvel. He's only—endless," Kate claims a bit earlier, conferring on him the power so ostensibly wanting in the recently dead Milly Theale but ultimately similar to the paralyzing legacy with which James's novel ends.[45] Lionel has clearly lost none of his powers to incite questions. (Densher "risks" asking, somewhat pointlessly, "What *has* he done?") And Lionel has lost none of his power to make his thoroughly modern daughter suffer, hesitate, and grow pale. There can be no better evidence of Lionel's ongoing power than the use of silence about him as a bargaining tool, even at this late stage, between Kate and Densher. Along with and as part of his state of terror, Lionel, in Kate's account, demonstrates an "awful quietness"—a state of stillness not unlike the quiet of the grave. And the principal active verb she uses about him is "to cry," which is employed in an unrelenting present tense.

One of the key effects of *The Wings of the Dove* noted by David Kurnick is what he terms "performative leveling," which is where characters, even when they have no immediate ties on the plane of realism (or even any ties at all) echo each other's vocabulary, often through the use of adjectives such as "wonderful" and "beautiful."[46] We might have an instance of this in the passage I just quoted when Kate claims that, on arriving at Miriam's door, Lionel looked "as wonderful as ever." I wonder whether Lionel's state of terror, his weeping and taking to his bed for a sepulchral three days, can be read, on the plane of performative leveling, as his uncanny response to the death of the utterly uncanny Milly Theale. I wonder whether his grief might be at the loss of the woman who, in Sedgwick's reading, completed his being in James's mighty text, because it might be right to say that Lionel is "trundled offstage" in favor of Milly as James's novel goes on.[47] But that very expulsion can also be read as a transformation. Lionel can be said to have *become* Milly rather than simply be replaced by her. Her death can be said, then, to return him to his former state. Perhaps, via Milly's burial, a power has been released, resulting in Lionel's terror. Listening to the phrase "trundled offstage," we can imagine Sedgwick's essay as something like a stage adaptation of *The Wings of the Dove* in which Lionel and Milly are thrillingly, disturbingly played by the same actor.

But in a novel where emotions, bodily states, and erotic dispositions are nothing, as Sedgwick herself noted, if not contagious, Lionel's terror might be said to have spread to Kate and Densher. By being buried in the ground, Milly's powers, newly released, are manifest in Lionel even as he grieves either a Milly he never met or a Milly he once was but is no longer. In taking to his awfully quiet bed for three days, Lionel might, Christlike, be read as preparing for a resurrection certainly (he is, after all, "only endless"). Or it might be that his powers, thus blended into Milly's, are being released precisely through his—perhaps voluntary, like Milly's—burial. Another way to read this scenario is spatially. James's text doesn't specify a locale for Lionel's bedroom in Marian Condrip's house, but it's far from overly speculative to assume that, by being in bed, he is upstairs, that he is above Densher and Kate, just as they are above the recently buried Milly Theale. A few pages later, emphasizing the extent to which her dead friend is now above them, Kate is to famously claim that Milly's wings "cover" both her and Densher.[48] Can we read the young lovers as, like Lionel and Milly, like Snediker's and Sedgwick's queer little gods, "covered" like the corpses of the dead, buried like the Catholic St. Anthony and efficacious only because this has taken place? And can we read this anxious discussion as a first, rather Poe-like recognition on their part that they have been buried? Perhaps Densher's question is incomplete. Perhaps he needs to ask not what Lionel has done but, rather, "What has he done *to us?*" A James outlined in that Gothic recognition of live burial is one to which Sedgwick would have been so responsive. The James outlined in that recognition would amount to powerful continuity between "Is the Rectum Straight?" and the essay to which it pays tribute, Bersani's "Is the Rectum a Grave?" The conceptual, literary, bodily, and phantasmatic use of the preposition "in" I've been outlining here echoes that very "fine and private place," as Andrew Marvell put it.[49] But it also makes of that fine quietude something awful, as Kate puts it, producing awe, not only by virtue of its power to contain, but also by virtue of its power, like Sedgwick's and James's cherished anus, to take in the world with a view to releasing uncanny powers.

NOTES

Acknowledgments: I am very grateful to Simon Swift and James Thurley for reading earlier versions of this essay. I am also grateful to Richard Hibbit for telling me about Jeremy Harding's translation of the sonnet by Verlaine and Rimbaud.

Epigraphs: John Updike, "The Rumor," in *The Afterlife and Other Stories* (London: Penguin, 1995), 214; Barbara Johnson, "Melville's Fist: The Execution of Billy Budd," in *The Critical Difference: Essays in the Contemporary Rhetoric of Reading,* by Barbara Johnson (Baltimore: Johns Hopkins University Press, 1981), 106.

1   Sedgwick uses this phrase as part of her account of the impact of reading Proust in the final chapter of *Epistemology of the Closet* when she writes, "I don't think I am the only reader on whom Proust has an almost coarsely energizing effect that is difficult to account for on any grounds of the purely kosher": Eve Kosofsky Sedgwick, *Epistemology of the Closet* (Berkeley: University of California Press, 2008), 242.

2   Updike, "The Rumor," 214.

3   Updike, "The Rumor," 201.

4   Updike, "The Rumor," 204.

5   All of these articles are in *Irish University Review* 40, no. 2 (2010).

6   Alaric Hall's work on the nineteenth-century meshing of encounters with Africa and perceptions of early medieval British history has drawn my attention to titles such as John Barrow's *Travels into the Interior of Southern Africa* (1806), Stephen Kay's *Travels and Researches in Caffaria* (1837), and Robert Moffat's *Missionary Labors and Scenes in Southern Africa* (1842).

7   Charles Dickens, *The Haunted House* (London: Oneworld Classics, [1862] 2009).

8 I say "surprisingly rare" because, despite the fact that three of the titles I have listed are the best known, as well as most frequently anthologized and critically discussed, of James's stories and the most identified with him, they represent, as a glance at the titles of his 112 stories and novellas shows, his only uses of the word "in" as part of their titles.

9 For a discussion of Sedgwick's decision to remain—as a woman married to a man and with a rather conventional sexual life—"closeted" in *Epistemology of the Closet*, see Jason Edwards, *Eve Kosofsky Sedgwick* (Abingdon, UK: Routledge, 2009), 124.

10 Scarry uses this term "instruction" to cover the interrelationship of mimesis, perception, and literary power when she asks, "How does it come about that this perceptual mimesis, which when undertaken on one's own is ordinarily feeble and impoverished, when under authorial instruction sometimes closely approximates actual perception?": Elaine Scarry, *Dreaming by the Book* (New York: Farrar, Straus and Giroux, 1999), 6. In making this analogy, I see James as a writer providing "instructions" not only for visually imagining phenomena but for conceiving, in a very sentient way, of forms of identity.

11 Edwards, *Eve Kosofsky Sedgwick*, 162.

12 Edwards, *Eve Kosofsky Sedgwick*, 74, emphasis added.

13 Leo Bersani, "Is the Rectum a Grave?," in *AIDS: Cultural Analysis/Cultural Criticism*, ed. Douglas Crimp (Cambridge, MA: MIT Press, 1988), 197–222; Edwards, *Eve Kosofsky Sedgwick*, 103.

14 I use the verb "to work" here in the sense of a familial proximity and ultimately financial, usually desperate, emotional motivation and a habitually draining set of consequences. This is the sense in which James uses it when he writes, for example, about Kate's sister, Marian, that "she desired her [Kate] to 'work' Lancaster Gate as she believed that scene of abundance could be worked": Henry James, *The Wings of the Dove*, ed. Donald Crowley and Richard A. Hocks (New York: W. W. Norton, 2003), 44.

15 Eve Kosofsky Sedgwick, *Tendencies* (Durham, NC: Duke University Press, 1993), 95.

16 Sedgwick, *Tendencies*, 94, emphasis added.

17 Sedgwick, *Tendencies*, 73, 75, 77.

18 Sedgwick, *Tendencies*, 96, 100.

19 Sedgwick, *Tendencies*, 74, 78, 89, 100.

20 Sedgwick, *Tendencies*, 77, 78, 81, 91, 96.

21 Sedgwick, *Tendencies*, 92–94, 96.

22 Sedgwick, *Tendencies*, 85.

23 Sedgwick, *Tendencies*, 75.

24 Sedgwick, *Tendencies*, 77–78, citing James, *The Wings of the Dove*, 43 [10].

25 Sedgwick, *Tendencies*, 77–78, citing James, *The Wings of the Dove*, 99 [58].

26 Sedgwick, *Tendencies*, 77–78.

27 Sedgwick, *Tendencies*, 43, emphasis added.

28 Sedgwick, *Tendencies*, 77.

29 As the essays in their special issue of *Representations*, particularly those by Mary Thomas Crane and Anne Anlin Cheng, show, the enterprise of surface reading is a way to discovery and surprise: see Stephen Best and Sharon Marcus, eds., "Surface Reading," special issue of *Representations* 108 (Fall 2009). The same is true of Marcus's work in *Between Women*, particularly that book's open and vivid reading of *Great Expectations*: see Sharon Marcus, *Between Women: Friendship, Desire and Marriage in Victorian England* (Princeton, NJ: Princeton University Press, 2007).

30 Sedgwick, *Tendencies*, 75, emphasis added.

31 Henry James, *The Notebooks of Henry James*, ed. F. O. Matthiessen and Kenneth B. Murdock (New York: Oxford University Press, 1947), 318, quoted in Sedgwick, *Tendencies*, 99.

32 Sedgwick, *Tendencies*, 101.

33 My reading of this passage owes much to Judith Butler's essay "The Force of Fantasy," in which she argues for the distribution of identity of the fantasizing *self* among various elements of a scene of fantasy. Interestingly, Butler's exemplary scenario of fantasy is dependent on a telling preposition. "I was sitting *in* the cafeteria," she writes, "and you came up to me": Judith Butler, "The Force of Fantasy: Feminism, Mapplethorpe and Discursive Excess," in *The Judith Butler Reader*, ed. Sarah Salih (Oxford: Blackwell, 2004), 188, emphasis added.

34 Arthur Rimbaud, *Selected Poems and Letters*, trans. Jeremy Harding (London: Penguin, 2004), 96.

35 Rimbaud, *Selected Poems and Letters*, 97.

36 Rimbaud, *Selected Poems and Letters*, 97.

37 James was in California, staying at San Diego's Hotel Coronado, when he wrote this note in March 1905. This was toward the end of a long return visit to the United States that was to result in the publication of his book *The American Scene*: Fred Kaplan, *Henry James: The Imagination of Genius: A Biography* (London: Hodder and Stoughton, 1992), 492–500.

38 Sedgwick, *Tendencies*, 99, emphasis added.

39 Eve Kosofsky Sedgwick and Michael D. Snediker, "Queer Little Gods: A Conversation," *Massachusetts Review* 49, nos. 1–2 (2008): 212–13.

40 Sedgwick, *Tendencies*, 90.

41 Sedgwick, *Tendencies*, 88.

42 Sedgwick, *Tendencies*, 89.

43 James, *The Wings of the Dove*, 395.

44 James, *The Wings of the Dove*, 395.

45 James, *The Wings of the Dove*, 395.

46 David Kurnick, "What Does Late Jamesian Style Want?" *Henry James Review* 28 (2007): 215, 218.

47 Sedgwick, *Tendencies*, 89.
48 James, *The Wings of the Dove*, 406.
49 Andrew Marvell, "To His Coy Mistress," in *The Norton Anthology of Poetry*, ed. Margaret Ferguson, Tim Kendall, and Mary Jo Slater (New York: W. W. Norton, 2018), 511.

Early and Earlier Sedgwick

In 2002, Stephen Barber and David Clark published an essay on Sedgwick's temporalities. "What remains evident . . . across the entire body of her work," they write, "is another conception and unfolding of temporality, a specifically queer temporality."[1] As far as I know, this represents the earliest occurrence in print of the now widespread phrase (and theoretical current) "queer temporality." Barber and Clark derive their notion of Sedgwick's queer temporality from the foreword to her book *Tendencies*; in that foreword she announces "a QUEER time," "the queer moment," "the moment of queer."[2] While Sedgwick in 1993 may be declaring the moment of queer, this is not your usual sort of moment. Close-reading Sedgwick's proclamation of the queer moment, Barber and Clark propose that "a problem about temporality may be for her a defining aspect of that moment. Sedgwick . . . initially seems to cast the span of 'queer' within a recognizably temporal frame, but what remains evident in the [foreword] to *Tendencies*, as across the entire body of her work, is another conception and unfolding of temporality, a specifically queer temporality." It is not just the moment of queer, but a queer sort of moment, indeed: as Sedgwick puts it in the foreword, "Queer is a continuing moment . . . recurrent, eddying, *troublant*."[3]

Inspired by Barber and Clark's formulation of Sedgwick's temporality, I produced a reading of *Tendencies* that I called "The Queer Temporality of Writing." This essay of mine appeared in the collection *Queer Times, Queer Becomings*, edited by Ellen McCallum and Mikko Tukhanen, and a revised version appeared as a chapter of *The Deaths of the Author*.[4] My reading of *Tendencies* focuses on Sedgwick's accounts of the temporality of her writing during the very period she dubs "the queer moment," a period around 1992, and there I find not only anachronistically "continuing moments," not only uncannily "recurrent" moments, but timing that is *troublant*, indeed—unsettling and even indecent. I mention this essay of mine because the essay you are now reading is a sort of sequel—or, rather, prequel—a continuation of my inquiry into Sedgwick's queer temporality of writing, looking now not at *Tendencies*, but at her earlier books.

Let me begin with a text that, while published in an "earlier book," was in fact written at almost exactly the same moment, the same queer moment, as the foreword to *Tendencies*. Eight years before *Tendencies*, in 1985, Sedgwick published *Between Men*, a book that has been given a certain originary status. According to *Rolling Stone*, it is "the text that ignited gay studies"; according to the *Voice Literary Supplement*, it is "the book that turned queer theory from a latent to a manifest discipline."[5] While *Tendencies* was published at the queer moment, *Between Men* had a place in bringing queer theory about. Thus Columbia University Press, at the same moment *Tendencies* appeared, brought out a version of *Between Men* "with a new preface by the author" (as it says on the cover and title page). This is not, in strict terms, a new edition; the interior pages remain the same, but the 1985 book, unchanged, is henceforth preceded by a preface, dated November 1992. This new preface, issuing from precisely the period Sedgwick has dubbed the "queer moment," has, in fact, a troubling effect on the temporality of the earlier book.

Readers who approach *Between Men* in this version—which is to say, most readers since 1993—have the disconcerting experience of the author relegating the book to some distant past before we even begin to read it. "From the 1990s vantage," she writes, "it's hard to remember what that distant country felt like. Rereading the book now, I'm brought up short, often, with dismay at the thinness of the experience on which . . . its analyses . . . are based."[6] As we read the preface, the book is still ahead of us, in our future, but the author quite insistently locates it in a past, one she characterizes as "distant." Since the book has not been in any way revised, brought up to date, we are being introduced to an anachronism. If such a preface were written by anyone other than the author, it would surely be seen as doing the book a disservice.

Sedgwick, however, has exhibited a taste for anachronism. In an interview with Barber and Clark in 2000, she said enthusiastically, "That's the wonderful thing about the printed word—it can't be updated instantly. It's allowed to remain anachronistic in relation to the culture of the moment."[7] Certainly this could be said about the 1993 reprinting of *Between Men*: it is in fact not updated but "allowed to remain anachronistic." This unusual enthusiasm for the anachronism of the printed word is part of what I find queer about Sedgwick's temporality of writing. And I see it manifest in the odd "new preface" to *Between Men*, which combines the author's sense of the book as an anachronism with real affection for the book.

The affection displayed in the 1992 preface is most striking, however, when directed not to the dated book but toward its "author." Although the preface begins in the first person—"I had in mind. . . . I started work on the book. . . . I was surprised, exultant, grateful. . . . I intended"—about halfway through, the "new preface by the author" refers to "the author of this book" in the third person. The preface to *Between Men* employs the formulation "the author of this book" on two occasions; it also twice refers to the author as "her." In the first instance of this, Sedgwick uses the phrase "the young author of this book." This phrasing makes it evident that between the author of the preface and the author of the book there is a marked age difference that is not just quantitative but qualitative.

"That there was something irrepressibly *provincial* about the young author of this book is manifest." Talking about her earlier self, Sedgwick italicizes "provincial." While that adjective generally connotes a condescending, superior attitude, the adverb "irrepressibly" that precedes it hints instead at admiration. The older author's relation to the younger author here combines superiority and affection; it is both patronizing and patronage.

Sedgwick continues: "But will it make sense if I describe that provinciality as not only a measure of her distance from the scenes of gay male creativity . . . but also a ground of her passionate, queer, and fairly uncanny identification with it?"[8] Much has been written about Sedgwick's identification with "gay male creativity"; it is surely central to her work and our appreciation of her. But in this passage I am more interested in another "queer and fairly uncanny identification"—the one that involves Sedgwick's writing about herself as an author, the one that uses the pronoun "I" for the author of the new preface ("I describe that provinciality") and "her" for the "young author of this book" ("her distance," "her passionate, queer . . ."). I find it fairly uncanny to hear Sedgwick talk about her young self in the third person.

The "new preface" goes on to say that the "founding narrative of a certain modern identity for Euro-American gay men . . . stretches from provincial origins to metropolitan destinies." In other words, gay male identity begins precisely in provinciality. Sedgwick confesses in the preface that "during the writing of *Between Men*, I . . . actually knew only one openly gay man." While this is precisely what dismays her as a "thinness of experience," by configuring this inexperience as "provinciality," Sedgwick ironically, perversely, makes her distance from gay men the very mark of her closeness to gay men.

That the "young author" can thus be coded as a young, inexperienced proto-gay man just arrived in the big city makes this identification not only perverse but erotic. We can recognize here a stock erotic scenario. The older, worldlier author looks with delectation at the young innocent from the provinces. This is a passionate, queer identification, to be sure, but also "fairly uncanny" in that the worldly writer and the young innocent are both Sedgwick.

While Sedgwick's "young author of this book" is certainly perverse, it may not even be the uncanniest author image in *Between Men*'s "new preface by the author." Aside from the two instances when Sedgwick refers to her earlier self as "the author of this book," the preface includes one (and only one) other use of the word "author." Just two sentences before her statement about the "young author of this book," in the same paragraph, Sedgwick lists the gay scholars on whose work the book depends—Jeffrey Weeks, Guy Hocquenghem, Paul Hoch, Mario Mieli, Alan Bray—and then says, "[T]hese texts appear in *Between Men* as . . . secondary sources by authors who might—for any sense *Between Men* gives of their contemporaneity—have been dead for a century."[9]

Contemporary authors who appear as if they "have been dead for a century." Sedgwick here is noting something peculiar about *Between Men*'s temporality: it treats these contemporary "authors" as belonging to a distant past. I would like to connect Sedgwick's referring to herself as "author" to this other use of the word, the only other use in the preface, which occurs immediately before the first time she refers to herself as "the author." And if I connect these two uses of "author," then her treatment of "the young author of this book" could be connected to the author as not only relegated to the distant past but "dead," to living authors appearing as if dead.

There is a reason I am drawn to make this connection. The chapter "Queer Temporality of Writing" in my book *The Deaths of the Author: Reading and Writing in Time* understands the peculiar temporality of Sedgwick's writing as an encounter with the death of the author, even though it does not look at this appearance of the living dead author in her 1992 preface to *Between Men*. The chapter centers on a text written the previous year, "White Glasses," a so-called obituary for her friend Michael Lynch that was in fact delivered while Lynch was still alive.

Named for the white-framed glasses Sedgwick wore in imitation of Lynch, "White Glasses" is all about Sedgwick's identification with him. "If what is at work here is an identification that falls across gender," Sedgwick writes, "it falls no less across . . . the ontological crack between the living and the dead."[10]

"White Glasses," written in 1991, is grappling not only with her friend's imminent death but also, at the same time, with the news that Sedgwick has advanced, metastasized cancer—thus placing Sedgwick and Lynch together in a queer moment in which the dead are not yet dead and the living are no longer quite living. The new preface to *Between Men*, written the next year, in fact mentions Lynch, identifying him as a "pioneer of gay studies," although it does not mention that he has recently died. What in "White Glasses" takes place through her identification with Lynch occurs in the preface to *Between Men* through her naming herself an "author" like the contemporary gay "authors" who appear as if dead.[11]

This might explain the unsettling figures of the author in the 1992 preface. We could chalk them up to the queer moment in which it was written, a moment in which Sedgwick is not only mourning gay friends dying of AIDS, but identifying with their dying because of her recent cancer diagnosis. We might attribute the sense of a temporal divide between herself in 1992 and the "young author" of the 1985 book as a gap opened up by her experiences of friends dying and perhaps especially by her own illness.

To thus explain these striking images by the moment in which this text was written would, however, be to forget that, while Sedgwick's queer moment might seem to be a recognizable point on a timeline (located around 1992), it is also part of "another conception and unfolding of temporality." Sedgwick's queer moment is "eddying, *troublant*"; Sedgwick's queer moment is "recurrent." While the dramatic events between 1985 and 1992 certainly provide a tempting explanation, they cannot account for how the new preface's vision of the author repeats an earlier authorial self-reflection, one in a text Sedgwick wrote early in 1986. While my essay thus far has read Sedgwick's preface to *Between Men* through its resemblances to her later book *Tendencies*, for the rest of this chapter I want to explore its resemblances to an earlier book.

Early and Earlier Sedgwick. Originary as it might be for queer theory, *Between Men* is Sedgwick's second book. Her first was *The Coherence of Gothic Conventions*, which began as a dissertation and was published in 1980 by Arno Press. A new edition of *Coherence* was published by Methuen in 1986, the year after the publication of *Between Men*. The success of her second book is likely responsible for this new edition of her first. The back cover of Methuen's *Coherence* not only tells us that Sedgwick is "the author of *Between Men*"; it also informs us that a "new introduction to this reprint of a 1980 study clarifies the connection between the . . . argument of the Gothic and its . . . crystallization of modern gender and modern homophobia"—which is to say that the new introduction "clarifies the connection between" the argument of this book and the argument of *Between Men*.

Early and Earlier Sedgwick. In the wake of her 1990 book *Epistemology of the Closet*, Columbia University Press asks Sedgwick to write a new preface to *Between Men*. About six years earlier, in the wake of *Between Men*, Sedgwick likewise wrote a new introduction to *The Coherence of Gothic Conventions*. In both cases, Sedgwick resituated an earlier book after a later book, prefaced the earlier book with a view that followed the later book. The temporality of Sedgwick's writing is queer indeed, not only progressing along a timeline but cycling back repeatedly—recurrent, eddying.

"Queer is ... recurrent, eddying, *troublant*." In both these instances, attempting to bring an earlier book up to date, Sedgwick experiences the anachronism of the printed word as a gap between preface writer and book author. What the back cover of Methuen's reprint of *Coherence* terms "a new introduction" is between its covers called a "preface." Dated January 1986, this preface by the author opens with these words:

> Rereading one's published work across a gap, for any reason especially marked, of time ... can feel like a family reunion, in which dramas of recognition careen unexpectedly off of shocks of disavowal. . . . No scene of reading could be more Gothic. . . . The past, the written word itself . . . would function, in such a scene, as forms of captivity, by the divisive and defining power of which something like distinct, doubled "selves" (the me reading, the me read) are generated. . . . Epicycles of the *unheimlich* . . . would make for the plot and thrills of this encounter.[12]

The 1986 preface begins by commenting on the experience of rereading herself "across a marked gap of time." This produces an uncanny doubling—*unheimlich*, she says, using Freud's German for uncanny—an uncanny doubling into "the me reading" and "the me read." While this experience of doubling may be uncanny (i.e., odd, peculiar), it is nonetheless presented as general: "rereading *one's* published work across a gap, *for any reason* especially marked, of time." Thus, we find in the beginning of this preface an explanation, perhaps even a theorization, of the situation we noted in the later preface, the one that caused Sedgwick to talk about herself in the third person, as "the author of this book," where the "marked gap of time" is represented by her reference to herself as "the young author of this book."

In 1992 she codes the "gap of time" as provinciality versus experience to cast the relation between the two selves as gay: "her passionate, queer, and fairly uncanny identification." Nearly seven years earlier, the relation is still uncanny, if in German, but uncanny connects not to queer but to Gothic. "No scene of reading could be more Gothic," she claims, hyperbolically.

The full sentence, which I truncated in the larger quote, reads: "No scene of reading could be more Gothic, in the sense of 'Gothic' formulated in this essay from the 1970s." Sedgwick is not just calling her relation to her earlier self "Gothic" loosely, as we might; she understands it as a version of the very notion her book is proposing. Thus, the relation to herself put forth in this preface is not just outside the book but also inside; it does not just comment on the book but is explained by the book.

What is this Gothic, uncanny encounter, formulated in Sedgwick's first book, repeated when the author rereads her published words? What is this relation between distinct, doubled "selves" that is at the heart of *The Coherence of Gothic Conventions* and can be found repeated at the heart of *Between Men*? A cogent answer would entail a more extensive reading of Sedgwick's first two books in view of an understanding of "the sense of 'Gothic' formulated in this essay from the 1970s" and how it plays out, a decade later, in her "crystallization of modern gender and modern homophobia." Since I am not prepared to do that here, let me just close with a quick and dirty evocation, a much too rough sketch.

At the beginning of the preface to *Coherence*, Sedgwick compares the experience of rereading her published work to a "family reunion," locates her relation to her earlier writings in the family. While the opening paragraph, quoted at length earlier, begins with the family drama (recognition and disavowal), it then leaves the family reunion image behind for the *unheimlich* encounter of doubled "selves." Four pages later, it traces a similar move from family to uncanny encounter when Sedgwick claims that "the family" in the Gothic is "a somewhat ephemeral stage on the way to the tableau that is seen as embodying primal human essence." She goes on to specify what this primal tableau is: "the tableau of two men chasing one another. . . . It is importantly undecidable in this tableau . . . whether the two men represent two consciousnesses or only one: and it is importantly undecidable whether their bond . . . is murderous or amorous."[13]

Not actually discussed in *The Coherence of Gothic Conventions*, this tableau is offered by the preface as the primal scene of what Sedgwick calls "the paranoid Gothic," the subgenre that is the subject of the middle chapters of *Between Men*, where it lays bare the homosexual panic of nineteenth-century homosocial relations. This image of the family that dissolves into relations between men, where we cannot tell whether they are murderous or amorous, cannot tell whether we are talking about one or two consciousnesses, is most precisely found in Sedgwick's reading of James Hogg's *Confessions of a Justified Sinner* (1824), the novel that occupies the exact middle of *Between Men*.

Sedgwick's rich and memorable reading of Hogg's novel finds its way into a scene in "White Glasses" where Michael and Eve are in bed together. I suggest that this paranoid Gothic tableau underpins Sedgwick's drama of reading herself. In that uncanny encounter, we cannot tell whether the author represents two consciousnesses or only one. Whether one or two, the author here identifies with this two men tableau. Two men chasing each other in a bond that is amorous—scene of gay male creativity—but possibly murderous as well, the author's identification is Gothically shadowed by death.

NOTES

1 Stephen M. Barber and David L. Clark, "Queer Moments: The Performative Temporalities of Eve Kosofsky Sedgwick," in *Regarding Sedgwick: Essays on Queer Culture and Critical Theory*, ed. Stephen M. Barber and David L. Clark (New York: Routledge, 2002), 2.

2 Eve Kosofsky Sedgwick, *Tendencies* (Durham, NC: Duke University Press, 1993), xi–xii.

3 Sedgwick, *Tendencies*, xii.

4 Jane Gallop, "The Queer Temporality of Writing," in *Queer Times, Queer Becomings*, ed. Ellen McCallum and Mikko Tukhanen (Buffalo: State University of New York Press, 2011), 47–74; Jane Gallop, *The Deaths of the Author* (Durham, NC: Duke University Press, 2011).

5 Both blurbs are on the back cover of the 1993 edition ("with a new preface by the author") of Eve Kosofsky Sedgwick, *Between Men: English Literature and Male Homosocial Desire* (New York: Columbia University Press, 1985 [1993]).

6 Sedgwick, *Between Men*, viii.

7 Eve Kosofsky Sedgwick, "This Piercing Bouquet: An Interview with Eve Kosofsky Sedgwick," in Barber and Clark, *Regarding Sedgwick*, 253.

8 Sedgwick, *Between Men*, ix.

9 Sedgwick, *Between Men*, viii–ix.

10 Eve Kosofsky Sedgwick, "White Glasses," in Sedgwick, *Tendencies*, 257.

11 One of the authors listed, Mieli, had died by the time *Between Men* was originally published; another, Hocquenghem, had died by the time the new preface was published. Both died very young. Sedgwick's "contemporaneity" is not a marker of whether the author is in fact alive or dead.

12 Eve Kosofsky Sedgwick, *The Coherence of Gothic Conventions* (London: Methuen, 1985), v.

13 Sedgwick, *The Coherence of Gothic Conventions*, ix.

Eve's Future Figures

In the spring 2010 semester, Michael Moon and I taught a graduate seminar at Emory University entitled "Reading Sedgwick." Almost from the start, questions of methodology were central to our discussions. By "methodology," our students meant to ask the question of how to use Sedgwick. These preoccupations crystallized almost immediately around a moment in the "Introduction: Axiomatic" to *Epistemology of the Closet* that addresses the question of method in just these terms: "If the book were able to fulfill its most expansive ambitions, it would make certain specific kinds of readings and interrogations, perhaps new, available in a heuristically powerful, productive, and significant form for other readers to perform on literary and social texts with, ideally, other results."[1]

The invitation offered in this sentence is certainly to be related to an experience to which many readers of Sedgwick's work can testify: a permission to think. It's on that permission that I want to focus here. To do so, it's important to notice that what's being asked of the reader at this moment in *Epistemology of the Closet* is to think in a way that will produce "other results" than those offered by Sedgwick herself. It was there, perhaps, that the conundrum arose for our students. Although the sentence gestures to "certain specific kinds of readings and interrogations," it does not define that specificity—that is, the reader is not told whether that specificity amounts to something generalizable as a model or paradigm or whether it inheres in specificities that remain specific and therefore presumably are non-generalizable. Moreover, it suggests that the methodological basis offered as "a heuristically powerful, productive, and significant form" is possibly new. To the degree that it might be new there attaches the further possibility—indeed, the likelihood—that it might be unrecognizable or ungraspable. Is a model to be imitated being proffered? If so, what form does it take?

One answer to that question comes in the introduction, in which Axiom 1 (*People are different from each other*) concludes: "Repeatedly to ask how certain categorizations work, what enactments they are performing and what relations they are creating, rather than what they essentially *mean*, has been my principal strategy."[2] Methodology here is strategy; performativity is preferred to meaning. Everywhere the sentence pluralizes. The "principal strategy" (a kind of general *categorical* imperative?) is offered in a past tense that seems to lag behind the verbal present of a plural activity with which it probably cannot keep up and that I perhaps named wrongly in the nominative. That is, the strategy is less the substantive "performativity" than "performing." If, once again, we ask the methodological question, it seems as if the sentence itself asks it too, or gestures toward such repetitions as the strategy deployed. A questioning that will not produce an answer seems to be the strategy to be deployed, since what one is attempting to grasp exceeds one's grasp—especially, that is, if "meaning" is the locus for the answer to the question, if grasping meaning is what it means to grasp.

Precisely because the "Introduction" in *Epistemology of the Closet* is offered as a series of declarative sentences arranged as axioms, one might assume that these are kernels of meaning, first principles to follow. Yet what kind of axiom is *"People are different from each other"* if not an invitation to ungraspable difference? What kind of generality inheres in a sentence so rooted in irreducible specificity?

The offer of a kind of general model could be claimed for the book that launched Sedgwick's career: *Between Men: English Literature and Male Homosocial Desire*. Its focus on triangular desire has offered many readers a template for understanding easily applied, and the success of the book could be chalked up to a methodological paradigm of just the sort that *Epistemology of the Closet* seems to render moot. Yet when one looks at a moment of methodological self-reflection early in *Between Men*, a model to be applied is not exactly what is on offer: "[T]he centrality of sexual questions in this study is important to its methodological ambitions. . . . I am going to be recurring to the subject of sex as an especially charged leverage point or point for the exchange of meanings, *between* gender and class (and in many societies, race), the sets of categories by which we ordinarily describe the divisions of human labor."[3]

The erotic triangle, which readers of this book might have supposed is something to be used, extended, applied to texts not discussed in *Between Men*, is not figured geometrically. Indeed, it is figured doubly, first as "an especially charged leverage point" and then as a "point for the exchange of meanings."

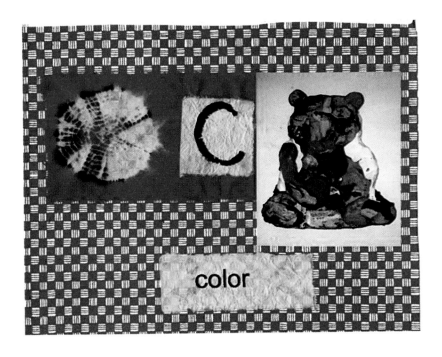

PLATE 1. Eve Kosofsky Sedgwick, *Panda Alphabet Card: Letter C*, date unknown. Collection of H. A. Sedgwick. © H. A. Sedgwick.

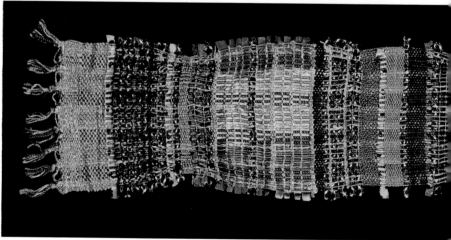

PLATE 2. Detail of *Untitled (Scarf)*. Photograph © Jason Edwards.

PLATE 3. Eve Kosofsky Sedgwick, *Untitled (Scarf)*, after 1996. Long, narrow, fringed wool weaving in orange, lavender, and green, using hand-painted kimono silk ribbons for weft. Photograph by Kevin Ryan. Collection of H. A. Sedgwick. © H. A. Sedgwick.

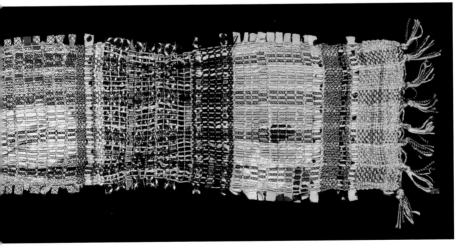

The text on the center-right panel reads:

THIS FINAL SCENE I'LL NOT SEE
TO THE END · MY DREAM
IS FRAYING

PLATE 4. Eve Kosofsky Sedgwick, *This final scene I'll not see to the end*, ca. 2002. Cyanotype and suminagashi on silk, 16 × 16 inches. Three panels of fabric, joined: brown, rust, and mustard-colored suminagashi (left); cyanotype bodhisattva (center); text of death poem by Choko in cyanotype (right). Photograph by Kevin Ryan. Collection of H. A. Sedgwick. © H. A. Sedgwick.

PLATE 5. Eve Kosofsky Sedgwick, *Untitled (Three Bodhisattvas)*, ca. 2002.
Quilted cyanotype of bodhisattvas on silk, 36 × 20 inches. Photograph by
Kevin Ryan. Collection of H. A. Sedgwick. © H. A. Sedgwick.

[OPPOSITE] PLATE 6. Eve Kosofsky Sedgwick, *Untitled*, between 1996 and 1998. Collaged
and quilted kimono scraps decoratively sewn with gold thread. Photograph by Kevin
Ryan. Collection of Eve Kosofsky Sedgwick Foundation. © Eve Kosofsky Sedgwick
Foundation. PLATE 7. Eve Kosofsky Sedgwick, figures from *In the Bardo*, ca. 1999. Silk,
cotton, and upholstery stuffing. Installation shot from *In the Bardo*. Collection of
H. A. Sedgwick. © H. A. Sedgwick.

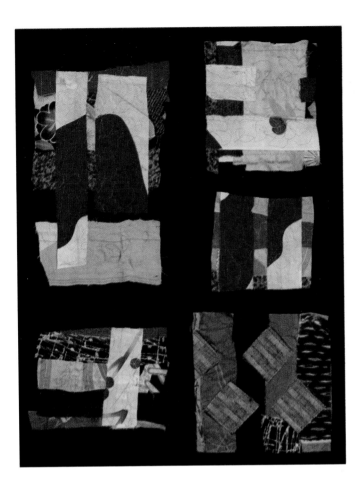

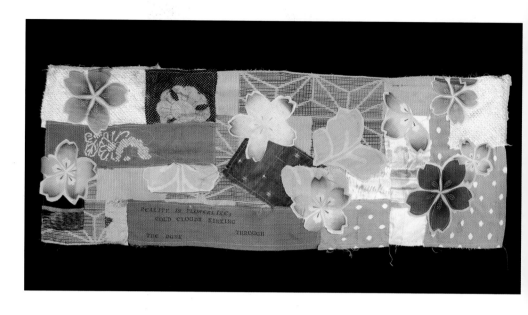

PLATE 8. Eve Kosofsky Sedgwick, *Reality is flowerlike*, ca. 1996–98. Collaged scraps of shibori, ikat, appliquéd flowers, and decorative sewing, stamped with text of Zen death poem. Collection of H. A. Sedgwick. © H. A. Sedgwick.

PLATE 9. Eve Kosofsky Sedgwick, *For beauty is a series of hypotheses*, ca. 2002. Sumanigashi on silk, with shibori techniques, 30 × 12 inches. Photograph by Kevin Ryan. Collection of H. A. Sedgwick. © H. A. Sedgwick.

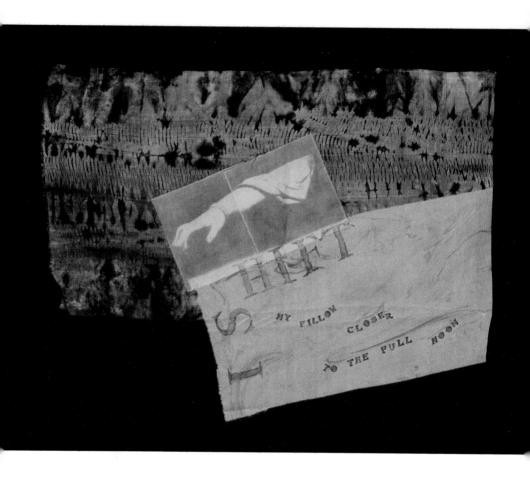

PLATE 10. Eve Kosofsky Sedgwick, *I shift my pillow closer to the full moon*, ca. 2002. Sumanigashi and printer ink on silk. Photograph by Kevin Ryan. Collection of Eve Kosofsky Sedgwick Foundation. © Eve Kosofsky Sedgwick Foundation.

PLATE 11. Eve Kosofsky Sedgwick, *Today, then, is the day the melting snowman is a real man*, ca. 2002. Shibori cloth and stamped, stenciled ink on silk. Photograph by Kevin Ryan. Collection of Eve Kosofsky Sedgwick Foundation. © Eve Kosofsky Sedgwick Foundation.

PLATE 12. Eve Kosofsky Sedgwick, back view of *This final scene I'll not see
to the end*, ca. 2002. Cyanotype and sumanigashi on silk. Photograph
by Kevin Ryan. Collection of Eve Kosofsky Sedgwick Foundation.
© Eve Kosofsky Sedgwick Foundation.

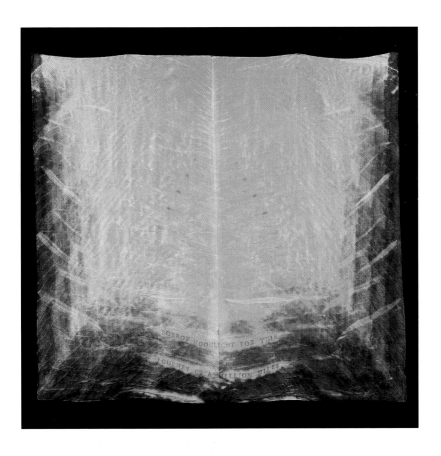

PLATE 13. Eve Kosofsky Sedgwick, *I borrow moonlight for this journey of a million miles,* ca. 2002. Shibori and stenciled ink on silk scarf. Photograph by Kevin Ryan. Collection of H. A. Sedgwick. © H. A. Sedgwick.

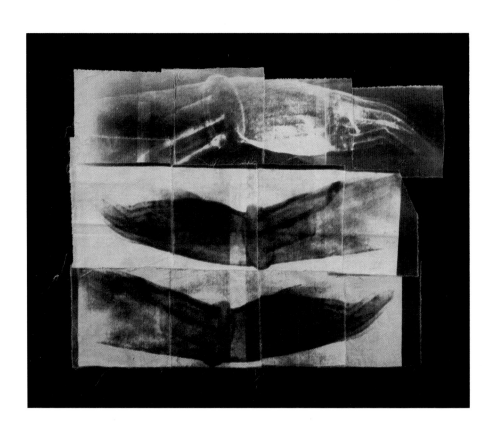

PLATE 14. Eve Kosofsky Sedgwick, *Untitled (Fractured Bodhisattva)*, ca. 2002. Scanned X-ray image quilted and cyanotyped on silk, 20 × 14 inches. Photograph by Kevin Ryan. Collection of H. A. Sedgwick. © H. A. Sedgwick.

PLATE 15. Eve Kosofsky Sedgwick, *Untitled (Prayer Flag 1)*, ca. 2002. Scanned bone scan, scanned photographs by H. A. Sedgwick, and printed text on handmade and sewn paper and kimono silk. Photograph by Kevin Ryan. Collection of H. A. Sedgwick. © H. A. Sedgwick.

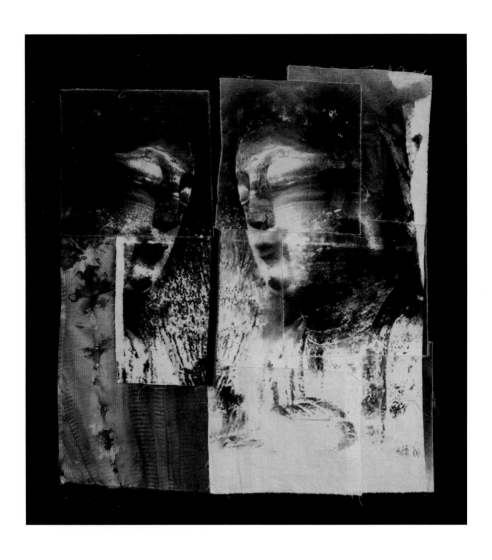

PLATE 16. Eve Kosofsky Sedgwick, *Untitled (Twin Bodhisattvas)*, ca. 2002. Cyanotype and sumanigashi on silk. Photograph by Kevin Ryan. Collection of Eve Kosofsky Sedgwick Foundation. © Eve Kosofsky Sedgwick Foundation.

PLATE 17. Eve Kosofsky Sedgwick, *Tender winds above the snow melt many kinds of suffering*, ca. 2002. Cyanotype, stencil, rubber stamp, and sumanigashi on silk. Photograph by Kevin Ryan. Collection of Eve Kosofsky Sedgwick Foundation. © Eve Kosofsky Sedgwick Foundation.

PLATE 18. Eve Kosofsky Sedgwick, *Untitled (For beauty is a series of hypotheses which ugliness cuts short when it bars the way that we could already see opening into the unknown)*, ca. 2002. Quilted cyanotype and stencil on cotton, 21 × 21 inches. Collection of H. A. Sedgwick. © H. A. Sedgwick.

"Leverage point" might remind us of (or anticipate) the strategic stance of *Epistemology of the Closet,* for it shares with it less the substantiveness of a definitive locale than something like a mobile place, something like a pressure point where a coming together, mutual implication, touching proximity makes it possible for something to happen. And the something to happen, insofar as this is a point of leverage, is to move something else, something that is movable precisely because it moves. The double similitude reworks this point as a point about meaning; indeed, it reworks it by repeating the word "point"—"leverage point," "point of exchange"—so that "point" does double duty. That's the point about meaning, that it is not a substantive, a given, there to be found. It is, in a word, performative, although the word is not used or available to be used in this text. At this point—at the point of "point"—an exchange takes place, an "exchange of meanings, *between* gender and class (and in many societies, race)." Extraordinarily, here, the feminist trope of the exchange of women, which is deployed throughout the analysis, is troped as the "exchange of meanings," while the book's title phrase has been transposed to "*between* gender and class," a betweenness that then gets complicated by the addition of a third term, "race," which renders "between" less attached to a dualism (like the two men in the triangle) than to a third term (as in the triangle with its identical three points, its asymmetrical two men and a woman). The template, that is, is not geometrical but algebraic. Yet, the calculus here pushes beyond how we "ordinarily describe" the categories (gender-class-race) that we think we know and think we think with. In other words, the methodological imperative in *Between Men* looks like the one in *Epistemology of the Closet* even if many terms have changed. The Marxist language of the earlier book is certainly eclipsed in the later one, and the historical framework is also quite different. If Gayle Rubin continues to be an ally and imaginative resource, "The Traffic in Women" has been overtaken by "Thinking Sex." All of this is evident as the paragraph closes, but what's also in evidence is a figuration that points to the future—that is, to productive possibilities to be found precisely in the absence of the definitive: "And methodologically, I want to situate these readings as a contribution to a dialectic within feminist theory between more and less historicizing views of the oppression of women."[4] Where would one locate this historical and theoretical "between" in relation to the betweenness of categories or the betweenness between men? Could these betweens be reduced to the singular? Evidently not.

The possibility of "meaning" eschewed is the kind on display in a devastating reading of "a dazzling . . . article by Catherine [*sic*] MacKinnon" where "there's a whole lot of 'mean'-ing going on. MacKinnon manages to make every manifestation of sexuality mean the same thing, by making every instance of 'meaning' mean something different."[5] Such chiastic reductiveness belies the plural and mobile conditions of meaning, the variability and obliquity that surround even as simple a figure as the triangle. It belies it precisely by assuming for language a constativeness that refuses figuration. Methodologically, the triangle is hard to apply when it moves.

In other words, MacKinnon is caught in what will be called a Christmas effect in *Tendencies* (the 1993 collection of essays), where everything is made to "line up," as if the only use of the point were to make a straight line. "What if the richest junctures weren't the ones where *everything means the same thing?*" is the question asked,[6] and in its way it is answered by its figuration: "richest junctures," places of meeting where necessarily there also is distance, crossing. The figure of juncture echoes in "Willa Cather and Others," which points to the "mazed junction" of sex and gender that Cather negotiates; "the thick semantics of gender asymmetry will cling to the syntax however airy of gender-crossing and recrossing—clogging or rendering liable to slippage the gears of reader or authorial relation with a special insistence of viscosity," the paragraph ends.[7] The "mazed junction" is also a rich juncture, not merely a crossing, but a double-cross, a recrossing of thick and thin, air and oil, author and reader. A crossing that opens up, this viscosity is still liable to a slipperiness, which perhaps makes the machine work but may baffle any possibility of settling on a meaning for the shuttle that is figured here in these intractable figurations. Nonetheless, they oil its gears.

What model, what method is this? If we wanted a word for it, it's available in *Tendencies* as it had not been in *Epistemology of the Closet*; the word is "queer." By this point, however, it should be clear that the desire for a word— the desire for a word that would be definitive and univocal—is not one we ought to be entertaining for any longer than a term can be used. In fact, in *Tendencies* the word is "Queer and Now"—that is, "queer" is marked for a present, coupled, doubled with a "now" that is therefore not exactly then, not exactly now either. (In the preface for the 2008 reissue of *Epistemology of the Closet*, the question of how a book said to be foundational for queer theory could have been so without the word is pondered.[8] Without it, before it, after it; these are, I've been suggesting, relations that inhere in the future figures I'm following.) "Queer and Now" can mean yet to come—and not necessarily in either term itself, maybe, more likely, in the copula. In *Tendencies*, one thing "queer" can do is mark "the open mesh of possibilities, gaps, overlaps, dissonances and resonances, lapses and excesses of meaning" when meaning does not mean one thing.[9] Figuration here attempts again the point and juncture, but this time as an open mesh, a net of reticulated crossings where there is not merely a maze of meetings but spaces, as well. These spaces might figure an outside to the meeting points but might also be refigured sonically as resonant or dissonant, as if the black and white of the mesh were a musical score rather than a text, unless, that is, the mesh figures a pair of stockings, where some meanings may lurk, as well. That figuration perhaps means to grasp and generalize the relation of sex and gender by way of a rather sexily gendered figure, a textile as much as a text.

Although it doesn't need saying, it nonetheless is worth saying that this initial list in *Tendencies* of what queer can do is followed by several more paragraphs, dense with thought and figure, in which "queer" moves in for a moment to be used in relation to questions of gay and lesbian identification; moves out to "the fractal intricacies of language, skin, migration, state"; and ends finally by glancing at another term, a performativity that can only ever connote rather than denote and can do so only *when attached to the first person.*"[10] If the first person brings us in proximity to Axiom 1: *People are different from each other*, we are also back to the methodological imperative "for other readers to perform . . . with, ideally, other results."[11]

Sedgwick wrote, "Part of the motivation behind my work . . . has been a fantasy that readers . . . would be variously—in anger, identification, pleasure, envy, 'permission,' exclusion—stimulated to write accounts 'like' this one (whatever that means)."[12] I cite the endnote to "A Poem Is Being Written"; in it, we can recognize again the methodological injunction and its figuration in the variousness of threads, points, positions that might nonetheless promote a tropism toward an identification, a writing-like, an attachment in the first person to a relationality that could be just as much a disidentification. The word here for all of this is "like," and it's in scare quotes, for to write "like" this is just as palpably to write unlike this, much as the terms placed in apposition in this list are—just as the way the figures of the wheels of Cather's writing and its reading relations are imagined. I want to turn now to "A Poem Is Being Written," less to discover how to write something "like" it than for its own self-likeness, which is, at once, its self-difference. And in thinking about future figures, it helps that the title of this essay is in the tense I seek to grasp and to which I want not so much to show Eve Sedgwick attached as (with her) us.

"This essay was written late," "A Poem Is Being Written" opens; it proposes that we start "with a few lines from *The Warm Decembers*," not a poem written by the nine-year-old Eve Kosofsky, who comes late in this essay. So the essay starts late but almost immediately suggests that "maybe we should go back," and having done that, and gotten a story told about Eve, it then suggests that the way to tell it would be to "jump ahead," only, some pages later, to suggest it would be better to "retreat."[13] All this to-ing and fro-ing is in the service of what is being written; it is to write in the tense of "A Poem Is Being Written." That time, that now, is where the story to tell is one in which "in fact the scars don't answer to the wounds" ("The Palimpsest"[14]), not a story then, not a straight line from then to now or from it to us; rather, what's told are various attempts to get to the "fundamental misrecognitions" central to the first person. This first person "has an art" in *The Warm Decembers*, an art that wasn't hers but is now:

> I "love" the work that lets me like the world,
> "love" the indenture that I call my "gift,"
> *almost* as much as simply fear
> the blinding loss of it.[15]

The asymmetry of love and fear, of having and losing, in the poem unfolds later in parenthesis—one of two sets of parentheses that appear some pages after the quotation from the poem. This is a page that Michael and I and our students pored over, passages brought to the seminar table by the students, still grappling with method. One of these ostensible parentheticals begins: "A will-to-live, per se, has seldom in me been more than notional,"[16] an almost unbearable remark were it not for the way it opens into what this paper seeks, for in that condition "a mother-lode" is identified precisely in the gap in existence in which she writes, those near-misses in which so many incommensurate energies cross. One particular site for this appears in parenthesis down the page. (This parenthetical has parentheses in it.) It begins, "Perhaps I should say that it is not to me as a feminist that this intensively loaded male identification is most an embarrassment," while the parenthesis within the parentheses ventures the generalization that such mismatching defines femaleness: "femaleness is always (though always differently) to be looked for *in* the tortuousness."[17] Two "always," always different; an assertion of a sameness-in-difference like the echo of "mother-lode" and "loaded male identification."

My language here comes too close to the terms of theory—of the kinds of theory in which Sedgwick was Yale-schooled. But unlike those lessons in the aporetic, hers do not lead to the impossibility of going further. As she said, in an interview with Stephen Barber and David Clark, "I'm always compelled by the places where a project of writing runs into things that I just can't say—whether because there aren't good words for them, or more interestingly because they're structured in some elusive way that just isn't going to stay still to be formulated."[18]

Where this leads us is the future into which Eve leads us:

beyond, beneath, and beside—
the peri-performative—
paranoid and reparative—
strong and weak theory—
the finger and the moon—
"vast unbridgeable gaps in meaning"—
"an aching gap in the real";
"tearing stretches must be invented"

and to do that means, to the degree that it is possible, to have some distance from the question of methodology insofar as it is tied to "an eerily thin Western phenomenology of knowing."[19]

I glance at and quote from *Touching Feeling*. These are among the texts that lie ahead as far as I have gotten here; they are not the same as the ones before, except that they, too, lie ahead and keep beckoning toward what is opened in Eve's future figures. Rather than continue this figural pursuit, I want now a bit more literally to describe work that lay ahead when I first wrote these words and that now could be in the reader's hands: *The Weather in Proust*, the volume of late writing that I edited as Eve's literary executor and that Duke University Press published in the winter of 2011–12.

The Weather in Proust gathers, in its first five chapters, the writing toward a book on Proust that occupied Eve in the last years of her life. I retained the title of that project for the entire volume, although only the opening essay has Proust as its central focus, because its capacious concerns with subjects as diverse as Neoplatonism, Bette Davis, affect theory, and puppet theater suggest that under that title much could be safely subsumed. "Cavafy, Proust, and the Queer Little Gods," which follows "The Weather in Proust," records Sedgwick's discovery of a madeleine moment: responding to an invitation to speak about C. P. Cavafy afforded her the chance recognition that Cavafy's peri-performative invocations of the "queer little gods" were the inspiring force behind her realization of their role in Proust. What is "in Proust," indeed, is likewise but differently in question in "Making Things, Practicing Emptiness." There, Eve's textile practices, while resistant to verbal translation, nonetheless involve texts, often citations from Proust; text and textile are warp and weft woven together in such forms as accordion books and looms. "Melanie Klein and the Difference Affect Makes" underscores one important theoretical strand in the Proust project. It is measured in "Affect Theory and Theory of Mind." Those theoretical relations are instantiated in this later chapter by a reading of the difficult fifth volume of Proust's À la recherche du temps perdu.

The next group of essays opens with "Anality: News from the Front," which contains what may have been the last sentence Eve composed, a parenthetical remark about the hope inspired by the inauguration of Barack Obama, which took place less than three months before Sedgwick's death on April 12, 2009. It is followed by two much earlier pieces, "Making Gay Meanings" and "Thinking through Queer Theory," valuable now for the ways in which Eve reviewed her career as a queer theorist, revealing for the citations from earlier work that she chooses to quote. Each piece also makes interventions into the scenes of their delivery, showing that her career as a queer theorist continued to the end of her life, as "Anality: News from the Front" certainly demonstrates, as well. The final essay, "Reality and Realization," written soon after her breast cancer had metastasized to her spine, provides the ground note encounter with impending death, and with Buddhism, that subtends much that comes before, including, centrally, the work on Proust.

Eve's Proust project is related to more explicitly political ruminations as much as to a rethinking of Western psychology and philosophy in light of Buddhist thought and practices. It expands the contours of possibilities for work one could go on calling "queer"; it gives permission, once again—as Eve's work always did (always does)—to think more boldly than one had thought one could. In Proust, around Proust, Eve contemplated the reality in which we exist, a reality that persists and toward which her future figures continually beckon. Reality presses on us, resists our attempts to reduce or refuse it, chastens grandiosity or fantasies of omnipotence. Eve's forays in the various fields that subtend her work in Proust—Buddhism, object-relations, Neoplatonism, material practices—were taken to open up a range of possibilities and agencies beyond aggrandizing zero-sum schemes of dichotomized modes of analysis whose effects are stultifying. What she lights upon is something—

but not one thing—between all and nothing, the "crucial middle ranges of agency" represented in Proust or Cavafy by the little gods who mitigate and populate ranges of experience: "To Call Up the Shades / One candle is enough. Its gentle light / will be more suitable, will be more gracious / when the Shades arrive, the Shades of Love."[20]

"Proust's reality orientation," Eve writes in "The Weather in Proust," "coincides with his mysticism."[21] This is a mysticism attached to the weather not just because the weather is a metaphor for an order of reality that corresponds to an order of propositional truth, as well as to the unexpected, but also because this external, material phenomenon serves as more than a metaphor for one's internal state—indeed, for a state within oneself that exceeds one's own. Its analogue—or, rather, its equivalent—is breath, and again not just one's own, but as a surround, a "supra-individual identity that persists at the moment of death."[22] Proust's mysticism is attached to this materiality, to a spirituality that infuses matter as its life, an unstoppable life. Eve characterizes this in Proust as "a cosmopolitan field of divinity" that includes the nonsentient, "a stone, a plant, a smell, or a song."[23]

This field includes writing—Eve's writing, too, it goes without saying. "*People are different from each other*," her first axiom in *Epistemology of the Closet*, means that Eve herself was irreplaceable. But also not singular. For ultimately how people are different is inflected precisely by what exceeds one's grasp. As she insists in "The Weather in Proust," one meaning of supra-individuality is that one is connected and constituted beyond oneself, connected thereby to versions of oneself that succeed oneself. That is, one lives not only various lives, so that the difference of people also comprehends one's own self-difference, but also as oneself in relation to others. In "Making Things, Practicing Emptiness," Eve approaches this point by way of weaving—for example, in techniques in which the same piece of fabric is totally different when folded and unfolded. From this she moves to fractals, a way of describing dimensionality that refuses to be daunted by the question of sameness and difference that the pairing folded-unfolded might pose. That pairing, moreover, was deployed by the physicist David Bohm in ways that Eve found inspiring as he posited the difference of life and death in similar terms of unfolding and infolding, implication and explication. In answer to the question of what happens after death, Eve quotes Bohm saying, "It doesn't make sense to say something goes on in time. Rather I would say everything sinks into the implicate order, where there is no time. But suppose we say that right now, when I'm alive, the same thing is happening. The implicate order is unfolding to be me again and again each moment. And the past me is gone."[24]

At the opening of "The Weather in Proust," Eve conjures up one of the great ekphrastic set pieces in À la recherche du temps perdu, the description of the Hubert Robert fountain found early in the fourth volume. There the flows, the jets, dying and being replenished, figure many things that could be drawn into this implicated order—Eve reads it for the ways in which it conjures up the *roman fleuve*, Proust's writing, and as the weather, too, as part of the flow of water and thereby the relations between insides and outsides, self and others. The fountain figures these and embodies them in its predictable and surprising spurts. It figures the life beyond life that inheres in relation that exceeds and constitutes the individual. Reading her reading that scene, it's impossible not to think as well of the pedagogy that continues reading Eve.

"That the universe along with the things in it are alive and therefore good; here, I think, is the crux of Proust's mysticism," Eve writes toward the conclusion of "The Weather in Proust." She continues: "Moreover, the formulation does not record a certainty or a belief but an orientation, the structure of a need, and a mode of perception. It is possible for the universe to be dead and worthless; but if it does not live, neither do the things in it, including oneself and one's contents. So put it comparatively: the universe itself is *as* alive as anything it holds."[25]

It holds Eve still. She holds us still.

NOTES

1 Eve Kosofsky Sedgwick, *Epistemology of the Closet* (Berkeley: University of California Press, 2008), 14.
2 Sedgwick, *Epistemology of the Closet*, 27.
3 Eve Kosofsky Sedgwick, *Between Men: English Literature and Male Homosocial Desire* (New York: Columbia University Press, 1985), 11.
4 Sedgwick, *Between Men*, 11.
5 Sedgwick, *Between Men*, 7.
6 Eve Kosofsky Sedgwick, *Tendencies* (Durham, NC: Duke University Press, 1993), 6.
7 Sedgwick, *Tendencies*, 171–72.

8 Sedgwick, *Epistemology of the Closet*, xvi.

9 Sedgwick, *Tendencies*, 8.

10 Sedgwick, *Tendencies*, 9.

11 Sedgwick, *Epistemology of the Closet*, 14.

12 Sedgwick, *Tendencies*, 214.

13 Sedgwick, *Tendencies*, 177–78, 182, 187, 195.

14 Sedgwick, *Tendencies*, 197.

15 Sedgwick, *Tendencies*, 201.

16 Sedgwick, *Tendencies*, 209.

17 Sedgwick, *Tendencies*, 209.

18 Eve Kosofsky Sedgwick, "This Piercing Bouquet," in *Regarding Sedgwick: Essays on Queer Culture and Critical Theory*, ed. Stephen M. Barber and David L. Clark (New York: Routledge, 2002), 246.

19 The quoted phrases are from Eve Kosofsky Sedgwick, *Touching Feeling: Affect, Pedagogy, Performativity* (Durham, NC: Duke University Press, 2003), 30, 33, 90, 168.

20 I cite the title and opening lines of C. P. Cavafy's "To Call Up the Shades," as quoted in Eve Kosofsky Sedgwick, "Cavafy, Proust, and the Queer Little Gods," in Eve Kosofsky Sedgwick, *The Weather in Proust*, ed. Jonathan Goldberg (Durham, NC: Duke University Press, 2011), 51.

21 Eve Kosofsky Sedgwick, "The Weather in Proust," in Sedgwick, *The Weather in Proust*, 4.

22 Sedgwick, "The Weather in Proust," 9.

23 Sedgwick, "The Weather in Proust," 15.

24 Sedgwick, "Making Things, Practicing Emptiness," in Sedgwick, *The Weather in Proust*, 101.

25 Sedgwick, "The Weather in Proust," 32.

Sedgwick's Perverse Close Reading and the Question of an Erotic Ethics

> Becoming a perverse reader was never a matter of my condescension to texts, rather of the surplus charge of my trust in them to remain powerful, refractory, and exemplary.
>
> —Eve Kosofsky Sedgwick, *Tendencies*

I learned how to close read by doing it with Jane Gallop. In fact, all of the graduate students in Gallop's 2007 seminar on Sedgwick were encouraged to join in the act as she routinely invited us, after her solo performance, to add our voices to the live event of a classroom close reading. With questions such as "What else do you all notice?" and "Is there anything here I've missed?" Gallop would beckon for us to slow down and savor the queer details of Sedgwick's writing. Together, we'd linger over the features of an unusual image or trace the way a minor phrase or odd word shifted in significance across a chapter. In this way, class often felt like a portal to an alternative pedagogy that not only enabled us to collectively attend to textual queerness but also to mess around with fixed notions of "teacher" and "taught." Were we learning from Gallop? Or she from us? Or were we all being schooled by Sedgwick's powerful texts? Whatever was happening, the atmosphere was definitely charged. It felt exciting, tense, responsive, and laced with the potential for self-shattering surprise—in short, somehow both erotic and ethical at the same time.

When Gallop's class ended, I wanted to know more about close reading. What, exactly, had we been doing? While Gallop never hesitated, in class, to identify her method as "close reading," she provided little historical context or theoretical insight into this term. In an attempt to fill this gap, I considered New Critical conceptualizations of this practice in the history of American literary studies and mused at the way deconstructionists such as Jacques

Derrida could use close textual analysis to achieve vastly different results. Most of all, I found myself drawn to queer feminist efforts to theorize an erotic ethics of close reading from an antifoundationalist perspective. When I mentioned this desire to Gallop, she handed me a copy of her article "The Ethics of Reading: Close Encounters."[1]

Although Gallop had been reticent to defend her use of this method in class, her thesis in this article is clear: close reading is ethical. Gallop begins her argument by distinguishing between what a text is "actually saying" versus our "projections" onto its surface. Close reading thus emerges as a tool to help us curb our tendency to distort the specificity of a text with our own "stereotypes" or "preconceptions." By directing our attention to "what is actually on the page," this practice can help readers respect difference (rather than ignore or erase it), be surprised, and actually "learn."[2] Importantly, Gallop positions this type of response as part of our "ethical obligation" or "duty" to "the other."[3] Toward the end of this article, she also claims that training in close reading has the potential to make "*all* our close encounters," not just textual ones, more fair and just—including those among "other humans" in everyday life.[4]

I appreciated the clarity of Gallop's argument and her effort to extend the theoretical discussion of close reading to the practical realm of everyday living. But I also found her sense of ethics to be dissatisfying in several ways. From the author of texts such as *Feminist Accused of Sexual Harassment* and "The Teacher's Breasts," I had expected at least some mention of the role of eros in her pedagogy of ethical reading.[5] My own experience in her seminar, where her teaching style seemed to combine an ethical *and* erotic charge, had only fed this anticipation. Yet in "The Ethics of Reading," Gallop offers a chaste sense of ethics that is not only devoid of eros but—startlingly—opposed to it. At the end of the essay, for example, Gallop depicts "passion," which she defines as intense feelings of love and hate, as a blinding emotional force that inhibits our ability to respond fairly to others and is thus in need of control by a more detached close reading.[6] Homing in on this point, Gallop asserts: "[I]f a person can bring passion to reading, then there is hope she can be taught to bring reading to passion."[7] This assumption, however, reinforces the harmful Cartesian logic of emotion as an unruly, negative force that threatens clear-headed, rational thought. Unlike my seminar experience, where passion seemed to feed ethics (and vice versa), here Gallop draws a clear line between the two dynamics and situates them in an adversarial relation where a dispassionate close reading is used to keep intense feelings in check. As a queer feminist, I was surprised to see this Cartesian logic at play in Gallop's work. Is there not a way to theorize *passion as a part of ethics* rather than its undoing?

Before I turn directly to this question, I want to raise a final concern with Gallop's essay. In "The Ethics of Reading," she repeatedly equates "the other" with a *presence* that is always ultimately visible (or audible) on the surface of "the text itself" or in what our interlocutor is "actually saying."[8] Given that there is a widespread tendency among many academic readers to project their own views onto a text, and thus erase its actual voice, there is much to admire in Gallop's insistence that we have a responsibility to try to hear what the other is actually saying (or writing). Yet framing alterity in this way also poses clear risks and disregards a long line of influential thinkers, such as Michel Foucault and Luce Irigaray, who insist that "the other" is precisely that which we can never fully know, and to presume otherwise is to betray the very possibility of an ethical encounter.

And so I emerged from Gallop's essay wondering: Is the exclusion of eros from ethics always necessary? And if not, where might we find a queer feminist example of an erotic ethics of close reading? It was at this point that Sedgwick's singular oeuvre came to mind, and I found myself returning to her writing. In particular, given my prior interactions with her work, I was now curious to see (1) whether Sedgwick's own close reading might be a kind of ethics that is enhanced by passion rather than opposed to it; and if so, (2) what such an ethics actually look like *in practice*. To begin to pursue these questions, I focused my attention on several key passages in *Tendencies* and *Touching Feeling* in which Sedgwick explicitly theorizes the stakes of her reading practice.[9]

Early in *Tendencies*, in the aptly titled section "Promising, Smuggling, Reading, Overreading," Sedgwick reflects on her unique way of interacting with texts. Importantly, in this section she situates her approach within the specific, terrorizing location of a twentieth-century heterosexist culture that is intent not only on eradicating gay and lesbian existence but also erasing the very traces of such lives from all social representation. Within such a context, Sedgwick wryly notes that for young people, "queer survival" means "surviving into threat, stigma, the spiraling violence of gay- and lesbian-bashing, and (in the AIDS emergency) the omnipresence of somatic fear and wrenching loss."[10] It is here, in this inhospitable realm where many queers literally see no future, that Sedgwick envisions *reading* as a tool for survival and resistance. Given that the stakes include matters of life and death, I would argue that Sedgwick is articulating an ethics of reading here. And yet it is a bit dizzying to realize that the very methods that Sedgwick lauds as essential to queer survival, such as "overreading" and "smuggling" queer representation into texts, could easily fit the definition of a "projective" or unethical mode of response that Gallop decries.

But Sedgwick has flipped the script, so to speak, and instead of evoking an abstract reader's obligation to the "text itself," as Gallop does, she focuses her attention on specific, marginalized individuals and highlights a mode of analysis that can help us persist and fight back. For Sedgwick, then, projecting one's own desires and expectations onto a text is not unethical; rather, it serves as a valuable survival tactic to counter cultural erasure. Speaking to this view, Sedgwick speculates that queer scholars likely share a commitment to "make invisible possibilities and desires visible; to make the tacit things explicit; to smuggle queer representation in where it must be smuggled and . . . to challenge queer-eradicating impulses frontally where they are to be so challenged."[11] Given the intensity of historical and contemporary forces of queer erasure, simply attending to what is *present* on the surface of a text is not enough. Rather, in *Tendencies* Sedgwick openly pursues a passion-driven form of ethical "overreading" to make "invisible . . . desires visible" and thus provide herself (and the larger queer community) with sustenance to survive.

Does Sedgwick's taste for "overreading," then, mean that she is not a close reader? To the contrary, in *Tendencies* Sedgwick insists that close reading is essential to her ability to smuggle queer representation *into* texts. Clarifying this somewhat counterintuitive claim, Sedgwick explains: "For me, a kind of formalism, a visceral near-identification with the writing I cared for, at the level of sentence structure, metrical pattern, rhyme, was one way of trying to appropriate what seemed the numinous and resistant power of the chosen objects."[12] In this passage, Sedgwick describes how an intense form of closeness or "visceral near-identification" with specific textual features, such as "sentence structure, metrical pattern, [and] rhyme," enables her not to respect the specificity of the other, but to "appropriate" the "resistant power" of a given object for her own use. In this specific context, "appropriation" acquires an unexpected *ethical* connotation as it allows Sedgwick, as a queer, to get the energy she needs to survive.

Ten years later, in *Touching Feeling*, Sedgwick depicts her reading practice in a strikingly similar way but now associates it with the reparative impulse as defined by the psychoanalyst Melanie Klein. Echoing her earlier definition of "overreading," Sedgwick now explains: "The desire of a reparative impulse is additive and accretive. Its fear, a realistic one, is that the culture surrounding it is inadequate or inimical to its nurture; it wants to assemble and confer plenitude on an object that will then have resources to offer to an inchoate self."[13] Similar to *Tendencies*, Sedgwick again situates her reading practice in the context of hostile culture and again ties it to a desire to invest energy *in* an object to extract sustenance for a marginalized self. While close reading is not the only tool for carrying out such a process (she also mentions queer camp), Sedgwick does name "the devalued and near obsolescent New Critical skill of imaginative close reading" as key to a reparative approach.[14] Across the span of Sedgwick's work, then, from *Tendencies* to *Touching Feeling*, we find evidence of an enduring passion-driven ethics of close reading.

But how exactly does *passion drive ethics* in Sedgwick's close reading? From *Tendencies* to *Touching Feeling*, Sedgwick consistently positions a queer reader's affective desires (for love, community, connection) as an enabling force of ethical response because these strong feelings enhance one's ability to smuggle queer representation into texts and also extract needed sustenance from them. Sedgwick is aware that such a practice counters a New Critical formalism that prizes readerly objectivity and emotional detachment. Discussing her unique twist on this method in *Tendencies*, she writes: "For me, this strong formalist investment didn't imply (as formalism is generally taken to imply) an evacuation of interest from the passional, the imagistic, the ethical dimensions of the texts, but quite the contrary: the need I brought to books and poems was hardly to be circumscribed, and I felt I knew I would have to wrest from them sustaining news of the world, ideas, myself, and (in various senses) my kind."[15]

Here Sedgwick clarifies how her own "formalist investment" departs from the normative sense of this practice which requires "an evacuation of interest from the passional, the imagistic, [and] ethical dimensions of texts." As a close reader, Sedgwick refuses to give up her own desires as they enable her ability to enact an ethical response and "wrest from [books and poems]" the "sustaining news" she needs. As a result, when Sedgwick describes herself as a "perverse reader" in the subsequent paragraph, this seems to be in the sense of one who deviates from the norm of traditional formalism and unabashedly brings their desire to bear on the textual encounter.[16] Although such a practice may seem odd in the eyes of mainstream criticism, in another twist Sedgwick adds that given "queer experience," such "ardent reading" is not really that "unusual" after all.[17]

I would argue, then, that Sedgwick provides one valuable example of an erotic ethics of close reading in which marginalized individuals bring their affective desires into an intense encounter with a text to obtain the energy they need to survive. At the same time, however, it is important to acknowledge that such an ethics is designed for a very specific context (marginalized readers seeking to resist cultural annihilation through identification); thus, it still leaves open the question of how to respond to *difference* in a way that does not reduce the other to the Same. In the face of societal erasure, Sedgwick's passion to smuggle queerness into texts is a laudable, ethical act. As a queer graduate student in Milwaukee in the early twenty-first century, I certainly did my share of overreading in an attempt to wrest from various texts sustaining news of "myself and my kind." However, it is also important to consider what may be lost in such a *reader-driven encounter* that is so intently focused on creating sites of *identification or sameness*. Lauren Berlant also speaks to this concern about Sedgwick's methodology when she writes, "I love the idea of reparative reading insofar as it is a practice of meticulous curiosity. But I also resist idealizing, even implicitly, any program of better thought or reading. How would we know when the 'repair' we intend is not another form of narcissism or smothering will? Just because we sense it to be so?"[18] Indeed, in a practice so driven by the goal of meeting the reader's needs for community, what happens to the other? Is Sedgwick's erotic ethics able to hear the forms of alterity that mark a limit to its own, potentially narcissistic desire?

Sedgwick's chapter "Willa Cather and Others" in *Tendencies* provides an opportunity to consider such questions more carefully. There Sedgwick reminds us of Cather's history as an "effeminophobic bully," given her violent, public condemnation of Oscar Wilde in 1895, and she brings this haunting biography to bear on Cather's short story "Paul's Case" (1905). In particular, Sedgwick wonders whether "Cather, with this story, does something to cleanse her own sexual body of the carrion stench of Wilde's victimization."[19] Somewhat surprisingly, Sedgwick proposes that, via this work of fiction, Cather ends up "*identifying with* what seems to be Paul's sexuality not in spite of but *through* its saving reabsorption in a gender-liminal (and very specifically classed) artifice."[20] While the vector of such a connection is clearly complex, it is also important to note that Sedgwick is ultimately trying to locate a point of queer *alliance* that can take into account past trauma and the particularities of a hostile society. To do so, she draws on evidence from Cather's personal life and enacts a close reading of her fictional texts to ultimately propose, "In what I am reading as Cather's move in 'Paul's Case,' the mannish lesbian author's coming together with the effeminate boy on the ground of a certain distinctive position of gender liminality is also a move toward a minority gay identity whose more effectual cleavage . . . would be that of homo/hetero sexual choice rather than that of male/female *gender*."[21] In this passage, Sedgwick describes a reunion of sorts—a coming together between Cather and her fictional character Paul. And what is the ground of their identification? Sedgwick argues it is the "gender liminality" that Cather and Paul *share* as a "mannish lesbian" and "effeminate boy" that brings them together via an alternative, "minority gay identity" that is distinct from homo/hetero sexual choice organized via gender separatism.

Sedgwick's effort to make visible this site of connection for "mannish lesbians" and "effeminate boys" is laudable. However, her effort to stake out a common ground between Willa Cather and Oscar Wilde around their "minority gay identity" also draws attention to the exclusionary effects of any community built on shared identity (no matter how queer). One could easily point out, for example, that in this chapter Sedgwick prioritizes bringing together *gay men and lesbians* around a "minority *gay identity*" that is not inclusive of trans individuals (who may identify as straight) or genderqueers (who reject the gender binary altogether). However, this problem will not be solved by simply broadening our awareness of all the identifications that must be included within our "LGBTQI+" queer community. Although such care is not without merit, a neverending moralizing quest to "exclude exclusion" can also keep us from acknowledging the unknowable forms of alterity and unreason that will *always* form the haunted ground of modern sexual subjectivity.[22] Given Sedgwick's strong devotion to queer identification, then, a key drawback of her erotic ethics is that it is unable to acknowledge the voices of unreason, or modes of repudiated alterity, that were excluded in the formation of the modern sexual subject in the West.

I wish to conclude this essay, then, by briefly highlighting a queer feminist scholar whose recent books offer great promise in supplementing this gap in Sedgwick's writing. In both *Mad for Foucault: Rethinking the Foundations of Queer Theory* and *Are the Lips a Grave? A Queer Feminist on the Ethics of Sex*, Lynne Huffer outlines a compelling antifoundationalist erotic ethics for our time.[23] In particular, in the final chapter of *Mad for Foucault*, "A Political Ethic of Eros," Huffer argues that Foucault's own archival practice, in which he analyzes official hospital records and police reports, sparks a close encounter with the "poem-lives" of individuals who were "reduced to ashes in the few sentences that struck them down."[24] By allowing the "erotic intensities" of these forces of unreason to act back on him, Foucault engages in a form of "sex play in the archives" in which, as a subject of Reason, he is undone in his "will to knowledge."[25] Huffer further notes that Foucault's "poetic refashioning of those [poem] lives" in his work forms "a part of love, of passion, and sexual pleasure."[26] With its attention to modes of alterity excluded in the production of the modern sexual subject, Huffer's erotic ethics addresses many of my concerns with Sedgwick's way of interacting with texts. Yet does Huffer link this more expansive erotic ethics to the particular practice of close reading?

At first glance, quite the opposite would seem to be true. In the introduction to *Mad for Foucault*, for example, Huffer is explicit about her own (and Foucault's) rejection of close reading. She writes:

> Some will interpret my analyses as a series of "close readings," although in my loyalty to Foucault I prefer to think of them otherwise and to give them a different name. For Foucault rejects in numerous interviews the belletristic sacralization of texts associated with the practice of poststructuralist close reading. Remembering Foucault's more explosive or utilitarian metaphors—firecracker, dynamite, toolbox—for the contact that occurs between books and their users, I call my approach a close encounter . . . that takes seriously the historical, conceptual, institutional, *and* rhetorical dimensions of [a text].[27]

What is striking to me in this passage is that it clarifies that there is a dominant idea of poststructuralist close reading that both Huffer and Foucault understandably wish to reject. The "belletristic sacralization of texts" that often occurs in Derridean textual analyses, for example, is to be rejected because this approach fails to appreciate the full range of dimensions at work in a text and frequently blocks the more practical explosive effects that Foucault and Huffer want their books to have in the world.

To be clear, I wholeheartedly agree that the normative and limiting concept of poststructuralist close reading needs to be set aside. However, I also wonder whether there might be value in acknowledging that many of the *minor tools* of close reading (such as giving careful attention to the specificity of a text, trying to hear what it is actually saying) might not still be of great value in sparking the very kinds of erotic close encounters that both Huffer and Foucault desire? Following Sedgwick, we might even call such an approach a "perverse close reading" in the sense that it would have no tolerance for poststructuralist pieties, given its open wish for a promiscuous alliance with other modes of textual analysis, including the historical. At long last, might the shape of a queer feminist erotic ethics of close reading be coming into view?

Epigraph: Eve Kosofsky Sedgwick, *Tendencies* (Durham, NC: Duke University Press, 1993), 4.

1 Jane Gallop, "The Ethics of Reading: Close Encounters," *Journal of Curriculum Theorizing* 16, no. 3 (2000): 7–17.
2 Gallop, "The Ethics of Reading," 11.
3 Gallop, "The Ethics of Reading," 12–15.
4 Gallop, "The Ethics of Reading," 17, emphasis added.
5 Jane Gallop, *Feminist Accused of Sexual Harassment* (Durham, NC: Duke University Press, 1997); Jane Gallop, "The Teacher's Breasts," *Discourse* 17, no. 1 (Fall 1994): 3–15.
6 Gallop, "The Ethics of Reading," 16.
7 Gallop, "The Ethics of Reading," 16.
8 Gallop, "The Ethics of Reading," 15.
9 Eve Kosofsky Sedgwick, *Touching Feeling: Affect, Pedagogy, Performativity* (Durham, NC: Duke University Press, 2003).
10 Sedgwick, *Touching Feeling*, 3.
11 Sedgwick, *Touching Feeling*, 3.
12 Sedgwick, *Touching Feeling*, 3.
13 Sedgwick, *Touching Feeling*, 149.
14 Sedgwick, *Touching Feeling*, 145.
15 Sedgwick, *Tendencies*, 4.
16 Sedgwick, *Tendencies*, 4.
17 Sedgwick, *Tendencies*, 4.
18 Lauren Berlant, *Cruel Optimism* (Durham, NC: Duke University Press, 2011), 124.
19 Sedgwick, *Tendencies*, 171.
20 Sedgwick, *Tendencies*, 171, emphasis added.
21 Sedgwick, *Tendencies*, 172.
22 I am using this term in relation to the introduction in *Are the Lips a Grave?* in which Lynne Huffer offers an astute critique of the "moral imperative to exclude exclusion" within contemporary intersectional analysis: Lynne Huffer, *Are the Lips a Grave? A Queer Feminist on the Ethics of Sex* (New York: Columbia University Press, 2013), 19–20.
23 Lynne Huffer, *Mad for Foucault: Rethinking the Foundations of Queer Theory* (New York: Columbia University Press, 2010); Huffer, *Are the Lips a Grave?*
24 Huffer, *Mad for Foucault*, 250.
25 Huffer, *Mad for Foucault*, 251.
26 Huffer, *Mad for Foucault*, 251.
27 Huffer, *Mad for Foucault*, 34.

On the Eve of the Future

I began writing this essay a little less than a year after our loss of Eve Sedgwick, at a time when I was just realizing that the legacy of her work had begun to take on some kind of life of its own. This struck me as comforting at first, but it also strikes me as being deeply weird, and that's part of what I want to attend to in these pages. The imponderable sources of writing, and its uncanny effects, were questions about which Eve had strong feelings. When a celebrated female French writer died some years ago, I mentioned to Eve that another friend, who had known this writer Back in the Day, had remarked, on hearing of her death, "Isn't it astonishing that someone who could write *classique* French prose apparently at will hadn't been sober since some time in 1958?" Eve looked pensive for a moment. "Ask your friend," she replied, "where he thinks *classique* prose comes from." Eve, no drinker herself, knew the sometimes intoxicating powers and sometimes harrowing and demoralizing demands of style from deep inside the practice of writing. Not for her to wonder at the idea that someone who could at times sit down and write directly to posterity had not maintained good mental and social hygiene for a very long time, or perhaps ever.

It was Jonathan Goldberg who first proposed the title of the present essay, for a joint presentation we were invited to make at the conference in honor of Sedgwick's work organized by her former graduate students at the City University of New York in February 2010. At the time, I was grateful to be reminded that there *is* an Eve of the future and that Eve and her work will continue to emerge for some time in the writing and art of other people drawing on the manifold strengths and beauties, aesthetic and ethical, of her art and writing. Musing on the durability of Eve's work, I was reminded of a remark that Walt Whitman made in his old age. Asked how, as he saw it, things had changed during his lifetime, the poet replied that when he was young, there had seemed to him to be hardly any other people like him, but with the passage of the intervening years, there had come to be more and more people like him. Whitman didn't explain exactly what he meant by his observation, but I take it to mean that he recognized that in spending his entire life writing and circulating the innovative, seductive, and often scandalous poetry of *Leaves of Grass*, he was helping bring into being more and more people who were (both) "different" and, in a sense, "like each other" in being "different" (recall Sedgwick's Axiom 1 in the introduction to *Epistemology of the Closet*).

I believe Eve was another such person, who, through the sheer intensity of her commitment and dedication to finding and helping found a community—and, eventually, numerous communities—of such initially insufficiently companioned and too thinly socially surrounded people, actually played a significant role in increasing the size of the population of those who in some powerful way shared her initial sense of there "not being very many people like me" and may have come to feel later that there were "more and more people like me" and "more and more people I'm like." In offering herself and her writing to her fellow feminist and antihomophobic readers as models of a new kind of relation between writing and agency, and between intimate and public desires, Sedgwick paradoxically become both more and less like the shy, ambitious, impassioned, depressive, longing-filled young person she had been when she first aspired to make a difference, and to help effect change in the world, through her writing.

In one of the first essays of hers that served notice that a remarkable new critical and ethical presence had arrived in the Anglophone literary academy, "A Poem Is Being Written" from 1986, Sedgwick closed by saying that she hoped the essay might inspire other people to experiment with producing similar projects. The numerous conferences that have occurred and the edited volumes that have appeared in the couple of years since her death are, I trust, only a first wave of response to that essay's invitation—a kind of public and collective response that Eve could not have anticipated receiving when she first published the piece twenty-five years ago. Or could she?

There is a second reason that I especially welcomed Jonathan Goldberg's suggestion for our title: years ago I had started reading a novel called, in translation, *The Eve of the Future*, and even though I hadn't finished it at the time, I remembered that reading its opening pages had made me laugh aloud repeatedly. The novel, as far as I could tell, wasn't supposed to be hilarious, but I found it so, and I have, absurdly, never found a more reliable heuristic for trying to identify *what it is I need to learn* at a given time than stopping when I read something that makes me laugh that I suspect wasn't supposed to have that effect and going back and asking, "What is it that I'm laughing at here?"

Those of you who already know this work will have recognized that it's the French novel *L'Eve future* (1886), variously translated into English as *The Eve of the Future*, *The Future Eve*, and *Tomorrow's Eve*.[1] It was written by the French decadent Villiers de l'Isle-Adam. The novel tells a story about Thomas Edison, very much in his "Wizard of Menlo Park" role. Lounging about his suburban New Jersey home in his magicianly purple robes at the beginning of the novel, toying with one and then another of his marvelous inventions in progress, Edison receives a visit from his dear English aristocratic friend Lord Ewald. Lord Ewald has good news and bad. He is madly in love with a young diva named Alicia Clary. Lord Ewald describes her charms and gifts to Edison: she is about twenty years old and magnificently beautiful, like a classical Greek sculpture of Venus come to life. Her face, her form, her voice, her acting and singing abilities—all glorious!

What's not to love? Edison asks his rhapsodic but clearly troubled friend. With anguish, Lord Ewald describes what has been for him the excruciating process of forming an intimate relationship with Alicia Clary. This fabulous-looking young woman, Lord Ewald informs Edison, has the soul of a petty bourgeois. Fleeing her family's home, she slept with the first businessman she met whom she thought might have money. She has taken up singing and acting not only because she has heard that it's lucrative, but also because she thought, correctly, that it might help her meet rich aristocrats such as Lord Ewald. He, it turns out, is her first titled catch, and she has let him know that she'll be satisfied with serving as his mistress as long as he keeps up his side of the bargain. Lord Ewald confides in Edison that he would have preferred that Miss Alicia be unfaithful—any sign of desire on her part for anything besides money and the appearance of high social status would have been better than this, he laments. But Miss Clary is all business, and that's breaking Lord Ewald's heart.

The redoubtable Edison springs into action on behalf of his friend, promising that, with the aid of some new hardware he has been working on, he can make poor Lord Ewald a perfect female companion, an automaton, a robot that will look every bit as fabulous as Miss Clary but will also have a high-minded and poetic "soul" programmed into her. Only three weeks later, Edison proudly presents Lord Ewald with a fully functioning simulacrum of Alicia Clary, renamed for some reason "Hadaly," the Persian word, he tells us, for "Ideal." Lord Ewald is enchanted with his new mechanical love and might happily have spent the rest of his life with Hadaly had the device not been destroyed in an accident at sea a while later. The novel ends with the Wizard of Menlo Park reading about the disaster in the newspaper, then receiving a telegram from Lord Ewald saying that he is absolutely inconsolable in his grief for his beloved Hadaly. Edison tosses the telegram aside and, in the closing gesture of the novel, shudders with some undefined disturbance of mind or spirit.

Why, we ask, doesn't Edison send a return telegram to Lord Ewald saying, "Don't feel bad, will have replacement off assembly line for you by Monday"? Here at the dawn of imagining Love in the Age of Mechanical Reproduction, why give up after one's first android lover crashes? Inexplicably, neither Edison nor Lord Ewald, who never discussed the ethical, aesthetic, or sexual implications of readily substituting a robot mistress for a human one, seems to be able to form the thought that there must be plenty more where Hadaly came from. Instead, at this novel's end, we get soap opera organ music and a vignette of Edison sitting and trembling slightly in the gathering dusk.

So I trust that you see what made me laugh both the first and second time I read Villiers's novel. Its misogyny is rank; its sex-and-gender politics may well strike a reader today as, in a phrase Eve used to deploy as needed, "a fly's supper." And yet, and yet. The question that formed in my mind on taking the novel up and actually finishing reading it this second time—a question not unrelated to my first one, which was: Can this novel be as ridiculous as it seems, and, if so, how?—has emerged as: "What may Villiers's *Eve of the Future* suggest to us about the future, the legacy, of Eve Sedgwick's work?"

Many readers have noticed that *L'Eve future* is in some obvious ways descended from E. T. A. Hoffmann's story *The Sandman*, about a cruel hypnotist who tricks the young poet Nathaniel into falling in love with a mechanical doll. Sigmund Freud launched his theory of the uncanny on a reading of the story. The relation between the *heimlich*, the *heimish*, the warm and friendly and even warm-and-fuzzy, and the *unheimlich*, the uncanny, the weird, for Freud also partakes of the relation between the living and the dead, the organic and the inorganic, and by extension, we may add, the writer and her books, the artist and her craft, not only but especially after the death of the writer and artist—exactly the territory we're revisiting in making these first tentative moves to assess the meanings of Eve's legacy and our various possible relations to it.

Some months after Eve's death, Hal Sedgwick had a memorial plaque placed on a bench in Madison Square in New York City inscribed with her name and dates and a line from Chaucer that she had once told him might serve as her epitaph: "The life so short, the craft so long to learn." What can we know about the relation between the life and the craft, besides the ironic knowledge that the one is "so short," the other "so long"? This kind of question we should probably approach with a lot of Proustian skepticism of the *Contre Sainte-Beuve* variety: What if the person we knew, her tastes, her behavior, her manner of dressing, walking, laughing, speaking, has precious little, perhaps nothing, to do with the more effectual and enduring aspects of what she wrote, made, thought? Eve took a lot of pleasure in sharing newly drafted writing with what she thought of as her *mishpuchah*; much of her work was produced in an atmosphere of group fun, of animated and sometimes perfervid interlocution. And yet I believe there was this other strong and distinct impulse that informed a lot of her writing of a kind memorably articulated by the young Gertrude Stein, when she says in *The Making of Americans*: "I write for myself and strangers."[2] And it was in this mode of virtual address that Sedgwick sometimes wrote in the manner that I called at the beginning of this essay "directly to posterity." About that highly uncanny process I believe Villiers's novel has something potentially vital to tell us, as does the more mature Stein, when, in her lecture "What Are Master-Pieces, and Why Are There So Few of Them," she opines that an artist or writer makes a masterpiece when she creates (at least in the moment of creation) without knowing identity, in a moment of the extinction of personal identity and the habits of thought and feeling that personal identity swathes us in most of the time.[3] It is an uncanny moment, surely, when the muse arrives and the writer's or artist's preliminary thoughts, plans, and sketches are swept aside and another set of forces takes over.

It is all too easy to participate in the mystification of something that often gets called "the creative process." Eve tended to fill what might otherwise have been idle hours with more down-to-earth mysteries—the procedural kind, the genre detective novel; it was her default reading material, as it has been for many other feminist academics. Despite her formative involvement in 1970s and '80s feminism, one of the strands of reading inculcated by the feminism of that period with which Eve uncharacteristically didn't get far was feminist science fiction. She for a while got very interested in the phenomenon of K/S slash fiction, stories of the otherwise unchronicled (but eventually massively chronicled) sex and love life that Kirk and Spock of *Star Trek* led with each other.[4] It was her own discovery of Silvan Tomkins's work and her emergence as a theorist of affect that determinately carried her work into the vicinity of science studies and systems theory; this movement, in turn, opens a path for us in thinking about the legacy of her work into the histories of science fiction and fantasy, feminist and otherwise, and of what one might call science culture, as well as cultured speculation about transformations of humans, of genders, of populations, of devices.

It is in this context that I want to reinvoke the novel *The Eve of the Future* and briefly chart the apparent tension in its author's life between his professed hatred of modernity and his fictional hero's at least ambivalent, if not downright positive, attraction to some of modernity's most characteristic virtual devices, such as successive technological forms of the mechanical bride.[5] Villiers was a member of a grandly aristocratic French family that had been polishing its escutcheon since the Middle Ages. The author's father dedicated himself to trying to amass a family fortune to pass on to his brilliant son, but all he succeeded in doing was wiping out the modest financial resources that the family had had. As Villiers entered adulthood, his previous pose as a bohemian rebel gave way to the actual grinding poverty, habitual hunger, and homelessness that most of his fellow bohemians experienced only as rich metaphors for their actually quite comfortable outward existences. With his bruised loyalties to his family's feudal past and faded fortunes, Villiers appears to have been drawn to the brand of French ultraconservative Catholicism of the time called ultramontanism, reactionary in the extreme, loathing and dreading every manifestation of liberalism and capitalism, along with the bourgeois hegemony they were making irreversible and inevitable during his lifetime.[6] So it is easy to understand, given this context, how in the novel Alicia Clary may be taken to represent the wave of money-grubbing lifestylists whom the novelist sees taking over his world, and Lord Ewald the heroically antimodernist reactionary who embraces the ghost of an android to escape the modern cult of what he and his author see as fast profits and low values.

But once again, the end of the novel brings the reader to an interpretive knife's edge: Has Lord Ewald indeed disappeared from the text into some ultrareactionary sublime into which he can escape from the evil bourgeois world? Or has he in fact at story's end fallen flat-out in love with the modern that he is supposed to loathe, fallen in love with that most indicative manifestation of the modern, the labor-saving, lifestyle-enhancing, even marital-aiding mechanical device? Have Lord Ewald's old-fashioned aristocratic values been fatally compromised by his passion for the love-automaton (Sándor Ferenczi's term) that Edison has custom-designed for him? Has Lord Ewald come to have the shocking feeling that bourgeois can have their McMansions and their SUVs, if you will, as long as he can have at least the perfect memory of his Mechanical Girlfriend? The possibility that Lord Ewald has re-confronted the modern world and this time not recoiled from it but gone techno-native potentially converts Villiers's novel into an intellectual comedy of a sort—in which case, the hilarity the novel first induced in me had perhaps been an invited response after all.

Around the time Sedgwick was publishing *Between Men*, which may certainly have had something to say about the overripe homosocial bond between Lord Ewald and Edison over the abjected person of Alicia Clary and the not-quite-live body of Hadaly, Annette Michelson published the article "On the Eve of the Future: The Reasonable Facsimile and the Philosophical Toy." In it she argued, on the basis of a fairly elaborate reading of Villiers's novel, that the early cinema and its makers had not only habitually *represented* "the mutilations, reconstitutions, levitations, and transformations" of an endless series of phantasmatic female bodies, but had cast the entire practice of early cinema, and the warped and twisted desires that compelled it, in the very image of this all-too-genuinely desired, all-too-ardently feared, despised, worshiped, and idealized fantasy of mechanically reproducible and hence technologically perfectible feminine corporeality.[7]

With Sedgwick's later work in mind, especially her work in fabric and textile arts, and in the fusion of writing and literary inscription with various forms of shibori and image transfer onto cloth, my calling the desires of early cinema and its makers in the previous sentence "warped and twisted" shouldn't place these desires off-limits to us, to any impulses we may feel to take these desires and warp and twist and thereby weave them into new designs or structures. I want to suggest that the set of questions around affect and technology, around the increasingly wide range of electronic and digital devices with which many of us in varying degrees have fallen in love over the years and perhaps even married, from our first personal computer to the iPhone we don't know how we ever lived without, is a potentially highly fertile field for further cultivation. In closing, I want briefly to relate this phenomenon of our own time to nineteenth-century spiritualism and mediumship, and to the possibility of getting the dead to speak to us, as well as to the "futuristic" fantasy of Villiers and many others of getting the inorganic to speak to us, to commune with us.

In her essay, Michelson would send us back to the philosophical toys that fascinated both the adepts of symbolist poetry (Baudelaire, Villiers, Mallarmé) and the founders of cinema (Edison, the Lumière brothers, Méliès, Feuillade). Attempting to channel some of Eve's energies for the moment, I want to propose sending us both forward into the present and backward to the generation before the founding of cinema, to Eve's native habitat, her be-loved if also often appalling Victorians. I want to leave us with two images that Eve loved: one from late in my long friendship with her and one from near its beginning.

In the first (and later) of these two images, Sedgwick's friend the artist and writer Brian Selznick reminds us in his book *The Invention of Hugo Cabret* that not all desired automatons are female, with his hauntingly illustrated tale of an orphaned and abandoned boy who painstakingly restores a ruined automaton and discovers that it—of all uncanny processes—*writes*, and writes a name.[8]

The other image I want to consider in closing is one that I remember show-ing to Eve when we were first sharing her house on Montgomery Street in Durham. It is a photograph of the nineteenth-century American poet Sarah Helen Whitman, richly dressed and veiled to lead a séance.[9] Whitman had been courted by Poe late in his life, and in the decades after his death she communed with his spirit; she also carried on correspondence with Mallarmé and other writers who revered her as both a living connection to the long-departed Poe and an accomplished and inspired poet herself. As you can see in the photograph (figure 8.1), her face and head are entirely covered. She is holding something before her face, perhaps a fan, perhaps a page or two of writing. Her eyes, barely perceptible through the veil, appear to be closed or downcast.

There is nothing casual about this photograph. The setting, the furniture, the costume, the pose, the gesture of holding a fan or a sheaf of poems to the head: Whitman's performance, like her apparel, is an elaborately composed and layered set of signs. Caroline Ticknor's biography of Whitman, published in 1906, quotes some of the poet's neighbors on Benefit Street to the effect that she wore the veil even when she was at home by herself and that she sometimes sat at the front window of her house in Providence, gazing out at Benefit Street from behind a veil. Did she really, one wonders, or is it the kind of "false memory" that neighbors produce years later, another way of saying "she was weird"? Although I'm skeptical about these neighbors' retrospective "recollections" of Sarah Helen Whitman "at home," I'm compelled by the col-lective perception they articulate of Whitman sitting in her front parlor or at her front window communing with herself and the spirits—dreaming not, in the words of the Glenn Campbell song, "The Dreams of the Everyday House-wife," but, perhaps, the dreams of the everyday prophetess or pythoness or sybil. Here, I believe, we are back in the vicinity of the demand of Eve's that

FIG. 8.1. The original of this photograph of Sarah Helen Whitman is
in the Special Collections of the Brown University Library. The photograph is reproduced in Barton Levi St. Armand, "Veiled Ladies:
Dickinson, Bettine, and Transcendental Mediumship," in *Studies in
the American Renaissance*, edited by Joel Myerson (Charlottesville:
University Press of Virginia, 1987), 1–51.

I began by quoting: "Ask your friend where he thinks *classique* prose comes from."

The occasion of my showing Eve this image was one of the first times that I remember getting a sense of the intensity of her own powers of channeling, of appropriative absorption, of unstinting incorporation, as she would later come to think of it, following Klein. The look of love was unmistakable in Eve's eyes as she gazed at this photo and began to speak about what it might have been like to practice both poetry and mediumship in a provincial New England capital city in the era of the Civil War, around the time of Henry James's Verena Tarrant. Eve went on to speak about how, for her, looking at the image also re-stimulated disturbing memories of seeing photos of nineteenth-century women hooded for hanging, their skirts modestly tied down lest the breeze lift them during the obscene spectacle of their execution. Showing her this photo of Sarah Helen Whitman was also, for me, one of the first experiences of textile fetish and textile love that I remember sharing with Eve: it was the exorbitance of the long white veil above the field of dark and heavily embroidered, lace-trimmed, frogged and fringed fabric—is it velvet?—of Whitman's mantle and the scant legibility of her face behind the veil that gave the image some of the erotic edge it had for both of us. But at the same time that the masses of rich and dark fabric suggest the luxury of a portrait of a Goya duchess, the veiled face and head of the figure suggest a woman not put on public display but withdrawn into an inner space accessible perhaps not even to summoned spirits. It is not the only one, but it is one of the figures I want to have to represent to myself some of the conditions and affordances that made it possible for Eve, at least momentarily, sometimes to depart from self-knowledge and self-identity and to write "beside" herself and "beside" her ordinary social and academic milieu. To legions of people who didn't and don't ordinarily read literary criticism or gender theory. And to the next generation, and to the future.

NOTES

1   *Tomorrow's Eve* is the title of Robert Martin Adams's translation of Villiers de l'Isle-Adam's *L'Eve future* (Carbondale: University of Illinois Press, 2000).
2   The young Gertrude Stein wrote, "I am writing for myself and strangers. This is the only way that I can do it. Everybody is a real one to me, everybody is like someone else too to me. No one of them that I know can want to know it and

so I write for myself and strangers": Gertrude Stein, *The Making of Americans* (Normal, IL: Dalkey Archive, 1995), 289.

3 "It is not extremely difficult not to have identity but it is extremely difficult the knowing not having identity. One might say that it is impossible but that it is not impossible is proved by the existence of master-pieces which are just that. They are knowing that there is no identity and producing while identity is not," Stein writes in one of her most succinct formulations of her theory of the creative process of making "master-pieces": Gertrude Stein, "What Are Master-Pieces and Why Are There So Few of Them," in *Writings and Lectures 1909–1945*, ed. Patricia Meyerowitz (Baltimore: Penguin, 1971), 153.

4 Sedgwick probably first learned of the phenomenon of K/S fan fiction from the essay "Pornography by Women, for Women, with Love," in Joanna Russ, *Magic Mommas, Trembling Sisters, Puritans, and Perverts: Feminist Essays* (Trumansburg, NY: Crossing, 1985), 79–99.

5 The relatively recent theoretical literature on gender, sexuality, and technology is vast, extending from Marshall McLuhan's *The Mechanical Bride* (London: Routledge and Kegan Paul, [1951] 1967) to Donna Haraway's "A Cyborg Manifesto: Science, Technology, and Socialist-Feminism in the Late Twentieth Century," in *Simians, Cyborgs and Women: The Reinvention of Nature* (New York: Routledge, [1985] 1991), 149–81, and, of course, well beyond. For a bracing and thoughtful survey of the textual history of such concepts as the mechanical bride and the *machine célibataire* (bachelor machine), see Allen S. Weiss, "Narcissistic Machines and Erotic Prostheses," in *Camera Obscura, Camera Lucida: Essays in Honor of Annette Michelson*, ed. Richard Allen and Malcolm Turvey (Amsterdam: Amsterdam University Press, 2003), 55–74.

6 The most readily accessible biography of the author in English is A. W. Raitt, *The Life of Villiers de l'Isle-Adam* (New York: Oxford University Press, 1981).

7 Annette Michelson, "On the Eve of the Future: The Reasonable Facsimile and the Philosophical Toy," *October* 29 (Summer 1984): 3–20.

8 The image appears in Brian Selznick, *The Invention of Hugo Cabret* (New York: Scholastic, 2007), 238–39.

9 The original of this photograph of Sarah Helen Whitman is in the Special Collections of the Brown University Library. The photograph is reproduced in Barton Levi St. Armand, "Veiled Ladies: Dickinson, Bettine, and Transcendental Mediumship," in *Studies in the American Renaissance*, ed. Joel Myerson (Charlottesville: University Press of Virginia, 1987), 1–51.

Race, Sex, and the Incommensurate

Gary Fisher with Eve Kosofsky Sedgwick

In my book *Cruising Utopia: The Then and There of Queer Futurity*, I argue that queerness does not yet exist.[1] I instead offer the proposition that queerness is an ideality or a figuration of a mode of being in the world that is not yet here. But I also argue on behalf of a revivification of queer politics. A question that follows both of these aspects of my larger thesis is something like this: If queerness does not exist, how can we have queer politics? In this essay, I take the opportunity to revisit this question of what the relationship between queerness and politics might be. I begin by reconsidering the role of politics and its relation to the lived experience of social inequality and economic asymmetry that people who understand their sexuality as marked by sexual alterity often share.

In an effort to reevaluate these questions around the (im)possible politics of queerness, I turn to a strange and compelling collaboration between Eve Kosofsky Sedgwick and her friend Gary Fisher. Gary Fisher was a graduate student in literature and a writer whose work Sedgwick supported and championed. Fisher died an unpublished writer in 1994 due to complications related to AIDS. Sedgwick took on the project of editing a collection of Fisher's short stories and poems after his death. This essay works through Fisher and Sedgwick's collaboration and the project's reception as an example of what I will describe as a queer politics of the incommensurable.

The publication of *Gary in Your Pocket* was met with what we perhaps can call some political unease by both queer studies and critical race studies.[2] Robert Reid-Pharr sums up the reception of the book by explaining that "responses have ranged from righteous indignation toward the text and its editor, Eve Sedgwick, to a rather maddening inarticulateness, a sort of collective shrug."[3] To understand the problems around the reception of *Gary in*

Your Pocket, we should turn to the question of a queer politics of life. The call for rights and the concerns about personal and collective value and devaluation that are articulated under the sign of LGBT activism in North America have been critiqued by queer theorists such as Jasbir Puar as often displaying homonationalist tendencies.[4] The inefficacy, or even impossibility, of these politics has everything to do with the way they are moored to a notion of value as equivalence.

But queerness—or, at least, what I am calling queerness today in relation to my readings of Sedgwick and my own lived experience of the term—is about the incommensurable and is most graspable to us as a *sense* rather than as a politic. Jean-Luc Nancy also suggests that there is something that exceeds politics, what he describes as nonequivalence, something incalculable that needs to be "shared (out)."[5] Nancy defines this unquantifiable integer as "the element in which the incalculable can be shared (out) [and that] goes by the names of art or love, friendship or thought, knowledge or emotion, but not politics."[6] Indeed, for Nancy politics is that thing that allows for the exercise of this other mode, which is a sharing (out). In place of gay politics, I wish to propose an understanding of *queerness as a sense of the incalculable* and, simultaneously, *the incalculable sense of queerness.*

I consider work produced by Fisher and shepherded by Sedgwick as a sharing (out) that helps us grasp a rich, complicated, and sometimes troubling collaborative scene. I am interested in Sedgwick's editing of and afterword for Fisher's posthumously published notebooks, fiction, and poetry published as *Gary in Your Pocket.* I also wish to consider Fisher on his own terms, paying attention to the challenge that his work presents today to calcified understandings of terms such as "queerness" and, more specifically, "queer of color." It is worthwhile to consider the erotics of racial humiliation and other pleasure-giving forms of sexual debasement that both Fisher and Sedgwick engage as productive sites of theorization. (As an aside, I should mention that it has taken me years to begin to "get" Gary Fisher and Eve's interest in his work. I found his highly stylized rendering of scenes of volitional and solicited racialized sexual debasement hard to attach myself to as a reader. While I identified interesting stylistic innovation, my own political mixed emotions made me shrug, too. Sedgwick's relationship to Fisher was only slightly clearer to me. But I knew her investment in this work went beyond politics or even friendship. There was something else there that escaped me. In this essay, I hope to describe that incommensurable something else that eluded me.) This task presents me with an opportunity also to describe a dynamic that partially transpires under the sign of "queer of color" that is routinely misread by the lens of a politics of equivalence, but that becomes newly accessible as a sharing (out) of a nonequivalent, incommensurable, and incalculable sense of queerness.

Fisher's work articulated a mode of desire that exemplified antiequivalence. His work, and the mode of relationality and desire it depicted, most certainly did not line up with his interest as a creative writer who saw himself as, at least in part, a participant in a black literary tradition and an antiracist scholar of literature. Fisher's politics did not align with his complicated and often unsettling relationship to his mode of desiring and being desired in the world. Our most anticipatable notions of "queer" and "queer of color" politics almost automatically register Fisher's "official" and "private" takes on the resonant linkage between race and sexuality as inconsistent, incoherent, and ultimately problematic. The critique of systemic racial subordination in collusion with the "fact" of a felt and, in the case of Fisher, vibrantly rendered account of actual erotics cohering around volitional racial humiliation and submission are generally understood as a problem. This problem is not simply due to a seeming contradiction between life and politics, or sex and sexual identity, or race and racism; it is due to the actual framing of queer and queer-of-color politics.

Let me set up a context for understanding the difficulty of Fisher's writing and Sedgwick's sponsorship, editing, and dissemination of his work. The word "sponsorship" is deliberate in this last sentence and is meant to index a history of African American cultural production that was not possible without a certain level of white patronage. Fisher and Sedgwick were always painstakingly aware of their place in a trajectory of American letters that arguably commenced with Phillis Wheatley. Reid-Pharr asks, "'How can we read Gary Fisher as a black man?' Given my argument that Fisher repeatedly takes up the particularly shocking notion of a Negro racial identity not only produced in direct relation to white hostility but produced in a manner that takes sublime pleasure in the white's domination, it taxes the imagination to place him neatly alongside Toni Morrison, John Edgar Wideman, James Baldwin, or even the growing number of self-identified black gay writers."[7]

I take Reid-Pharr's question "How can we read Gary Fisher as a black man?" as a provocation for a reconsideration of this shrug-inducing text. Our knowing of Fisher and his startling and powerful authorial effect through Sedgwick can benefit from some brief biographical contextualization. Fisher met Sedgwick when he took a course with her at the University of California,

Berkeley. Sedgwick's afterword to *Gary in Your Pocket* devotes quite a bit of time to narrating the movement from teacher and student to friendship. Before Berkeley, Fisher had received a degree in English at the University of North Carolina, Chapel Hill. His journals talk about his years of study there in the Wilson Library. This coincided with something of a flashpoint in early years of the HIV/AIDS epidemic. The library was an almost legendary cruising and public sex site on campus. In his journals, Fisher suggests that this library is the place where he contracted the virus that would lead to his eventual passing in 1993. The library is narrated in his journals as the space where his sexuality took a certain form, and the young, smallish, black man began to understand his own sexual desire as the impulse to be mastered by older, larger, dominant, white men.

It is not only the identitarian contours of his object choices that make Fisher's writing hard to take within the parameters of gay black men's writing practices, which are predominantly associated with tropes of redemption and nobility. It is also, as I have mentioned, his careful description of explicit sexual acts of voluntary sexual submission and degradation. All of Fisher's sex writing highlights the fantasy of his small frame being overwhelmed by larger, white bodies, about his oral servicing of a white master who would be fully in control in a sexual scenario, and, beyond that dominant trope, his submission to any and all sexual acts that the man topping him would demand, no matter how much or how little direct sexual pleasure specific acts would generate for him. Indeed, his desire was for the scene of submission, and this scene was often played out before an imaginary backdrop that reflected the scene of North American chattel slavery. His voluminous writing was intricately linked to this experience of the self as a racialized sexual object. Sedgwick wrote that Fisher did not represent sex but instead wrote sex in a fashion that pushed representation itself, "stretching every boundary of what sex can represent."[8]

A nonequivalent yet nonetheless relational dynamic animates Fisher's writing, and Sedgwick employed the tools of the adept literary scholar to make a kind of sense of the sense that Fisher made in the world:

> Like others gone before him, he forged a concrete, robust bodily desire in the image of historical dispossession, humiliation, compulsion, and denigration, among other things. Probably any sexuality is a matter of sorting, displacing, reassigning singleness or plurality, literality or figurativeness to a very limited number of sites and signifiers. Tenderness (here, brief, contingent, illuminating); a small repertoire of organs, orifices, and bodily

products; holding, guiding, forcing; "your" pleasure and "my," different and often nonsynchronous, pleasure . . . the galvanized, the paralyzed; the hungry, impartial, desiring regard in which ugliness may be held as intimately as beauty, and age as youth: these are among the elements here splayed through the crystal of anonymity.[9]

Many things strike me when I consider this account of Sedgwick's reading of Fisher, which is conterminously Sedgwick's reading of the choreography or "literality or figurativeness" that we know as sex. Sedgwick's ability to render a phenomenologically salient account of what sex feels like in relation to an "image of historical dispossession" that can be understood as undergirding any account of racialization we can access is, I want to suggest, an important move to hold on to when we consider the actual performative force or lack thereof that concepts such as "queer" or "queer of color" may hold. Reading Fisher is a challenge for those of us who toil in the archives of collective historical dispossession. In the long passage from Sedgwick, we find a certain choreography of sex and race that aligns itself with questions of the literal and the figurative, the singular and the plural that help track just how we might read and know Fisher. I contend that Fisher's writing leads to an understanding of queerness as incalculable.

A reconsideration of Fisher today, fifteen years after the publication of *Gary in Your Pocket*, might produce something more than a shrug. Let's think of Fisher, and Sedgwick's reading of his works, in relation to Nancy's mapping of "sense" as a useful philosophical concept that potentially helps to know queerness in a way that moves beyond some familiar stumbling points in queer politics. Nancy imagines a philosophical practice that dispels a fundamental and foundational "ontology of the Other and the Same" and instead highlights an understanding of ontology as world that is unmediated multiplicities of singular "ones,"[10] a collectivity of others co-appearing in irreducible plurality. This is essentially Nancy's notion of "being singular plural." It is a call for an interruption of a familiar Hegelian formulation of the Other/Same dichotomy. Standing in its place would be a consideration of crisscrossing and intersecting vectors of singularity. At times, Nancy formulates this as a finite thinking of the infinite. Nancy's point is that we have exceeded the politics of equivalence that is so at the center of the foundational conflict between the Other and the Same.

I could not keep Hegel out of these proceedings if I wanted to. Fisher, of course, cannot escape the thematic of Master/Slave, either, and his sexualized prose is haunted by the specter of this most poignant moment from Hegel. In his journal, Fisher fantasizes about the knowledge that reading Hegel might bring him: "I haven't read Hegel yet. Why haven't I read Hegel when I'm somewhat in love with this? I'm afraid to know. Half of this is the wandering, the obscurity, the possibility of surprise (and yet the other half is a fixed equation, inevitable)—when I get there I'll be able to say I've always known this would happen to me—but I'll come to that admission as through a dream, still half unbelieving."[11]

Fisher envisions a Hegelian Master/Slave dynamic that he anticipates always to have known in advance. He feels that he will inevitably arrive at a certain understanding of this famous formulation in philosophy in a way that he describes as both "inevitable" and "unbelieving." In *Hegel: The Restlessness of the Negative*, Nancy reads Hegel as a source of understanding for a being singular plural that we experience as a sharing (out).[12] Nancy offers us a Hegel that diverges from the way in which he is often cast in surveys of the history of Western philosophy: "Hegel has often been read as if he exhibited the auto-development of an anonymous Subject or Reason, foreign to us, the big Other of an autistic self that, moreover, would only be the fantasmatic correlate of the subject of a proprietary and securitary individualism: two subjects each the mirror for the other, each one as stupid and wretched as the other."[13]

In Nancy's account of this important Hegelian formation, the scene of recognition concludes not with individualism but, instead, with the "*truth* of a self-knowing that must be the knowing of manifestation, of the desire of the other, and of decision [which] cannot be a truth that simply returns to itself."[14] So we no longer look for our autistic self in the Other but instead find the truth of our being singular plural. Truth is not about transcendence or totality. It is not about possession or incorporation. It is more nearly about the proximity of different senses of the world. We know the world through our sense of it. While sense is always about singularity, this singularity is thinkable and knowable as plurality, which gets us back to what Fisher "knows" about Hegel. Or what Eve "knows" about Gary. And what Gary "knows" about Eve. This knowing is akin to a sense of the world that isn't about the dyad of Same and Other, Master and Slave, Lord and Bondsman. Nor is it about an anticipatable calculus of equivalence ending in some recognition of the self in the Other. Instead, it is about the incommensurable. It is about trajectories and intersections between our senses of the world that make the world. This is to suggest that what Sedgwick sees in Fisher is not herself but instead a sort of sharing (out) of the unshareable in which she, too, participates. In *Epistemology of the Closet*, Sedgwick writes about her own motivation for writing "A Poem Is Being Written" as being a fantasy that "readers or hearers would be variously— in anger, identification, pleasure, envy, 'permission,' exclusion—stimulated to write accounts 'like' this one (whatever that means) of their own and share."[15] Nancy's somewhat dramatic formulation, "the sharing (out) of the unshareable," sounds a lot like a translation of Eve's statement in the lexicon of classic deconstruction.[16] Sedgwick's editing of Fisher's writing ensured that his unshareable sense of the world would be shared.

Ellis Hanson published an essay on Fisher and Sedgwick titled "The Future's Eve: Reparative Readings after Sedgwick."[17] One of the immediate goals of my essay is that Sedgwick's work on Fisher and race be taken up again, that the Fisher volume be considered a weighty and dense moment in Sedgwick's oeuvre. In this most general sense, I welcome Hanson's work. Furthermore, his essay contains evidence of thoughtful archival work. Hanson spent time in the San Francisco public library and read all of Fisher's unpublished papers. He clearly holds the work in great esteem and does not seem to be as hesitant about engaging it as I am. Certainly, Fisher's work is important on its own terms, within the context of black gay men's writing practices in the AIDS epidemic. But I am clearly more interested in the ways in which Sedgwick and Fisher looked at the world through the strange optic allowed by their communion with each other. To this end, I take issue with the way in which Hanson describes their connection. When characterizing the different eulogizing moments in Sedgwick's work where she discusses deceased gay men, he writes: "While her elegies for Lynch and Owens celebrate the bond between feminist and queer men, her elegy for Fisher, her editorial monument to him, celebrates the connection between not only a black gay man and a married woman but a submissive gay man and the white woman who agreed to dominate him."[18]

This sentence gives me pause. The descriptive language deployed to render an image of the relationship between the two writers seems reductive: a "married white woman" and a "black gay man." In his writing, Fisher became a self-abjected black object, renouncing "manhood" or "personhood" for the sustaining sexual fantasy of being a chattel slave or another historically disposed character. And while Sedgwick would refer to herself as a married woman, it was often in an effort to show how conventional language failed to grasp her own fundamental sense of queerness. Interestingly, Fisher is not always exactly black in his writing. A notable example would be the short story "Arabesque," where he narrates a sexual scenario in which he is made to play the role of a sexually abused "Arab boy" who describes himself as a captive of a champion of Israel. I will return to that story. The trickiest part of Hanson's line is the sentence's second descriptive movement, where he describes the relationship as one in which Sedgwick "agrees" to dominate the submissive Fisher. Suddenly Sedgwick becomes one of the cruel white daddies that Fisher craves in his fiction and sexual role-playing. This strikes me as an imprecise description. Yes, Sedgwick agreed to publish Fisher's work posthumously, and in this way we can perhaps see him "submitting" his writing to her editorial control. But that reading seems especially forced, and Sedgwick's gender seems to be the integer that suddenly falls out of Hanson's formula.

Perhaps Hanson is referring to some kind of structural domination that was implicit in the relationship between a teacher and a former student. But as a lucky recipient of Sedgwick's pedagogy, I can testify that the word "domination" seems to have no descriptive force in rendering our relationship. What is lost in Hanson's description is the actual stuff of their deep communion, which is about the ways in which they actually shared more of what Nancy would call a literary communism between a woman who famously wrote about the coterminous pleasures of poetic enjambment and being spanked in "A Poem Is Being Written" and a younger black man who is also deeply interested in the convergences of bodily mortification and literary style. In Hanson's formulation, submission stands in for identification, and the impression of the substitution begs commentary. The sentence leads Hanson to one of the main points of his argument. He explains that with *Gary in Your Pocket*, "Sedgwick engages in her most elaborate reparative project the one that has attracted the harshest criticism."[19]

The elaboration of Melanie Klein's notion of the reparative was one of Sedgwick's great later contributions. Sedgwick famously outlined the reparative as a way out of the rote dominance of paranoid readings that traded in a hermeneutics of suspicion. "Reparative" was meant to help us consider something other than the unveiling of that thing we kind of already knew anyway. The reparative is a theoretical stance in which we use our own psychic and imaginative resources to reconstruct partial or dangerously incomplete objects that structure our reality into a workable sense of wholeness. The reconstructed sense of an object offers us a kind of sustenance and comfort. One cannot dismiss Hanson's idea that *Gary in Your Pocket* is a reparative project *tout court*. In his essay on Fisher, he calls on Tim Dean to suggest that there is no sex or race without fetishism.[20] He quotes Dean's argument that fetishism need not be dehumanizing but is, instead, just impersonalizing.

I certainly agree that sexual rhetorics of impersonalization can be highly erotic for all sorts of people. But, of course, impersonalization as a process does not then preclude different individuals or groups from a very real sense of dehumanization in relation to systemic cultural and political logics such as racism. Certain shared or collaborative projects of impersonalization are not automatically wounding and are often sexually generative, but these scenarios, for the most part, include a shared and volitional script. I think of this aspect of queer sex, or just sex, as a kind of communism of the incommensurate. Hanson correctly identifies Fisher as a racialized subject who enjoyed being sexually dominated and fetishized by older and larger white men. Hanson argues that "most academic writing on racial fetishism" has "calcified into a defensive fetishistic ritual in its own right."[21] He suggests that an understanding of Sedgwick's reparative beside Fisher's writing on sexual fetishism might offer us some cues for how to move beyond the impasse in thinking about sexual fetishism that he perceives. In a footnote, he refers to two other writers and me as being among the few queer-of-color writers who employ the reparative.

Indeed, I do find the reparative to be a productive theoretical stance. For me, it is a resource to imagine something else that might follow social stigma or even ruination. While I am interested in the work that the reparative might offer groups who have experienced some version of social violence or death, I would certainly agree that the reparative is not automatically about the integrity or sense of wholeness for which a collective or group may long. It may indeed be about the individual imaging some sort of personal redress, or the carving out of what Hanson calls "a sustainable life."[22] Fisher's writing does tell a moving story about submitting to and even flourishing within a force field of racial fetishism. But the example of Fisher in Hanson's article does not telescope out to consider the world outside the page; it fails to consider the damage that racial fetishism does within the social or the ways in which racial fetishism can easily be a byproduct of racial oppression. To the contrary, his reading of the text attempts to hold this knowledge at bay.

Using Fisher as an example of a more complex understanding of a racial fetishism that is not racist does not acknowledge the moments in which the author admits his volitional involvement in a script that we might initially consider "impersonalizing" but not necessarily "dehumanizing." In the story "Arabesque," the narrator endures a scene in which he is being suffocated by his imaginary role-playing slave master's prick. As the top in the scene orders the narrator to "Choke! Choke!" the bottom cognitively steps back and reflects, "He drove with desperation that actually amused me more than it frightened me, but then I was outside myself and somewhat embarrassed with myself and needed to laugh at it to keep from blacking out. I'd laugh for a moment more, then politely mention my need to breathe—didn't know how I would do either, but at the time this didn't seem to bother me—it all seemed so funny, my fucked-up priorities, especially the need to laugh at this man's desperation before I took another breath."[23]

Fisher's narrator is certainly submissive; he craves and relishes the "impersonalization" the scene engenders. But something else is happening here beyond pure submission or domination. Hanson's reading of Fisher tells us that racial fetishism can be erotic and not be a symptom of racial bias. I partly agree insofar as racial difference can be and often is erotic. But these fetishistic erotics don't exist in a vacuum or unmoor themselves from the fact of systemic racism. In white male culture, the erotic value bestowed on men of color is often linked to devaluing them in other aspects of their being. This is a problem not because people of color demand to be desired as a whole person in some naive fashion. The ways they are devalued matter in a much more socially damaging manner. Working through trauma and finding real pleasure in that process, as Fisher does, is worth considering not because it enacts a complicating of the fetishism's relationship to systemic racism.

Racial bias can and does coexist with the erotics of racial fetishism, as irreconcilable integers. Furthermore, their incommensurability is a ground-level fact in so many people's erotic imaginaries, sexual lives, and broader life practices. Fisher imposes a structure (a script) within the structurelessness of sex itself, not because he is attempting to delink sexual fetishism and sex oppression. The scene from "Arabesque" that I describe features a literalizing of incommensurability, a refusal of reciprocity or equivalence that becomes a communism of the incommensurate. In Fisher's work, we glimpse a commons of the incommensurate signaling something that goes beyond a politics of equivalence. Fisher's relationship with his sexual partners and Sedgwick was not about equivalence, but there is a powerful idea of a commons in these relational lines. This commons, this experience of being-in-common-in-difference, offers readers a map of life where singularities flow into the common, enacting a necessary communism.

I use the term "communism" to help us think a certain communing of incommensurable singularities that can be enacted through even impersonal sex. But I also mean just plain communism. But let me be more exact: by "just plain communism" I do not mean to invoke the communism of a mythical society of equals but, instead, the communism of living within a sense of the commons, a living in common. Michael Hardt describes this idea of the common in communism as "the affirmation of open autonomous biopolitical production, the self-governed continuous creation of humanity."[24] In the work of Nancy, we encounter a communism that is most immediately summarized as a being singular plural. Nancy explains that communism "means the common condition of all the singularities of subjects, that is, of all the exceptions, all the uncommon points whose network makes a world (a possibility of sense)."[25] He goes on to suggest that this notion of communism does not belong solely to the political, but precedes it. It is important to emphasize that "not belonging" to politics in Nancy's sense is not an escape or refusal of the political. It is just the opposite.[26]

Here I return to the auto-examination of my book with which I began this essay. How are queer politics possible? When I call for a reinvigoration of the queer political imagination, I am turning to communism or, maybe better put, naming something that I failed to name with enough force in my book. Communism is an idea that is almost as old as utopia. Communism is first and foremost about the precondition for emancipation. But emancipation from what? we might ask. Here we come to understand emancipation as freedom from historical forces that dull or diminish our sense of the world. Nancy points out that Marx himself argued that the commune was the antithesis of empire.[27] Communism would therefore be antithetical to our inner and outer colonialism, those blockages that disallow our arrival at an actual sense of the world, which is the world as a plurality of senses. This sense can be impersonal or even structured around the figurations of dehumanization and submission that Fisher longed for. Indeed, as Sedgwick has pointed out, so much can be "splayed through the crystal of anonymity,"[28] and includes impulses that can be equally tender and destructive. Indeed, they are simultaneously both.

I am interested in thinking about both Fisher and Fisher with Sedgwick as offering us the option to think beyond the register of the individual subject. Implicit in this line of argumentation is the idea that ideologies that enable empire are shored up by a reification of the individual sovereign subject who can think of itself as differentiated from a larger sense of the commons. Thinking of the self as purely singular enables a mode of imagining the self as not imbricated in a larger circuit of belonging, what I call an actual sense of the world where we grasp the plurality of the senses, which is not one's own senses but instead the multiple senses of plural singularities. Such a logic of the singular that eschews plurality is able to self-authorize oneself to dispossess those outside any particular logic of the singular. Sedgwick and Fisher perform and map a relational schema that is based not on commensurable singularities but, instead, on a vaster commons of the incommensurable.

Thinking about incommensurability is not meant to cleanse or make Fisher's sex, desire, or writing antiseptic. The crisscrossing trajectories of singular being are certainly full of violent collision, especially when we think about the history of dispossessed people, and we must not fail to understand these crashes as being traumatic or violent. I don't want to simply suggest that the incommensurable is a ludic mode where our desire and ethics can be easily worked out. Indeed, the incommensurable can lead to annihilating violence like that which in the past two years took the lives of Lindon Barrett, a talented theorist of race and value who was killed by a man the police described as an acquaintance, and the writer Don Belton, who wrote a beautiful introduction to *Gary in Your Pocket*. Don was murdered by a young man who, when tried for the murder, used a sexual panic defense that was not unlike those analyzed and described by Sedgwick in *Between Men*.[29] Yet without denying the implicit and explicit violence of certain scenes and acts, we can nevertheless see something else in Fisher's insistence on the incommensurable over equivalence, which may be a certain kind of freedom. In this instance, we can revisit Sedgwick's sentence one last time: "Probably any sexuality is a matter of sorting, displacing, reassigning singleness or plurality, literality or figurativeness to a very limited number of sites and signifiers." Sex and sexuality in this passage are "a matter of sorting, displacing, reassigning singleness or plurality," and it is this somewhat structural account of the structurelessness of sex that resonates with the larger ontological mapping of a world that exceeds equivalence.[30] Nancy remarks that it was Karl Marx who best understood that man produces himself and that this production is worth infinitely more than any measurable evaluation.

I haven't forgotten Reid-Pharr's query, "How can we read Gary Fisher as a black man?" I cannot be certain that my response will be satisfactory, but I think we can read Gary Fisher as a gay black man whose sense of self was incommensurable with an immediately available notion of black male identity. Instead, let us think of Gary Fisher and the writing he has left behind as a testament to the very limits of understanding his life as a black gay man solely through politics. The layering of acts of mastery and submission he narrates doesn't make sense within the logic of recognition, equivalence, and value. Instead, I suggest that there is something else to be gleaned through incommensurability. At the heart of Fisher's writing we encounter a quality that was meant to mirror the sex through which he so often came to know and describe himself. Fisher and Sedgwick's project, the book we know as *Gary in Your Pocket*, is the sharing of the unshareable, which for some is the shock of Gary Fisher, and for a growing number of others, one hopes, the sense of Gary Fisher.

NOTES

1   José Esteban Muñoz, *Cruising Utopia: The Then and There of Queer Futurity* (New York: New York University Press, 2009).
2   Gary Fisher, *Gary in Your Pocket: Stories and Notebooks of Gary Fisher*, ed. Eve Kosofsky Sedgwick (Durham, NC: Duke University Press, 1996).
3   Robert Reid-Pharr, *Black Gay Man: Essays* (New York: New York University Press, 2001), 149.
4   Jasbir Puar, *Terrorist Assemblages: Homonationalism in Queer Times* (Durham, NC: Duke University Press, 2007).
5   Jean-Luc Nancy, *Being Singular Plural* (Stanford, CA: Stanford University Press, 2000), 17.
6   Nancy, *Being Singular Plural*, 17.
7   Reid-Pharr, *Black Gay Man*, 139.
8   Fisher, *Gary in Your Pocket*, 282.
9   Fisher, *Gary in Your Pocket*, 284.
10 Nancy, *Being Singular Plural*, 53.
11 Fisher, *Gary in Your Pocket*, 203.
12 Jean-Luc Nancy, *Hegel: The Restlessness of the Negative* (Minneapolis: University of Minnesota Press, 2002).
13 Nancy, *Hegel*, 76.
14 Nancy, *Hegel*, 76.
15 Eve Kosofsky Sedgwick, *Epistemology of the Closet* (London: Harvester, 1991); Eve Kosofsky Sedgwick, "A Poem Is Being Written," *Representations* 17 (Winter 1987): 137.
16 Jean-Luc Nancy, *The Truth of Democracy*, trans. Pascale-Anne Brault and Michael Naas (New York: Fordham University Press, 2010), 17.
17 Ellis Hanson, "The Future's Eve: Reparative Reading after Sedgwick," *South Atlantic Quarterly* 110, no. 1 (Winter 2011): 101–19.
18 Hanson, "The Future's Eve," 109.
19 Hanson, "The Future's Eve," 109.
20 Tim Dean, *Unlimited Intimacy: Reflections on the Subculture of Barebacking* (Chicago: University of Chicago Press, 2009).
21 Hanson, "The Future's Eve," 114. Hanson presented work at University of Michigan's Queer Shame conference in 2005. During a talk on Plato and pedagogy,

he played gay Latino porn. The porn was not addressed in the paper and merely served to achieve a spectacular effect, according to Hiram Perez, who wrote a description of Hanson's performance: Hiram Perez, "You Can Have My Brown Body and Eat It, Too!," *Social Text* 84–85 (Fall–Winter 2005): 171–91. Lawrence La Fountain-Stokes also cited this incident in another critique of the conference: Lawrence La Fountain-Stokes, "Gay Shame, Latino/a Style: A Critique of White Queer Performativity," in *Gay Male Latino Studies: A Critical Reader*, ed. Michael Hames-García and Ernesto J. Martínez (Durham, NC: Duke University Press, 2011), 55–80. Finally, J. Jack Halberstam wrote a critique of the entire conference, mentioning Hanson's performance: Judith [Jack] Halberstam, "Shame and White Gay Masculinity," *Social Text* 84–85 (Fall–Winter 2005): 219–34. When considering the controversy that hung over Hanson's performance at the Queer Shame conference, one cannot help but wonder whether his reading of Fisher is somehow meant to address the kind of moralizing that he relates to critiques of racial fetishism that automatically equate it with racial oppression. There is a common move in some pages of queer studies and the world of few people who produce and consume it: the labeling of queers of color who challenge white gay men's racist practices, fetishistic or otherwise, as moralizing or self-righteous. While Hanson offers a theoretical argument, Michael Warner has off-handedly quipped that the Michigan conference became an occasion for mutual shaming, where the participants "missed the point": Michael Warner, "Queer and Then?," *Chronicle of Higher Education*, January 1, 2012, http://chronicle.com/section/The-Chronicle-Review/41. For Warner, people of color offering interventions about race and racism seems to be doing nothing but shaming for shame's sake or simply exercising self-righteousness. This is a familiar defensive maneuver seen in those who have clung to minority status and suddenly find themselves questioned about their own insensitivity and bias. While Hanson attempts a reparative maneuver through Sedgwick and Fisher's work, Warner indulges in a predictable exercise of an epistemological privilege of unknowing.

22 Hanson, "The Future's Eve," 102.
23 Fisher, *Gary in Your Pocket*, 66.
24 Michael Hardt, "The Common in Communism," in *The Idea of Communism*, ed. Costas Douzinas and Slavoj Žižek (London: Verso, 2010), 144.
25 Jean-Luc Nancy, "Communism, the Word," in Douzinas and Žižek, *The Idea of Communism*, 149.
26 Nancy, *The Truth of Democracy*, 17.
27 Nancy, *The Truth of Democracy*, 146.
28 Fisher, *Gary in Your Pocket*, 284.
29 Eve Kosofsky Sedgwick, *Between Men: English Literature and Male Homosocial Desire* (New York: Columbia University Press, 1985).
30 Fisher, *Gary in Your Pocket*, 284.

Sedgwick Inexhaustible

The work of Eve Kosofsky Sedgwick has attached itself to so many different kinds of inquiry, and has been with me so long, that I had a hard time finding a good way to talk about it for the MLA panel in January 2011 from which this essay developed. Preparing for that panel on Sedgwick's uses of the Gothic, I was dismayed to find I no longer knew how to read Sedgwick's work in the way I once believed I could. It took me a bit to realize that for me, interpreting Sedgwick—her ideas, her prose, her commitments—is now a compelling historical puzzle.

I should say what I mean by this. When I first read Sedgwick, it was as a graduate student in the first decade of the AIDS epidemic, the era of ACT UP and Queer Nation, at the moment of a delicate and fortuitous convergence between queer work inside and outside the academy. Now, though, that convergence is more an ideal than a reality; queer politics no longer feels like movement politics, and the sweet head rush of early forms of queer institution building inside the academy has been displaced by the dread of a systemic crisis in the academy itself. I think differently now; we all do. So the occasion of these beautiful panels has prompted me to ask myself, if I'm not going to read Sedgwick nostalgically—that is, so as to be able to imagine myself as a gay man, or a queer person, or as a critic poised to elide the difference between criticism and activism—then how should I read her? As a Marxist? As a Buddhist? As a poet? What *does* endure in the work? What changes?

These are big questions; in the brief span of this essay I'll try to answer them two different ways. First, I'd like to think about some changes, across Sedgwick's career, in her ideas about the relationship of structure to texture. Second, I'd like to pay attention to a small but interesting shift in how she periodizes. Together, these two approaches will allow me to touch, very lightly, on the question of how she handled the competing claims of structuralism, poststructuralism, and Marxism in her work. More to the point, though, my split emphasis on texture-structure and on periodization will allow me to begin to think historically about Sedgwick—to think of her as liable to reinterpretation in changed circumstances. For the one, I'll turn to passages from *The Coherence of Gothic Convention, Epistemology of the Closet,* and *Touching Feeling*; for the other, I'll take a look at *Between Men* and *A Dialogue on Love*.[1]

So let's turn for a moment to the question of texture in Sedgwick's work. I'd like to suggest that from the publication of *The Coherence of Gothic Convention* in 1980 to that of *Touching Feeling* in 2003, Sedgwick maintains a theoretical interest in how figures confound structures but changes her mind about where the scene of this confounding is most significant, shifting her attention from figure-structure play in carceral settings to its activity in everyday life. In between these settings—the carceral and the everyday—lies the great middle scene of her career: the scene of movement activism.

To begin at the end: for the Sedgwick of *Touching Feeling*, the significance of texture lies in how it mixes sensations, or media, or genres, and this mixedness produces a modulation, or "middle range," of experience and subjectivity, the spacious center that Lauren Berlant in particular has discussed. This middle range is more than spacious. For Sedgwick, it's potentially infinite. The texture of two fabrics laid alongside each other, say, or the *frisson* of poetry as it's set inside a novel—to experience these is to experience utopia in miniature.[2] So there's a movement, you could say, from Sedgwick's interest in the Gothic, which is such a wild amalgam of genres and modes, to her interest in shame, which for her is most delightfully excited in Henry James—especially when he struggles to mix or conjoin modes and media, the visual and the narrative.[3] I return to this theme in late Sedgwick later.

First, though, I'd like to supply its background. Take this passage from the first chapter of *Gothic Convention*, in which Sedgwick is discussing the claustrophobic and paranoiac effects of Giambattista Piranesi's mid-eighteenth-century drawings of prisons, his *Carceri d'invenzione*, which, she notes, were influential for the Gothic. Here Sedgwick is thinking about the way the *Carceri* make it difficult for the viewer to establish a clear sense of what's inside and what's outside the prison—indeed, to establish whether the viewer herself is inside or outside its confines. "Sometimes . . . there seem to be clouds in the background," she writes, "but in other plates the density of detail and the complete lack of open 'sky' space make it impossible to imagine them as being in any sense outside. The incoherent, indefinite, apparently infinite space depicted cannot, however, be perceived as inside either."[4]

Later in *Gothic Conventions*, these problems of perception reemerge as a related literary problem of how to depict character. At the end of the book, Sedgwick claims that this was the Gothic's great contribution to the history of the novel, the history that for so long deliberately occluded it: for Sedgwick, the Gothic forces the issue of what counts as character in literary representation. A certain minimum of description? If so, what kind? A foreground of physical detail? A background of psychological states? The answer the Gothic proposes, Sedgwick suggests, is an unstable admixture of all of these: "The issue of what constitutes the character—what internecine superposition of a length of words, the image of the body, a name, and, on the countenance, an authenticating graphic stamp—had never before the Gothic been confronted so energetically in these terms. . . . It was from the Gothic novel that this drama of substance and abstraction made its way into more easily intelligible, modern-sounding fictional forms."[5]

These passages don't add up, quite, to a de Manian bid for the subversiveness of figures, which for de Man upend foreground-background distinctions or disrupt a stable sense of the difference between structure and texture, logic and rhetoric. Neither does the first passage quite amount to a Foucauldian argument about how the power of the prison lies in its ability to imply that it might be everywhere. But if these two strands of French poststructuralism seem uncannily present in this early work, it is perhaps because structuralism itself, to which Sedgwick had more access in 1980, was already invested in a certain language of disruption, in a certain uncanniness. On one political front, structuralist anthropology meant to counter what disaffected Marxists on the French left took to be Marxism's overly hasty projection of progress onto a history that was more legible as repetition across scale than development across time. On another front, the discovery, in work such as Claude Lévi-Strauss's *The Savage Mind* (1962), of the past in the present—of "primitive" behaviors in the heart of modernity—was meant to disrupt the colonial hubris of France's arrogation of "modernity" only to the metropole. So even before the rise of poststructuralism, there were quietly post-Marxist and anticolonial overtones in the gestures of the kind Sedgwick makes in *Gothic Conventions*. Her crediting the emergence of "intelligible, modern" literary character to the disavowed, thick texture of the "premodern" Gothic performs a kind of rescue of the Gothic's dignity by way of a structuralist jab at the presumption of the "modern" to autochthony.

By the time of *Epistemology of the Closet*, ten years later, Sedgwick was writing into a vastly different academic and political context. English translations of the key works of poststructuralism were by now widely available in the US, and queer activism had replaced feminism on Sedgwick's political map as the movement context into which left-leaning academic work on literature and sexuality might speak. *Epistemology of the Closet* was also, of course, published at the height of direct-action AIDS activism, at a moment of great ferocity and anguish among gay men, as well as their lesbian, queer, and straight allies. So much has changed, in fact, that it's startling to see the continuity of Sedgwick's interest in structure and texture from *Gothic Conventions* to *Epistemology of the Closet*, but it's present nonetheless.

The continuity is possible to see even in the famous "Introduction: Axiomatic" chapter of *Epistemology of the Closet*, the one that diverges most fully from literary readings. Even there Sedgwick's manifesto-like identification of the "hetero-homo" binary, and her call for its disruption by way of nourishing many different relations to sexuality, is structurally akin to her observations about inside and outside, or figure and ground, in Piranesi and the Gothic. What changes is the tone and the implicit politics: whereas in the case of Piranesi the upsetting of a distinction between inside and outside is a dark tactic of carceral power, in the case of Gothic character the upsetting of the figure-ground divide is already taking on shadings of advocacy—advocacy for the literary dignity of a discarded genre. By the time of *Epistemology of the Closet*, the proliferation of avenues of identification, over and against the rigid homo-hetero binary, transposes the earlier genre-based valorization of the many over the binary into the scene of movement politics and into a different, humanist tone: not only are "people different," in the language of *Epistemology of the Closet*'s famous axiom, but scientific worries over the origins of homosexuality should be replaced, Sedgwick argues in this period, by a wish that there be *more gay people* in the world.[6]

Elsewhere in *Epistemology of the Closet* the traces of the Gothic, and of Sedgwick's relation to it, appear as figures or in political gestures. At the end of her chapter on *Billy Budd*, for instance, Sedgwick highlights the ineradicability of homosexuality, which she is concerned to counterpoise to what she takes to be the genocidal fantasies of the period's most homophobic and AIDS-phobic discourse. "As gay community and the solidarity and visibility of gays as a minority population are being consolidated" in the epidemic, she asks, "how can it fail to be all the more necessary that the avenues of recognition, desire, and thought between minority potentials and universalizing ones be opened and opened and opened?"[7] Here the call for diversity and dignity is figured as a kind of light-filled obverse to the multiplying avenues of Piranesi's prisons, infinitely extensive but no longer carceral.

Later, in a chapter that undermines modernist hostility to sentimental discourse, Sedgwick describes the persistence of sentiment as a kind of endangered residue built up from traces of a now pathologized affection for male bodies, superscripted now by medical narratives that nevertheless continue to depend on it—much the way Gothic character was disavowed but still present in latter-day, "modern" literary techniques of representing personhood.[8] And in the famous chapter on Henry James's "The Beast in the Jungle," Sedgwick reads the story's closing lines, in which John Marcher throws himself onto May Bartram's tomb, as the Gothic consequence of his self-ignorance: Marcher never admitted to himself that he loved men, so he kept May waiting for him all her life and ends up making a hapless, belated gesture in her direction that mimics the "live burial" Sedgwick found so alluringly disturbing in Gothic narrative. Here, though, Marcher's attempt to force oneself into the past—"become Gothic," as it were—elicits Sedgwick's pity: his attempt to entomb himself is the cost of internalized homophobia.[9] In this last case, James's plot serves as structure to the gesture's texture, and, as in Sedgwick's other work in this most politically charged part of her career, the contrast elicits pity and compassion.

So in the transition from *The Coherence of Gothic Conventions* to *Epistemology of the Closet* we can see, first, analogies between the sentimentality of recuperating Gothic convention and the antimodernism of French structuralist anticolonialism and post-Marxism. Then we see a modulation of those analogies between Sedgwick's reading practice and the aims of the structuralists into a new key: although Gothic is still analogized to the premodern, ruthlessly cast aside in the assembly of modernity, in the later work Gothic is also analogized to homosexuality, itself rendered as a premodern residue that won't be, can't be, erased but that, because of modernizing attempts to erase it anyway, makes it worthy of solicitude. The implied theoretical narrative moves from being structures against hubris to structures *as* hubris, or structure against texture, and this implied movement is a trace of Sedgwick's movement from a committed academic feminism that quietly allied itself with structuralist anticolonialism to a movement-grounded antihomophobia that allied itself with the *soixant-huitard* energies of post-Marxist student movements— which, in an ironic passing of the torch from the French students to their professors, had made it possible to imagine "texture" as principally located in *texts.* Although my formulations here are primarily about academic theory, it is impossible not to see, in the years from 1980 to 1990, movement politics grow more immediate and more ferocious in Sedgwick's work.

By the time of *Touching Feeling*, though, in 2003, homosexuality had all but disappeared as a ground for progressive social movement, leaving behind valuable queer culture, queer critique, and queer (non-)identities that, however radical, were nonetheless no longer hitched to mass mobilization (Sedgwick called this "the strategic banalization of gay and lesbian politics").[10] Like a wave receding from shore, though, the aftermath of gay, lesbian, and queer movement politics left behind a surprising array of figures and concepts useful for thinking about what endures beyond the momentary syzygy of texts, politics, and sexuality. Chief among these are figures for the everyday, for everyday life, including a revivified use of "texture," which serves as both figure and concept in *Touching Feeling*, and an elaboration of "affect" drawn from the work of the psychologist Silvan Tomkins. They are both figures for variety: as Sedgwick relayed to humanist scholars in a 1995 essay included in *Touching Feeling*, Tomkins imagined eight or nine basic affects, which multiplied when experienced in combination. Elsewhere in the volume, Sedgwick discusses texture by way of the proliferation of its types: "sedimented, extruded, laminated, granulated, polished, distressed, felted . . . fluffed up."[11]

But texture and affect, as figures for variety, are also figures and concepts for everyday life. As Sedgwick puts it, "If texture and affect, touching and feeling seem to belong together, then, it is not because they share a particular delicacy of scale, such as would necessarily call for 'close reading' or 'thick description.' What they have in common is that at whatever scale they are attended to, both are irreducibly phenomenological."[12] That for Sedgwick the phenomenological is linked to the everyday is evidenced in the paragraph that follows this passage, in which she notes that she is less interested in sexuality and shame than she used to be and more interested in pedagogy; in happiness; in Buddhism.

And in a particularly Buddhist image, she notes that the many senses involved in experiencing texture are what give it its actuality: "We *hear* the brush-brush of corduroy trousers or the crunch of extra-crispy chicken."[13]

From thick description to crispy chicken: the rejection of structuralism in favor of phenomenology could not be more pronounced. But the things that affect and texture end up offering Sedgwick, in the aftermath of the great drama of queer politics—actuality and the ordinary—don't quite add up to "everyday life," I realize. That's because "everyday life" as a key phrase is linked, in French phenomenology and post-Marxism, to arguments about historical consciousness on which I haven't touched. So let's take a brief look at how

Sedgwick, in the years when her thinking about structure was changing so rapidly, thought about history.

Famously, of course, in the movement from *Between Men* in 1986 and *Epistemology of the Closet* in 1990, Sedgwick turns from a story about the mediating role of women in exchanges between men to a story about the polarization of those exchanges into a stark and unstable binary, hetero-homo. In his contribution to the 2011 MLA panels on Sedgwick, Jonathan Goldberg pointed out that the historical frames are different in the two books, that there's a movement in Sedgwick that parallels the shift from Gayle Rubin's early emphasis on "the traffic in women" to something more like Rubin's argument in "Thinking Sex," which turned on how cultures binarize the values they attach to sex practices. Jonathan's account of the shift in Sedgwick's historical frame, and how it tracks the shifts in feminism from the mid-1970s to the mid-1980s, seems just right to me. But I'm also interested in the historical method that *Between Men* and *Epistemology of the Closet* actually share, which is to shift back and forth between an account of the transition from rural to industrial capitalism, and an account of how a cluster of related phenomena—the Gothic, paranoia, and homosexuality—mediated that transition. For Sedgwick, the action is always with the story of mediation.

So in *Between Men*, for instance, the narrative of the polarization of male-male relations into hetero and homo depends on another narrative of the shifting role of women in mediating those relations; what is easy to forget, reading after the rise of poststructuralism, is that the story about women's role in male homosociality is a story about how women mediate the shifts in the class valences of those male-male relations—specifically, a shift in how to manage men's relationships in the transition from the rural and feudal to the industrial and the modern. In a reading of Thackeray's *Henry Esmond* and George Eliot's *Adam Bede*, Sedgwick puts it this way: "In *Bede* and *Esmond*, a magnetic and preemptive drama of heterosexual transgression occasions even as it obscures a transfer of power between classes."[14] So to be clear: if the one role of women is to obscure the nature of relations between men, one role of the eventual polarization of those relations into hetero and homo is itself to mediate and obscure changes in class relations—that is, the emergence of a polarized hetero-homo binary serves the rise of capital. And it does so by creating a kind of paranoia among men that is specific to modernity. As Sedgwick puts it, "No man must be able to ascertain that he is not (that his bonds are not) homosexual."[15]

Compare that story of nested mediations that facilitate period transitions to how she describes the cross-period fortunes of the trope of unspeakability in its relation to the Gothic. Tracing the associations between homosexuality and aristocratic bearing in *Between Men*, Sedgwick follows this trope from early to late Gothic novels, suggesting that what begins as arcana ends as spectacle, and that it's Oscar Wilde who makes all the difference. She puts it this way: "What had been the style of homosexuality attributed to the aristocracy... now washed through the middle classes, with... complicated political effects. The Gothic, too, changed: homosexual implications in [earlier novels] had been esoteric; parts of Dorian Gray... were used as... a handbook of gay style and behavior."[16]

Sedgwick follows this making-parallel of the Gothic and homosexuality with a further periodization, this time from the late nineteenth to the late twentieth century. Recalling a story told by the author Beverly Nichols about his father confronting him, outraged, with the boy's copy of *Dorian Gray*, Sedgwick writes, "It is hard to imagine today that a Gothic novel... could have such a pivotal and mystifying force. For the Nichols circle, the Gothic acted as an electrified barrier between generations, between classes, between sexual choices; for the middle-class reader today it is something to pass up at the supermarket."[17]

This anecdote rounds out the arc of the surprisingly familiar historical story to which the Gothic is attached: motley literary arcana becoming the ground on which realist tales of the transition to capitalism are built, spiking back up to visibility as aristocratic codes are made accessible to a middle class through an early form of mass-cultural spectacle, then disappearing once more from properly literary view as that spectacle, along with many others, is universalized and made banal, made American. In this larger historical tale, homosexuality and the Gothic twine into and untwine from each other around the central stalk of a pretty linear history of capitalism.

To look back for a moment: when she's thinking about the Gothic and its relationship to homosexuality as an ambivalent structuralist, on her way to taking her leave from its terms, Sedgwick thinks of both the genre and the sexual identity as buried, occluded, overwritten by systematization—live-buried, that is, and in need of rescue. When she's thinking about homosexuality and the Gothic as a historicist, though, Sedgwick thinks of them as having *lost their excitement*. They've become banal; commodified; everyday in a negative sense.

So there's a tension—actually, I'd say a contradiction—between Sedgwick's stucturalist and her historicist approaches, one that poses practical questions for her latter-day readers. If the place Sedgwick leaves the Gothic—the place she leaves *us*—is in the everyday, what is its quality? Is it a zone of actuality, the zone of experience as "crispy chicken," free from melodrama? Or is it the zone of "banalization," of the becoming universal of the commodity? Which chicken are we left with here?

The problem is that, although Sedgwick's career has ended, the ambivalent framework she came to adopt is not a terminus. It is, rather, an unstable formulation, of French provenance, where it signaled, in the work of Henri Lefebvre and (later) Michel de Certeau, a commitment not only to phenomenology but to a humanist Marxism opposed to structuralism. Sedgwick's sense of the everyday overlaps with de Certeau's, especially. Just as he was interested in how the average city dweller became a tactician of the commodity, retooling it to her own uses, so did Sedgwick come to find the object-world most interesting for the stories it could tell us about how things had been handled ("sedimented, extruded, laminated"). And her humanist axiom that "people are different" finds echoes throughout de Certeau, as when he tries to prise the theory of consumer society away from a presumption of the passivity of the consumer, writing that "it is always good to remind ourselves that we mustn't take people for fools."[18]

Again, though, the problem is that these formulations were produced to meet the challenge of the Pax Americana, of the relative economic stability of the 1950s and 1960s, when the question of whether capitalism could survive by producing consumer goods rather than industrial goods and the question of what kind of person consumption made you were central to certain critiques of capitalism. But that era is over, and whatever meanings "the everyday" takes on now will have to meet a different set of conditions. The commodification of everything—the Gothic, homosexuality—turns out not to be the end of the story, which has pretty clearly modulated into a tale of what the sociologist Randy Martin calls "the financialization of daily life."[19] The rise of contemporary finance, and the crises it has generated, have major implications for how we think of contemporary capitalism, and not because finance is what "comes after" industrial capital. Rather, this new era of volatility and crisis demonstrates all too brutally how close the link actually *is* between finance and industry: housing crises and food shortages caused not by actual underproduction, but by the collapse of speculative opportunities for the financial classes. In our era, crisis and volatility *are* "everyday life" in the global North—not something we're used to up here.

It is a question for me, every day, whether my academic training in early-1990s queer theory, or my brief participation in a liberationist mode of lesbian and gay politics, can help me think through the politics of this new period, can help me think about political economy. By and large, I don't think so. But my coming out into the residue of liberationist LGBT politics gave me an experience of solidarity, lived and potential, that will never leave me, and queer theory, whatever its limits, was friendly to poetry, which has structured my intellectual life since then. So the place I find I'm still able to read Sedgwick for the present—maybe for the future—is the place where she's begun to let a certain poetry enter her work. It is the place where the Gothic, ever present, is less novelistic and more lyric and where that openness to poetry facilitates a meditation on whether and how her writing can be said to address—even to be written by—a "we" that is the source and scene of solidarity.

Describing the trope of live burial in *The Coherence of Gothic Conventions*, Sedgwick writes that the buried self, sundered from the activity of the world outside, has only one route to reintegration with that world: "Only violence or magic, and both of a singularly threatening kind, can ever succeed in joining them again."[20] This is, of course, a description of psychoanalysis; but it's also a description of the Gothic writing practice of *A Dialogue on Love*, Sedgwick's 1999 account of her own therapy, which intersperses narrative prose concerning, among other things, her own sadomasochistic fantasies with poetic fragments and triangulated commentary from her therapist, this last printed all in small caps, like the Ouija board messages of the mischievous spirit Ephraim in James Merrill's poem *The Changing Light at Sandover*.

At a key point in *A Dialogue on Love*, Sedgwick recalls the bliss and safety she experienced while spending time out in the world with her older sister. In a short poem that's set indented from the main narrative, and in a less formal, sans serif typeface, Sedgwick describes these joint outings as "sealed with my / favorite pronoun: the dear / first person plural." The line break implies that there might be a pronoun in English that signifies "the dear," in the way that *tu* can signify intimacy in French when used in the place of *vous*. Sure enough, in the paragraph that follows the poem, Sedgwick writes, "It never surprised *me* that 'we,' in French, means yes."[21] Then, in a sudden dilation of we-as-two to we-as-anyone that owes more than a little to the heyday of queer theory, Sedgwick returns to her sans serif poem stanza and concludes the book's chapter this way:

Promiscuous we!
Me, plus anybody else. Permeable we!

This sense of the plural as affirmative, which has recently resurfaced in French intellectual life in the work of Jacques Rancière, and that structures the most hopeful moments of Michael Hardt and Antonio Negri's *Empire* trilogy, is not Marxist per se, but it's as strong a reminder as I could possibly hope for that the politics, and the theory politics, of the era in which I came of age are not entirely discontinuous with the avenues of study, and the sense of politics, that feel urgent to me today. It's a mark of Sedgwick's intellectual suppleness—her inexhaustibility, really—that I find myself so curious about what she would have made of this new era.

There's no time now to do the thing I know would honor Sedgwick best, which would be to do a close reading of her most poetic prose. *A Dialogue on Love* would merit that. Instead, I'll just suggest that the kind of subject Sedgwick can now begin becoming, free of cancer, after queerness, in late capital, at the feet of the Buddha—that implausibly spacious, impossibly gracious subject—is hiding in plain sight on the front cover image for *A Dialogue on Love*. It's a close-up photograph of the shadowed seam between two blank pages of an open book.

NOTES

1 Eve Kosofsky Sedgwick, *The Coherence of Gothic Conventions* (London: Methuen, 1985); Eve Kosofsky Sedgwick, *Epistemology of the Closet* (Berkeley: University of California Press, 1991); Eve Kosofsky Sedgwick, *Touching Feeling: Affect, Pedagogy, Performativity* (Durham, NC: Duke University Press, 2003); Eve Kosofsky Sedgwick, *Between Men: English Literature and Male Homosocial Desire* (New York: Columbia University Press, [1985] 1993); Eve Kosofsky Sedgwick, *A Dialogue on Love* (Boston: Beacon, 2000).

2 Sedgwick, *Touching Feeling*, 16.

3 Sedgwick, *Touching Feeling*, 46.

4 Sedgwick, *The Coherence of Gothic Conventions*, 26.

5 Sedgwick, *The Coherence of Gothic Conventions*, 170.

6 See Eve Kosofsky Sedgwick, "How to Bring Your Kids Up Gay," *Social Text* 29 (1991): 18–27.

7 Sedgwick, *The Coherence of Gothic Conventions*, 130.

8 Sedgwick, *The Coherence of Gothic Conventions*, 180.

9 Sedgwick, *The Coherence of Gothic Conventions*, 212.

10 Sedgwick, *Touching Feeling*, 13.

11 Sedgwick, *Touching Feeling*, 14.

12 Sedgwick, *Touching Feeling*, 21.

13 Sedgwick, *Touching Feeling*, 15.

14 Sedgwick, *Between Men*, 137.

15 Sedgwick, *Between Men*, 89.

16 Sedgwick, *Between Men*, 95.

17 Sedgwick, *Between Men*, 95–96.

18 Michel de Certeau, *The Practice of Everyday Life*, trans. Steven Rendall (Berkeley: University of California Press, 1984), 176.

19 Randy Martin, *Financialization of Daily Life* (Philadelphia, PA: Temple University Press, 2002).

20 Sedgwick, *The Coherence of Gothic Conventions*, 13.

21 Sedgwick, *A Dialogue on Love*, 106.

The Age of Frankenstein

Science seems to have as its always possible outcome an escaping of sexual difference, not a reinforcement of it, so that what seems like a biological invariant can be gotten around. That, in fact, is one of the aims of science, and perhaps also what makes science seem like a not entirely benign force (*Frankenstein*: "I thought I held the corpse of my dead mother in my arms").

–Barbara Johnson, *Mother Tongues*

This essay began as a talk for one of several MLA sessions in 2011 that honored Eve Kosofsky Sedgwick's life and work following her death in April 2009. A revised version was given a year later as the second annual Sedgwick Lecture at Boston University, and then once more at the invitation of the University of California, Irvine, English Department. I am as grateful today as then to my hosts for these opportunities to reflect on aspects of Eve's work that I never had the chance to speak with her about. This version—the last one, I hope— concludes with questions I began to frame in the conclusion to *The Theorist's Mother*, questions that have since opened onto a series of others about concepts of mechanism and gender difference in post-Romantic literature and philosophy.[1] I wonder, of course, what Eve would have made of these recent musings, especially as they revisit concerns that date from some of her earliest writings.

I should also note at the outset that Eve was my colleague, collaborator, frequent co-conspirator, and one of my dearest friends. I don't think I've solved very well the problem of whether to refer to her throughout this text as "Eve" or as "Sedgwick," so I decided finally and arbitrarily to do both. You'll encounter in any case a great deal of her own writing here, which seems a fitting way to honor someone who always strongly promoted Sándor Ferenczi's essay "Confusion of Tongues."[2]

Readers of Eve Kosofsky Sedgwick's *Epistemology of the Closet* will no doubt recall the centrality of the phrase "the Age of Frankenstein" to the book's overarching preoccupation with forms of homophobia, mediated by the "male paranoid plots" of the Gothic novel that emerged in nineteenth-century Euro-American culture.[3] The Age of Frankenstein—the proper name sometimes italicized and sometimes not, but always appearing with a big A and a big F—clearly functioned for Sedgwick as a periodizing concept, naming as a single and coherent epoch the hundred-odd years between the closing of the English molly-houses in the late eighteenth century and Oscar Wilde's late nineteenth-century trial and incarceration. And yet the Age of Frankenstein also never simply frames its epoch, confining this period to itself. The phrase first occurs in *Epistemology of the Closet* with reference not, as we might expect, to Mary Shelley's novel but to Friedrich Nietzsche, who is said to provide "an exemplar for the Gothic-marked view of the nineteenth century as the Age of Frankenstein"—"an age," Eve continued memorably, "philosophically and tropologically marked by the wildly dichotomous play around solipsism and intersubjectivity of a male paranoid plot" in which two men chase "one another across a landscape evacuated of alternative life or interest, toward a climax that tends to condense the amorous with the murderous in a representation of male rape."[4] If it is Nietzsche, somehow, who exemplifies the Age of *Frankenstein* even better than *Frankenstein*, and this despite the fact that, to my knowledge, nowhere in Nietzsche's writing do two male characters chase each other across a landscape devoid of alternative life or interest,[5] then there is something provocatively askew in Sedgwick's choice of *Frankenstein* as the eponym of an era. I'll be looking in what follows at several instances in Eve's work where Shelley's novel repeatedly morphs, as in this first instance, into something or someone other than itself. Sedgwick's discussions of *Frankenstein* not only are surprisingly infrequent but also regularly shift their attention from the novel to another person or work, thereby posing for her readers the question of how *Frankenstein* can stand for an era when it always seems to be turning into something else. What kind of an Age can this be?

Here, for example, is the later, longer, and far more cited passage from *Epistemology of the Closet* on the narrative conventions of "the paranoid Gothic," Eve's shorthand for the canon of "Romantic novels in which a male hero is in a close, usually murderous relation to another male figure, in some respects his 'double,' to whom he seems to be mentally transparent."[6] For Sedgwick, the paranoid Gothic was an ideal vehicle for promoting homophobia not because the genre provided a platform for expounding an already formed homophobic ideology—of course, it did no such thing—but through a more active, polylogic engagement of "public" with "private" discourses, as in the wildly dichotomous play around solipsism and intersubjectivity of a male paranoid plot like that of *Frankenstein*. (This is a verbatim repetition of the phrase that occurred twenty-three pages earlier in the passage about Nietzsche.) The transmutability of the intrapsychic with the intersubjective in these plots where one man's mind could be read by that of the feared and desired other; the urgency and violence with which these plots reformed large, straggly, economically miscellaneous families such as the Frankensteins in the ideologically hypostatized image of the tight oedipal family; and then the extra efflorescence of violence with which the remaining female term in these triangular families was elided, leaving, as in *Frankenstein*, a residue of two potent male figures locked in an epistemologically indissoluble clench of will and desire—through these means, the paranoid Gothic powerfully signified, at the very moment of crystallization of the modern, capitalism-marked oedipal family, the inextricability from that formation of a strangling double bind in male homosocial constitution. Put another way, the usefulness of Freud's formulation, in the case of Dr. Schreber, that paranoia in men results from the repression of their homosexual desire has nothing to do with a classification of the paranoid Gothic in terms of "latent" or "overt" "homosexual" "types." But it has everything to do with the foregrounding, under the specific, foundational historical conditions of the early Gothic, of intense male homosocial desire as at once the most compulsory and the most prohibited of social bonds.[7]

I want to linger for a moment on this long and complex passage, certainly one of the signature moments in Sedgwick's entire corpus, both for what it does and for what it doesn't do conceptually and linguistically. Her analysis focuses on the novel's plotting, its reduction of a remarkably large cast of characters (male and female) to just two, Victor and his monstrous creation, whose identities blur into each other when seen from a distance at the novel's end. This reduction is simultaneously intrapsychic and familio-economic: as in Eve's contemporary reading of George Eliot's *Adam Bede*, the indistinguishability of prescribed and proscribed bonds between men, with its murderous effects on women, is shown to have become an urgent (if unconscious) cultural problem at the moment when, at the start of the Industrial Revolution, the Oedipalized nuclear family first assumed its modern form. Besides the sheer poetry of this passage (I'll pause here only to savor again the cadence and consonance of "the extra efflorescence of violence"), the passage is astonishing in the interpretive power it musters in disclosing, in its stark schematization, what had never been said before about either *Frankenstein* or the paranoid and homophobic culture that its plot is said to metonymize. I will have more to suggest about the conclusion of the passage in a moment.

When subsequent critics speak of Eve's "reading of *Frankenstein*," it is to this schema that they refer. In point of fact, the passage contains the most that she ever said in print about *Frankenstein*. It is certainly a powerful and useful crystallization of an important dimension of the novel's plot, but it is not, as Eve would have been the first to acknowledge, a *reading*. It isn't difficult, for example, to itemize many of the novel's elements that could have been incorporated into the schema of "two men chasing each other around the ice" but somehow weren't: the novel's other pairs of intense male-male relationships (Victor and Clerval, as well as Victor and Walton, each with a woman at the hinge of a homosocial triangle); the parallel homosocial triangle composed of Mary Shelley and her demanding breakfast companions, her husband Percy and Lord Byron, who asked her each day to report on the progress of her story; the novel's intensely eroticized bonds between its *female* characters (Elizabeth and Justine above all); and the national allegory introduced with the interpolated story of the De Lacey family and Safie, their prospective Turkish daughter-in-law. While Sedgwick was hardly the first to extract Victor Frankenstein and his monstrous creation from the novel's larger formal context, it still is fascinating to consider just how much of that context was available for theoretical use but wasn't. Among other rich possibilities, there's the moment of the monster's birth, which we could call explicitly homoerotic except for the fact that, as a still lifeless assemblage, the monster has no gender as yet:

> It was on a dreary night of November that I beheld the accomplishment of my toils. With an anxiety that almost amounted to agony, I collected the instruments of life around me, that I might infuse a spark of being into the lifeless thing that lay at my feet. It was already one in the morning; the rain pattered dismally against the panes, and my candle was nearly burnt out, when, by the glimmer of the half-extinguished light, I saw the dull yellow eye of the creature open; it breathed hard, and a convulsive motion agitated its limbs.[8]

This passage, when read aloud in class, never fails to reduce the room to silence—especially the students who, minutes before, had been so curious about the nature of Victor's experimental methods. We can perform Sedgwickian readings of many other such moments, such as the declaration Victor makes to Elizabeth late in the novel:

"I have one secret, Elizabeth, a dreadful one; when revealed to you it will chill your frame with horror, and then, far from being surprised at my misery, you will only wonder that I survive what I have endured. I will confide this tale of misery and terror to you the day after our marriage shall take place; for, my sweet cousin, there must be perfect confidence between us. But until then, I conjure you, do not mention or allude to it. This I most earnestly entreat, and I know you will comply."[9]

I can hear Eve playfully ventriloquizing Elizabeth's unrecorded response, *relieved*, finally, that her betrothed's dark secret was nothing more than the unholy creation of new life. My point, again, is simply that Eve never included such passages in any of her few discussions of *Frankenstein*. Nor did she remark on the novel's famous nesting of narrative frames—the monster's story inside Victor's inside Walton's—as if the paranoid Gothic only ever appears as a static and expungable tableau (an important term for her, as we will see) and not as an integral part of a larger narrative.[10]

Never plentiful or prolonged in any case, references to *Frankenstein* and/or its Age dwindle in Eve's work after *Epistemology of the Closet*. There are none in *Tendencies*, none in her long introduction to *Novel Gazing*, none in *A Dialogue on Love*, and only two brief allusions in *Touching Feeling* in discussions of Henry James. In some ways, the concept of the Age of Frankenstein may simply have outlived its usefulness in Eve's later thinking. In nearly every instance of its appearance in her corpus, Sedgwick focused on the novel just long enough so as to arrive at Dr. Schreber, who, like Nietzsche, seemed to her a better emblem for "the Age of Frankenstein" than *Frankenstein*. The long passage cited previously from *Epistemology of the Closet* moves abruptly at its conclusion from *Frankenstein* ("put another way") to the Schreber case as *the* privileged instance of Gothic paranoia. Indeed, this transposition is already legible in *Between Men*, where every Gothic novel appears to have been erected over a Schreberian chassis:

> Particularly relevant for the Gothic novel is the perception Freud arrived at in the case of Dr. Schreber: that paranoia is the psychosis that makes graphic the mechanisms of homophobia. In our argument about the Gothic in the next chapter, we will not take Freud's analysis on faith, but examine its grounds and workings closely in a single novel. To begin with, however, it is true that the limited group of fictions that represent the "classic" early Gothic contains a large subgroup—*Caleb Williams, Frankenstein, Confessions of a Justified Sinner*, probably *Melmoth*, possibly *The Italian*—whose

plots might be mapped almost point for point onto the case of Dr. Schreber: most saliently, each is about one or more males who not only is persecuted by, but considers himself transparent to and often under the compulsion of another male.[11]

Frankenstein is the only one of this group of novels not to have its grounds and workings examined closely in an extended analysis of its own. What accounts for its omission? Is it possible to read here an avoidance of a reading? What, finally, would be "made graphic" were Frankenstein mapped "almost point for point" onto the Schreber case? This essay concludes with some speculative responses to these questions.

But first, I want to consider briefly one of Eve's earlier and less well-known texts, her 1986 preface to the reprinting of The Coherence of Gothic Conventions. The preface is where the phrase "the Age of Frankenstein" was coined, in fact, and it serves in some ways as a dress rehearsal for the substance and syntax of the long passage from Epistemology discussed earlier:

> The fate of the family in Frankenstein and throughout the paranoid Gothic presents the pared-down nuclear or Oedipal family, first, as compulsory, but second, as a somewhat ephemeral stage on the way to the tableau that is seen as embodying primal human essence or originary truth: the tableau of two men chasing each other across a landscape. It is importantly undecidable in this tableau, as in many others like it in Gothic novels, whether the two men represent two consciousnesses or one; and it is importantly undecidable whether their bond—in the first place, as in Melmoth, ancestral—is murderous or amorous. I would argue out from the first of these central indecisions that the entire, many-pronged Romantic and nineteenth-century philosophical project of embodiment that centered on the question of solipsism, the question of the very existence of other minds, took its deepest impetus from the crystallization of this paranoid, i.e., specifically homophobic, tableau; surely one could call the nineteenth century philosophically, as much as technologically, the Age of Frankenstein.[12]

"Tableau," again and again, which, already, never seems to appear without "paranoid" and "homophobic"—as if these adjectives were part of "tableau"'s definition. But even as this passage hints at the very large claims proposed by Epistemology of the Closet in its opening pages,[13] the preface turns into a discussion that departs radically from the historiographic premises of the later version of the Age of Frankenstein. For one thing, that age is not over and done with even after the historical emergence, with Oscar Wilde, of a modern "homosexual role or culture." Where we might choose today as one example of its persistence the US media's lurid coverage of the Rutgers University student Tyler Clementi's devastating suicide, Eve focused in 1986 on the "extra efflorescence of violence" squeezed out by journalists in their coverage of the emerging AIDS pandemic: "The current discourse of AIDS in the United States, apparently on the point of transforming a biological wastage of lives into a cultural and legal holocaust of liberties and meanings and lives, confronts the reader of the Gothic with an uncircumnavigable familiarity, made only the more paralyzing by the 'bizarreness' of the nightmare-intimate shocks dealt by every morning's newspaper."[14] Sedgwick chose one such newspaper on which to comment, William F. Buckley's column from December 1985 fantasizing the state's inscription on the bodies of HIV-positive men a sign that would warn others, "so to speak, [to] Keep Off The Grass." Eve wrote this remarkable sentence in response: "Pornographically sly and mendacious and pornographically gendered as is, ultimately, probably any at least modern public discourse of privacy, Buckley's fantasy is classically Gothic in the compulsiveness with which it insists that it takes one to know one; deadeningly, uncannily familiar in its insistence that that is true only because he, the unknown knower, will have it so."[15]

At once, then, historically finite *and* anything but that, the Age of Frankenstein lives on, overlapping or fusing with (and perhaps surviving) later regimes of knowledge. If we're not done with this Age—or if it's not done with us—that may have something to do with the new forms of gender binarism that Eve located early on at the heart of the Gothic novel: "Call, for convenience's sake, the heroine of the Gothic a classic hysteric, its hero a classic paranoid."[16] This taxonomy is understood as merely convenient on account not of the fragility of the gender distinction itself but of the psychoanalytic terms that it places in opposition:

> "Hysteria" and "paranoia," as psychoanalytic entities, are kept distinct by, among other things, an insistent gender marking, whose half erasure is then a project of gender critique: "Is" there a female paranoia? "Is" there a male hysteria? The verbs are put in quotation marks as a way of asking again about the temporality of "psychoanalytic entities," but in fact it has been through approaches to the question of gender distinctiveness that the feminist-marked Gothic criticism of the last half dozen years, not re-

flected in the early essay, has made its most refined progress toward a historicized reading of the Gothic.[17]

Sedgwick is thinking at the beginning of this passage about recent essays by Naomi Schor and Neil Hertz on, respectively, the cross-dressed possibilities of female paranoia and male hysteria.[18] Today, perhaps, we would call such entities simply "paranoia" and "hysteria," dropping their gendered attributes. In fact, Eve did precisely that in her later Kleinian work, where paranoia is opposed no longer to hysteria (as male to female) but to *reparation* as the potential subject positions of the infant. In the passage from *Coherence*, however, strict gender division remains a given, even a presupposition, so much so that it underwrites what becomes in the preface a departure from the terms of recent feminist readings of *Frankenstein*—Eve was thinking especially of Barbara Johnson's influential essay "My Monster/My Self," among others—which proposed that the novel is its female author's autobiography in the guise of a male birth fantasy. "The story of *Frankenstein*," wrote Johnson, "is after all, the story of a man who usurps the female role by physically giving birth to a child."[19] Johnson was taking issue here implicitly with Sandra Gilbert and Susan Gubar's reading of the novel in *The Madwoman in the Attic*, which suggested not only that Victor and monster are "Eve and Eve all along," but that all of the novel's male characters are "female in disguise." How else, indeed, could Victor have given birth?[20] Unlike Gilbert and Gubar, Johnson fully credited Victor's (and the monster's) maleness, if only to allegorize the preclusion of women's authorship as a male usurpation of birth. Sedgwick obviously admired Johnson's reading, recognizing that in it *Frankenstein* becomes "a critical meditation on the emergence of a technological subject and of a colonial subject [that] can be appropriately embodied finally only, though never seamlessly, in a narrative that takes the maternal work of embodiment as its manifest subject."[21] "Finally only, though never seamlessly": a curiously strenuous phrase occurring in a sentence in which embodiment happens twice, if at all, through the novel's transposed figurations of maternity.

This is what Sedgwick called the "feminocentric" reading of *Frankenstein*. Her own thinking about the novel, with its focus on male paranoia, would seem to depart from the terms of Johnson's reading, or it would if it fully could: "In a text like *Frankenstein*, as arguably in most Gothic novels, the male paranoid plot is not separate from the maternal or monstrous plot; instead there is articulated within the text a male paranoid reading of maternity, a reading that persistently renders uncanny, renders as violence of a particular kind, the coming-to-body of the (male) individual subject."[22] I take this to be, once more, a "finally only, though never seamlessly" moment, where male and female are complexly and violently *intra*related rather than simply opposed. And yet, separating what she just described as inseparable, Eve distinguished her own interest in the novel from Johnson's through a logic in which difference *between* replaces difference *within*: "If 'my monster, my self' is the slogan of the feminocentric or hysterically-oriented reading of the Gothic, that of the masculocentric or paranoiacally oriented reading would have to be 'it takes one to know one.'"[23] Thus, where Johnson's version of *Frankenstein* gave us an allegory of gendered hysteria without paranoiac homophobia, Sedgwick's *Frankenstein* has plenty of the latter but very little of the former. Neither analysis seemed then to have been capable of imagining feminist and antihomophobic analyses simultaneously.

This is, I'm speculating, the predicament that *Frankenstein* posed early and often for Sedgwick—a predicament made manifest not only in the absence of a reading that would justify the name of an Age but also in the development of queer theory in the ensuing decade. Eve would speak later in *Epistemology of the Closet* of the tactical differences between feminist and antihomophobic analyses, and we can see, perhaps, the origins of that distinction—and some of what that distinction costs—in the partiality of her treatment of *Frankenstein*. The "full fruity ripeness" of the novel's "indicatively male" paranoia, with its recurrent scenes of "fearful, projective mirroring recognition," is what may have extended the Age of *Frankenstein* well past Oscar Wilde, Nietzsche, and Schreber at least to William F. Buckley and arguably to today.[24] I wonder, however, whether Eve might have left us with a different understanding of that Age (one not predicated on a choice between the critique of gender binarism and the critique of homophobia) if she read Freud on Schreber differently—indeed, if Eve addressed Schreber's text itself and not (only) Freud's homophobic analysis of it. Schreber's strange account of his impregnation by divine rays certainly supports Freud's glossing of a male paranoid plot that will look to Sedgwick very much like the plot of *Frankenstein*—a paranoid plot that reflects the indiscernibility of the most and least reprobated bonds between men. But Schreber's text is also an account of a pregnant man, and some recent readings, my own included, suggest that the possibility of men giving birth, and not (only) homosexual panic, may be what is newly readable in it.[25] With male pregnancy now no more (or less) fantasmatic than female pregnancy, the choice between feminist and antihomophobic analyses may have become, in some ways, less acute today. Testing that conjecture would be a reason to return again to *Frankenstein*, this time with Shulamith Firestone along with Eve Sedgwick, to ask whether the Age of Frankenstein has finally reached closure.[26]

NOTES

Epigraph: Barbara Johnson, *Mother Tongues: Sexuality, Trials, Motherhood, Translation* (Cambridge, MA: Harvard University Press, 2003).

1 Andrew Parker, *The Theorist's Mother* (Durham, NC: Duke University Press, 2012).
2 Sándor Ferenczi, "Confusion of Tongues between Adults and the Child," *Contemporary Psychoanalysis* 24, no. 2 (2013): 196–206.
3 Eve Kosofsky Sedgwick, *Epistemology of the Closet* (Berkeley: University of California Press, 1991).
4 Sedgwick, *Epistemology of the Closet*, 163.
5 Unless, and not altogether implausibly, we were to consider *Nietzsche contra Wagner*, a story about two men chasing each other across a landscape evacuated of alternative life or interest.
6 Eve Kosofsky Sedgwick, *Between Men: English Literature and Male Homosocial Desire* (New York: Columbia University Press, 1985), 186.
7 Sedgwick, *Epistemology of the Closet*, 186–87.
8 Mary Shelley, *Frankenstein; or, The Modern Prometheus*, rev. ed., ed. Maurice Hindle (London: Penguin, 1992), 58.
9 Shelley, *Frankenstein*, 193.
10 My heart leaped up recently when I came across a folder of materials from a 1986 multi-section literature class that Eve and I taught with others at Amherst College. In addition to *Frankenstein*, the syllabus included Pope's "Eloisa to Abelard," Tennyson's "The Princess," Browning's *Aurora Leigh*, Merrill's *Divine Comedies*, Plato's *Meno*, James's *The Pupil*, and Freud's *Dora*—all of them EKS favorites. In the middle of the folder was our writing assignment for *Frankenstein*, which turned out to be one of the few that Eve did *not* write for the course.
11 Sedgwick, *Between Men*, 91. On the Sedgwickian "graphic," see Sharon Marcus, "Gen/Ten: Eve Kosofsky Sedgwick's Between Men at 30," Columbia University Academic Commons, 2015, accessed February 10, 2019, doi: 10.7916/D8BZ65M6.
12 Eve Kosofsky Sedgwick, *The Coherence of Gothic Conventions* (London: Methuen, 1985), ix–x.
13 "The book will argue that an understanding of virtually any aspect of modern Western culture must be, not merely incomplete, but damaged in its central substance to the degree that it does not incorporate a critical analysis of modern homo/heterosexual definition; and it will assume that the appropriate place for that critical analysis to begin is from the relatively decentered

perspective of modern gay and antihomophobic theory": Sedgwick, *Epistemology of the Closet*, 1.

14 Sedgwick, *The Coherence of Gothic Conventions*, xii.

15 Sedgwick, *The Coherence of Gothic Conventions*, xiii–iv.

16 Sedgwick, *The Coherence of Gothic Conventions*, vi.

17 Sedgwick, *The Coherence of Gothic Conventions* (1985), vii. The "early essay" is her 1975 dissertation for Yale University. Published as *The Coherence of Gothic Conventions* (New York: Arno Press, 1976), the text would be augmented a decade later when it was reprinted under the same title.

18 Naomi Schor, "Female Paranoia: The Case for Psychoanalytic Feminist Criticism," *Yale French Studies* 62 (1981): 204–19; Neil Hertz, "Medusa's Head: Male Hysteria under Political Pressure," *Representations* 4 (1983): 27–54.

19 Barbara Johnson, "My Monster/My Self," *Diacritics* 12, no. 2 (1982): 8. The posthumous publication of *A Life with Mary Shelley* indicates that, for Johnson, *Frankenstein* was to remain a constant companion: Barbara Johnson, *A Life with Mary Shelley* (Stanford, CA: Stanford University Press, 2014). In the age of Thomas Beatie, that men can give birth may be less usurpation than relief.

20 See Sandra M. Gilbert and Susan Gubar, *The Madwoman in the Attic: The Woman Writer and the Nineteenth-Century Literary Imagination* (New Haven, CT: Yale University Press, 1979), 213–27.

21 Sedgwick, *The Coherence of Gothic Conventions* (1985), vii.

22 Sedgwick, *The Coherence of Gothic Conventions* (1985), ix.

23 Sedgwick, *The Coherence of Gothic Conventions* (1985), viii.

24 Sedgwick, *The Coherence of Gothic Conventions* (1985), viii.

25 See Parker, *The Theorist's Mother*, esp. the coda.

26 Shulamith Firestone, *The Dialectic of Sex: The Case for Feminist Revolution* (New York: William Morrow, 1970). On Firestone's renewed contemporaneity as a theorist of reproductive technologies and their political possibilities, see Mandy Merck and Stella Sanford, eds., *Further Adventures of the Dialectic of Sex: Critical Essays on Shulamith Firestone* (New York: Palgrave Macmillan, 2010).

Queer Patience

Sedgwick's Identity Narratives

Is there a difference between writing queer theory and being a queer theorist? And if so, what does it mean to *be* a queer theorist? This is a discernible concern in Eve Kosofsky Sedgwick's writing. Queerness itself is an infamously difficult concept to pin down. It arguably has always involved an engagement with sexuality, but where the limits of this sexuality are to be set and what sexuality itself entails is by the very definition of queer theory (if there is such a thing) a notion that will and should continually be problematized. If stripped down to its most abstract basis, the queer is a space where the private becomes public—our most secret desires are transformed into generalized concepts and theoretical terms. But it is also the means by which more public concerns may become intimately personal or private, and this is where Sedgwick's writing stands at the very forefront of the theoretical movement. Especially in her later work, and in her poetry, Sedgwick often leaves her own writing persona, body and mind, utterly exposed to her reading audience.

Discussing the definition of "queer" may seem superfluous, as in the more than twenty-five years that have passed since the term was first coined it has been extensively theorized, debated, and dissected—and further defining already overly contextualized definitions is far from what this chapter is attempting to do. My interest is in what "queer" meant to Sedgwick and how this is reflected in her writing. As Jason Edwards recognizes in his Routledge Critical Thinkers introduction to Sedgwick's work, her various modes of writing often throw her readers slightly off-balance.[1] It is not entirely easy to get a grip on what, exactly, her body of work as a whole attempts to do. Erin Murphy and J. Keith Vincent put this down to the "polyvocal nature" of her work.[2] Whereas, on the one hand, *Between Men* and *Epistemology of the Closet* present rather technically conventional analyses or modes of sexual and gendered communication in past and present Anglo-American culture, *Fat Art, Thin Art* and *A Dialogue on Love* provide an entirely unconventional engagement with Sedgwick's more personal experiences of gender and sexual discourses. *Tendencies* and *Touching Feeling* reside somewhere in between the academic and the personal. Not surprisingly, perhaps, critical engagement with Sedgwick's work thus tends to be divided into an academic and theoretical stream and a more autobiographical and creative stream—and her poetry has received very little critical attention at all.

Although combining the critical and the creative parts of Sedgwick's work is not unproblematic, it is nonetheless highly rewarding—and I particularly investigate this in relation to Sedgwick's discussion of queerness and her several personal and theoretical notions of identity categories and what it means to identify. I focus on her roles as writer, teacher, patient, and poet. I trace the emergence of a distinctly discernible and queer stance that emerges throughout the oeuvre, which I choose to call Sedgwick's "queer patience." This is not as "passive" as it may sound; it is rather a specific relationship to experiences, encounters, and other people's processes of identification through her persona and her work, as well as her own identifying processes.

QUEERNESS AND IDENTITY

In his book *Second Skins*, which maps the inconsistencies among various gender studies discourses and ideas of embodied being, the transgender theorist Jay Prosser develops a critical perspective on queer theory and queer approaches to identity.[3] He claims to spot a set of contradictions in early queer theory, and especially in Sedgwick's writing. Although Sedgwick argues that the strict identity categories of contemporary Western society should be exploded in favor of "the open mesh of possibilities, gaps, overlaps, dissonances and resonances, lapses and excesses of meaning where the constituent elements of anyone's gender, of anyone's sexuality aren't made (or can't be made) to signify monolithically,"[4] Prosser spots a growing concern in Sedgwick's writing to find an identity for herself and to justify her role in queer academia. He acknowledges that Sedgwick not merely writes about the lives and concerns of people generally categorized as queer but, at different points in her writing, builds up a discourse of identification both with gay victims of the AIDS epidemic and butch lesbians.[5]

Prosser is not the only critic who has reacted to Sedgwick's identity narratives. Sociologically inclined readers such as Joshua Gamson and Stephen Valocchi similarly consider these concepts with an air of confusion.[6] Why should the sexual identity of the queer theorist have any bearing on his or her text? The many confessional prefaces to canonical queer texts and the often hostile reactions to what has become known as "straight queer" show that to some extent it does.[7] Despite (especially early) queer theory's emphasis on the fluidity and inessential nature of sexual and gender identities, the distinctly directive emphasis on categories of queer prevails in many of the texts that are produced under its umbrella. According to Prosser, Sedgwick's determination to identify with the subjects of her life's work—to find direct points of connection—although she technically did not belong to an aberrant sexual identity category is evidence of the inadequacies and inconsistencies of queer theory as a philosophical discipline. Queer theory may claim to be a practice rather than a label, a doing rather than a being, but when it comes down to it, the various intertextual identity discourses that evolve within queer theorization testify to the fact that being is always going to be at its forefront.

As Edwards confirms, Sedgwick's sexuality and gender identity was a point of concern to her at several points in her career, but she used these moments as critical points of transport and self-reflection rather than stabilizing identity categories.[8] Prosser, Gamson, and Valocchi are not recognizing the narratological nuances and ethos behind Sedgwick's writing. In the same section of "Queer and Now," in *Tendencies*, in which she argues that queer is the space where gender and sexuality cannot be made to "signify monolithically," she also describes queer as "the experimental linguistic, epistemological, representational, political adventures attaching to the very many of us who may at times be moved to describe ourselves."[9] Acts of identification do not necessarily involve final stable identities—and they certainly never become such in Sedgwick's work. Queer for Sedgwick was the mode through which identification—not just single acts, but continual processes of identification—take place at the same time that it is the means by which any illusion of stability is broken down.

There certainly are processes of identification within queer scholarship; implicit coming-out narratives appear throughout the queer canon, but although such narratives may be inconsistent with a strict anti-essentialism, they are not inconsistent with Sedgwick's conception of queerness.[10] Identifying discourses are formulated as a means of reflection and reconsideration. The moments of identification that Prosser refers to in Sedgwick's writing are not merely reminiscent of the coming-out trend in queer texts of the 1990s but contextualize, challenge, and reflect on it. Like many of the most innovative writers in the history of Anglo-American literature,[11] Sedgwick uses a pre-existing genre to problematize boundaries and generic specification. For example, the differences and similarities that are played out between the social implications of Sedgwick's fatness and Michael Moon's homosexuality and AIDS in the reprinted "Divinity" section of *Tendencies* both break down and further emphasize the uniqueness of socially ostracized groups—and they do this through a type of narrative that is usually used to signal simplistic collective otherness.

There is more to Sedgwick's coming-out narratives than mere critique, however. Throughout her work, Sedgwick measures and explores the very depths and limits of self-narration. In adherence to the poststructuralist tradition she comes out of, Sedgwick does not consider narratives merely expressions of identifying processes. Her narratives are her identity, and, like any good story, they are constantly being reread, rewritten, reconceived, and redisseminated. As she confirms in "A Poem Is Being Written," reprinted in *Tendencies*, Sedgwick never considers her identity narratives finished texts. Just as "change as well as vicariousness" take the place of the traditional subject,[12] insertions, exclusions, and continual poetic additions take the place of the traditional story. Texts, like identities, cannot and should not be erased, but they will never remain the same from one moment to the next or from one reader to another.

"A Poem Is Being Written" finishes with a poem in which the older Eve of the present speaks to the young Eve of the past, expressing a simultaneous wish and fretful resistance to give life to her voice one more time: "I like standing in, / in unconscious magic, for your pay, / your turd, your baby; but more, I'm scared / by the scalding rush to the eyes, the rush to finish—and your / resistance to it."[13] The authorial persona that emerges here simultaneously reveals and eludes its origin. Neither her past nor her present identity is ever fully stabilized. She fantasizes about a passionate conjunction of these two characters, "a night we can spend together, a night to make good what so far is only the raging sift of the detail of impatient arousal," but she recognizes that even such a moment will not make her identity more stable, coherent, or real: "It won't be more our own than other nights."[14] This writing practice, in which Sedgwick allows herself and all the ghosts of herself to form and uniform, to embrace and yet remain separate, is in several ways undeniably queer.

Identity narratives are not solely about self-identification, however. They are also about community and connection, and if there is one thing Sedgwick's work has accomplished, it is a sense of shared intimacy. Sedgwick asks in *Touching Feeling*, "What does it mean to fall in love with a writer? What does it mean, for that matter—or maybe we should ask, *what else* could it mean to cathect in a similar way a theoretical moment not one's own?"[15] What else, indeed, does it mean to fall in love with Eve Kosofsky Sedgwick? Could it be that we yearn to embrace the intensely intimate outside of ourselves?

Most readers of Sedgwick's work express an intensely personal relationship to her, and although for many of the contributors to this volume this stems from a significant friendship and intimate love, most of her avid readers have merely come in contact with Sedgwick through her writing. Her writing communicates in a way that "touches" in several senses of the word. Sedgwick has the ability to speak not merely to us but also for us—and this "us" simultaneously becomes an individual and a shared concept. As Annamarie Jagose acknowledges in a discussion of Sedgwick's writing, the experience of reading Sedgwick is "something like what I imagine it would feel to be fired from a cannon, spangled and spectacular, newly aerodynamic, holding everything together—including a temporarily aerial perspective—courtesy of an extrinsic propulsive force."[16] It is a feeling of existing simultaneously in yourself and around yourself—and to be aware that this sphere is both strictly your own and a point of connection.

Sedgwick argues that "people who fall in love with someone wish at the same time to exhibit themselves to others as *being loved*."[17] Interestingly, many of her readers choose to come out about their love and their relationship to Sedgwick. Those who knew her often give a short account of a particularly pertinent comment she made or an occasion on which she spoke, laughed, or reacted in a specifically Eve-esque manner. Those who neither had the privilege to know her beyond the pages of her books nor to hear her speak tend to openly admit to this—and point out that their reading will be colored by this fact. This is certainly not unrelated to the fact that many of the recent publications in relation to Sedgwick's work have been parts of what can more or less be termed memorial special issues, celebrating the important role she has played in academia—and to the fact that she became renowned as a mesmerizing speaker—but it is an interesting trend all the same. Not many writers, academic or otherwise, evoke this degree of personal exposure in their readers. Can it be that we respond to Sedgwick's own practice of narrative exposure?

Personally, I belong to the group of readers who neither knew Sedgwick nor saw her speak, but her writing touches me on a particularly personal level all the same. Her intimate accounts of her childhood and her struggles against social conventions of beauty and health speak to me in a way that hardly any other writing does (be it poetry, theory, or prose). Sedgwick's writing becomes a means through which we simultaneously find ourselves and allow ourselves to become slightly other. It is not dissimilar to what she herself does when she gives life and commences a conversation with her nine-year-old self in "A Poem Is Being Written." We all have our own personal Eves with whom we enter into dialogue and who become our wonderfully intimate, although more or less imaginary, friends. We all give birth to what Kathryn Bond Stockton recognizes as Eve's queer little love children,[18] and this little love child provides a means through which our relationships to her texts—or any texts—will never remain simple.

As Nikki Sullivan acknowledges, this type of writing creates something similar to what we would usually refer to as reader-author identification, but in some ways it is actually closer to what Jean-Luc Nancy called the "being-plural."[19] There is a sense in which readers of Sedgwick's work become individual little parts of the continually expanding set of relations that is Sedgwick: "One cannot be distinguished from the other; which does not mean that they are indistinct."[20] As Stephen Barber and David Clark recognize in their introduction to the collection *Regarding Sedgwick*, a social space is "mobilized around the signifier 'Sedgwick,'" where new ways of relating to the academic individual, existing scholarship, and the act of writing in general are made possible.[21]

Sedgwick herself becomes a queer hub, an "open mesh," through which identity becomes reconceptualized in terms of continual reformation, and the boundaries between writer and reader are made indistinguishable. The act of coming out and the various points of exposure function like generators of further making strange, or strangening, of identity. It is never solid. Sedgwick moves from spot to spot, level to level, and adds more and more voices to her subjective cascade, but when it comes down to it, the concept that connects them is the compulsion that keeps her moving, the urge to expand and expose: "If the night finally / comes when you and I, one sleepless darkness / mimicking another darkness, penetrate / from room to room, or into breathless / room, I needn't wonder if your voice hollows / under mine, sounding delicate, or absent, / the glutted body of that voice being here."[22]

Her identity formation is never stagnant, and each new voice yearns to appear in her texts—in a here and now entwined with the past and the future.

QUEER INTERLUDES

Sedgwick's strangening of identity is negotiated through a type of queer tutelage that leads both author and reader in new directions. As Cindy Patton recognizes, her language thus does not strictly function as a means of communication.[23] It is the instrument through which Sedgwick and each reader of Sedgwick will find their own way to communicate pedagogically and affectively. It functions like a classroom or a catalyst rather than a straightforward set of signposts and signifiers. This is where a reader like Prosser gets lost. Although he engages extensively with poststructuralist theory and acknowledges that the relationship of subject, reality, and discourse cannot be read simplistically, he does not recognize the pedagogic power of identification.

Up to this point I have written primarily about Sedgwick's role as an academic and autobiographical writer, but Sedgwick's texts cannot and should not be separated from her role as teacher. Teaching and writing about identity are both ways to reconfigure it pedagogically; to make it simultaneously strange and real. Sedgwick's idea of pedagogy in *Touching Feeling* positions the writer/teacher as a catalyst, and this pedagogic stance is visible especially in her later work. She writes that she has gradually aimed to take on the role of the disturber of her readers' and students' consciousnesses rather than the distributor of knowledge, and, in the assumption of such a role, she also disturbs her own sense of identity. In the section suggestively titled "Interlude, Pedagogic," she recounts an episode in which she finds herself in the middle of a political disturbance and experiences a wish to leave the bounds of her subjectivity to become part of the mass of protesting people who form the event. She translates this dizzying experience in terms of her classroom. As she is finding herself "as teacher . . . to be less and less at the center of [her] own classroom, [she] was also finding that the voice of a certain abyssal displacement."[24] Every time she enters the "condensing and complexly representative" arena of the classroom, she does so in a new and less authoritative fashion and lets herself be informed by the pedagogic performance in which she takes part.[25] She finds that the role she plays, as well as the purpose of the performance, made more and more strange. She takes part in a continual strangening of each space she inhabits, and as her performances, pedagogy, and writing change, the identities that appear "provide effects that might sometimes wrench the boundaries of discourse around in productive if not always obvious ways."[26]

The most remarkable discursive reversal, or "wrench," Sedgwick produces arguably stems from her power to switch pedagogic perspectives. When forcing her students and readers to reconsider their culturally conditioned ideas of reality, she simultaneously reconceives her own. Sedgwick is a prime example of what Jacques Rancière calls an "ignorant schoolmaster."[27] She abandons didactic pedagogies in favor of a classroom negotiated through mutual exchange. She affects her students by virtually becoming one of them. In *Tendencies*, she argues that "knowledge is not in itself power, although it is the magnetic field of power. Ignorance and opacity collude or compete with it in mobilizing the flows of energy, desire, goods, meaning, persons."[28] The greatest privilege of the teacher is the power to affect, and to affect she has to be prepared to be affected.

The act of pedagogically interluding thus is not merely disruptive but also subjectively disorienting. Sedgwick uses affective encounters as lines of flight. Combining Silvan Tomkins's idea of directionless affect and Gilles Deleuze and Félix Guattari's "interest in planar relations," she forms a theory of injunction in which the "beside" takes center stage, invoking "a number of elements" that "lie alongside one another, though not an infinity of them."[29] For Sedgwick, "Beside comprises a wide range of desiring, identifying, representing repelling, paralleling, differentiating, rivalling, leaning, twisting, mimicking, withdrawing, attracting, aggressing, warping, and other relations."[30] It is the concept of relationality itself; a space where self and other are simultaneously distinct and indistinguishable. In these moments Sedgwick continually transforms herself and finds new, interlinked modes of becoming. As in "A Poem Is Being Written," the different Eves walk hand in hand, beside one another. As she becomes abstract, she becomes intimate; as she becomes teacher, she becomes student; and as she becomes older and frailer, she becomes young and healthy once more.

QUEER PATIENCE

The image that appears in the diffracted sections of this chapter are of an Eve Kosofsky Sedgwick emerging through three primary modes of becoming— her role as theorist and teacher, her role as friend and autobiographical writer, and her role as patient and student. I believe Sedgwick herself would argue that the most pivotal of these is her role as patient and patiently open-minded student. In her semiconfessional memoir *A Dialogue on Love*, she writes,

"Apparently it's as a patient I want to emerge."[31] Sedgwick certainly assumed the role of patient on various occasions and for various reasons throughout the 1990s and early 2000s, and in many ways it is as such that the public as well as the private persona her work discloses *does* emerge—and it is in this form that her writing becomes most powerful. As Elizabeth Stephens suggests, the Sedgwick who appears in *A Dialogue on Love* is not only the most narratologically subversive but also the queerest in late twentieth- and early twenty-first-century queer theory.[32]

Sedgwick's "A Poem Is Being Written," "Divinity," and "White Glasses" in *Tendencies*, *Touching Feeling*, and *A Dialogue on Love*, respectively, are the instigators of a new form of writing, a queer patienthood and patience that functions as a narratology of continual emergence. Her strong yet passive "I" voice, which Edwards distinguishes as "neither a simple, settled, congratulatory 'I,' nor a fragmented postmodernist, post-individual—never mind an unreliable narrator," continually pushes the boundaries of what we consider critical/creative/theoretical and autobiographical writing.[33] Edwards recognizes that she has "employed her subjectivity as an example of the almost grotesquely unintelligent design of every human psyche."[34] The self-imposed interdependence and active passivity of the patient is also indicative of the way Sedgwick positions herself to her reading, writing, and teaching. She continually reiterates the importance of not merely interpreting, but letting herself be interpreted. Sedgwick's texts attempt to open up a space for productive communication and affective encounters rather than provide definitive answers. She "draws her readers' attention to the impossibility of the fascination at the center of her own writing, and of the (auto)biographical act in which it is grounded: autobiography is a public account that produces particular aspects of a life as personal and private in order to 'reveal' them to the reader."[35]

Sedgwick's queer patience develops a particular relationship to reading and writing about her body—a stance through which these two modes become practically indiscernible. It involves becoming the passive intermediary of one's own writing and reading experience, allowing them to communicate and correspond and accept the way they transform themselves. According to the emerging field of scholarship known as narrative medicine, reading and writing practices are active means of care and cure. In her seminal book *Narrative Medicine*, Rita Charon argues that the act of writing about pain and illness and the resulting narratives of patienthood open their authors up to new connections between their own changing bodies and the bodies of the people surrounding them.[36] This type of writing is queer in itself, by virtue of the fact that it changes the way readers and writers consider their relationship to each other, but this queerness gains particular valence for Sedgwick because she continually queers herself and her writing even as she writes. Her bedside stories are littered with queer "besides"; thus, she leads queer theory back to its most pivotal basics: the breakdown of normative and "healthy" conceptions of reality, relationships, and the body.

Queer theory has always taken a keen interest in medical discourses of health and embodiment. Indeed, if the genealogy of queer theory is traced to Michel Foucault, queer embodiment and queer practices directly respond to the dominant medical tropes of normality. Sedgwick's writing draws queer resistance to the medicalized view of the body in Western culture in a new set of directions. Her writing about embodiment and illness is no longer a matter of pathologization; it is a transformative process of speaking, writing, and scarification. Charon argues that wounded patients usually attempt to hide themselves, building a secret fortress, or space of communication, between themselves and their bodies. The act of writing tears down the walls of this space, opening it up to connections that will expose the wounded flesh to further pain, but in the end may lead to the construction of a hardier stretch of scarified skin.[37] Sedgwick's texts leave the scarified areas of her body visible. Her processes of becoming can be traced through the patterns that emerge on her skin. These scars are not signs of self-pity or pain. They tell stories of resistance, empathy, and connection.

The queer patience of *Tendencies*, *Touching Feeling*, and *A Dialogue on Love* is thus a spatial narrative practice. Sedgwick's illness-riddled body is an affective space, where her readers may find comfort and support. It is a narrative hideout in which non-normative bodies and selves can gather strength from each other's experiences. As Rosi Braidotti puts it, each painful experience becomes a "location," or site, of connection: "It is a collectively shared and constructed, jointly occupied spatio-temporal territory."[38] These locations are affective building blocks, negotiated through differently patterned "revisitations and retakes" of shared encounters.[39] Sedgwick weaves a pattern of narratives—a pattern of scarified bodily inscriptions that open her up to further networks of shared strength.

Rita Felski reminds us that anti-spaces and shared vulnerability are not necessarily entirely positive. She suggests that specific and vulnerable spaces define their inhabitants in terms of a compulsory marginality and oppression.[40] According to Felski, there is a tendency among marginal and wounded writers to give what Judith Butler refers to in her eponymous book as "an account of oneself" to claim ownership and agency over certain types of experiences.[41] Resistant hiding spaces can easily turn into guarded territories—or, at worst, impenetrable prisons of pain. They develop conceptions of exclusivity, secrecy, and interiority that close them off from other modes of communication. Scarified spaces function differently. Scars are loci of exteriority rather than interiority. The patterns on the body open themselves up to infinite interpretations. As mentioned earlier, Sedgwick's writing tends to form pluralistic clusters, and her illness narratives are no exception. She uses her times of distress and pain as departure points for discussions of concepts as disparate as Zen Buddhism (*Touching Feeling*) and the AIDS epidemic of the 1990s (*Tendencies*). Her be(d)side stories receive their power from a formative sense of distress.

The emphasis on pain in queer theory has been heavily criticized, not least by Sedgwick herself, but in her illness narratives allusions to pain give rise to affirmative reparation. In the poem "The Use of Being Fat," from her collection *Fat Art, Thin Art*, she momentarily allows the same fatty folds that have caused her so much pain throughout her social life to become the spaces that enfold and protect her loved ones: "[N]o one I loved could come to harm / enfolded in my touch— / the lot of me would blot it up, / the rattling chill, night sweat or terror."[42] In a subsequent poem, she describes her fat in terms of a "mourning" that to an extent parts but more urgently attaches her body to her husband's, a "warm elastic membrane, between us. The girl of 19 who doesn't bear thinking about, for instance; the patience of her young husband, the inexperience and violence, the patience succeeding patience."[43]

It is through this patience that Eve Kosofsky Sedgwick finally becomes a poet—and I now return to the point where I started. Poetry, according to Sedgwick, is a space of love: "'Loving' in truth, I take its shape."[44] This is where we all connect as readers and lovers of Sedgwick's work. We find one another in the poetic flow of her phrases, words, and inflections. In "A Poem Is Being Written," she tells us that it is the love of her present and past selves that lets her speak, and it is love that shapes her narrative flow in *A Dialogue on Love.*[45] Poetry and love are never far from pain in Sedgwick's work. Love nurtures "the finger however loving that sets the harmonic glass to vibrate—and that stays it—the finger however loving on the string, the string's however swollen bite of the finger."[46]

Sedgwick's be(d)side identity narratives are multifaceted and fractured, but in this disparity they find their connective and formative power. Her writing is a space that simultaneously opens us up and brings us together. We find ourselves writing about her and our experience of her over and over again—and throughout our lives and careers, we sense her walking steadily beside us.

NOTES

1 Jason Edwards, *Eve Kosofsky Sedgwick* (Abingdon, UK: Routledge, 2009), 121.
2 Erin Murphy and J. Keith Vincent, eds., "Honoring Eve" (special issue), *Criticism* 52, no. 2 (Spring 2010): 166.
3 Jay Prosser, *Second Skins: The Body Narratives of Transsexuality* (New York: Columbia University Press, 1998).
4 Eve Kosofsky Sedgwick, *Tendencies* (Durham, NC: Duke University Press, 1993), 8.
5 Prosser, *Second Skins*, 96.
6 Joshua Gamson, "Must Identity Movements Self-Destruct? A Queer Dilemma," *Social Problems* 42, no. 3 (1995): 390–407; Stephen Valocchi, "Not Yet Queer Enough: The Lessons of Queer Theory for the Sociology of Gender and Sexuality," *Gender and Society* 19, no. 6 (2005): 750–70.
7 See, e.g., the preface to the 1999 reprint of Judith Butler's *Gender Trouble: Feminism and the Subversion of Identity* (New York: Routledge, 1999) and the introduction to Jack/Judith Halberstam's *In a Queer Time and Place* (New York: New York University Press, 2005). On the controversy of straight queer, see Nikki Sullivan, *A Critical Introduction to Queer Theory* (Edinburgh: Edinburgh University Press, 2003), 141–42.
8 Edwards, *Eve Kosofsky Sedgwick*, 124. Edwards argues that she underwent what he refers to as "painful pedagogies" of self-realization, writing, "These included teaching a women's studies class in which, introducing a section on lesbian issues, Sedgwick apologized that as a non-lesbian she felt at a disadvantage at understanding the material; and in response to which a group of students told her, firmly but kindly, that she mustn't do *that* again."
9 Sedgwick, *Tendencies*, 8.
10 Adele Scholock investigates these at great length in "Queer in the First Person: Academic Autobiography and the Authoritative Contingencies of Visibility," *Cultural Critique* 66 (2007): 127–59. Although the anti-essentialism of queer theory is often reiterated in introductions and references to queer theory, it is nowhere to be found in most of the canonical queer works. The concept of anti-

essentialism infers an active rejection of any essentialism of identity. Sedgwick, for example, is more a non-essentialist than an anti-essentialist; she denies the existence of an unchangeable essential identity, but she still embraces and takes a great interest in processes of identity formation.

11 This is possibly particularly true for Henry James, whose work Sedgwick, of course, writes about and engages with extensively. Sedgwick also makes the link between genre and (both gender and sexual) identity on several occasions: see, e.g., Eve Kosofsky Sedgwick, "A Poem Is Being Written," *Representations* 17 (Winter 1987): 117.

12 Sedgwick, *Tendencies*, 178.

13 Sedgwick, *Tendencies*, 214.

14 Sedgwick, *Tendencies*, 213.

15 Eve Kosofsky Sedgwick, *Touching Feeling: Affect, Pedagogy, Performativity* (Durham, NC: Duke University Press, 2003), 117, emphasis added.

16 Annamarie Jagose, "Thinkiest," PMLA 125, no. 2 (April 2010): 379.

17 Sedgwick, *Touching Feeling*, 117.

18 See Kathryn Bond Stockton, "Eve's Queer Child," in *Regarding Sedgwick: Essays on Queer Culture and Critical Theory*, ed. Stephen M. Barber and David L. Clark (New York: Routledge, 2002), 181–200.

19 Jean-Luc Nancy, *Being Singular Plural* (Stanford, CA: Stanford University Press, 2000), 54.

20 Nikki Sullivan, "Being, Thinking, Writing 'With,'" *Cultural Studies Review* 9, no. 1 (2003): 55.

21 Stephen M. Barber and David L. Clark, "Queer Moments: The Performative Temporalities of Eve Sedgwick," in Barber and Clark, *Regarding Sedgwick: Essays on Queer Culture and Critical Theory*, 31.

22 Eve Kosofsky Sedgwick, *Fat Art, Thin Art* (Durham, NC: Duke University Press, 1994), 214.

23 Cindy Patton, "Love without the Obligation to Love," *Criticism* 52, no. 2 (2010): 215–24.

24 Sedgwick, *Touching Feeling*, 34.

25 Sedgwick, *Touching Feeling*, 34.

26 Sedgwick, *Touching Feeling*, 34.

27 Karin Sellberg and Lena Wånggren, "Intersectionality and Dissensus: A Negotiation of the Feminist Classroom," *Equality, Diversity and Inclusion* 31, nos. 5–6 (2012): 549–51.

28 Sedgwick, *Tendencies*, 23.

29 Sedgwick, *Touching Feeling*, 8.

30 Sedgwick, *Touching Feeling*, 8.

31 Eve Kosofsky Sedgwick, *A Dialogue on Love* (Boston: Beacon, 2000), 1.

32 Elizabeth Stephens, "Queer Memoir: Public Confession and/as Sexual Practice in Eve Kosofsky Sedgwick's *A Dialogue on Love*," *Australian Humanities Review*

48 (2010), http://press-files.anu.edu.au/downloads/press/p41611/html/04 .xhtml?referer=1295&page=5.

33 Edwards, *Eve Kosofsky Sedgwick*, 122.

34 Edwards, *Eve Kosofsky Sedgwick*, 122.

35 Stephens, "Queer Memoir."

36 Rita Charon, *Narrative Medicine: Honoring the Stories of Illness* (Oxford: Oxford University Press, 2006), 85–86.

37 Charon, *Narrative Medicine*, 91–92.

38 Rosi Braidotti, *Metamorphoses: Towards a Materialist Theory of Becoming* (Cambridge: Polity, 2002), 12.

39 Braidotti, *Metamorphoses*, 12.

40 Rita Felski, *Beyond Feminist Aesthetics* (London: Hutchinson Radius, 1989), 47.

41 Judith Butler, *Giving an Account of Oneself* (New York: Fordham University Press, 2005), 3.

42 Sedgwick, *Fat Art, Thin Art*, 15.

43 Sedgwick, *Fat Art, Thin Art*, 35.

44 Sedgwick, *Fat Art, Thin Art*, 201.

45 Sedgwick, *Fat Art, Thin Art*, 214.

46 Sedgwick, *Fat Art, Thin Art*, 151.

Weaver's Handshake

The Aesthetics of Chronic Objects
(Sedgwick, Emerson, James)

> We are the photometers, we the irritable goldleaf and tinfoil that measure the accumulations of the subtle element. We know the authentic effects of the true fire through every one of its million disguises.
> —Ralph Waldo Emerson, "Spiritual Laws"

In his essay *Nature* (1836), Emerson invokes what he calls a "theory of nature," inviting us to think about a theory as problematic and surprising as nature itself.[1] Beyond the boilerplate of the double genitive, the flexibility of this "of" between theory and nature speaks to Emerson's interest in minimizing the ontological distance between the theorizing and the thing being theorized. The unabsorbable appeal of this "of" recalls Paul Grimstad's account of what in Emerson most lends itself to the radical empiricism of William James. "For such a philosophy," James writes, "the relations that connect experiences must themselves be experienced relations, and any kind of relation experienced must be accounted as 'real' as anything else in the system."[2] If the "of," as an object, belongs to theory and nature alike, it's not entirely clear how one might best think through this category of objects between, as Jacques Lacan might say, the glove and the hand.[3]

As a grammatical unit, "of" ordinarily vanishes into the words it holds together. Here, it is an experience as much as theory is an expression and act of nature. In the wake of "our Cartesian moment,"[4] the difficulty posed to thinking by objects about which one doesn't quite know how or what to think describes the neither-quite-subject-nor-object of a particular strain of queer theory connecting the work of Emerson to that of Eve Kosofsky Sedgwick. Along related lines, Jordana Rosenberg has recently analyzed queer theory's involution with theories of materialism, informed by William James no less than by Alfred North Whitehead or Baruch Spinoza. Rosenberg argues that this ontological turn conceals a primitivism bound to the separation of objects from the social sphere. Of queer theory's recent fascination with "the object"—specifically, that queerly, aleatorily resistant object, the molecule—Rosenberg asks, "Would it be unorthodox to suggest that what was once a methodological question attending queer theory at its outset—what is theory's relation to its object?—has now taken on the character of an a priori answer? In other words, we no longer ask: *what is the object of queer studies?* Rather, the object of queer studies—at the present moment—appears to be *the* object."[5] The slippery nonequivalence of "[queer] theory's relation to its object" and "the object of queer studies" suggests the shiftlessness of the shift that Rosenberg describes, an unresolved set of remainders that equally subtend and undermine what Emerson calls our most unhandsome condition.

Elsewhere in *Contingent Figure*, I ask what difference genre makes in terms of Elaine Scarry's inclination in *The Body in Pain* to think about pain as a question of narrative rather than poetics.[6] I similarly wonder how a turn from narrative to poetics might open along an edge of Rosenberg's thinking a place for the kind of Emersonian objects that sustain Sedgwick's attention. For instance, in reminding us that "'the object' has been a foundational question for queer studies," Rosenberg points to Judith Butler's "unsettling the appearance of [the] ontological reality" of the "object" that "was sex/gender."[7] An inverting of Emerson, Butler's reading takes an object previously supposed natural—through an atavism strategically posited beyond the social frame—and restores our sense of its theoretical constitution. Butler's analysis yields a performative object consigned to constant iterations of what in the guise of the natural it had professed to be. Even as performativity and iterability are no less essential to the following lines from Sedgwick's early essay, "Privileges of Unknowing," the object to which they accrue, by contrast, isn't theoretical or abstract so much as figuratively vivid:

> In fact, the delineation of "the sexual" in this convent, in this reading, is done by a process that resembles gravestone-rubbing. The dense back-and-forth touch of the crayon leaves a positive map not of excrescences but of lines of absent or excised matter. And the pressure of insistence that makes a continuous legibility called sexual knowledge emerge from and take the shape of the furrows of prohibition or of stupor is, most powerfully, the reader's energy of need, fear, repudiation, projection.[8]

Notwithstanding its correspondence to the object that is Butler's "sex/gender," "the sexual" here is all but eclipsed by the passage's translation of it into the continuous present tense—what I am inclined to call the chronic object—of the aestheticized and aestheticizing figure of gravestone rubbing. That the predicate of the sentence under way is "the sexual" gratuitously amplifies the erotic energy inherent in the process that these lines describe. Sedgwick's metaphorical vehicle and tenor catch and drag, even as the fidelity of the grave-robbing—if not as vehicle than as nonfigurative practice—depends on the maintenance of the uniformity of the hand that effects it. Sedgwick seems to introduce gravestone rubbing as an approximately transparent medium; we are asked, after all, to read the furrows as though they were "made legible," rather than written. And yet the ingenious extravagance of the comparison also implies that the more it helps us see what is otherwise occluded, the more what we are seeing might be on account of the weight of a hand. If, in the case of Butler's "sex/gender," what had seemed material reappears at the end of a process of reading as abstract, Sedgwick's comparison demonstrates the interesting difficulties that arise when such inversions become the coefficients of an analogy. This difficulty of knowing how to distinguish the properties of the sexual from "the sexual" from the equivocally material and only somewhat transparent medium out of which either appears returns us to the Emersonian project of minimizing if not quite dissolving the differences between theory and nature.

The dense "back-and-forth touch" of Sedgwick's analysis anticipates the activity at the lightning-rod heart of *Tendencies*'s notorious chapter, "Jane Austen and the Masturbating Girl," in which Sedgwick juxtaposes passages from *Sense and Sensibility* with examples such as the following from "Onanism and Nervous Disorders in Two Little Girls": "In addition to the practices already cited, X . . . provoked the voluptuous spasm by rubbing herself on the angles of furniture, by pressing her thighs together. . . . One night she succeeds in rubbing herself till the blood comes on the straps that bind her."[9] While Sedgwick doesn't entirely discount the authenticity of this "narrative structured as a case history," or, for that matter, its publication in 1881, I expect that the *frisson* that her writing registers for these lines actually is intensified by their implicit (and eventually, confirmed) fraudulence.[10] The text's titillating frustration of a reader's assumption of veracity leads me to think about the counterfeit Foucauldian document in terms of what Daniel Tiffany, following Susan Stewart, calls the distressed genre of the imitation ballad. The lurid recoil of not being able to tell an authentic text from a sham generates, for Tiffany, the flinch of kitsch.[11]

The possible imbrication of kitsch with the surveillant rise (circa 1881) of the Foucauldian sexual subject is an important context for Sedgwick's own influential articulation of kitsch's relation to queerness. As I note in this essay's next section, that Sedgwick's writing has given us a theory of kitsch is not separable from the frequency with which she seems to have induced something like a kitsch response in many of her critics. Sentimental and florid: a way to describe both the theory and the style of the writing in which the theory occurs. It is arguably in this confluence (of, we might say, radical empiricism and aesthetics) that Sedgwick's queer theory is most Emersonian. But to return to the rubbing at hand: that the girls waver in and out of seeming real as subjects of history in general and medical scrutiny in particular isn't incidental to how Sedgwick helps us think about their rubbing themselves to bloody distraction. Like Hawthorne's "discovery" of the artifact that is the scarlet letter, Sedgwick's attention to this spurious text is all the keener because of the possibility that its insatiably rubbing subjects—stand-ins, not insignificantly, for Sedgwick herself—might not be "real" at all. That the rubbing surveilled in the fake case study could seem ontologically compatible with the rubbing as which Sedgwick describes the sexual lends this flickering connection between scenes the feel of substantial presence, at once established and hollowed out by a chronicity figured in and across both scenes as out of thin air.

Even though this scene does not belong to the object-world in the sense understood by Rosenberg and the object-oriented ontology (OOO) theorists she critiques, it's an object-world nonetheless. Its terms resonate with those of Rosenberg's admonitory claim that "the turn to ontology" is an "origin narrative . . . that takes the form of appearance of a methodology, but that is, in essence, driven by a figural logic."[12] And yet the figural logic by which Sedgwick's lines are driven is of a different granular order from the one Rosenberg describes in part because it is, in a certain sense, literal. To adapt Leo Bersani's formulation, "the dense back-and-forth touch of the crayon" is an inaccurate replication of Sedgwick's pen or her fingers on an early computer keyboard. Nonetheless, it's hard not to imagine Sedgwick inside the scene being conjured. This is all the more the case insofar as grave rubbing, somewhere between writing and craft, uncannily compresses her evolution to and from the high stylistic verve associated with *Epistemology of the Closet* and *Tendencies*, of which this passage is exemplary. Far more than is usually acknowledged, Sedgwick's investment as a critic in her own writerly style is unthinkable apart from her lifelong sense of poetry as a first calling. At the same time, Sedgwick's eventual migration to the differently capacity-making medium of textiles—

precipitated by what she sometimes describes as a waning investment in authorial control—is as much an intensification of her long-standing attachments as it is a turning away. What follows traces some of the continuities between her earlier and later conceptions of herself as poet, theorist, and artist.

First, though, I want to return to Emerson and the Orphic chant that concludes *Nature*. As a mythology of the fall of man *as* the birth of objects, the chant complements Sedgwick's attention to what in the gravestone passage she hauntingly calls "excised matter." In its conjuring the cutting off of a limb or organ, Sedgwick's "excised" is homologous with what in "Experience" Emerson calls "caducous": "So is it with this calamity: it does not touch me: something which I fancied was a part of me, which could not be torn away without tearing me, nor enlarged without enriching me, falls off from me, and leaves no scar. It was caducous. I grieve that grief can teach me nothing, nor carry me one step into real nature."[13] The disorienting alacrity of this caducous falling away is a variation on the Orphic chant's myth of externizing:

> Man is the dwarf of himself. Once he was permeated and dissolved by spirit. He filled nature with his overflowing currents. . . . The laws of his mind, the periods of his actions externized themselves into day and night, into the year and the seasons. But, having made for himself this huge shell, his waters retired; he no longer fills the veins and veinlets; he is shrunk to a drop. He sees that, the structure still fits him, but fits him colossally. Say, rather, once it fitted him, now it corresponds to him from far and on high. He adores timidly his own work.[14]

I appreciate this passage next to Sedgwick's account of "the sexual" because it suggests that the spatial relations literalized in grave rubbing's paper over stone belong to a spectrum of the ever dilating centrifugal distance between correspondences. Unlike Sedgwick's figurative words "magically" arising in the feel of a crayon for what it passes over, Emerson's myth of the waters retiring is like a *Trauerspiel* that never quite comes to life. That it doesn't come to life is precisely the point. The extravagance of the myth is an amplifying symptom of the exaggeration the myth describes, as though hyperbole and observation were different in degree rather than kind.

What this pathos of cosmic estrangement is least able to conjure is what Sedgwick, following Henry James, calls the middle range. In Emerson's lines, the middle range is experienced, if at all, as the cavernousness of its qualities grown imperceptible. It is like air—neutral, abstract—or like "like" or "of." Bearing in mind the botany of caducousness, we might say that Emerson encounters the textures of the world as if they were phantom pains. "The wholeness we admire in the order of the world," he writes, "is the result of infinite distribution. Its smoothness is the smoothness of the pitch of the cataract. Its permanence is a perpetual inchoation. Every natural fact is an emanation also, and from every emanation is a new emanation."[15] Another way to describe the situation this cataclysm hyperbolically stands in for is that the suffering of the loss of a relation to an object isn't distinguishable from suffering the loss of the object and is symptomatic of the loss itself. This confusion of categories pervades the strangeness of Emerson's claim in "Experience" that he grieves that grief can teach him nothing, as though the loss of his son were mistakable for the grief that follows the loss of his son, in turn mistakable for grief over the insufficiency of grief.

Although the Orphic chant doesn't explicitly mention feeling, it's nonetheless "permeated and dissolved" by it insofar as feeling, like reading, is so often synonymous for Emerson with the intractable perception of distance between one's self and the world for which one feels. It's not that Emerson is asking us to believe in the primordial ruin as a historical fact, not least because the logic of facts is coextensive for him with confronting the world as though it were a set of objects and we the scrutinizing subject.[16] Rather, I take Emerson to be suggesting that this scalarly disorienting vision is how a certain relation to objects *feels*. I've elsewhere discussed chronic pain as a realism of hyperbole; even if these lines don't mention pain per se, they illuminate how pain shapes a world that is neither internal nor external to it. Lacan thinks about pain—chronic pain in particular—in analogous terms, as an inhabiting of the landscape one has become:

> The complex character of pain, the character that, so to speak, makes it an intermediary between afferent and efferent, is suggested by the surprising results of certain operations, which in the case of some internal illnesses, including some cancers, allow the notation of pain to be preserved, when the suppression or removal of a certain subjective quality has been effected, which accounts for the fact that it is unbearable. . . . I will . . . limit myself to suggesting that we should perhaps conceive of pain as a field which . . . opens precisely onto that limit where a living being has no possibility of escape.
>
> Isn't something of this suggested to us by the insight of the poets in that myth of Daphne transformed into a tree under the pressure of a pain from which she cannot flee? Isn't it true that the living being who has no possibility of escape suggests in its very form the presence of what one might

call petrified pain? Doesn't what we do in the realm of stone suggest this? To the extent that we don't let it roll, but erect it, and make of it something fixed, isn't there in architecture itself a kind of actualization of pain?[17]

Not only does Lacan, like Emerson, imagine pain as both more and less than the object it might otherwise have been. He also, like Emerson, thinks about the vicissitudes of the objects of pain in terms of the poet, who, for Emerson, "stands one step nearer to things, and sees the flowing or metamorphosis."[18] Looking ahead to Sedgwick's predilection for lyric, chronic objects, the poet's "insight" is most salient for Lacan because it intuits a relation between trying to imagine the experience of pain and the experience (such as that might be) as though it were inseparable from the pulsation—perpetual inchoation, incessant capsizing of unending movement into stasis—of anthropomorphosis.

The recent decision to take notes in my original copies of Sedgwick's books in ink instead of pencil feels surprisingly drastic.[19] Floating beside the new marks are the earlier ones in pencil, from when trying to make sense of her writing had all the imagined, *Nachträglichkeit* urgency of learning the language of the country unfolding from under me. What was the language, that first summer, for carrying *Epistemology of the Closet* less as book than transitional object, like the book with which Charlotte Stant steels herself, fleeing unsuccessfully to a garden's canicular heat from the terms, strictly speaking, she, no less than James, at some earlier point might have claimed proudly as her own?[20] What was the language for having brought with me, that afternoon of reading on the University of California, Berkeley, campus, a neon yellow and quickly fading neoprene messenger bag bought at the gift shop from my first and only visit to the Louvre, or, as I sat under a tree absorbed in the woeful and fruitless first efforts at cruising, for coming to the mortifying realization that the bag, surely flung with the insouciance of some new variation on the inveterate rhythms of the compensatory, was lying in a new pile of dog shit, as though the olfactory under the right conditions were as affectively susceptible to slow motion as vision or sound? The language and the country, it turns out, belonged to what Sedgwick, several years after *Epistemology of the Closet*, would call queer performativity: that of the demolishing interruption of self-spending theatricality both by and as an experience of shame transformable perhaps only by a subsequent version of the readerly self of which that younger one up until this very moment was unaware.[21]

In ink, even desultory marks seem to contradict note taking's spirit of off-the-cuff, what Sedgwick following Flaubert might call note taking as *idée recue*: "The interpretive paths by which there is any sense to be made of him are completely paved, as I'm afraid I may be unable to stop demonstrating, with the *idées recues* of homophobic 'worldly wisdom.'"[22] In other hands, this peppering of English with French might register as cacozelia, "a stylistic affectation of diction, such as throwing in foreign words to appear learned."[23] Cacozelia, from the Greek κᾰκοζηλία (unhappy imitation), sounds like something Sedgwick would appreciate—after all, it names a species of the snobbish habit that makes minor James and Proust characters recognizable as such.[24] Contra J. L. Austin's sense of theatricality as performatively nullifying (e.g., a wedding performed within a play), "unhappy imitation" bespeaks the inseparability of style from thinking about the performative felicity of mimetic acts. More generally, it calls our attention to the affective gamut on which any given imitative act might fall. That some forms of imitation are unhappy or make us so (and some are/make us happy) recalls in its deceptive simplicity the empirical vigor, revolutionary as the Wittenberg theses on the sale of indulgences, of the axioms at the outset of *Epistemology of the Closet*. In the manner of indulgences, my speculation on what Sedgwick might hypothetically appreciate helps me appreciate, among other things, the difficulty sometimes of telling imitations apart.

Insofar as Quintilian's definition of "cacozelia" conjures the lavishness toward which Sedgwick's critics and devotees equally gravitate, it may be unsurprising how closely it lines up with the spoken and unspoken criteria of *Philosophy and Literature*'s "bad writers of the year." "Unhappy imitation" manages to describe the potential indistinguishability of what Dennis Dutton calls "kitsch theorists" from the real thing.[25] The fault line that sets Quintilian's definition apart from Dutton's is that of sincerity. Amid all the licenses bad writing might take, one of Dutton's few requirements for contest entries is that they "be non-ironic," since "deliberate parody cannot be allowed where unintended self-parody is so wide-spread."[26] Like Jack Spratt's wife (although in stylistic terms, Dutton and Quintilian alike occupy the nonuxorious position of *eat no fat*), Quintilian oppositely insists that cacozelia is allergic to sincerity, even as the prodigiousness of Sedgwick's style seems nothing if not sincere. Cacozelia, Quintilian writes,

> or perverse affectation, is a fault in every kind of style: for it includes all that is turgid, trivial, luscious, redundant, far-fetched or extravagant, while

the same name is also applied to virtues carried to excess, when the mind loses its critical sense and is misled by the false appearance of beauty, the worst of all offenses against style, since other faults are due to carelessness, but this is deliberate. This form of affectation, however, affects style alone. For the employment of arguments which might equally well be advanced by the other side, or are foolish, inconsistent or superfluous, are all faults of matter, whereas corruption of style is revealed in the employment of improper or redundant words, in obscurity of meaning, effeminacy of rhythm, or in the childish search for similar or ambiguous expressions. Further, it always involves insincerity, even though all insincerity does not imply affectation. For it consists in saying something in an unnatural or unbecoming or superfluous manner.[27]

If Sedgwick suggests that the difference between kitsch and camp is the difference between *who on earth would ever want that* and *this has my name all over it*, then somewhere between these modes, to borrow one of Sedgwick's *mots justes*, is the vicariating impulse of *this has* her *name all over it* (she would *love* that), which this passage does.

The finality of the blue ink sets into relief the pencil's earlier scenes of reading, which retrospectively seem both mystified and trusting, tentative and zealous. To move from *Epistemology of the Closet* to Sedgwick's essay on queer performativity: "The first of these scouring depressions was precipitated in 1895 by what James experienced as the obliterative failure of his ambitions as a playwright, being howled off the stage at the premiere of *Guy Domville*."[28] No pencil there. The pencil is waiting for "narcissism/shame circuit," which it circles. It underlines "in the prefaces is using reparenting or 'reissue' as a strategy for dramatizing and integrating shame, in the sense of rendering this potentially paralyzing affect narratively, emotionally, and performatively productive."[29] The blue pen circles "scouring," whose economy conjures the upstairs-downstairs drama of feeling's textural relation to the person who feels it. As a singular verb of exasperatingly repetitive action, "scouring" choreographically forces depression to its hands and knees—or does depression do this to James?—immersed (physically if not otherwise), red-knuckled, in a labor whose *fata morgana terminus* we hear in *Annie*'s "And if this floor don't shine like the top of the Chrysler Building, your backsides will." At the same time, scouring won't tell us whether depression is being compared to a scullery maid or the Bon Ami (signature combination of tallow soap and feldspar) at her side, the hermeneutic challenge of which, Sedgwick suggests in *A Dialogue on Love*, is constitutive:

"It's just so much easier for me to envision things in discrete parts. But then you come along and smudge up the barriers, and it's really different. It's important for you to keep doing that—I really think I am getting it."

Deconstruction 101, I do *not* say impatiently.

Then he asks, when I was involved in these scouring devaluations of myself, could I tell whose voice it was that I was hearing in my head?

Me: "I think that's an important question"—meaning I can't answer it—"but there's something else I want to say about it."[30]

Perhaps because the image in my head is of *Guy Domville* wiping James's floors clean, my first inclination is to think of scouring in terms of detergent, the root of which, *tergo*, denotes both the wiping and the backside in need of it. Only subsequently do I remember scouring's less abrasive, epistemological register, the scavenging of a landscape as for clues.[31]

As Beatrix replies to Trollope in Sedgwick's Victorian novella in verse *The Warm Decembers*, "Oh, Uncle Cosmo will stay out / Nimrodding while there's light anywhere—/ scouring his horizons."[32] Sunlight and Cosmo alike are scourers, as are acolytes of cacozelia, "childishly search[ing]" for expression. As object of scrutiny, the horizon (let alone "horizons") illuminates the rigor with which scouring searches out texture in a field of vision worn epistemo-logically smooth: in the case of James, a smoothness itself the synchronous result of depression's scrubbing fervor. Epistemologically, scouring locates texture where there had been none (the stubble of a field versus "the flat, the blueless / aerated tones of earth—and glazed, like pastry," as the field appears on the horizon), even as scouring detergently wears down buildup to a smooth polish.[33]

In an essay that is contemporary with Sedgwick's "A Poem Is Being Written," Jonathan Culler distinguishes between two modes of reading: the lyrical and the descriptive. Culler's terminology clarifies my understanding of Sedgwick's high critical style, its gregarious enactment of charisma, its bottomless car-pet bag of rhetorical intensities. Specifically, the lyrical—and in "A Poem Is Being Written," the lyrical as inextricable from Sedgwick's sense of herself as a poet—gives us a way to think about style in terms of its relation to the ob-jects it mobilizes. "Critics," Culler writes, "have characteristically translated apostrophe into description ('O Rose, thou art sick,' is an intensified way of describing the rose as sick), but what the lyric or a lyrical reading (to use Paul de Man's term) does is to translate description into apostrophe and anthropomorphism."[34] If "scouring depression" operates "not as a truth or assertion but as dramatized experience of a consciousness," the scouringly "corrosive but magical substance" of this consciousness belongs to neither James nor Sedgwick but to the scouring, an exemplarily tergiversating quilting point between read and written texts.[35]

Lacan's quilting point—"the point at which the signified and signifier are knotted together, between the still floating mass of meanings"[36]—describes a space imaginable as having been expansive only in the precise moment of being compressed to an approximation of that single point. I take this to be the force, in part, of Lacan's observation that it "enables everything that happens in this discourse to be situated retroactively and prospectively."[37] The quilting point incessantly converts what it holds together from two dimensions to three and back again; this back and forth between dimensions corresponds to the quilting point's own pulsation between being a word and being an object, an animation not unrelated to Culler's understanding of anthropomorphosis. Its simultaneous implying and collapsing of intermediate space repeats the play of pressure and surface from which emerges the grave rubbing, the scouring's pulverizing crystallography. Lacan's own attention to the fractal dimensions of the materiality of language is evident throughout his seminars, as in the possibility of "see[ing] the various dimensions in which the phenomenon of the sentence—I am not saying the phenomenon of meaning—unfolds."[38]

This dimensional mutability helps us differently visualize the oddness of figuration when it seems neither quite metaphorical nor literal. Such is the coalescing, animating force of "the weaver's handshake," a gesture that Sedgwick describes in "Making Things, Practicing Emptiness," published posthumously in *The Weather in Proust*:

> But really I've always loved textiles. I used to sew my own clothes (though ineptly), back in college when I had time for it and no money, and the feel of any kind of fiber between my thumb and fingers—in a gesture I probably got from my grandmother, who also taught me to crochet and embroider—just is the rub of reality, for me. It's funny that the same brushing-three-fingers gesture is mostly understood to whisper of money, the feel of the coin, as a bottom-line guarantee of reality. I've learned that this gesture is also called "the weaver's handshake," because of the way a

fabric person will skip the interpersonal formalities when you're introduced and move directly to a tactile interrogation of what you're wearing.[39]

As a Masonic salute of sorts between textiles and the tactually sensitive
people who love them, this not quite clandestine greeting recalls Sedgwick's
account in *Between Men* of "Whitman" as a "Victorian homosexual shibboleth": "Photographs of Whitman, gifts of Whitman's books, specimens of his
handwriting, news of Whitman, admiring references to 'Whitman' which
seem to have functioned as badges of homosexual recognition, were the currency of a new community that saw itself as created in Whitman's image."[40]
We find in this "currency of a new community" a way to make sense of the
gesture's "whisper of money." The resemblance between these two forms of
address is most striking, not in the way either functions as currency, but in
Sedgwick's intuition of the shibboleth as a kind of quilting point caught in the
act of making fiber art. "In England," Sedgwick writes, "to trace the path of
individual copies of the book, beginning with the remaindered copies of the
1855 *Leaves* scattered abroad by an itinerant pedlar, would be to feel like the
eye of a needle that was penetrating from layer to layer of the literate social
fabric . . . around the connecting thread of manly love."[41]

This plangent and bizarre passage reads like the activation of a heteroge-
neous vision only subsequently reduced to a series of discrete movements from
poet to critic to theorist to fiber artist. "We begin" in a periphery or interruption of literary history, the sort of lost days that Emerson describes as "interca-
lated."[42] In this nearly unimaginable moment, not least in terms of the Emersonian approbation with which the 1855 *Leaves of Grass* is greeted, Whitman's
work wakes (if we might allow it even this animating percipience) to discover
itself unread and undesired: remaindery in England as a dead letter office. It's
in this incapacity that it appears as an object other than the one as which it has
been imagining itself. What is most startling in Sedgwick's passage isn't that
Whitman's poetry is no longer being handled like a body; after all, by the last
lines of "Song of Myself," the poem foresees a version of this ghostliness: "I be-
queath myself to the dirt to grow from the grass I love, / If you want me again
look for me under your boot-soles."[43] What it *can't imagine* (even redistributed
as dead leaves or "drift[ed] . . . in lacy jags") is not having a body, not having a
voice, as though dropped from an anthropomorphosis that may well have been
the figurative move least possible for Whitman himself to shake.

The voice that narrates this scene is as little a reader as the book, in Whitma-
nian terms, is a book. Thus, the eye that traces the book's path (rather than reads

its pages) so quickly gives way to the unseeing eye of a needle. These lines are as much a reversal of Emerson's transparent eyeball as the mute, insensate book is a reversal of Whitman's Emersonian agenda. They are disorienting in part because they treat words, texts, and names as though they were objects without quite knowing how best to navigate a relation to them; we might, for that matter, say that the experience of words as objects is precisely this experience of unmooring. What is the ideal distance or vantage from which to read becomes a question of how many vantages one can sustain more or less at the same time? The sinuous terrain of Sedgwick's sentence does not ask us to choose between the long view of tracing a transatlantic path and the micro-attention by which a needle is threaded. Rather, the coincidence of these ocular orders suggests that as early as *Between Men*, Sedgwick is thinking about simultaneities of reading in terms of fractals and thinking, more specifically, about fractals as the mutual constitution across multiple figurative registers of textile and text. This is not least the case in the turbulence of a reader's eye as it tries to imagine as continuous what otherwise is experienced as the jolts of distance and dimension. What on earth would it "feel like" to be the eye of this needle as it penetrates "layer to layer of the . . . social fabric"?[44] The Whitman with which we are familiar would keen at the touch, let alone pierce, of a needle. But can this remaindered, transatlantic *Leaves of Grass*, the one without a voice (which is to say, at least in Sedgwick's imagination of the scene, without consciousness), still feel this sharpness to which we—at least, as readers—are privy?

Taking *Leaves of Grass* in terms of the first titular half of *Fat Art, Thin Art*, we might also imagine Sedgwick's vision of Whitman as a remediating engagement with James's preface to "The Beast in the Jungle," a text never far, it seems, from Sedgwick's mind, "where every object was as familiar to [her] as the things of [her] own house and the very carpets were worn with [her] fitful walk very much as the desks in old counting-houses are worn by the elbows of generations of clerks."[45] As James writes, "It takes space to feel, it takes time to know, and great organisms as well as small have to pause, more or less, to possess themselves and be aware. Monstrous masses are, by this truth, so impervious to vibration that the sharpest forces of feeling, locally applied, no more penetrate than a pin or a paper-cutter penetrates an elephant's hide."[46] The relations among the social fabric, the poem, the poem's readers, the thread and needle—they all blur and bleed together at the precise point at which the needle, such as it is and we are, makes contact. Turning to a trope so similar one wonders whether Sedgwick is paying homage, James writes in the preface of *Roderick Hudson* that "really, universally, relations stop nowhere," and the exquisite problem of the artist is eternally but to draw, by a geometry of his own, the circle within which they shall happily *appear* to do so. He is in the perpetual predicament that the continuity of things is the whole matter, for him, of comedy and tragedy; that this continuity is never, by the space of an instant or an inch, broken, and that, to do anything at all, he has at once intensely to consult and intensely to ignore it. All of which will perhaps pass but for a supersubtle way of pointing the plain moral that a young embroiderer of the canvas of life soon began to work in terror, fairly, of the vast expanse of that surface, of the boundless number of its distinct perforations for the needle, and of the tendency inherent in his many-coloured flowers and figures to cover and consume as many as possible of the little holes.[47]

It is in the spaciousness of these relations (including those among Sedgwick and Whitman and James), rather than the comparably obvious overdetermination of "penetrating," that Sedgwick locates the queerness of the sexual. Over and against the de-apostrophization of Whitman's book, the needle translates the social into fabric and that fabric into an art we are unable to name. In the manner of Emily Dickinson's fascicles, is the fabric becoming a book, or a garment? Or something else altogether?

Like Whitman as shibboleth, the weaver's handshake occurs in the text as a double movement between absorption and late bloomingly, Strether-like outward interest. Alongside the gravestone rubbing, I try to take the needle and the weaver's handshake on their own terms. Even as these are the sorts of passages that most bear for me Sedgwick's signature, we don't yet have an idiom for conceptualizing just how fundamental their singularity is to the quality of her thinking. As an attempt to treat this figurative elaborateness as nonornamental—or, at least, nonsubsidiary—this essay is an effort to think about style as theory as the theory looks from one vantage onto poetry and from another onto textiles. The compressed emblem of this practice, for me, is the weaver's handshake, the unfamiliarity of which brings to mind the question that opens "Pedagogy of Buddhism." *What does it mean when our cats bring small, wounded animals into the house?*[48] Cross between *Hamlet*'s play within a play and a Buddhist koan, the question posits a scene of pedagogy about a scene of pedagogy. Our balking at the little carnage is an inflexible extension of the narcissism that presupposes it is a gift. Like Ronald Reagan not knowing French, we are ungrateful when our obstinate language of gratitude misses the point of the cat—to be sure, an imperious creature conversant only in *its* language—who isn't proffering an object for us to accept so much as heuristically performing an action for us to repeat. We are (unaware that we are) being treated, that is, as kittens in need of training rather than masters or parents deserving tribute. "Is it true," Sedgwick asks, "that we can learn only when we are aware we are being taught? How have we so confused the illocutionary acts of gift giving and teaching?"[49]

Adopting what Sedgwick calls "the relations of near-miss pedagogy," I try to take the weaver's handshake, like the cat's mouse, on its own terms. Whereas strong theory, as Sedgwick understands it, corresponds to the graspiness of Emerson's "clutching hard," the weaver's handshake seems to propose a new, necessarily minor chirography. I would be inclined to describe the latter's endgame as incompatible with strong theory's language of possession were the weaver's handshake not so resolutely nonteleological. The rubbing back and forth of thumb and fingers translates grasping into a motion potentially as chronic as scouring or grave rubbing. What's more, the gesture's intervention in other, more aggressive forms of handling is inseparable from its replicability. The pleasure that Sedgwick finds in the gesture has less to do with its secrecy than with its self-pollinating ubiquity. Analogously, when someone in Victorian England unexpectedly works Whitman into polite conversation, it's not quite the *beginning* of friendship or otherwise between likeminded souls so much as the effortless extension of a sodality almost magically already in place. That one falls gently into a sympathy one has done little to achieve likewise conjures the felicitous meeting, one afternoon in Weatherend, of John Marcher and May Bartram. (That the friendship that follows seems so asymmetrically May's doing is another story.) It's possible that something momentous had been conveyed between them in the past to account for their present inimitable intimacy, but it's also as plausible that their relation is founded on the unspoken, shared belief that something along those lines *might* have happened. We can almost imagine in its description, "between my thumb and fingers," of the "brushing-three-fingers" gesture, that the passage anticipates the irresistibility with which its future readers will try the gesture out themselves.

As I type (or rather, importantly, in the interstices between typing), I find myself performing the weaver's handshake in front of the passage that incessantly teaches it to me. And yet, what most strikes me about the passage's "rub of reality" is that it comes on the heels of the following lines:

Actually it was just before this diagnosis that I was finding I had fallen suddenly, intrusively, and passionately in love with doing textile work. That is, before the *diagnosis*, but I think it may have happened after I'd started having the neck pains that were misdiagnosed for several months before they turned out to represent the cancer recurrence. I can't exactly remember the order in which things happened, actually. I just found myself cutting up fabrics, especially old kimonos, which I've always been fond of, to make into other fabrics—appliqués, collages (fig. 1) and an odd kind of weaving that used scraps of already-woven cloth as its weft material (in fig. 2 and fig. 3 [detail], the warp on the scarf is silk yarn, and the weft is kimono scraps and other materials).[50]

This neck pain is another kind of quilting point. In the fall of 2005, for instance, Sedgwick and I (along with my then partner and Sedgwick's friend and former student, John Emil Vincent) meet in Cambridge, Massachusetts, where she is undergoing an experimental procedure at Brigham and Women's, and I'm having nerves in my neck cauterized at Harvard's Pain Clinic. After our treatments, the three of us end up, I think, in the candy aisle of Walgreen's. The neck pain is a relay switch, as powerful a site of identification and cross-identification as the lyric and narrative sensitivities of the backside through which Sedgwick understands her "identification 'as' a gay man": "And in among its tortuous and alienating paths are knit the relations, for me, of telling and of knowing."[51] We risk losing the textural specificity of pain and desire alike (not to mention that of textural specificity itself) in straining to make this earlier figurative knitting line up too much with the later "odd kind of weaving that used scraps of already-woven cloth as its weft material." At the same time, I can't help but think that the literal and figurative vicissitudes of figuration are precisely what is at stake in Sedgwick's citing in "Making Things, Practicing Emptiness" of "(fig. 1)," the first such figure not only in *The Weather in Proust*, but of her decades-long career as "'an important writer of / fiction and poetry,—' / of *criticism* / and poetry, of course it's meant to say, / but 'fiction,' in this empty register, / scans, so 'fiction' in my head it always is . . . / Waking as an adult, now, who has an art."[52]

"So I've always loved textiles," Sedgwick tells us again, "without doing much about it, but something different was happening right around then, something that kept kidnapping me from my teaching and writing tasks and pinning me to my kitchen table with a mushrooming array of 'arts and crafts' projects and supplies. Why? Here's one thing that was different: I think I was finally giving up the pretext of self-ornamentation, to which my love of textiles had always clung before."[53] The complexity of such a claim begins "right around then" in the simultaneously specific (*before the* diagnosis) and slippery (*I can't exactly remember the order in which things happened*) temporality of a pain whose diagnostic elusiveness conjures its own scene of near-miss pedagogical encounter. We can perhaps hear the echo of a lyric poem being written inside "Making Things, Practicing Emptiness" in the pleasure of its sound pattern: how the *app* of *happening* becomes the second syllable of *kidnapping*, how the double *p* of both becomes the opening sound of *pinning*, whose double *n* amplifies the one in the middle of those previous words. The reservation of *perhaps hear the echo of* responds to what de Man might call the phenomenal difference between the compression of "scouring" and this triple rhyme, which nonetheless arguably belongs less to the domain of anthropomorphosis than to that of description. The difference is telling.

"A Poem Is Being Written" stitches together at least four temporally specific Eves: the nine-year-old poet who masters "two-beat Untermeyer-rhythm"; the "eleven-year-old redhead" who experiments with the further lyrical resistance of enjambment; the "twenty-four-year-old graduate student" at Cornell for whom the narrative poem "enacts . . . the generic leap to the social and institutional framing as narrative of exactly the same scene";[54] and finally— and ultimately, not final at all—the thirty-five-year-old assistant professor at Amherst who presents "A Child Is Being Beaten" at a Columbia University colloquium. In "Making Things, Practicing Emptiness," the Sedgwick who has spent "two decades of thinking, lecturing, and writing [queer theory]" finds herself not in Amherst or Durham but a few streets up from Washington Square in New York.[55] That the fantasy is one of being kidnapped evokes the crossed wires of masochism and self-infantilization, the particular richness of what Sedgwick has elsewhere taught us about her fantasy life. While "pinn[ed] to the kitchen table" resonates with the excitement of being held turning into being held *down*, it no less strikingly intimates that the fantasy on some other fractally synchronic level involves becoming the very kind of fabric scrap that this other self, having pinned it, might stitch to something else. As telling, we find in the fantasy's proliferation of gerunds—doing, kidnapping, teaching, writing, mushrooming, giving—the temporal preference that marks so much of Sedgwick's work, including "A Poem Is Being Written," *Touching Feeling*, and the essay at hand, "Making Things, Practicing Emptiness." The ongoing-ness of the verb formation is an expression of Sedgwick's long-standing investment in the chronic, a point all the more emphatically made in the formulation "kept kidnapping." It's not quite that the kidnapping's reiteration follows the logic of repetition compulsion. After all, it's not that the fantasy repeats, but that the fantasy itself is one of repeating, the kidnapping happening chronically, again and again, within the single moment of the fantasy's frame.

This forty-six-year-old Sedgwick isn't discovering so much as remembering the art most saliently present in that earlier essay in lines cited from "Two Arts," the last chapter of *The Warm Decembers*:

It *is* strange:
the way the art of our necessity
makes precious, the vile things—
the finger's-breadth by finger's-breadth
dearly bought knowledge
of the body's lived humiliations,
dependencies, vicarities
that's stitched into the book
of The Sexualities, wasteful
and value-making specificity.[56]

Finger's breadth by finger's breadth, a version of the once and future fabric lover's thumb against fingers. If we think about "fat art, thin art" in terms of "criticism and poetry" (although as strong a case can be made for the correspondence of "poetry and criticism"), how then do we make sense of this third art that governs the stitching, knotting, and weaving of the literal figures embedded in *The Weather in Proust*? What has happened—what was happening—involves an ontological shift away from an experience of writing (as ambitious, spoiled, spoiling, ebullient, effervescent) as a scene (both source and expression) of power. In her preface to *Tendencies*, for instance, Sedgwick writes that "for me, a kind of formalism, a visceral near-identification with the writing I care for, at the level of sentence structure, metrical pattern rhyme, was one way of trying to appropriate what seemed the numinous and resistant power of the chosen objects."[57] "A Poem Is Being Written" further articulates the specific power of poetic utterance as eventful and immanent: "But I was genuinely in love with something in this poem: it gave me power, a kind of power I still feel, though I no longer feel it in this poem. The name of that power—I know it now, and I knew it not long after I got this [Untermeyer] anthology at age nine—is, enjambment."[58] But what happens to this notion of poetic power in the obsolescing wake, if not of power itself, then of power at that particular ratcheting? Compare these passages, for instance, with this one from *A Dialogue on Love*:

> She feels that one of the things she has gotten in therapy is a more real-istic sense and understanding of her power. She feels less and less that power (intellectual, spiritual, artistic, etc.) is either boundless or nothing, either the overblown balloon or the suddenly deflated balloon. "More like a sleeping bag with many separate air compartments—a single puncture won't flatten it." Relates this to emphasis on talents rather than genius. Also related to handicraft passion?[59]

"As Cyndi Lauper might put it," Sedgwick writes apropos Milly Theale, "ill-ness changes everything." Milly was never a writer (that calling falls at least notionally to Densher), but when James's dying heroine—famously, scath-ingly, heartbreakingly, triumphantly—"turn[s] her face to the wall," she is being radicalized not as poet but as lyric poem, insofar as this is precisely the embodiment of lyric's paradigmatically apostrophic gesture.

That it's hard to read Sedgwick's essay on "The Beast in the Jungle" without imagining her "as" May Bartram is as much to say that it's hard not to imagine Sedgwick imagining herself "as" May Bartram. Having *had* imagined? Which Sedgwick does one imagine when, by her own count, there are so many? *The death of the author* never seemed so mathematically simplifying. Sedgwick, after all, has told us countless times that the place of her own "will-to-live . . . often aggressively absent" is "taken, when it is taken at all, by an also aggressive will-to-narrate and will-to-uncover, each with a gay male siting."[60] For Sedg-wick to identify with Bartram is for her to identify, in part, with a will to live that is ontologically fused with the ideally interminable project of carving out—locating, claiming, lighting, inhabiting—the space in which she and Marcher together might meditate on the queer contingency of what might have been the past on what might become the future. This meditation, founded as it is on a cultivated practice of lavish attention, is a respite, if not for Marcher, then for us from Marcher's comparably foreclosing, melodramatic idiom of girding-for and deliberation. The queerness of this contingency, as conceivably interminable (and interminably conceivable) as the meditation on it, is in turn a respite from the comparably terminating "diagnosis" of homosexuality that waits in the story's wings, as different from the rigors of May's interminability as the coercion of an overly firm handshake from the weaver's deft rubbing.

James writes that "it was only May Bartram who had, and she achieved, by an art indescribable, the feat of at once—or perhaps it was only alternately—meeting the eyes from in front and mingling her own vision, as from over his shoulder, with their peep through the apertures." Marcher's "mask" of "the social simper" is haunted (and not entirely unhappily) not only by Bartram over Marcher's shoulder, but also by James over Bartram's and Sedgwick over James's, and like Marcher's interminable queerness, this leap-frog pajama game—"the chain stretched and stretched"—could go on forever. Kevin Ohi is right to align the mask's dissimulating properties with those of a Janus-faced closet; that the mask in the first place is chronically, mendaciously enabling gives way to a new pleasure whose brazenness marks precisely the extent to which the mask no longer tethers Marcher to the social world, no longer renders, like a scuba mask, that world's air as at least fleetingly breathable. Rather, Bartram's appearance on either side of it takes it out of social circulation, thereby repurposing its capacity as interface. A bit like Charlie Chaplin's flagrant and ingenious repurposing of objects, Marcher and Bartram take advantage of the masks' ability to refine the contours of proximity.

If the mask's incipient function (Marcher less aware of it than we) still bears some relation to the chronically prevaricative, its import is less ontic than ontological. To this end, the mask's outpacing of its original use resembles the literal creativeness of what Bersani indispensably calls the Jamesian lie: "And she achieved, by an art indescribable, the feat of at once—or perhaps it was only alternately—meeting the eyes from the front and mingling her own vision, as from over his shoulder, with their peep through the apertures."[61] Ohi writes that "'perhaps . . . only alternately' prevents this multifaceted gaze from being 'merely' figural—or merely 'figural.'"[62] This attention to dissimulation's movement from the logic of true-false to some more slippery coupling of literal-figurative illuminates the mask's newly calibrated aesthetic import. As important, the difference between "at once—or . . . only alternately" is also one of chronicity. "Only alternately" breaks down the staring-contest mesmerization of a sustained glance and alchemizes it into a motion, a back-and-forth. Just as the mask literalizes an evolving of the properties of space, the back-and-forth literalizes the repetitive labor not of literal but of figurative action. And if Bartram alternates between the two sides of the mask, she might in the scopic feat blurringly manage to catch a glimpse of herself, catching a glimpse, around the corner.

Of "The Beast in the Jungle," Sedgwick notes the "story's negative virtue of not pretending to present [May] as rounded and whole," insofar as not articulating May's desire seems preferable to displacing it with the normative proscription, in Sedgwick's words, of "what she Really Wanted and what she

Really Needed."[63] To entertain the possibility of May catching a glimpse of herself from behind Marcher's fractally recalibrated mask is to imagine May's roundedness in terms of not psychical complexity so much as of Emersonian sphericity, as being dimensional enough for her to go behind herself. The possibility of going behind not just characters—"for routing the authorial point of view austerely through the eyes of characters as they in turn view other characters"[64]—but one's self clarifies, in part, what strikes Sedgwick as most enigmatic in an early characterization of Kate Croy in *The Wings of the Dove*: "A striking phrase, 'her eyes aslant no less on her beautiful averted than on her beautiful presented oval.' But, as my favorite Lynda Barry character would say, what does it even mean? Is Kate looking at her butt in the mirror? Is she watching the back of her head? . . . A moralistic formulation would be that the pressure of want and disgrace has made her two-faced. And that's not far from true, if you can subtract *its* punitive patness: the simple fact of *sidedness*, double-sidedness, presented and averted, recto and verso, seems not just to be lodged in Kate's person but to radiate out from it across the novel."[65] Bearing the alternations of Marcher's mask in mind, we might also imagine that Kate's eyes, aslant, catch a glimpse of themselves through themselves, or that Kate, in her roundness, is perceiving her own roundness, as though turned oval in the slant speed of anamorphosis.

Going behind one's self is an apt way to describe James's relation, in both his prefaces and his tripartite autobiography, to himself. The idiom figures a capacity for an author to go behind his younger self with the acquired ability, through the differently dimensionalized distance of years, to see what that younger self couldn't. In this sense, the anal erotics of going behind that Sedgwick traces in "Is the Rectum Straight?" speaks also to the possibility of selves treated in the text not as characters, per se, but as three-dimensional, "rounded" objects, capable not so much of being penetrated as of going round. This dimensionalizing of one's relation to one's self is as literally revolutionary as James's conversion of shame of and over his earlier self into pleasure. We ought, in this context, to recall the source of the shame that is the nominal subject of Sedgwick's essay on queer performativity. In Sedgwick's words, the younger James is abashed by "his mortifyingly extravagant miscalculations concerning the length of (what he had imagined as) a short story: "Painfully associated for me has 'The Spoils of Poynton' remained, until recent reperusal, with the awkward consequence of that fond error. The subject had emerged . . . all suffused with a flush of meaning; thanks to which irresistible air, as I could but plead in the event, I found myself . . . beguiled and led on."[66]

I quote this passage at length because the lines Sedgwick cites from the preface of *The Spoils of Poynton* exemplify the figuratively elaborate language from which, mortifyingly, James's textual excrescency is inseparable. After all, the James who writes *The Spoils of Poynton* in 1896 isn't going over the word limit because he can't resist just one more element of plot. James's stories are most susceptible to "going over" not because of too much action but because of too much of the "too much" that characterizes both James's and Sedgwick's writing. As James writes in the preface to *The Lesson of the Master* about his liberating lack of word limit in *The Yellow Book*:

> I was invited, and all urgently, to contribute to the first number, and was regaled with the golden truth that my composition might absolutely assume, might shamelessly parade in, its own organic form.... One had so often known this product to struggle, in one's hands, under the rude prescription of brevity at any cost, with the opposition so offered to its really becoming a story, that my friend's emphasised indifference to the arbitrary limit of length struck me, I remember, as the fruit of the finest intelligence. We had been one—that we already knew—on the truth that the forms of wrought things, in this order, *were*, all exquisitely and effectively, the things.[67]

That "the forms of wrought things ... were, all exquisitely and effectively, the things" isn't an argument for understanding Jamesian style as nonornamental. Rather, the repetition of "things" suggests that when it comes to Jamesian style, the ornamental is constitutive. Such a claim is unsurprising in the context of *The Spoils of Poynton*, given the novel's distinction between not the ornamental and nonornamental but the ornamental and decorative. The flush of prodigiousness is as fundamental to James's sentences as the ivory is to Mrs. Gereth's Maltese cross.

When *Poynton*'s narrator notes that "Maltese," as ascription of provenance, is "technically incorrect," he echoes a self-reproach that is related to James's inability to keep his stories short: he frequently can't remember the anecdote or "real-life" person or place out of which any given tale emerges. As James notes of "The Lesson of the Master," his stories "make together, by the same stroke, this other rather blank profession, that few of them recall to me, however dimly, any scant pre-natal phase." Or as he notes of "The Beast in the Jungle," "I remount the stream of time, all enquiringly, but ... come back empty-handed."[68] In the context of the necessarily unverifiable origin of Marcher's and Bartram's relationship, the missing provenance of the stories, like that of the Maltese cross, acquires a specifically psychical value, which is as much to say treats style and psychical value as though they were one and the same. It's along these lines that I think of James's prose in conventionally lyrical terms. Unlike an origin story of *who did what to whom* but like a lyric poem, the Jamesian line cannot be paraphrased. "Let it pass that if I am so oddly unable to say here, at any point, 'what gave me my idea,' I must just a trifle freely have helped myself to it from hidden stores." The line's scare quotes mark the difference between a paraphrasable sense of plot and the sensibility of text freed from the burdens of plot per se. We might, in fact, hear "what gave me my idea" not in James's own voice at all but, rather, the voice of devoted reader not quite catechized into the difference between the "idea" and the ideationally saturating objects of which James's work in so many ways consists. The thing is the thing is the thing, and if shame arises in response to its largesse, it has less to do with miscalculation than with the eminently queer sense of style as altogether irrevocable because it's as much a thing as the things it describes, a theory of nature pitched at a level of grandeur ambitious enough to do both Emersonian theory and nature justice.

James's writing resists paraphrasing for the same reasons a poem resists paraphrasing—namely, because its descriptive value is inextricable from the abstractions it enacts. I borrow these terms from Jonathan Culler, who distinguishes between a criticism that "translate[s] apostrophe into description" and "lyric or lyrical reading [that] translate[s] description into apostrophe and anthropomorphosis." Along these lines, "The Beast in the Jungle" might be said to translate the description of a mask into an anthropomorphosis of one. For that matter, we might analogously say that Bartram herself translates—*enacts*—Marcher. In both cases, the transformation involves a multiplication of the modes of relation one might sustain in, around, or with a given object. The object—even Marcher, who implicitly thinks about himself as though he were a (nonrhetorical) question—becomes an answer different from what it was not because it changes but because the questions we ask it change. In moments such as these, Jamesian text salubriously breaks free from the air of omnipotence that Sedgwick comes to associate with writing, and in terms of which she describes her evolving detachment from it in favor of the wabi-sabi of textile art. "Unlike making things," Sedgwick writes, "speech and writing and conceptual thought impose no material obstacles to a fantasy of instant, limitless efficacy. Nor for that matter is there anything to slow down the sudden, utter spoiling of such fantasy . . ."[69] This desire for obstacles is inseparable from the real-toads-in-imaginary-garden desire of materiality embedded in the texture of fantasy, from the more general, tacit counter-fantasy of inefficacy and limit. James's writing seems most persuasive not in its mimetic fidelity to a world outside itself but in the sense that it is self-responsive, self-negotiating.

The nearly simultaneous pedagogical and erotic exhilarations of constraint are evident in Sedgwick's writing from outset. I think of this line from the opening of *Epistemology of the Closet*, which on first and second read I knew I loved without understanding why. Here was my first encounter with Sedgwick's transfixing theatricalizing of a need for and magnetizing justification of our readerly attention:

> Accordingly, one characteristic of the readings in this book is to attend to performative aspects of texts, and to what are often blandly called their "reader relations," as sites of definitional creation, violence, and rupture in relation to particular readers and particular institutional circumstances. . . . It has felt throughout this work as though the density of their social meaning lends any speech act concerning these issues—and the outlines of that "concern," it turns out, are broad indeed—the exaggerated propulsiveness of wearing flippers in a swimming pool: the force of various rhetorical effects has seemed uniquely difficult to calibrate.[70]

Not having worn flippers in a pool for some time, I can only imagine (which is precisely the point) the particular form of attentiveness that they ostensibly bring to and encounter in Sedgwick's swimming pool library. Another name for this attentiveness is resistance, as though the prosthetic appendages made one newly or differently aware of the neither attraction nor repulsion of one's feet, ankles, shins in and against the (somewhat euphemistically) appreciated wear of the water. This flipper effect speaks not only to the density of social meaning but also to the incessant grip and pulsive give of Sedgwick's own writing as a site where writing itself—some illuminated exchange between its most material and phantasmatic selves—experiences its own campy, complexly lovable torpor. The fantasy of *feeling writing* as both more and less than itself, of trusting the vitality of a text to the extent that one feels its (or is it one's own?) strain, suggests the mutual constitutiveness for Sedgwick of resistance's outer valence as it flickers in and out of literal and figurative registers. "The book aims to resist in every way it can the deadening pretended knowingness by which the chisel of modern homo/heterosexual definitional crisis tends, in public discourse, to be hammered most fatally home."[71] Sedgwick's writing, that is, seeks to resist the velocity (and instantaneous-seeming hurt) of knowledge as chisel by exposing scenes to, as well as being an environment where, the physics of resistance more visibly occurs. To paraphrase Claggart, resistance is as resistance did it. Or as that text's narrator says of Vere, "No more trying situation is conceivable than that of an officer subordinate under a Captain whom he suspects to be, not mad indeed, but yet not quite unaffected in his intellect. To argue his order to him would be insolence. To resist him would be mutiny."[72]

The problem against which Sedgwick's mutiny of resistance arises isn't that knowingness is pretending but that this specific form of pretend lacks the nonabstracting feeling that resistance confers:

> Then, of course, I am disquieted at this tectonic shift in what I've presumed were the fixed zones of permission and prohibition.
>
> Also, though, I feel somehow restored to an adult size—in relation, that is, to the spectral figure of my fear and rage. Which I've always associated with my father in his own rage: a figure who's abstract to me in the particular sense that it could never have occurred to me to resist or push back against him, or to wrestle him to a standstill or to anything else.[73]

As Sedgwick observes in the eponymous essay of *The Weather in Proust*, "It's worth noting here that in requiring support from the elements, the subject also lays a claim on their reliable ability to resist pressure from it or damage by it. In Barbara Johnson's paraphrase of Winnicott, 'The object becomes real because it survives, because it is outside the subject's range of omnipotent control.'"[74] Sedgwick's observation translates the Cartesian cogito into something along the lines of "I resist, therefore I am," a haptic vividness in comparison to which the Winnicottian "I survive, therefore I am" tautologically pales in comparison. Sedgwick's gravitation to an ontology of resistance makes sense insofar as it slows down and expands a terrain of writing that otherwise gets reduced to the dualisms of active and passive, subject and object. "Any verb, aside from the verb 'to be,' generates a doer and done-to. And by this simple, built-in grammatical feature it thus makes it almost impossible for any language user to maintain a steady sense of the crucial middle ranges of agency: the field in which most of consciousness, perception, and relationality really happen."[75] Even as Sedgwick's investment in a "'wabi-sabi' aesthetic that prefers funky craft to finely done craft" marks a turn, for her, away from her "vocation as a writer and theorist,"[76] it also rearticulates the love of resistance that had been there all along. In this context, Sedgwick's practice of suminagashi and shibori is an experiment in resistance's middle ranges of literal and figurative expression, even as this surprise of the middle range regularly collates figuration's specifically haptic unpredictability not only with resistance but also with a capacity to feel and be felt: "I used a resist to cover the shape of each letter. . . . I wanted reading it to involve a series of hypotheses."[77] "Here the mark of the scissor works as the marks of dye and resist do in *shibori*: they gain a kind of material purchase, in one moment and dimensionality, that persists, albeit transformed and even unrecognizable, into a changed one. And neither folded nor unfolded state can be called realer than the other."[78]

Imagining Bartram as anthropomorphically enacting Marcher is thus to encounter lyric reading as it approaches the patience (as opposed to finished perfectibility) of the middle ranges of craft:

> The rest of the world of course thought him queer, but she, she only, knew how, and above all why, queer; which was precisely what enabled her to dispose the concealing veil in the right folds. She took his gaiety from him—since it had to pass with them for gaiety—as she took everything else; but she certainly so far justified by her unerring touch his finer sense of the degree to which he had ended by convincing her. *She* at least never spoke of the secret of his life except as "the real truth about you," and she had in fact a wonderful way of making it seem, as such, the secret of her own life too. That was in fine how he so constantly felt her as allowing for him; he couldn't on the whole call it anything else.[79]

The meticulousness with which Bartram "dispose[s] the concealing veil in the right folds" both literalizes the middle range that her relation to Marcher occupies and figures the particular care that I imagine Sedgwick may have imagined between herself and others (broadly and infinitesimally conceived). Like the resists, such folds become a way to inhabit a theory of writing from which Sedgwick's subsequent interest in textile art isn't a departure so much as a rededication. Sedgwick's thinking about artistic folds in terms of the dimensionality of fractals corresponds to James's account of Bartram's "indescribable art," insofar as the art by which she is able to see through the mask's apertures translates the mask's two-dimensional surface enough into three that she can go behind it. "The fractal, the fractionally dimensional, seems like, among other things, a language invented exactly to talk about texture."[80] It's this three-dimensionality of Bartram's art that makes it possible for Marcher's "finer sense"—"that was in fine how he so constantly felt her as allowing for him"—to be "justified by her unerring touch."

In both Sedgwick's earliest and last writings, the difficulty of doing justice to the pathos of dimensionality (reflected back to itself as the dimensionality of feeling) arises in or as the waver of perspective. "In pictorial terms," the passage continues, "a fractured dimensionality might be a way of describing the struggle staged in perspectival realism, between the receding space of illusion and the fractal space of the picture plane."[81] In "A Poem Is Being Written," Sedgwick imagines the feel of this struggle between telescopingly complex, competing visions as the "'thud / of longing' with which the contracted, bodily siting of the drama of enjambment is displaced back outward onto the sheepish hungry gaze from the wedged-open door."[82] Analogous scenes appear throughout Sedgwick's poems. Here's the opening of a 1973 poem titled "An Essay on the Picture Plane," whose surficial preposition converts the notion of subject (an essay about a given topic) into a Magritte-like encounter between differently dimensioned media:

> The vertical plane makes the absence present
> to you, who are absent both from the horizon
> and from the fabric itself before you
> which is too articulate. Be thankful
> for the absence is at least here, because it is stretched,
> stretching clear to the edges, and immobile.
> Be grateful too when sometimes it resolves
> as a woven thing with just a woven depth.[83]

That the relation between Marcher and Bartram is structured, as Bersani suggests, like an analytic encounter makes it all the more tempting to hear in a later poem, titled "Snapsh," the susurrus by which Sedgwick refers in writing to her therapist, Shannon, as "SH." The last lines of "Snapsh" take the form of two questions whose emotional and aesthetic proximity to "The Beast in the Jungle" recalls Sedgwick's interest in a fractal's capacity both to expand and contract along a single fold:

> Why won't the proffer of such comforts
> comfort me?
> Why mask out, at each viewing, with my hand,
> the smooth, huge foreshortening of his own?[84]

Such points of contact among genres, authors, and years complicate our sense of the relation between Sedgwick's insatiably various career and itself. It illuminates my sense that if Sedgwick "fastens" on a photograph of Judith Scott, and if this identification "is less as the subject of some kind of privation than as the holder of an obscure treasure," it's not quite because Scott's embrace of her art traces the same curve as Bartram's embrace of Marcher. Not quite, to the extent that the causal narrative of "because" overlooks the irresistible, middle-range textures we've been tending. We are told that the beginning of one of Scott's sculptures is a central object, but I think instead that the sculpture begins when the possibility of a core is buried enough that its never having been there strikes us as no less plausible than its being. We might at this point not be surprised that Scott's sculptures repeat that pattern of Bartram and Marcher's art of friendship, predicated on the possibility rather than fact of their having met before.

Scott's sculptures anthropomorphically rewrite Galatea as an aesthetic of ongoing attention. That Galatea and Pygmalion make each other out of each other makes me think of the aestheticizing self-distance inherent in what Sharon Cameron calls beautiful work: "To be competent to speak of pain is to speak of pain that isn't yours. This requires experiencing pain that is yours. Pain experienced *as if* it were your own."[85] The moment at which the sculpture seems to come to life is the endlessly repeatable, scouring, scrubbing, flickering of aesthetic duress, the expression of both one's calling and one's resistance to it. To turn this screw one thread more: Judith Butler writes about the heroine of James's *Washington Square* that if Catherine Sloper "'takes up life as it were,' we are asked to understand the life she takes up as a figural one, a life that is as proper to fiction as, say, the life of a fictional character must be."[86] Catherine's earlier gluttony—"In her younger years she was a good deal of a romp, and though it is an awkward confession to make about one's heroine, I must add that she was something of a glutton"[87]—leads to the falling curtain of the novel's last line with an air almost of inevitability: "Catherine, meanwhile, in the parlour, picking up her morsel of fancy-work, had seated herself with it again—for life, as it were." The life that we take up in the end is the life not of a fictional character but of a lyric figure. And figuration is what happens in the blurring between what at once again and again makes one one's self and what keeps one from becoming:

> If the night finally
>
> comes when you and I, one sleepless darkness
> mimicking another darkness, penetrate
> from room to room, or into breathless
>
> room, I needn't wonder if your voice
> hollows under mine, sounding delicate, or absent,
> the glutted body of that voice being here.[88]

NOTES

1 Ralph Waldo Emerson, *Essays and Lectures* (New York: Library of America, 1983), 7.

2 William James, "A World of Pure Experience," *Journal of Philosophy, Psychology, and Scientific Methods* 1, no. 20 (1904): 534.

3 Jacques Lacan, *The Ethics of Psychoanalysis 1959–1960: The Seminar of Jacques Lacan*, vol. 7, ed. Jacques-Alain Miller, trans. Dennis Porter (New York: W. W. Norton, 1997), 61.

4 Michel Foucault, *The Hermeneutics of the Subject: Lectures at the Collège de France, 1981–1982* (New York: Palgrave Macmillan, 2005), 14. See also Leo Bersani, "'Ardent Masturbation' (Descartes, Freud, and Others)," *Critical Inquiry* 38 (Autumn 2011): 1–16.

5 Jordana Rosenberg, "The Molecularization of Sexuality: On Some Primitivisms of the Present," *Theory and Event* 17, no. 2 (2014), accessed February 12, 2019, https://muse.jhu.edu/article/546470.

6 Michael D. Snediker, *Contingent Figure: Aesthetic Duress from Ralph Waldo Emerson to Eve Kosofsky Sedgwick* (Minneapolis: University of Minnesota Press, forthcoming Fall 2020).

7 Rosenberg, "The Molecularization of Sexuality."

8 Eve Kosofsky Sedgwick, *Tendencies* (Durham, NC: Duke University Press, 1993).

9 Sedgwick, *Tendencies*, 120–21.

10 In his *New Republic* rant against Sedgwick and queer theory, Lee Siegel treats her (heuristically motivated) disregard for the inauthenticity of this Chatterton-like document as *pièce de résistance*. For an efficient account of Siegel's stink, see Vincent Quinn, "Loose Reading: Sedgwick, Austen, Critical Practice," *Textual Practice* 14, no. 2 (2000): 305–26.

11 Daniel Tiffany, *My Silver Planet* (Baltimore: Johns Hopkins University Press, 2014), 65–69.

12 Rosenberg, "The Molecularization of Sexuality."

13 Emerson, *Essays and Lectures*, 473.

14 Emerson, *Essays and Lectures*, 46. I am reminded by this passage of lines from "The Garment," a poem by Louise Glück that draws out the resonance between Emerson's vision of extraordinary, simultaneous dilation and contraction and *Fat Art, Thin Art*, the title of Sedgwick's only book of poems:

> My soul withered and shrank.
> The body became for it too large a garment.
>
> And when hope was returned to me
> it was another hope entirely.

(Louise Glück, "The Garment," in *Poems, 1962–2012* [New York: Farrar, Straus, and Giroux, 2012], 382.)

15 Emerson, *Essays and Lectures*, 119. Emerson's sensitivity to the evanescing texture of the interface, the nonequivalence of smoothness and textual lack, recalls Sedgwick's fondness for Renu Bora's essay "Outing Texture." She wrote, "One consequence of Bora's treatment of the concept: however high the gloss, there is no such thing as textual lack": Eve Kosofsky Sedgwick, *Touching Feeling: Affect, Pedagogy, Performativity* (Durham, NC: Duke University Press, 2003), 15.

16 "But the best read naturalist who lends an entire and devout attention to truth, will see that there remains much to learn of his relation to the world, and that it is not to be learned by any addition or subtraction or other comparison of known quantities, but is arrived at by untaught sallies of the spirit, by a continual self-recovery, and by entire humility": Emerson, *Essays and Lectures*, 43.

17 Lacan, *The Ethics of Psychoanalysis*, 60.

18 Emerson, *Essays and Lectures*, 456.

19 Drastic (*adj.*), 1690s, originally medical, "forceful, vigorous, especially in effect on bowels," from Greek *drastikos*, "effective, efficacious; active, violent," from *drasteon*, "(thing) to be done," from *dran*, "to do, act, perform," in *Online Etymology Dictionary*, accessed February 12, 2019, https://www.etymonline.com /word/drastic#etymonline_v_15885. Looking ahead to Sedgwick's growing interest in fractals, I think of these new marginal notes beside the older ones in terms of Cole Swensen's observation (in the context of Susan Howe) that the margin "is the dividing line made extra-dimensional, inhabitable": Cole Swensen, *Noise That Stays Noise: Essays* (Ann Arbor: University of Michigan Press, 2011), 33.

20 Henry James, *The Golden Bowl* (New York: Penguin Classics, 1987), 530.

21 I am imagining (if not quite trying to justify) the flagrance of this recollection (and this essay more generally) as an effort to respond to the concluding note of Sedgwick's essay "A Poem Is Being Written" (*Representations* 17 [Winter 1987]: 110–42). "Part of the motivation behind my work on it," she writes, "has been a fantasy that readers or hearers would be variously—in anger, identification, pleasure, envy, 'permission,' exclusion—stimulated to write accounts 'like' this one (whatever that means) of their own, and share those": Sedgwick, *Tendencies*, 214.

22 Sedgwick, *Tendencies*, 79.

23 "Cacozelia," in *Your Dictionary*, by Michael D. Snediker, accessed November 12 2017, http://www.yourdictionary.com/cacozelia.

24 "'They had no opportunity of going into society; they formed no relations.' This was one of a certain number of words that the Baroness often pronounced in the French manner": Henry James, *The Europeans* (New York: Penguin Classics, 2008), 105.

25 Jonathan Culler and Kevin Lamb, "Introduction," in *Just Being Difficult? Academic Writing in the Public Arena*, ed. Jonathan Culler and Kevin Lamb (Stanford, CA: Stanford University Press, 2003), 6.

26 Culler and Lamb, "Introduction," 6.

27 Quintilian, *The Institution Oratoria of Quintilian*, vol. 3, trans. H. E. Butler (New York: G. P. Putnam's Sons, 1922), 241–43.

28 Sedgwick, *Touching Feeling*, 38.

29 Sedgwick, *Touching Feeling*, 44.

30 Eve Kosofsky Sedgwick, *A Dialogue on Love* (Boston: Beacon, 2000), 31.

31 Cf. Elizabeth Bishop, "The Sandpiper" (*New Yorker*, July 21, 1962), 30:

> The roaring alongside he takes for granted,
> and that every so often the world is bound to shake.
> He runs, he runs to the south, finical, awkward,
> in a state of controlled panic, a student of Blake.
>
> The beach hisses like fat. On his left, a sheet
> of interrupting water comes and goes
> and glazes over his dark and brittle feet.
> He runs, he runs straight through it, watching his toes.
>
> Watching, rather, the spaces of sand between them
> where (no detail too small) the Atlantic drains
> rapidly backwards and downwards. As he runs,
> he stares at the dragging grains.

32 Eve Kosofsky Sedgwick, *Fat Art, Thin Art* (Durham, NC: Duke University Press, 1994), 95.

33 Sedgwick, *Fat Art, Thin Art*, 95.

34 Jonathan Culler, "Reading Lyric," *Yale French Studies* 69 (1985): 99.

35 Jonathan Culler, "Lyric Continuities: Speaker and Consciousness," *Neohelicon* 13, no. 1 (1986): 108, 114.

36 Jacques Lacan, *The Psychoses 1955–1956: The Seminar of Jacques Lacan*, vol. 3, ed. Jacques-Alain Miller, trans. Russell Grigg (New York: W. W. Norton, 1997), 268.

37 Lacan, *The Psychoses 1955–1956*, 268.

38 Lacan, *The Psychoses 1955–1956*, 100.

39 Eve Kosofsky Sedgwick, *The Weather in Proust*, ed. Jonathan Goldberg (Durham, NC: Duke University Press, 2011), 71.

40 Eve Kosofsky Sedgwick, *Between Men: English Literature and Male Homosocial Desire* (New York: Columbia University Press, 1985), 206.

41 Sedgwick, *Between Men*, 206.

42 Emerson, *Essays and Lectures*, 471.

43 Walt Whitman, *Leaves of Grass: The First (1855) Edition*, ed. Malcolm Cowley (New York: Penguin, 1986), 86.

44 Sedgwick, *Between Men*, 206.

45 Henry James, *Complete Stories: 1898–1910* (New York: Library of America, 1996), 513.

46 Henry James, *The Art of the Novel* (Chicago: University of Chicago Press, 2011), 244.

47 James, *The Art of the Novel*, 5.

48 Sedgwick, *Touching Feeling*, 153.

49 Sedgwick, *Touching Feeling*, 154.

50 Sedgwick, *The Weather in Proust*, 71.

51 Sedgwick, *Tendencies*, 209.

52 Sedgwick, *Tendencies*, 201. I hear Sedgwick's happy misrecognition of herself as "writer of / fiction and poetry" in the same register as James's insistence, regarding Milly Theale's death, that "the poet essentially *can't* be concerned with the act of dying": Sedgwick, *Tendencies*, 100.

53 Sedgwick, *The Weather in Proust*, 71.

54 Sedgwick, *Tendencies*, 185, 187.

55 Sedgwick, *The Weather in Proust*, 69.

56 Sedgwick, *Fat Art, Thin Art*, 149.

57 Sedgwick, *Tendencies*, 3.

58 Sedgwick, *Tendencies*, 182.

59 Sedgwick, *A Dialogue on Love*, 203.

60 Sedgwick, *Tendencies*, 209.

61 James, *Complete Stories*, 511.

62 Kevin Ohi, *Dead Letters Sent: Queer Literary Transmission* (Minneapolis: University of Minnesota Press, 2015), 164.

63 Eve Kosofsky Sedgwick, *Epistemology of the Closet* (Berkeley: University of California Press, 1991), 200.

64 Sedgwick, *Tendencies*, 97.

65 Sedgwick, *Tendencies*, 84.

66 Sedgwick, *Touching Feeling*, 41.

67 James, *The Art of the Novel*, 219.

68 James, *The Art of the Novel*, 221, 246.

69 Sedgwick, *The Weather in Proust*, 79.

70 Sedgwick, *Epistemology of the Closet*, 3.

71 Sedgwick, *Epistemology of the Closet*, 12.

72 Herman Melville, *Billy Budd and Other Stories* (New York: Penguin Classics, 1986), 353.

73 Sedgwick, *A Dialogue on Love*, 94.

74 Sedgwick, *The Weather in Proust*, 11.

75 Sedgwick, *The Weather in Proust*, 79.

76 Sedgwick, *The Weather in Proust*, 79.

77 Sedgwick, *The Weather in Proust*, 84.

78 Sedgwick, *The Weather in Proust*, 101.

79 James, *Complete Stories*, 510.

80 Sedgwick, *The Weather in Proust*, 90.

81 Sedgwick, *The Weather in Proust*, 90.

82 Sedgwick, *Tendencies*, 195. Compare this with James's speculation on consecu-
    tively dimensionalized selves in terms of the jamming of a door. James wrote,
    "[And] I was to regard [this experience] . . . as the marked limit of my state of
    being as a small boy. I took on, when I had decently . . . recovered the sense of
    being a boy of other dimensions somehow altogether, and even with a new
    dimension introduced and acquired; a dimension that I was eventually to think
    of as a stretch in the direction of essential change or of living straight into a part
    of myself previously quite unvisited and now made accessible as by the sharp
    forcing of a closed door. The blur of consciousness imaged by my grease-spot
    was not, I hasten to declare, without its relenting edges and even, during its
    major insistence, fainter thicknesses; short of which, I see, my picture, the pic-
    ture I was always so incurably 'after,' would have failed of animation altogether":
    Henry James, *A Small Boy and Others: A Critical Edition*, ed. Peter Collister
    (Charlottesville: University of Virginia Press, 2011), 314.

83 Sedgwick, *Fat Art, Thin Art*, 72.

84 Sedgwick, *Fat Art, Thin Art*, 24.

85 Sharon Cameron, *Beautiful Work* (Durham, NC: Duke University Press, 2000), 1.

86 Judith Butler, "Values of Difficulty," in *Just Being Difficult: Academic Writing in
    the Public Arena*, ed. Jonathan D. Culler and Kevin Lamb (Stanford, CA:
    Stanford University Press, 2003), 214.

87 Henry James, *Washington Square* (New York: Oxford World's Classics, 2010), 9.

88 Sedgwick, *Fat Art, Thin Art*, 75.

Eighteen Things I Love about You

I. YOUR HUMOR

Please pardon the title of this *Lover's Discourse*–style elegy. I realize it echoes Anne Sexton. Once upon a time, I asked you if you liked the confessional poets, Anne Sexton and Sylvia Plath.

You replied: "Sylvia Plath was the Kurt Cobain of my generation."

II. YOUR LOVE OF POETRY

Empty My Heart, of Thee . . .
Erase the root—no tree.
–Emily Dickinson, "Empty My Heart, of Thee"

Emily Dickinson's words have never been more powerful to me than they are right now. Your love of poetry, our shared love of poetry, always a source of pleasure in conversation together, has become the place I turn to alone, in deep grief, missing you. I remember meeting Stephen Barber at your house one night, the three of us a small minyan of Cavafy lovers, reading aloud our favorites. If lines of poetry could be totems, I nominate James Merrill's "how generous love makes one" as yours.

III. YOUR GENEROSITY

At your memorial, I looked around at the attendees and thought, "How many people here owe their success, their university teaching jobs, their university tenure, their accepted book manuscripts, their positive reviews, their fully flowered theses, their nascent ideas made better to the caring, time-giving, help-giving generous hard work of you?"

IV. SHARING FOOD WITH YOU

As I write this, I am defrosting a slice of smoked salmon to put on a bagel with cream cheese. For me, strangely, it is the ultimate comfort food, the thing I want when I want nothing else. The week of April 12, whole days passed without food. On what would have been your fifty-ninth birthday, May 2, 2009, I went out to Dillard's, a palace of southern comfort food where you loved to go, and ordered smothered chicken over rice, proceeding to cry over it like the wedding-cake baker in *Like Water for Chocolate*. Food had always been such a part of our togetherness. Dinners at Craft, at Babbo, at Danube, where we celebrated Stephen's tenure. At the Boulevard in San Francisco, where you gave me a box of marrons glacés. Drinking Red Zinger iced tea with you. Finding soothing soups for your sore throat after radiation treatment. Getting your still cherished email when you discovered that runny Brie and oily sundried tomatoes hastily conveyed to the mouth go down rather easily. Telling me that you almost took a bath in the homemade vegetable soup I brought you. Telling Stephen that when little else worked, "God bless Kraft Macaroni and Cheese."

V. YOUR GENIUS

Before I knew you, before I met you, an acquaintance in New York gave me a photocopy of your essay "Privileges of Unknowing." Reading this essay was one of the most exciting intellectual experiences of my life. It redefined how to read and especially how to write, and it is not exaggeration when I say that neither practice has ever been the same for me since. I am so grateful to you for the gift of your exquisite, extraordinary genius. I am so lucky to have the tremendous good fortune in learning, and continuing to learn, from you. No writing has ever given me more pleasure!

VI. YOUR FRIENDSHIP

I count your friendship as one of the dearest of my life.

You once wrote that almost all you had to do to make a person interesting to you was to imagine that person as gay. For me, in the deep loss of missing you, almost all I have to do to become interested in a new acquaintance is to hear that that person knows you, admires you, loves you. This is true at on-campus interviews in Timbuktu and true in the dentist's chair at your former dentist's office in Durham, North Carolina. You continue giving me friendship even now, Eve.

VII. YOUR EXQUISITE TASTE

VIII. YOUR RE-CONCEPTION OF FAMILY

You once described Charles Dickens's character Little Dorrit as having an uncanny ability to magnetize new people toward her, to form friendships with them, and to keep such friendships whole. You described this as a "nutty cluster" effect, likening it to nuts and caramel stuck together in delicious affinity. Little Dorrit formed a new family out of friends who met her, gravitated toward her, and stuck with her ever after. I couldn't help noticing, after spending time with you, that other people also gravitated toward your irresistible sweetness and that, for you, the concept of family dearly included those who formed this nutty cluster with you.

IX. YOUR GIFT IN SPREADING HAPPINESS TO OTHERS

You once told me that when you taught Sarah Orne Jewett's *The Country of the Pointed Firs*, your students sat quietly when you asked if there was eroticism in the writing. We were, during this conversation, eating several dozen raw oysters, gorgeously cold and luscious, and laughing like crazy. I can't remember ever being happier. Even your eyes were turned upward, smiling.

X. YOUR BEAUTY

XI. YOUR VULNERABILITY

Once in Boston, after a public lecture, a genuine curmudgeon asked you what she thought was a question, starting with the word "But!" and leading with a quasi-argumentative tone. Watching you respond, I wrote an ode to your grace and tact under fire. I mutter, under my breath, in a furious falsetto, George Eliot's line from *Daniel Deronda*: "What dost though think I am, minced offal?"

(A line that you—incidentally—thought was an Anglo version of "What am I, chopped liver?")

In an alternative universe, I take liberties with part of a poem by Mary Oliver, remembering that "every soft thing / that walks through the world / yourself included" needs rachmones.

But who knew better than you?

XII. YOUR CANDOR

Once, as I bemoaned reading a bad book that reified gender in migraine-giving repetition, I described to you an added insult: the positioning of the author's imaginary or so-called women was not just reductive and straitjacketing but also familiarly masculinist in orientation. I was in the mood to rail and said, "You'd think this named professor would know better!"

"Why?" you quipped in delicious hell-no irony, "because he must just be so post-feminist?"

XIII. YOUR TACT

XIV. GIVING YOU THINGS

The things that pleased you, and the thought of pleasing you, thrilled me. Learning restraint in this matter was next to impossible, even on the occasions when you would steal my thunder. For example, when the very best miniature poodle in all of poodledom became available, I offered her to you, only to see you turn right around and offer her to me. My house is filled with your gorgeous art, with Sculpey beads, resist-dyed silk shibori, handmade tiles, scarves you made, scarves from the South of France. My last present to you, a delivery of no-cook nibbles so you wouldn't have to bother, became in turn your gift to me. My credit card received a mysterious refund. When I called the purveyor, she said—apologetically—"Professor Eve Sedgwick counted the items in her delivery box, compared it to the packing list, and called to tell us the smoked salmon was missing so that we would be sure to refund you for it."

My eyes filled with tears. I did not want you to have to bother. I would never have known about the salmon or cared about the money. Yet you cared about it for me.

XV. YOUR ART

XVI. YOUR INSPIRATION

My work, I'm very careful about it, and I love it.
−C. P. Cavafy, "Pictured"

Your mother still worries and wonders whether she did the right thing when she prevented you, in elementary school, from publishing a letter to the editor in the Bethesda newspaper in defense of your gay teacher who was being persecuted for his homosexuality. At the time, she understood herself to be rightfully protective of you, still a child, who would be caught in the middle of public debate if such a letter were to be published. Now she worries that she picked the wrong side of right, especially given your career path and your own intellectual, emotional, and political interests. I suggested the possibility that her prohibition was a kind of foundational turning point without which your future might not have progressed in the direction it did. Did you promise yourself something in childhood that you made come true in adulthood? Would we have *Epistemology of the Closet* if you had not?

XVII. YOUR MOTHER

I just do.

XVIII. YOUR PEDAGOGY

Of the many creative assignments you dreamed up for students in your Experimental Critical Writing class, the assignment to write an obituary comes back to haunt me. At the time, your own brilliant "White Glasses" lived by my bed's side, its pages more instructive, bar setting, than any student practice could be. It never occurred to me then that you might be the subject of my attempt. You were, in those years, spared the knowledge that would come soon enough, that your cancer would return, metastasized as bone cancer. Furthermore, despite what you had been through, despite the lurking threat that cancer represents even to so-called survivors, I know that then (and even now) I could not, and still cannot, fathom this world without you. Instead, I wrote about a friend I lost, a man who committed suicide at work, my office just down the hall from his at Macmillan Publishers, where I paused briefly in my early twenties, where he paused briefly in his late thirties. He was a graduate student in his spare time, and I still have a book of his, complete with marginalia and witty doodling in the pages of an essay by Barbara Herrnstein Smith. I could not even look at, or touch, this book for a long time after losing him.

At his funeral, I began to learn something that reading "White Glasses" later taught me best—namely, that writing eulogies is an art. A meaningful one is hard to find. A bad one is a bruise to the soul.

My friend's boss stood up at the podium and told his family of mourners, including his six-year-old daughter, that my friend was remarkable for his success in having persuaded some mapmakers to contribute their work free of charge to a multivolume reference encyclopedia. I held another colleague's hand as we looked at each other in disbelief.

At your memorial, I thought, "We owe you 'White Glasses.'"

NOTE

Epigraphs: Emily Dickinson, "Poem 587," in *The Complete Poems of Emily Dickinson,* ed. Thomas H. Johnson (Boston: Little, Brown and Company, 1960), 287; Constantine Cavafy, "Pictured," in *C. P. Cavafy: Collected Poems,* rev. ed., trans. Edmund Keley and Philip Sherrard, ed. George Savidis (Princeton, NJ: Princeton University Press, 1992), 59.

Eve's Triangles
Queer Studies Beside Itself

I met Eve Sedgwick on a bridge in Chicago in December 1990.¹ My friend
Tom Yingling, who knew he was dying, saw her in the distance. "That's Eve,"
he said in a voice filled with pleasure at everything he had just been lamenting: being on a bridge, at the Modern Language Association conference, in
Chicago, in the freezing cold. She was the only woman coming toward us in
a group of three—much shorter than the others, covered entirely in coat.
I had seen Eve Sedgwick once, the year before, at a conference Tom and I
attended at Yale when her session erupted in a contested shout-out about her
sexuality.² *"Are you a lesbian?"* Audience members demanded to know. That
was Eve at a different distance—at a table in the front of a regular classroom,
with a soft, almost ethereal voice, softer still in the raucous space in which the
authority of her person was being called into question for the very authority
she was taken to exert over a field that had finally found itself at Yale.³

I talked to Eve twice after that meeting on the bridge. When Tom died
in 1992, she helped me secure a contract for his work at Duke University
Press and encouraged me to use his personal writing as a way to represent
and mourn him. That book—*AIDS and the National Body*—arrived in print
in 1997, shortly after the genocidal emergency of AIDS in North America had
been "downgraded" and people began to imagine living with and not simply
dying from the disease.⁴ What had been struggled for in the earliest years of
the epidemic—the PLWA (Person Living with AIDS)—was thus emerging for
the first time as a medical possibility. In one of her last published essays, Sedgwick described the affective density of the summer of 1996 when the "brutally abbreviated temporality of the lives of many women and men with HIV
seemed suddenly, radically extended if not normalized. . . . [R]elief, hope, ex-
pansiveness, and surprise set the tone."⁵ Today, of course, the normalization

of the disease remains incomplete, if not a First World luxury, but the point is that by the time Tom's book came out, a year after the controversial *Gary in Your Pocket*, which Sedgwick edited to memorialize the very talented and never published Gary Fisher, AIDS was being reinvented in popular and public health discourses as a chronic illness.[6]

I want to emphasize the use of the word "normalizing" here, because it is a strange feature of our present that the route that so much queer inquiry would take after Eve turned its political gaze increasingly against normalization of every kind, becoming less and less exacting about which norms a minoritized community can and cannot live without and why the choices are never its alone. In this, the field that has emerged to claim an institutional domain called queer studies can sometimes appear immune to the complexities that HIV/AIDS presented to political analysis and activism alike, where the necessary engagement with various institutions—the state, medicine, and the corporate health industry—challenged, if not defied, many of the assumptions guiding radical sexual politics since the 1960s.[7] In Sedgwick's recollection of the summer of 1996, normalization is not a synonym for the narrow vision of state-based civil rights that underwrites gay liberation politics in the US today—what scholars now call "queer liberalism," "homonormativity," and "homonationalism"—but a referent for the irreducible value of survival.[8] While she would likewise lament the assimilationist agenda of the mainstream gay/lesbian movement, her critique of its normalizing impulses took aim at the way it contracted the meaning of the political by abandoning the historical and hermeneutic lessons of AIDS. "Believe it or not," she wrote in the posthumously published essay "Thinking through Queer Theory," "AIDS has disappeared as a public issue, and also as a gay issue. . . . Except for a few queer activists, the entire society seems to believe that AIDS is now being cured—which it is not—and that the number of people with AIDS has gone down—which it has not."[9] In this context, where the normalization of AIDS remained (and remains still) a cogent and much needed political goal, Sedgwick renewed the call for a "queer analysis, not a strictly gay one," to address a "disease that respects no simple boundaries of identity."[10]

In what follows, I return to Sedgwick's contribution to the origins of queer theorizing by inhabiting the critical distinction that lives in the paragraph just quoted, where the contrast between a conservative gay politics of normalization and a politically queer one confounds the nearly canonical equation between queer inquiry and antinormativity that anchors the contemporary self-definition of queer studies. This equation is ubiquitous across various domains of academic writing, from scholarly monographs to blogs, journal essays, conference themes, and program mission statements, making antinormativity the single most resonant feature of the field's depiction of its own political, critical, and epistemological achievements. Even a quick survey of institutional documents in North America underscores this point. In one program description, for example, queer studies is presented as an interdisciplinary field that focuses on the "histories, contemporary experiences, and community-based knowledges of lesbians, gay men, bisexuals, transgender people, intersexed people, queers, and others who occupy non-heterosexist and non-normative gender positionalities."[11] Other programs promise an interdisciplinary range of courses to address "the relationship between the normative and the transgressive," thereby defining the mission of the field as the study of "norms" and "how [they] are produced and come to be taken for granted." In still other institutional documents, queer studies is described as the only academic arena that "denaturalizes heterosexuality and interrogates analyses of sexuality normativity."

To be sure, the very postulation of antinormativity as canonical is at odds with the political disposition at stake in the historical cultivation of the antinormative thesis. For scholars writing before the field's institutional consolidation, "queer" held critical promise precisely because its antinormativity was bound to a refusal of institutional forms of all kinds, including those most familiar in discipline-oriented terms.[12] For David Halperin, for instance, "queer" was valuable "not as a positivity but as a positionality, not as a thing, but as a resistance to the norm."[13] Scholars today continue to cite queer inquiry along these lines, objecting to more familiar disciplinary protocols that would designate proper objects of study and methodological guarantees in favor of the field's antinormative intuitions and political priorities. As Donald E. Hall and Annamarie Jagose put it in their introduction to the *Routledge Queer Studies Reader*, "Queer Studies' commitment to non-normativity and anti-identitarianism, coupled with its refusal to define its proper field of operation in relation to any fixed content," make it "potentially attentive to any socially consequential difference that contributes to regimes of sexual normalization."[14]

My interest in emphasizing the axiomatic antinormativity of queer studies is not meant to dismiss the political commitments that have shaped the field or to disavow my own history of being enthralled by them.[15] Nor do I want to challenge prevailing opinion by repeating the political formulations that incite it, as if the problem to be faced today is *the normativity of antinormativity* as the field's most disciplining (inter)disciplinary rule. In line with conversations begun elsewhere, my aim is to undermine altogether the security of antinormativity as an inherently radical critical position by revising our understanding of scholarly work long taken to invite—and underwrite—the field's antinormative thesis.[16] A key passage for this investigation is Sedgwick's own. In "Queer and Now," the introduction to her 1993 book *Tendencies*, Sedgwick addresses in print for the first time the conceptual rubric that had come to frame her scholarship in the aftermath of *Epistemology of the Closet*.[17] To answer the resonant question, "What's 'queer'?" she ruminates on the holiday season—Christmas—in which she was writing, lamenting "the monolith" created as "religion, state, capital, ideology, domesticity, [and] the discourses of power and legitimacy" all come to "speak in one voice." "What if," she posits, "there were a practice of valuing the ways that meanings and institutions can be at loose ends with each other? What if the richest junctures weren't the ones where *everything means the same thing?*"[18] By reading this provocation as a necessary intervention into consolidations of every kind, my essay casts doubt on the capacity of antinormativity to engage the political, historical, and psychic complexities of the very social relations at stake in contemporary queer studies.[19]

To that end, my discussion turns first to the book that is now taken to have inaugurated an interdisciplinary field of study, *Epistemology of the Closet*, to review its appetite for contradiction, incoherence, and the political double bind before reconsidering the famously vexed lesbian (and) feminist critical inheritances that underwrite Sedgwick's contribution to queer studies—inheritances that are stunningly at stake in the contentious scene Tom and I witnessed at Yale. To read this scene in all of its affective and critical entailments, I trace Sedgwick's response to the criticism her work inspired, beginning with the book that first drew lesbian (and) feminist contention, *Between Men: English Literature and Male Homosocial Desire*.[20] My specific focus is on the figure foregrounded in my title—the triangle—which has significance across the body of Sedgwick's work in multiple ways: not only as a convention of canonical narration in *Between Men*, but as a metaphor for the work of interpretation and as a pedagogy for exploring the incommensurabilities of identity and identification. By following "Eve's Triangles"—on the bridge with Tom and me; in conversations with her texts and their lesbian readers; and in the feminist, queer, and antihomophobic inquiries she crafted—there is much to be said about why Sedgwick never refused to respond to the question that both inscribed and exiled her from identity's prevailing terms. *"Are you a lesbian?"* On more than one occasion she offered a simple, resonant "no."

It might be hard today to recapture the audacity of Sedgwick's proclamation in the second sentence of *Epistemology of the Closet* that "virtually any aspect of modern Western culture must be, not merely incomplete, but damaged in its central substance to the degree that it does not incorporate a critical analysis of modern homo/heterosexual definition."[21] This provocation follows Michel Foucault's *The History of Sexuality, Volume 1* but raises the ante of his historicizing claims by pondering the consequences of the story he tells on the discursive shape of the present. Sedgwick is chiefly concerned with the fact that, among the many different figures Foucault discerns in the nineteenth-century rise of *scientia sexualis*—the masturbator, hysteric, fetishist, pedophile, and homosexual—it was "precisely one, the gender of object choice, [that] emerged from the turn of the century, and has remained, as *the* dimension denoted by the now ubiquitous category of 'sexual orientation.'"[22] Discarding, as did Foucault, the pursuit of an explanation for this radical contraction of sexual definition, Sedgwick seeks instead to revise the contemporary critical uptake of his famous declaration that "the homosexual was now a species" by probing the perspective from which late twentieth-century scholars approach the seeming coherence and legibility of homosexuality.[23] What, she asks, *is* the homosexuality that we think we know? For Sedgwick, this is the question submerged in scholarly arguments about the impact of Foucault's famous volume, which undermined gay and lesbian studies projects that looked to homosexuality as a historically continuous identity by exposing the disciplinary apparatuses that wed homosexuality to modern personhood. As she frames the matter in the fifth of her seven field-generating axioms in *Epistemology of the Closet*: "*The historical search for a Great Paradigm Shift may obscure the present conditions of sexual identity.*"[24] Sedgwick's goal instead is to "denaturalize the present, rather than the past—in effect, to render less destructively presumable 'homosexuality as we know it today.'"[25]

As is well known, *Epistemology of the Closet*'s turn toward interrogating the coherence of homosexuality as a category of identity was foundational to the anti-identitarian hermeneutics that now serve as a signal characteristic of queer critique. While one can find this commitment across the entire body of Sedgwick's work, its critical force emerges most profoundly in *Epistemology of the Closet*'s explication of the qualifying phrase used earlier, as Sedgwick seeks to render homosexuality "less destructively presumable" by parsing its discursive, political, and institutional complexities.[26] This entails defining the double binds that shape contemporary sexual politics, where what we inherit from the "architects of our present culture," she writes, are two spellbinding contradictions that are "internal to all the important twentieth century understandings of homo/heterosexual definition, both heterosexist and antihomophobic."[27] These contradictions—between a minoritizing and universalizing view of homosexuality, on the one hand, and a gender-separatist and gender-integrationist view of same-sex object choice, on the other—frame the critical dilemma that governs the book and mark its most compelling challenge to contemporary understandings of critical practice and politics.[28] "The purpose of this book," she writes in the opening pages, "is not to adjudicate between the two poles of either of these contradictions, for, if its argument is right, no epistemological grounding now exists from which to do so. Instead, I am trying to make the strongest possible introductory case for a hypothesis about the centrality . . . of [these] definitional issues to the important knowledges and understandings of twentieth-century Western culture as a whole."[29] In these terms, any attempt to judge the form that sexual politics should take is compromised from the outset by the complexity of the contradictions that characterize the political and conceptual field.

In thus parsing the political demand *on* criticism as a demand to articulate the contradictions that shape the present, *Epistemology of the Closet* achieves its most exacting critical precision by deferring political mastery over its subject. One catches a glimpse of the critical impact of this deferral at the end of "Reality and Realization," an essay in the posthumous volume of her work edited by Jonathan Goldberg. In charting her turn toward Buddhism and its critical as well as affective value, Sedgwick considers how "respect for realization as both process and practice" stands in contrast to the epistemological pursuits of Western critical theory.[30] She writes:

> The stuttering, exclusive perseveration of epistemological propositions in contemporary critical theory reads as a stubborn hysterical defense. Whether it comes in the form of anti-essentialist hypervigilance or, say, of the moralizing Marxist insistence that someone else is evading a true recognition of materiality, all this epistemological fixation, with all its paralyzing scruples or noisy, accusatory projections, can also seem like a hallucinatorily elaborated, long-term refusal to enter into realization as into a complex practice. Rather, it can't stop claiming mastery of reality as a flat, propositional object of a single verb, shivering in its threadbare near-transparency: the almost fatally thin "to know."[31]

In this reference to two seemingly divergent critical traditions—poststructuralism and Marxism—Sedgwick casts prominent contemporary forms of left critique as not simply impoverished but belligerently, even willfully so, as both draw their political credibility from the pretense "to know" the truth about "reality," no matter how differently conceived. Hence, for her the hypervigilance required to ward off theoretical error for the poststructuralist is as epistemologically driven as the moralizing noise of the Marxist's accusatory proclamation that the theoretical stakes of theory are materially real. In this textual terrain of paralyzing scruples, Buddhism is compelling for Sedgwick precisely because it inhabits the limit questions of humanism not by turning its back on knowing, but by trying to attend to what that "single verb" pursuit is so desperate to elude.

While there is much to say about the way that "thin" and "fatally" collide in the quote to conjure a set of relations found throughout Sedgwick's writing, it is her emphasis on the epistemological fixation of critical theory that interests me the most.[32] One can hear a similar "stubborn hysterical defense" in the rhetorical habits of contemporary queer studies where the repeated—and repeatedly unquestioned—declaration of antinormativity as the field's most formidable theoretical intervention cloaks the epistemological power it thereby secures through the deeply affective and intensely aspirational claim to political transgression and transformation; this, after all, is what the invocation of the political as the value of critical thought so optimistically confers.[33] But the cost of this security is high, as the very proliferation of antinormativity has entailed a striking condensation, transforming normativity from its early status as an object of study into *the* political position against which the field articulates its own institutional ambitions.[34] In this condensation, normativity is overwritten by the ahistorical presumption that it is always regressive and constraining—in short, that it is always politically bad. The problem here is simple, if perplexing: that no matter the ongoing affiliation of queer inquiry with the itinerant, unstable, unintelligible, fluid, negative, backward, unproductive, low, open-ended, or out of sync, the political imaginary that antinormativity yields as the defining politics of queer studies exacts a disciplinary toll on critical practice, rendering the contingent relationship between knowledge and politics in noncontradictory, if not wholly determinist terms. As a consequence, we might say that the political pursuit of queer studies today is epistemologically driven, as critical authority is dispensed (or withheld) on the basis of *always knowing* the difference between normativity and the value of being queerly set against it. It is this kind of guarantee—this certainty about the political capacity of critical judgment—that I reference when I call Sedgwick's critical practice something other than "political mastery."

To be sure, Sedgwick never aimed her antiepistemological commitments toward the question of normativity per se, and one would be hard pressed to argue that her scholarship had no impact on orienting queer inquiry toward the antinormative dispositions that now characterize it.[35] "Queer" was an adjective attached to the activity of her criticism in the aftermath of the publication of *Epistemology of the Closet*. By the time she embraced it in the introduction to *Tendencies*, it served as the framework for self-nomination and explanation, providing the necessary vehicle for responding to the identity expectations we now take as endemic of those years. If, today, we consider her as a foundational figure in the field *and* if we regard queer studies as premised on an opposition to identity-oriented thought, this twin billing is possible only because the struggles over Sedgwick's identity have been largely muted by casting the early demand on her to be a lesbian as decidedly different from the demand the field now exerts on practitioners to claim antinormativity as the epistemological and political value of the designation "queer." As strange as it might now seem, "queer" amassed power in Sedgwick's work *as a defense* against the charge of sexual normativity, providing the framework for distinctions that would be as important to her own position in the field as they would become to the field's institutional self-definition, for in "valuing the ways that meanings and institutions can be at loose ends with one another," Sedgwick was able to distinguish the meaning of her identifications with gay men from the institutions of marriage and heterosexuality to which the question *"Are you a lesbian?"* threatened to keep her bound.[36] To say this is not to diminish the importance of Sedgwick's queer critical inquiries but to establish with greater clarity one of the potent forces that compelled them. As she put it in 1993, "What it takes—all it takes—to make the description 'queer' a true one is the impulsion *to* use it in the first person."[37]

To think about Eve Sedgwick in this way is to encounter her at a different distance, one that locates her self-defense in the context of queer inquiry's institutional history, where antinormativity has served not only as the framework of its most passionate political commitments, but also as an identity-laden metric for determining and establishing critical authority in the field, albeit one that continues to be roundly disavowed. A quick comparison with the queer embrace of Judith Butler's *Gender Trouble: Feminism and the Subversion of Identity* (1990) is especially telling in this regard, as its foundational status was never predicated on a defense of its object attachments or underwritten by a personal narrative that established the author's lesbian-feminist inheritances as the warrant to challenge them.[38] And yet it was Butler who made famous her own resistance to going "to Yale to be a lesbian" in the essay "Imitation and Gender Insubordination," which extended her critique of identity as a regulatory regime to include sexual identity, including her own.[39] This is not to say that Butler was spared critiques of her work—far from it.[40] But it is to magnify the way that contestations concerning the relation between identity and identification—evoked most dramatically by the specter of Sedgwick's presumptive heterosexuality—have been complexly implicated in the pursuit of antinormativity as a critical and political ideal. It is not a hallucination to claim, in fact, that the greatest critical mobility for anti-identitarianism in the field has issued from the most secure identity quarters, as if the propulsion not to "be" a lesbian required the claim to the category as precondition for its transgression. The implications of this—the disavowed identity relations of queer critique—are enormous, especially today as the ongoing political value of the field is being defined against the complicity of various "queer" identifications with normativity. In the political imaginary that antinormativity has institutionalized in the field, nothing has escaped suspicion except the belief in antinormativity itself.

Let's return now to the scene at Yale, where Eve's triangulated identification as a married woman who loved and studied gay male life in the context of Western cultural organization was taken as a political as well as a professional threat to feminist and lesbian-feminist audiences. I must confess that I was conflicted about the prominence of gay men in the critical imaginary of sexual studies as it unfolded in those years, even as Sedgwick's *Between Men: English Literature and Male Homosocial Desire* had taught me to read the asymmetry of homosociality in patriarchal social orders as crucial to my own dissertation interests in the racialized nexus of masculine bonds in the US.[41] But while I had some hint of how the scene of interracial male bonding was serving in my own work as a means to identify with the women-of-color feminism that had brought me to the topic of race and masculinity in the first place, I had no idea how to deploy that identification as a central part of my inquiry.[42] Instead I feared it: feared attending to the way that black male bodies were part of a project of routing my affinities away from whiteness and the potent compact across sexual difference that has constituted white racial formation and undermined feminism at every turn—feared, that is, what it might mean for me, as a white woman, to seek an allegiance with black men in a history in which white women have been deadly to them.[43] It was easier to concern myself with the question of the legibility of the lesbian where the authority of my claim to the category could defer the difficulty of exploring the actual and at times awful explosiveness of political alliances, or the discomfort that can accompany identification, or the confusion that can follow the errant itineraries of desire—that is, all the ways in which who we are, what we want, what we feel, and what moves or makes us are not commensurate with either our social identities or the political subjectivities we critically seek.

Sedgwick, as we know, was never unaware of these complexities. In the early days of institutionalizing identity-oriented knowledges, when discerning an identity object of study from the vantage point of "being it" *was* what identity studies meant, Sedgwick understood well the dicey terrain in which her first book, *Between Men*, maneuvered.[44] In the introduction she wrote, "As a woman and a feminist writing (in part) about male homosexuality, I feel I must be especially explicit about the political groundings, assumptions, and ambitions of this study. . . . My intention throughout has been to conduct an antihomophobic as well as feminist inquiry."[45] In doing so, Sedgwick sought to intervene in the existent literature on the relationship between women and male homosexuality, which had suffered, she writes, from one of two overdetermining assumptions: "either that gay men and all women share a 'natural,' transhistorical alliance . . . or else that male homosexuality is an epitome, a personification, an effect, or perhaps a primary cause of woman-hating."[46] By reading both of these assumptions as false, Sedgwick set out to develop an analytic that could help "shed light" on the "alliance" between "feminism and antihomophobia" by attending to the distinctly gendered history of homosocial desire in the modern West.[47]

This agenda entailed setting feminism's own analysis of the continuum that shaped the relationship between "women loving women" and "women promoting the interests of women" in a wider frame of reference, one capable of accounting for the radical discontinuity that underwrote male bonds, where there had been no modern cultural or political discourse aimed at negotiating the divide between "men loving men" and "men promoting the interests of men."[48] On the contrary, male homosocial bonds were structured by homophobic prohibition, denial, and violent negation—not generically but as a primary characteristic of twentieth-century Western patriarchy. By detailing this structure through careful readings of (mostly) canonical Western literature, *Between Men* made a feminist case for rethinking the familiar but historically specific relationship between the injunction against homosexuality and the patriarchal production and sustenance of masculine bonds.

Sedgwick's key focus was the "erotic triangle"—a figure she drew from René Girard's well-regarded study *Deceit, Desire, and the Novel*, which explored the plot lines of major European texts in which two men enter into a rivalrous relationship with one another for the attention/love/devotion of the same woman.[49] What engaged Sedgwick was *Deceit's* "insistence that, in any erotic rivalry, the bond that links the two rivals is as intense and potent as the bond that links either of the rivals to the beloved. . . . In fact, Girard seems to see the bond between rivals . . . as being even stronger."[50] Hence, the social relations produced through "the bonds of 'rivalry' and 'love' . . . are equally powerful and in many senses equivalent," thus raising important issues about the circulation of desire, the psychic work of identification, and the power relations produced, reconfigured, and confirmed in the erotic triangle.[51]

According to Sedgwick, such issues could not be fully answered from within Girard's framework, as his analysis suffered from an inability to consider the ways in which gender and sexuality were always pertinent to the calculus of power through which the erotic triangle functioned—not simply in literary narratives but also in the Oedipal scenario that informed his project as a whole, where the familiar triangle of father-mother-child was importantly differentiated by the child's sex and by the routes of attachment and identification that produce or prohibit sexual object choice.[52] *Between Men* resituated the erotic triangle to contend with these issues, addressing the interplay of gender and power that structures modern patriarchal formation, first, by giving the relationship between the rivalrous men a name, "homosocial desire"; second, by establishing that desire as on par with, if not at times more socially valuable than, the heterosexual bond that was otherwise taken to found the triangle's erotic life; and third, by undermining the structuralism of Girard's account by engaging the historical variability of gender and its meanings, especially as it shaped radically incongruent conceptions of homosexuality across time.[53] Sedgwick thus made visible what Girard's analysis of the erotic triangle could not: that the structuring prohibition that barred the men from choosing one another as sexual objects existed in dramatic tension with the priority afforded masculine bonds in Western modernity—and further, that this tension was routinely defined by, if not organized through, relationships to women, whether real or imagined, rejected or pursued. As she put it, "The status of women, and the whole question of arrangements between genders, is deeply and inescapably inscribed in the structure even of relationships that seem to exclude women—even in male homosocial/homosexual relationships."[54] In developing this claim, Sedgwick argued for the importance of addressing the historical variability of the meaning of "men's genital activity with men," noting that the "virility of the homosexual orientation of male desire seemed as self-evident to the ancient Spartans, and perhaps to Whitman, as its effeminacy seems in contemporary popular culture."[55] In chapters that moved from Shakespeare's sonnets to the novels of Laurence Sterne, George Eliot, and Charles Dickens, among others, *Between Men* argued convincingly that "the etiology and the continuing experience of male homosexuality . . . [is] inextricable from the changing shapes of the institutions by which gender and class inequality are structured."[56]

Today, *Between Men* can be read as a generative contribution to what was a decade-long feminist reconsideration of the structure, history, and operation of "patriarchy," perhaps the most important term in the feminist theoretical lexicon in the 1980s.[57] But in 1992, when Sedgwick wrote a new preface to accompany the book's post–*Epistemology of the Closet* reprint, she had ample reason to believe that its distinctly feminist commitments had been underappreciated, if not completely obscured. This was a book, as we now know, that "evoked rage . . . on a continuing basis," especially from "other feminist scholars"—the very readers whom Sedgwick imagined as her primary audience.[58] In the 1992 preface, Sedgwick reinforced this point by describing the environment of her everyday critical passions while *Between Men* was being composed: "I was very involved with lesbian-inflected feminist culture and critique, but I actually knew only one openly gay man."[59] In this context, Sedgwick was keen to consider the critical limits of what identity imposed on a "feminocentric field . . . in which the subjects, paradigms, and political thrust of research, as well as the researchers themselves, might all be indentified [*sic*] with the female."[60] Expressing these limits in language that readers of *Tendencies* would come to know as characteristic of her investment in "queer," she explained: "Participating in each of these contingencies, I still needed to keep faith . . . with an obstinate intuition that the loose ends and crossed ends of identity are more fecund than the places where identity, desire, analysis, and need can all be aligned and centered."[61] *Between Men* was meant "very pointedly as a complicating, antiseparatist, and antihomophobic contribution to a feminist movement with which, nonetheless, I identified fairly unproblematically."[62] In these terms, the preface performs its own commitment to an analysis of triangulated desire by foregrounding the transferential relations that mobilize Sedgwick's critical practice, where optimism, disappointment, and prohibition mark the complexities of the contingent identifications she claims: feminism, lesbian-inflected critique, and male homosexuality.

As I read, the triangle thus becomes much more than a structure of conventional narration; in the context of her retrospective reflection, it offers a conceptual framework to engage the affective intensity of the response her work repeatedly generated, confounding the story that has been told about the complexity of her own identifications.[63]

To be sure, we do not need Sedgwick's 1992 ruminations on the reception of *Between Men* to understand the force of the triangle as a theoretical lever for attending to her work's broader interventions into the complexities not simply of identity but of identification. The final axiom of *Epistemology of the Closet* is devoted to the matter at hand, albeit in a different rhetorical key and with a much fuller rendering of the complexities of identification both across identities and within them: "*The paths of allo-identification,*" she writes, "*are likely to be strange and recalcitrant. So are the paths of auto-identification.*"[64] To explicate this axiom, Sedgwick begins by citing her earlier discussion in *Between Men* when she first took on the question of what it means to be "'a woman and a feminist writing (in part) about male homosexuality.'" She wrote, "My account was, essentially, that this was an under-theorized conjunction, and it was about time that someone put her mind to it. . . . [T]he intervening years have taught me more about how important, not to say mandatory, such an accounting must be—as well as how almost prohibitively difficult."[65] One lesson entails rejecting what she calls the "abstractive formulations" used in the introduction to *Between Men* in favor of attending to "the way political commitments and identifications actually work. Realistically, what brings me to this work can hardly be that I am *a* woman, or *a* feminist, but that I am this particular one."[66] In addition, because the routes of attachment and investment move in multiple directions, the reader is likewise bound to critical desires and analytic animations that arise from her own particularities. Hence, while "it takes deeply rooted, durable, and often somewhat opaque energies to write a book," it also takes them, Sedgwick contends, not only "to read it" but "to make any political commitment" at all.[67]

To illustrate this point in the critical idiom she implicitly calls for, Sedgwick recalls a graduate seminar she taught in gay and lesbian literature that fractured on the impossibility of the female participants to cohere as a group: "Throughout the semester all the women, including me . . . , attributed our discomfort to some obliquity in the classroom relations between ourselves and the men. But by the end of the semester it seemed clear that we were in the grip of some much more intimate dissonance. It . . . was among the group of women, all feminists . . . that some nerve of individually internal difference had been set painfully, contagiously atremble."[68] Sedgwick describes this nerve as arising from "differences among our mostly inexplicit, often somewhat uncrystallized sexual self-definitions," such that "each woman in the class possessed . . . an ability to make one or more of the other women radically and excruciatingly doubt the authority of her own self-definition as a woman; as a feminist; and as the positional subject of a particular sexuality."[69] From this scene of "intimate denegation," Sedgwick engages the familiar but intensely unresolved feminist dilemma of identification in which the possibility of identifying *"as* must always include multiple processes of identification *with.* It also involves identification *as against*."[70] These multiplicities interrupt and confound investments in identity as a source of collective political relief by making apparent the very challenge that identification raises to the security and authority of identity itself. No one in queer studies has attended more fully and forcefully to the pedagogical implications of this than Eve Sedgwick.

The introductory chapter of *Epistemology of the Closet* thus ends, fittingly, in the classroom, where several new triangles emerge—the first being Sedgwick, her female students, and the men in the class; the second being Sedgwick, her feminist readers, and the gay male subjects who populate her text and define its most powerful attachments. To the extent that her feminist readers are also lesbian ones—and it is this that I hear in the charged language of the classroom, where the "positional subject of a particular sexuality" is put under stress—it becomes possible, even necessary, to learn to read *Epistemology of the Closet* again, against the accusation that has shaped a great deal of its distinctly lesbian-feminist critical reception.[71] It seems to me now, twenty years since Yale, that the book's address, like that of *Between Men* before it, emerges from within the deep identificatory lineages of the kinds of triangulation that Sedgwick taught us to explore, as precisely a response to the interpellation of Yale, if not also an exercise in its inhabitation. "It is not only identifications *across* definitional lines that can evoke or support or even require complex and particular narrative explanation; rather, the same is equally true of any person's identification with her or his 'own' gender, class, race, sexuality, nation."[72] If this is the case, as Sedgwick's work repeatedly asserts, then the point is not that the itineraries of auto- and allo-identification live apart or separate from one another but, rather, that their interaction, their diffuse and powerful intersections, their hesitations and deferrals are complexly—indeed, intimately—interwoven. We might even say, following Sedgwick, that there is no epistemological grounding from which to adjudicate them, no matter the importance, in her work and elsewhere, of accounting for the ways that identifications generate the substance—and raise the stakes—of intellectual and political commitments. This is what it means to think of the triangle not simply as a narrative convention, but also as a means for engaging the relational, one that can attend to the various ways that identity can be disrupted, confirmed, congealed, doubted, rebuked, and celebrated but never simply outpaced or overcome—not even in queer studies. *"Are you a lesbian?"* The import of the question lies in the value its answer continues to deliver.

The last time I spoke to Eve was in the book exhibit at a conference in a year that I cannot decisively identify. We exchanged a few words, including my thanks for her help with Tom's book, which had been out for several years but with few reviews and increasingly sparse sales—the dim reality of nearly all academic work on AIDS in this century. People vied for her attention, but I stood there awkwardly, not moving away when I should have, as if some other conversation was about to be had, given how much I thought I knew about her: from reports about the advance of her cancer offered by friends we shared to my own engagement with the increasingly acute reflections on embodiment, identification, and affect that characterized all of her writing after *Epistemology of the Closet*. I want to say—though I have no idea if this is really true—that in the moment before she appeared, I had been thumbing through *Touching Feeling*, fixated as I still am by the textual interruption, "Interlude, Pedagogic," that sits both before and imaginatively *beside* the arguments of the five chapters that comprise the book. The piece opens with an excerpt from a poem by Randall Jarrell called "Hope," the same title as a poem of Tom's, which I included in AIDS *and the National Body*.[73] In it, Jarrell's narrator describes a childhood scene in which his mother faints: "Mother's . . . face no longer smiled at us / Or frowned at us. Did anything to us. / Her face was queerly flushed / Or else queerly pale; I am no longer certain. / That it was queer I am certain." In the pages that follow, Sedgwick rather uncharacteristically says nothing about the poem.[74] Instead, it hovers evocatively over the scene she narrates in which she, too, faints—at a rally against the North Carolina PBS station that had refused in 1991 to air Marlon Riggs's important film on black gay male life, *Tongues Untied*. "This was a fight," she writes, "about blackness, queerness, and (implicitly) AIDS: properties of bodies, some of them our bodies, of bodies that it seemed important to say most people are very willing, and some people murderously eager, to see not exist."[75]

In the space of eight pages, Sedgwick tells the story of the protest by meditating on the insecurity of referentiality and the unsettling work performed by a series of "displacements" that not only accompany but *circulate* meaning as her faint enacts a health emergency in the midst of a protest aimed in part at representing one.[76] As a collaboration between the Ad Hoc Coalition of Black Lesbians and Gays and ACT UP Triangle, the protest was designed "to discredit the pretense at representing the public maintained by our local 'public' broadcasting station." But "our object," she writes, "was not merely to demand representation . . . [but] to *be* representation: somehow to smuggle onto the prohibitive airwaves some version of the . . . dangerous and endangered conjunction, queer and black."[77] How this might be done, under the authoritarian gaze of state troopers and the specularizing gaze of local TV reporters, when "a majority of our smuggling-intent bodies were not themselves black" is the key question that inaugurates the interlude, marking the distance between Sedgwick's own political desires and the embodied particularity that simultaneously marks and unsettles her. Like the other white protesters, Sedgwick was "haplessly embroiled in the processes of reference: reference to other bodies standing beside our own, to the words on our placards, to what we could only hope would be the sufficiently substantial sense—if, indeed, even *we* understood it rightly—of our own intent."[78] In the end, she makes no claim to resolve the ethical dilemma that ensues, where her fainted body—"a mountainous figure, supine, black-clad, paper-white, weirdly bald . . . apparently female, uncannily gravid with meaning (but with what meaning? what usable meaning?)"—places her "at the center of the work of protest" but without volitional intent, as the activity of fainting plunges her into "the deep pit of another world" from which she finds herself "surfacing violently . . . with a state trooper taking my pulse."[79] She is certain about only one thing: that the meaning of her body—"so dense, too dense" in that place—"was indeed not a usable one . . . in relation to the complexly choreographed performative agendas and effects of that demonstration."[80]

In the challenging and disappointing displacements of reference that the interlude maps—white skin, black queer presence; female embodiment, the identity implosions of female baldness; cancer iconicity, AIDS—Sedgwick points in the end toward a "certain magnetic queerness," by which she means a queerness "productive of deviance" to characterize the events that interrupted the protest.[81] This deviance is not destined for celebration, as "queer" provides no clear compass for interpreting either the critical or political stakes of the scene she narrates. On the contrary, the pedagogical force of the story arises from the unsettling relations that incite it, implicitly revising the "axiom" that governs her work—where "the loose ends and crossed ends of identity are more fecund than the places where identity, desires, analysis, and

need can all be aligned"—by demonstrating that such fecundity is as peril-
ous to the possibility and security of meaning as it is inviting.[82] This is, at the
very least, how I read Sedgwick's complex textual choreography as she becomes not only the pale, fainted figure of Jarrell's poem but also its narrator,
the adult who finds in the designation "queer" a way to name the failure of
interpretative precision that resides in the memory that continues to haunt
him. She is also the writer whose meditation on the centrality of her balded
whiteness bears witness to the failure of identification and intention to found
even the most cautious and contingent interpretative agency offered by the
first-person form that framed her deployment of "queer." The meditation ends
with what I am inclined to describe as a terminal kind of hope, as Sedgwick
evokes the value of her own displacement not only in the protest scene but
in the classroom where, finding herself to be "less and less" at its center, she
"was also finding that . . . displacement . . . could provide effects that might
sometimes wrench the boundaries of discourse around in productive if not
always obvious ways."[83] In the triangle thus staged among "Hope," the protest
scene, and the classroom, the interlude eschews the more familiar argument-
oriented and concept-driven itineraries of critical practice to perform the affective densities of its chief concerns: activism, race, gender, sexuality, illness,
death. Affective density, not epistemological proposition. A writer's text, not
a critic's argument. Touching feeling, not "knowing" it.

Today, of course, I am—we are—reading Sedgwick in the context of the
most inevitable displacement. That she tried to prepare us for this is certain, as
her work increasingly compelled readers to abandon their interpretative dependencies, along with the resentments that routinely traveled with them. At
first this meant learning to let go of the object orientations that anchored and
affirmed feminist criticism's own sense of political agency in order to pursue
the circulations of desire that linked male bonds in the midst of monumental
prohibitions. If the triangle served as the narrative form that figured this pursuit, its pedagogical impact drew more than my generation of scholars toward
a feminist practice that is far more capacious than the one we first knew. In
Epistemology of the Closet, Sedgwick challenged the political imaginary of
leftist criticism altogether by honing an appetite for the double bind, which
meant learning how to withstand the insecurity of a present that offered no
epistemological grounding from which to adjudicate the contradictions that
characterized it. Less an intended performance of "queer theory" than a revi-
sion of what theory could do as part of an avowedly "antihomophobic" enterprise, *Epistemology* reconfigured the relations among sex, sexuality, and gender

to displace the centrality of identity categories for a deeper inquiry into the scope and complexity of the hetero-homosexual distinction itself.[84] By the time *Tendencies* appeared three years later, she was writing in the midst of both new and ongoing threats: breast cancer and a readership still coming to terms with her insistence on identification, posed more extensively and ever more precisely in the richly contextualized language of "this particular one."[85] "Queer" would emerge here as the resonant figure of "now," as Sedgwick turned what was tacitly a defense of her critical authority into an explication of the profound pleasure she found in putting her pleasure in writing on display.[86] Retrospectively, we can take much of the work after *Epistemology of the Closet* as a performance of the genre of criticism she would name "*experimental* critical writing."[87] Under its auspices, readers have been invited into "the circuit of contagion, fun, voyeurism, envy, participation, and simulation" that such writing promises to deliver as it seeks out "spaces of thought and work where everything doesn't mean the same thing!"[88]

In taking permission from Sedgwick to shift my focus to the density of the relations that her writing engages, I have offered less an argument against the antinormative thesis that now anchors the field's political self-conception than an exploration of what it means to read her abiding interest in contradiction and incommensurability in a new way: as a pertinent reminder in our own critical moment of the limitations of configuring any dualistic account of the political as a transformative ideal. My concern with this, the most disciplinary rule in queer studies today, has not been forwarded as an exercise in rescuing normativity from collective condemnation, for even the most basic deconstructive lesson would demonstrate that standing on one side or the other of the prevailing distinction between normativity and its antithesis revises nothing in the larger critical ecology in which we write and think. The issue this essay raises is more simple if vexing precisely because any effort to consider normativity a complex object of study is so decisively at odds with the transgressive fictions that underwrite the field's sovereign declarations: *this* is what we choose, *this* is what we refuse, *this* is what we/they are.[89] In light of these assertions, it is increasingly the case that a studied approach to the complexity of normativity as it operates across the spheres of social and psychic life is precisely what antinormativity enables the field to most actively resist. While much more needs to be said about the affective density of such resistance, my essay has turned its attention elsewhere, finding in "Eve's Triangles" and the antiepistemological dispositions that shaped her pedagogical reflections a way to hear, twenty-five years after Yale, the impasse that antinormativity now poses as the field's most stubborn defense: *Are you a lesbian?*

NOTES

1 A slightly different version of this essay was published as part of a larger project on the possibility of "Queer Theory without Antinormativity": see Robyn Wiegman and Elizabeth A. Wilson, *Queer Theory without Antinormativity* (Durham, NC: Duke University Press, 2015).

2 This was the Third Annual Lesbian and Gay Studies Conference in 1989. The previous two were also held at Yale. In 1990, the conference moved to Harvard and then to Rutgers in 1991. The final "annual" conference—the sixth—was held at the University of Iowa in 1994. The field name under which Sedgwick would hold foundational status had been revised toward Teresa DeLauretis's nomination, "queer theory," in 1991: see Teresa DeLauretis, ed., "Queer Theory: Lesbian and Gay Sexualities," *Differences* 3, no. 2 (1991): iii–xviii. Sedgwick herself did not use "queer" in print to refer to her own work until 1993, in "Queer and Now," the introduction to *Tendencies* (Durham, NC: Duke University Press, 1993). For her, as I discuss here, the queer theory project was deeply intertwined with AIDS political activism. As she explained in an interview in 1995, "The historical links between the emergence of queer theory and the emergency of AIDS are very close. For one thing, theory is important with this disease, because the self-evident categories that we had before don't work about this virus. AIDS, among all of the tragedy and devastation, also makes a huge problem for thinking, and in AIDS activism the interpenetration of theory and activism is extensive and very productive": Mark Kerr and Kristen O'Rourke, "Sedgwick Sense and Sensibility: An Interview with Eve Kosofsky Sedgwick," *Thresholds: Viewing Culture* 9 (1994), http://nideffer.net/proj/Tvc/interviews/20.Tvc.v9.intrvws.Sedg.html. For a discussion of the Yale conference in 1987, see Siobhan B. Somerville, "Feminism, Queer Theory, and the Racial Closet," *Criticism* 52, no. 2 (Spring 2010): 191–200.

3 Numerous scholars have discussed Sedgwick's relation to the lesbian—as object of study, personal identification, or political affiliation—from a variety of critical perspectives. See, e.g., Terry Castle, *The Apparitional Lesbian: Female Homosexuality and Modern Culture* (New York: Columbia University Press, 1993); Teresa DeLauretis, *The Practice of Love: Lesbian Sexuality and Perverse Desire* (Bloomington: Indiana University Press, 1994); Jason Edwards, *Eve Kosofsky Sedgwick* (Abingdon, UK: Routledge, 2009); Annamarie Jagose, "Eve Kosofsky Sedgwick," in *Key Contemporary Social Theorists*, ed. Anthony Elliott and Larry Lay (Malden, MA: Blackwell, 2003), 239–45; Annamarie Jagose, "Feminism's Queer Theory," *Feminism and Psychology* 19, no. 2 (2009): 157–74; Melissa Solomon, "Flaming Iguanas, Dalai Pandas, and Other Lesbian Bardos

(A Few Perimeter Points)," in *Regarding Sedgwick: Essays on Queer Culture and Critical Theory*, ed. Stephen M. Barber and David L. Clark (New York: Routledge, 2002), 201–16; Blakey Vermeule, "Is There a Sedgwick School for Girls?" *Qui Parle* 5, no. 1 (Fall–Winter 1991): 53–72.

4 Tom Yingling, AIDS *and the National Body* (Durham, NC: Duke University Press, 1997). In defining 1996 as a "nodal point" in the history of HIV and AIDS, Sedgwick notes how "news from the Eleventh International AIDS Conference in Vancouver [that summer] indicated for the first time that . . . HIV could plausibly be treated as a chronic disease": Eve Kosofsky Sedgwick, "Melanie Klein and the Difference Affect Makes," *South Atlantic Quarterly* 106, no. 3 (Summer 2007): 639.

5 Sedgwick, "Melanie Klein and the Difference Affect Makes," 639. In what Sedgwick calls a "strange chiasmus," it was also during the summer of 1996 that she received a terminal diagnosis when her breast cancer, first treated in 1991, "spread and bec[a]me incurable. So my own temporality and mortality came into an unexpected kind of focus—informed by my own immersion in the AIDS emergency, but experienced, as it also happened, through a very different set of affective frameworks": Sedgwick, "Melanie Klein and the Difference Affect Makes," 639.

6 For the general shape of the controversy over Gary Fisher's work and Sedgwick's publication of it, see Ellis Hanson, "The Future's Eve: Reparative Reading after Sedgwick," *South Atlantic Quarterly* 110, no. 1 (Winter 2011): 101–19; Dwight A. McBride, *Why I Hate Abercrombie and Fitch: Essays on Race and Sexuality* (New York: New York University Press, 2005), esp. 94–98; Robert F. Reid-Pharr, *Black Gay Man: Essays* (New York: New York University Press, 2001).

7 The language I use to connote field formation is purposely meant to differentiate two terms that are often conflated in contemporary scholarship: "queer theory" and "queer studies." I take the former as a distinct genre of critical analysis that emerged largely in English departments in the US university in the late 1980s, when a complex brew of identity knowledges, cultural studies, and critical theory revised accepted notions of identity's political compass in academic leftist discourses, challenging long-standing philosophical and literary traditions of humanism and liberalism. The influence of AIDS activism on the anti-identitarian and antihomophobic political imaginary of queer theory was profound and—as this essay hopes to suggest—ongoing, if at times disavowed, as Sedgwick has argued in her work on the topic. Queer studies, by contrast, is the name of an interdisciplinary project that is increasingly institutionalized in formal terms, with undergraduate programs of study, faculty directors, and various degree-granting capabilities (certificates, undergraduate minors, and, in some cases, a major). It typically houses courses in queer theory, but its interdisciplinary commitments draw on much broader disciplinary traditions,

some of which are deeply antithetical to the anti-identitarian and posthumanist inclinations of queer theory. For an elaboration of the stakes of these distinctions for understanding the genealogy of queer inquiry as it relates to both disciplinary formation and academic left political aspirations, see Robyn Wiegman, "The Vertigo of Critique: Rethinking Heteronormativity," in *Object Lessons*, by Robyn Wiegman (Durham, NC: Duke University Press, 2012), 301–43.

8 For the most important formulations of these concepts, see, respectively, David Eng, *The Feeling of Kinship: Queer Liberalism and the Racialization of Intimacy* (Durham, NC: Duke University Press, 2010); Lisa Duggan, "The New Homonormativity: The Sexual Politics of Neoliberalism," in *Materializing Democracy: Toward a Revitalized Cultural Politics*, ed. Russ Castronovo and Dana D. Nelson (Durham, NC: Duke University, 2002), 175–94; Jasbir Puar, "Mapping U.S. Homonormativities," *Gender, Place and Culture* 13, no. 1 (February 2001): 67–88; Jasbir Puar, *Terrorist Assemblages: Homonationalism in Queer Times* (Durham, NC: Duke University Press, 2007).

9 Eve Kosofsky Sedgwick, "Thinking through Queer Theory," in Eve Kosofsky Sedgwick, *The Weather in Proust*, ed. Jonathan Goldberg (Durham, NC: Duke University Press, 2011), 202. Even in this context, Sedgwick would also say that "the conservative mainstream of the gay/lesbian movement is achieving some successes, and I do not want to diminish the importance of any success in an antihomophobic undertaking. Such successes are all too rare": Sedgwick, "Thinking through Queer Theory," 202. In 2004, in a review of *The L Word*, she similarly reflected on the antihomophobic effects of mainstream projects, finding "novelty in normalcy," as the title of the review put it. Detailing the poverty of the show's narrative engagement with contemporary politics, she nonetheless asserted that the success of *The L Word* mattered to "queer cultural politics." She wrote, "The series should make a real and unpredictable difference in the overall landscape of the media world. Palpably, the quantitative effect of a merely additive change—dramatizing more than one lesbian plot at a time—makes a qualitative difference in viewers' encounter with social reality. The sense of the lesbian individual, isolated or coupled, scandalous, scrutinized, staggering under her representational burden, gives way to the vastly livelier potential of a lesbian ecology": Eve Kosofsky Sedgwick, "The L Word: Novelty in Normalcy," *Chronicle of Higher Education*, January 16, 2004, B10.

10 Sedgwick, "Thinking through Queer Theory," 202.

11 My interest in these program documents is in their representative status as institutionalized formulations of the field, not their specific origin. Hence, I have purposely eschewed the usual rules of citation.

12 Michael Warner's introduction to the 1991 special issue of *Social Text* used the concept of "heteronormativity" for the first time in print: Michael Warner, "Introduction: Fear of a Queer Planet," *Social Text* 29 (1991): 3. Two years later, an edited volume under the same title, *Fear of a Queer Planet*, appeared, followed at

the end of the decade by his influential *The Trouble with Normal*: Michael Warner, ed., *Fear of a Queer Planet: Queer Politics and Social Theory* (Minneapolis: University of Minnesota Press, 1993); Michael Warner, *The Trouble with Normal: Sex, Politics and the Ethics of Queer Life* (New York: Free Press, 1999). Along the way, Warner and Lauren Berlant published the extensively cited essay "Sex in Public," which deliberates with analytical precision on the meaning of heteronormativity. It also introduces the concept of "homonormativity" to the field—a fact that is largely forgotten in citational histories of the term. "Heteronormativity," they write, is "a concept distinct from heterosexuality. One of the most conspicuous differences is that it has no parallel, unlike heterosexuality, which organizes homosexuality as its opposite. Because homosexuality can never have the invisible, tacit, society-founding rightness that heterosexuality has, it would not be possible to speak of 'homonormativity' in the same sense": Lauren Berlant and Michael Warner, "Sex in Public," *Critical Inquiry* 24, no. 2 (1998): 548n2. See also Lauren Berlant and Michael Warner, "What Does Queer Theory Teach Us about X?," PMLA 110, no. 3 (May 1995): 343–49.

13 David Halperin, *Saint Foucault: Towards a Gay Hagiography* (New York: Oxford University Press, 1995), 66. Halperin would lament, rather quickly, what he took to be a contraction of *queer*'s critical capacity wrought by its increasing deployment as a category of identity, as in the elaboration of lesbian, gay, and bisexual to include queer: see David M. Halperin, "The Normalization of Queer Theory," *Journal of Homosexuality* 45, nos. 2–4 (2003): 339–43.

14 Donald E. Hall and Annamarie Jagose, eds., *The Routledge Queer Studies Reader* (New York: Routledge, 2013), xvi.

15 For a critique of the centrality of antinormativity in queer theory on the grounds of its historical presentism, see Karma Lochrie, *Heterosyncrasies: Female Sexuality When Normal Wasn't* (Minneapolis: University of Minnesota Press, 2005).

16 See Wiegman, "The Vertigo of Critique."

17 Eve Kosofsky Sedgwick, *Epistemology of the Closet* (Berkeley: University of California Press, 1991). In 1993, Sedgwick also published two other essays that embraced the conceptual rubric of queer: see Eve Kosofsky Sedgwick, "Queer Performativity: Henry James's *The Art of the Novel*," GLQ 1 (1993): 1–16; Eve Kosofsky Sedgwick, "Socratic Raptures, Socratic Ruptures: Notes toward Queer Performativity," in *English Inside and Out*, ed. Susan Gubar and Jonathan Kamholtz (New York: Routledge, 1993), 122–36.

18 Sedgwick, *Tendencies*, 5–6.

19 Janet Jakobsen's prescient "Queer Is? Queer Does? Normativity and the Problem of Resistance" argues against binary understandings of norms and normativity in favor of more relationally grounded theorizations of power in order to interrupt the conceptual simplicity of invocations of resistance in queer scholarship. While her essay's goal is different from mine—she seeks to animate queer

forms of social activism by interrupting rhetorical invocations of resistance in favor of more robust enactments—our interests converge in her call for queer inquiry to attend to "the relation among a particular set of norms, the regime of power that is normativity, and the inducement and enforcement of normalization." As she puts it in what could easily be a Sedgwickian axiom, "Not all norms are related to normativity and the normal in the same fashion": Janet Jakobsen, "Queer Is? Queer Does? Normativity and the Problem of Resistance," GLQ 4, no. 4 (1998): 517.

20 Eve Kosofsky Sedgwick, *Between Men: English Literature and Male Homosocial Desire* (New York: Columbia University Press, 1985).

21 Sedgwick, *Epistemology of the Closet*, 1.

22 Sedgwick, *Epistemology of the Closet*, 8.

23 Michel Foucault, *The History of Sexuality, Volume 1: An Introduction*, trans. Robert Hurley (New York: Random House, 1978), 43.

24 Sedgwick, *Epistemology of the Closet*, 44. The other axioms are (1) "People are different from each other"; (2) "The study of sexuality is not coextensive with the study of gender; correspondingly, antihomophobic inquiry is not coextensive with feminist inquiry. But we can't know in advance how they will be different"; (3) "There can't be an a priori decision about how far it will make sense to conceptualize lesbian and gay male identities together. Or separately"; (4) "The immemorial, seemingly ritualized debates on nature versus nurture take place against a very unstable background of tacit assumptions and fantasies about both nurture and nature"; (6) "The relation of gay studies to debates on the literary canon is, and had best be, tortuous"; and (7) "The paths of allo-identification are likely to be strange and recalcitrant. So are the paths of auto-identification": Sedgwick, *Epistemology of the Closet*, 22, 27, 36, 40, 48, 59.

25 Sedgwick, *Epistemology of the Closet*, 48.

26 Sedgwick, *Epistemology of the Closet*, 48.

27 Sedgwick, *Epistemology of the Closet*, 1.

28 The first contradiction, Sedgwick writes, arises "between seeing homo/heterosexual definition on the one hand as an issue of active importance primarily for a small, distinct, relatively fixed homosexual minority (what I refer to as a minoritizing view), and seeing it on the other hand as an issue of continuing, determinative importance in the lives of people across the spectrum of sexualities (what I refer to as a universalizing view)": Sedgwick, *Epistemology of the Closet*, 1. The second contradiction exists "between seeing same-sex object choice on the one hand as a matter of liminality or transitivity between genders, and seeing it on the other hand as reflecting an impulse of separatism . . . within each gender": Sedgwick, *Epistemology of the Closet*, 1–2. The transitive view would subordinate the gender difference between gay men and lesbians in favor of privileging the similarity of their same-sex desire, while the gender separatist view would see same-sex object choice as definitionally reliant on

gender alliances, thereby wedding lesbians primarily to the identity category of women and gay men to the category of men. In her discussion of Sedgwick's work, Annamarie Jagose glosses the second contradiction in slightly different terms: "Gender-liminal understandings of homosexual desire posit homosexual as an intermediary gender category, neither wholly masculine nor feminine; gender-separatist understandings represent homosexuals as the very epitome, the defining heart of their gender": Jagose, "Eve Kosofsky Sedgwick," 242.

29 Sedgwick, *Epistemology of the Closet*, 2. Later, Sedgwick writes, "The book will not suggest (nor do I believe there currently exists) any standpoint of thought from which the rival claims of these minoritizing and universalizing understandings of sexual definition could be decisively arbitrated as to their 'truth.' Instead, the performative effects of the self-contradictory discursive field of force created by their overlap will be my subject": Sedgwick, *Epistemology of the Closet*, 9.

30 Eve Kosofsky Sedgwick, "Reality and Realization," in Eve Kosofsky Sedgwick, *The Weather in Proust*, ed. Jonathan Goldberg (Durham, NC: Duke University Press, 2011), 212.

31 Sedgwick, "Reality and Realization," 212–13.

32 In the proximity between "thin" and "fatal" I hear resonances of Sedgwick's various deliberations on her own embodiment, whether as a fat woman or as a breast cancer survivor, but most profoundly as both, as each of these self-explications has appeared as an important form of translation and identification in her critical alliances with gay men: see esp. Eve Kosofsky Sedgwick and Michael Moon, "Divinity: A Dossier, A Performance Piece, A Little-Understood Emotion," *Discourse* 13, no. 1 (Fall–Winter 1990–91): 12–39.

33 Lee Edelman's now famous resistance to the discourse of the political in queer critique—often cited as queer negativity, or the antisocial thesis—is interesting to consider here. In *No Future*, Edelman argues for embracing the long-standing affiliation of homosexuality with death by rejecting projects that seek gay and lesbian rehabilitation. In his terms, the political aspiration toward a transformed future wagers the political from within the auspices of heteronormativity, crafted as it is on a reproductive logic that ensures the so-called survival of the species by sanctifying the figure of the child as the emblem of historical transcendence: Lee Edelman, *No Future: Queer Theory and the Death Drive* (Durham, NC: Duke University Press, 2004). Various scholars have challenged Edelman's formulation to embrace negativity and the antisocial by retaining the utopian force of a political investment in the future: see esp. Jack Halberstam, "The Anti-Social Turn in Queer Studies," *Graduate Journal of Social Science* 5, no. 2 (2008): 140–56; José Esteban Muñoz, *Cruising Utopia: The Then and There of Queer Futurity* (New York: New York University Press, 2009). For a compelling discussion of how Edelman and his detractors are actually quite closely aligned through the value they collectively, if differentially, ascribe to the capacity of "queer," see Annamarie Jagose, "Counterfeit Pleasures: Fake Orgasm and

Queer Agency," *Textual Practice* 24, no. 3 (2010): 517–39. For a more complete commentary on negativity and the antisocial thesis, see my "Sex and Negativity; or, What Queer Theory Has for You," *Cultural Critique* 95 (Winter 2017): 219–43.

34 Other scholars have worried, at length and well before me, about the heady political conjuncture between queer and antinormativity, though without my focus on the force of institutionalization and the consequences of anchoring a field's epistemological guarantee in its political pursuit: see esp. Cathy J. Cohen, "Punks, Bulldaggers, and Welfare Queens: The Radical Potential of Queer Politics?" GLQ 3, no. 4 (1997): 437–65; Biddy Martin, "Extraordinary Homosexuals and the Fear of Being Ordinary," *Differences* 6, nos. 2–3 (1994): 100–25; Biddy Martin, "Sexualities without Genders and Other Utopias," *Diacritics* 24, nos. 2–3 (Summer–Autumn 1994): 104–21.

35 To be sure, Judith Butler is most often cited as the chief purveyor of the field's antinormative thesis—except when Foucault's signature is offered. In the introduction to *Frames of War*, she rehearses her long-standing interest in norms by summarizing her argument about the normative construction of the subject—which should not be conflated with Foucault's commitment to historicizing the production of a normalizing culture through his delineation of biopolitics. Butler writes:

> Subjects are constituted through norms which, in their reiteration, produce and shift the terms through which subjects are recognized. These normative conditions for the production of the subject produce an historically contingent ontology, such that our very capacity to discern and name the "being" of the subject is dependent on norms that facilitate that recognition. At the same time, it would be a mistake to understand the operation of norms as deterministic. Normative schemes are interrupted by one another, they emerge and fade depending on broader operations of power, and very often come up against spectral versions of what it is they claim to know. (Judith Butler, *Frames of War: When Is Life Grievable?* [London: Verso, 2009], 3–4)

In these terms, there is no social order without norms and the normative practices they generate and sustain; at the same time, there is no guarantee that a norm will operate to normalize in any predetermined way. In fact, Butler's project is rather rigorously set against the idea that norms stabilize either subjects or social orders. Her interest lies instead in the cultural legibility that norms offer and the possibility, for critical practice, of bringing those operations into view. Nevertheless, Butler *has often been read* in ways that reproduce the rather simple equation between antinormativity and queer political and critical intervention that her emphasis on an antihumanist account of subjectivity would eschew.

36 Sedgwick, *Tendencies*, 6.

37 Sedgwick, *Tendencies*, 9. See also Eve Kosofsky Sedgwick, "Imitation and Gender Subordination," in *Inside/Out: Lesbian Theories, Gay Theories*, ed. Diana Fuss (New York: Routledge, 1991), 18.

38 Judith Butler, *Gender Trouble: Feminism and the Subversion of Identity* (New York: Routledge, 1990).

39 Interestingly, Butler refers in a note to the 1989 venue as "the Conference on Homosexuality at Yale": Sedgwick, "Imitation and Gender Subordination," 29.

40 As is well known, Butler was asked to respond on various occasions to questions about her rendering of performativity, especially in relation to trans identities and identifications, in ways that repeatedly challenged her externality to the category and its embodied experience. This aspect of the reception of her work importantly reinforces my point here about the way that queer critique's anti-identitarian aspirations are critically authorized from the very epistemological guarantee that identity confers. For its engagement with Butler, see Jay Prosser, *Second Skins: The Body Narratives of Transsexuality* (New York: Columbia University Press, 1998); Ki Namaste, "'Tragic Misreadings': Queer Theory's Erasure of Transgender Subjectivity," in *Queer Studies: A Lesbian, Gay, Bisexual, and Transgender Anthology*, ed. Brett Beemyn and Mickey Eliason (New York: New York University Press, 1996), 183–203. See also defense of Butler's theoretical position in Gayle Salamon, *Assuming a Body: Transgender and the Rhetorics of Materiality* (New York: Columbia University Press, 2010).

41 The book that would emerge, *American Anatomies: Theorizing Race and Gender* (Durham, NC: Duke University Press, 1995), followed Sedgwick by taking up the figure of the interracial male bond in US literary and popular culture. But while Sedgwick focused on the erotic triangle in its paradigmatic formula, with male homosocial bonds being solidified through the circulation of heterosexual desires marked by the narrative presence of a woman, I was interested in how the history of white supremacy produced different narrative configurations. Most notably, the American celebration of homosociality required women's banishment—think here of Leslie Fiedler's influential study *Love and Death in the American Novel* (New York: Stein and Day, 1960), which reads the US literary tradition as the story of interracial masculine democracy founded in the flight from civilization to the territory. With women paradigmatically displaced, I focused instead on discourses of sexual difference as they mediated contradictions between patriarchy and white supremacy. The emphasis on discourse was very much a piece of the reconfiguration in the 1980s of literary studies under the auspices of cultural studies as it intersected with critical theory.

42 This failure is not mine alone but a reflection of the difficulty in leftist criticism in general of addressing identificatory traffic between dominant and subordinated identity positions—as in white racial identifications with blackness, straight men's identifications with women or the feminine, or bourgeois alli-

ances with the working class. The critical vocabulary for doing so is sparse and most often tuned to suspicion. Much more needs to be said, following Sedgwick, about the complexities of such cross-identifications in their political and psychic capacities.

43 I am not alone among scholars who have found *Between Men* useful for thinking about race and racial formation, whether in conjunction with feminist concerns or not. But racialization was never a primary axis of analysis in Sedgwick's work, leading some scholars to interpret her understanding of sexuality and sexual subjectivity as predicated on an implicit whiteness. Marlon Ross has been most decisive in this regard, casting *Epistemology of the Closet* as paradigmatic in its deployment of the "claustrophilic assumptions of (white)queer theory": Marlon B. Ross, "Beyond the Closet as Raceless Paradigm," in *Black Queer Studies: A Critical Anthology*, ed. E. Patrick Johnson and Mae Henderson (Durham, NC: Duke University Press, 2005), 182. Recently, Siobhan Somerville has returned to Sedgwick's work, via Ross, to consider when, how, and to what ends Sedgwick addresses racial formation and hierarchy directly, arguing that Sedgwick's very formulation of feminist theory bears within it critiques offered by women of color feminism. "The particular ways in which Sedgwick positions her work in relation to feminist theory have implications for understanding how she situated not only questions of sexuality but also questions of race in *Epistemology of the Closet*": Somerville, "Feminism, Queer Theory, and the Racial Closet," 196.

44 In the introduction, she addresses the issue head on, writing, "The isolation, not to mention the absolute subordination, of women, in the structural paradigm on which this study is based . . . is a distortion that necessarily fails to do justice to women's own powers, bonds, and struggles. The absence of lesbianism from the book was an early and, I think, necessary decision, since my argument is structured around the distinctive relation of the male homosocial spectrum to the transmission of unequally distributed power. Nevertheless, the exclusively heterosexual perspective of the book's attention to women is seriously impoverishing in itself, and also an index of the larger distortion": Sedgwick, *Between Men*, 18.

45 Sedgwick, *Between Men*, 19.

46 Sedgwick, *Between Men*, 19–20.

47 Sedgwick, *Between Men*, 20.

48 Sedgwick, *Between Men*, 3. In subsequent critical discussions, it is this claim that would become a central point of contention for many scholars invested in lesbian studies, who read Sedgwick's acceptance of Adrienne Rich's idea of the "lesbian continuum" as both a subordination of sexual relations between women and a refusal to take seriously the homophobia that lesbians experience. My own sense is that if Sedgwick erred, she did so actually by giving greater priority to lesbian feminist discourses in her representation of the structure and force of women's social bonds than they might actually wield in the operation

of Western culture. For a discussion of this issue in Sedgwick's work, see esp. Castle, *The Apparitional Lesbian*.

49 Sedgwick, *Between Men*, 21.

50 Sedgwick, *Between Men*, 21.

51 Sedgwick, *Between Men*, 21. In "Capacity," Judith Butler glosses Sedgwick's use of Girard and its significance by writing, "Her point was to show that what first appears to be relation of a man who desires a woman turns out to be implicitly a homosocial bond between two men. Her argument was not to claim . . . that the homosocial bond comes at the expense of the heterosexual, but that the homosocial (distinct from the homosexual) is articulated precisely through the heterosexual. This argument has had far-reaching consequences, . . . confounding the identificatory positions for every 'actor' in the scene. The man who seeks to send the woman to another man sends some aspect of himself, and the man who receives her, receives him as well. She circuits, but is she finally wanted, or does she merely exemplify a value by becoming the representative of both men's desire, the place where those desires meet, and where they fail to meet, a place where that potentially homosexual encounter is relayed, suspended, and contained?": Judith Butler, "Capacity," in *Regarding Sedgwick: Essays on Queer Culture and Critical Theory*, ed. Stephen M. Barber and David L. Clark (New York: Routledge, 2002), 112. In my reading, *Between Men* is indeed interested in how the circulatory dynamics of the erotic triangle confound any simple—indeed, singular—reading of the routes of desire and the identificatory positions of the players that constitute it, but I would contend that Sedgwick does not mean to minimize the value of women's circulation in the way that Butler's use of "merely" would otherwise suggest. Quite the contrary.

52 While the Oedipal scenario is classically understood as a triangle that orders desire and power hierarchically, many psychoanalytically inclined thinkers find it more useful to encounter its identifications as circulations that produce, narrate, and subordinate multiple triangulations: among father, mother, son; father, mother, daughter; mother, son, daughter; and the siblings themselves. In a great deal of contemporary scholarship, the nuclear structure of the Oedipal has been superseded altogether, whether by considering the fractured kinship relations inaugurated by slavery in the Americas or the emergent forms of family wrought by queer kinship. For the former, see esp. Hortense Spillers, "Mama's Baby, Papa's Maybe: An American Grammar Book," *Diacritics* 17, no. 2 (Summer 1987): 64–81; for the latter, see Judith Butler, "Is Kinship Always Already Heterosexual?" *Differences* 13, no. 1 (2002): 14–44.

53 Sedgwick, *Between Men*, 1.

54 Sedgwick, *Between Men*, 25. The importance of this insight cannot be overstated, as it pushes the discussion of the patriarchal "traffic in women" first deployed by Gayle Rubin beyond both its originating framework and some of its most potent feminist appropriations. In her now classic essay of the same name, Rubin

argues against using the concept of patriarchy as a generic, transhistorical description of the social structure that produces and sustains women's oppression. "It is important—even in the face of a depressing history—to maintain a distinction between the human capacity and necessity to create a sexual world, and the empirically oppressive ways in which sexual worlds have been organized. Patriarchy subsumes both meanings into the same term." For this reason, Rubin claims that "patriarchy" should be restricted to referencing the social organization generated by the "institution of fatherhood," which establishes and legitimates the patriarch's "absolute power over wives, children, herds, and dependents." In its place, Rubin offers—famously—the "neutral" concept of the "sex/gender system" through which feminist theorists can track the historical production of gender and sexuality in "specific social relations": Gayle Rubin, "The Traffic in Women: Notes on the 'Political Economy' of Sex," in *Toward an Anthropology of Women*, ed. Rayne R. Reiter (New York: Monthly Review, 1975), 168. Luce Irigaray likewise uses the Lévi-Straussian idea of the "exchange of women," but her emphasis locates the commerce in women at the heart of patriarchal practice. "The trade that organizes patriarchal societies takes place exclusively among men. Women, signs, goods, currency, all pass from one man to another. . . . Homosexuality is the law that regulates the socio-cultural order. Heterosexuality amounts to the assignment of roles in the economy. . . . Why then consider masculine homosexuality as an exception, while in fact it is the very basis of the general economy?": Luce Irigaray, "When the Goods Get Together," trans. Claudia Reeder, in *New French Feminisms: An Anthology*, ed. Elaine Marks and Isabelle de Courtivron (New York: Schocken, 1981), 107. Sedgwick's argument works in the space of the difference between these accounts, taking from Rubin the insistence on a rigorous historical specificity in determining the organization of patriarchy, while pursuing what Irigaray must sublimate—"the quicksilver of sex itself"—in the "expensive leap of register" that generates her understanding of "the relation of heterosexual to male homosocial bonds": Sedgwick, *Between Men*, 26.

55 Sedgwick, *Between Men*, 26–27.

56 Sedgwick, *Between Men*, 27. Careful readers will note that this quote identifies the relations of class inequality as equally important to those of gender. My inattention to this aspect of Sedgwick's argument reflects the identifications around sexuality and gender that I mean to discern and is not intended to subordinate the way her analysis of the erotic triangle is profoundly shaped by political economic concerns. Indeed, *Between Men* is highly attentive to how class status— along with ideations about the ethics of genital relations among men—is part of the often stunning historical transformations by which male homosexuality has been represented and understood in Western culture.

57 Sedgwick affirms this interpretation of the book's contribution to feminist theory, writing, "In fact, *Between Men* was one of a group of theoretical projects

in the 1980s that very much put in question the usefulness of the overarching concept of patriarchy. Nevertheless, it was able to offer the following as an explicit axiom: that the historically differential shapes of male and female homosociality—much as they themselves may vary over time—will always be articulations and mechanisms of the enduring inequality of power between women and men": Sedgwick, "Thinking through Queer Theory," 195.

58 Sedgwick, *Between Men*, x, vii.

59 Sedgwick, *Between Men*, viii.

60 Sedgwick, *Between Men*, viii.

61 Sedgwick, *Between Men*, viii. Sedgwick will use this language again, later, to define queer politics. "'Queer,' to me, refers to a politics that values the ways in which meanings and institutions can be at loose ends with each other," she writes, "crossing all kinds of boundaries rather than reinforcing them. What if the most productive junctures weren't the ones where *everything means the same thing*?": Sedgwick, "Thinking through Queer Theory," 200.

62 Sedgwick, *Between Men*, viii. In an interview in 1995, Sedgwick reiterated this point. *Between Men* "was very clearly to me an intervention in feminist theory," she said, "because at that time there was so little of it that you couldn't even distinguish between feminist theory and other kinds of feminist stuff. I basically didn't have the sense of addressing, or of there even being, a community of gay studies for the book. There were people doing it, but there were very few people publishing books in it yet. . . . But it wasn't written into that scene; it was written into existing feminist scholarship": Kerr and O'Rourke, "Sedgwick Sense and Sensibility."

63 It is important to emphasize that these intimacies are loaded with negative affects—aggression, betrayal, anger, hatred—and hence that my argument for reengaging the triangle is in part an attempt to challenge the moral order that the discourse of antinormativity installs in its dyadic approach to both criticism and politics. In positing the triangle as a figure for the incommensurate relations of politics, identification, pedagogy, reading, and desire, I am embracing the difficulty it presents to any simple adjudication of right and wrong, good and bad, inside and out, complicity and innocence.

64 Sedgwick, *Epistemology of the Closet*, 59.

65 Sedgwick, *Epistemology of the Closet*, 59.

66 Sedgwick, *Epistemology of the Closet*, 59. Here, Sedgwick cites several of her own particularizing narratives, the lengthiest being "A Poem Is Being Written," which addresses the socially ignored topic of women's anal eroticism. See also "Tide and Trust" (*Critical Inquiry* 15, no. 4 [Summer 1989]: 745–57), which appeared as chapter 4 of *Epistemology of the Closet*, and "Privilege of Unknowing" (*Genders* 1 [Spring 1988]: 102–24), which appeared as the first chapter in Sedgwick, *Tendencies*.

67 Sedgwick, *Epistemology of the Closet*, 59.

68 Sedgwick, *Epistemology of the Closet*, 61.

69 Sedgwick, *Epistemology of the Closet*, 61.

70 Sedgwick, *Epistemology of the Closet*, 61.

71 Sedgwick, *Epistemology of the Closet*, 61.

72 Sedgwick, *Epistemology of the Closet*, 60–61.

73 Jarrell was killed in 1965 along Highway 15–501 in Chapel Hill, North Carolina, the road that connects that university town with Durham, where Sedgwick taught and lived. He suffered for years from vaguely defined "mental illnesses," and many of his closest friends thought his death was a suicide. His book of poems *The Woman at the Washington Zoo* (1960) won the National Book Award. One of his most loved writers was Proust.

74 Quoted in Eve Kosofsky Sedgwick, "Interlude, Pedagogic," in *Touching Feeling: Affect, Pedagogy, Performativity* (Durham, NC: Duke University Press, 2003), 27. "Interlude, Pedagogic" is essentially an excerpt from a longer and much earlier essay, "Socratic Raptures, Socratic Ruptures," which opened with the story of Sedgwick's fainting as a preamble to her deliberation on "*experimental* critical writing" and the queer performativity of the classroom: Eve Kosofsky Sedgwick, "Socratic Raptures, Socratic Ruptures: Notes toward Queer Performativity," in *English Inside and Out*, ed. Susan Gubar and Jonathan Kamholtz (New York: Routledge, 1993), 133. By reprinting only the first section for *Touching Feeling*, Sedgwick offers "Interlude, Pedagogic" as a performative instance of the kind of writing for which the earlier essay called. My reading of it here emphasizes its significance to the volume as a whole, not as an excerpt of what came before but precisely as an interlude that speaks in a different idiom to the book's contemplation of the three terms triangulated in its subtitle: affect, pedagogy, performativity. However, it is noteworthy that in "Socratic Raptures, Socratic Ruptures," Sedgwick did engage the Jarrell poem directly. "That the effects of such experiments are radically unpredictable is, obviously, to the point of their queer performativity; 'that they are queer I am certain,' as Randall Jarrell would put it; but how, by whom, and in what relations 'queerness' itself may be constituted is still up for grabs": Sedgwick, "Socratic Raptures, Socratic Ruptures," 133.

75 Sedgwick, "Interlude, Pedagogic," 29.

76 Sedgwick, "Interlude, Pedagogic," 33.

77 Sedgwick, "Interlude, Pedagogic," 31.

78 Sedgwick, "Interlude, Pedagogic," 32.

79 Sedgwick, "Interlude, Pedagogic," 32–33.

80 Sedgwick, "Interlude, Pedagogic," 33.

81 Sedgwick, "Interlude, Pedagogic," 33.

82 Sedgwick, *Tendencies*, viii.

83 Sedgwick, "Interlude, Pedagogic," 34.

84 Sedgwick, *Epistemology of the Closet*, 14.

85 Sedgwick, *Epistemology of the Closet*, 59.

86 Sedgwick, *Tendencies*, 19.

87 Sedgwick, "Socratic Raptures, Socratic Ruptures," 133. It is more often the case that scholars refer to Sedgwick's critical practice after *Epistemology of the Closet* as reparative, following her influential critique of the hermeneutics of suspicion first published in 1997 in "Paranoid Reading and Reparative Reading; or, You're So Paranoid You Probably Think This Introduction Is about You," the introduction to *Novel Gazing: Queer Readings in Fiction*, ed. Eve Kosofsky Sedgwick (Durham, NC: Duke University Press, 1997), 1–37. For a discussion of the history of Sedgwick's engagement with the reparative-paranoid relation, especially as it is reflected in recent queer feminist criticism, see Robyn Wiegman, "'The Times We're In': Queer Feminist Criticism and the Reparative 'Turn,'" *Feminist Theory* 15, no. 1 (April 2014): 1–24.

88 Sedgwick, *Tendencies*, 19–20.

89 This is not to say that all scholarship in the field conforms to such sovereign reductions. Both Lauren Berlant and Annamarie Jagose have been keenly interested in the way that normativities are historically made and psychically lived, and neither repeats the injunction to understand queer politics in strictly antinormative terms. Still, I would say, especially in the case of Berlant, that the organizing concern of *Cruel Optimism*—"the problem of detaching from the normal"—has a resonance within the broader auspices of antinormativity because of the difficulty, for readers in queer studies, to take "the problem of detaching from the normal" as anything other than a command: Lauren Berlant, *Cruel Optimism* (Durham, NC: Duke University Press, 2011), 21. For Jagose, see Annamarie Jagose, *Orgasmology* (Durham, NC: Duke University Press, 2013).

Afterword

In times of stormy weather
She felt queer pain.
–Langston Hughes, "Strange Hurt"

A tree is a new thing at every instant; we affirm the *form* because we do not seize the subtlety of an absolute moment.
–Friedrich Nietzsche

The weather surrounding our loss is lifting, into subsequent patterns of losing. This is the story emerging in this volume: of an enormity giving way to subtleties, channeling into runnels of pain, which are hard to calibrate and no less extravagant for their mercurial, liquid spread. How to account for the loss we've gained?

Let me delineate two forms of loss, neither subtle on its face: we are deprived of Eve's need for us; we are bereft of her replenished prose. (*The Weather in Proust* is Eve's last say.) In other words, the call and response of our relation, as we've known it, has concluded. What do we have in having this conclusion?

What we have in losing Eve is losing Eve to myth. We are left feeling she is disappearing, slipping into forms, even as our grief is running into subtleties. This strange mix is our sorrow, and necessity. Myth is a graspable form that we make of even living beloveds when evoking them. Even our relations with the living— via images, words, and sensations, daily renewed—are reduced and summarized by signs that will fit inside our heads. This is how we take a beloved with us, also in us, through the day, and what we use to produce that person, hold that person, in our minds—a circumstance intensified when a person's dead.

Eve has been mythologized for a long time. But the myth I hear in these pages and my head is of *Eve's* capacity to reach for crucial forms on a very large scale, on a monstrous scale, and then seize on subtleties among enormities. No one has better ranged along these scales. No one has so broadly carried what she's found. Therefore, I imagine that she'd love our mourning as rendered in this book.

Fittingly, that is, the movement of our grief from Gothic deluge to capillary drama, and back again, is the weather in Eve. Such strong shifts are the nimbus of her thought. And they make a cube. Cubist climatology? I think so, in the sense that what is thought by Eve as she moves from one set of claims to another, book to book, is not left behind like a climate event or point on a line but gathered along in a forward spread. Strikingly, and tenderly, she performed this gathering early on. One especially saw it when she named as "parallel" the movements of "gay" activism, on the one hand (to which she says she "owed" "the space of permission for [my] work and the depth of the intellectual landscape in which it might have a contribution to make"), and, on the other hand, the queer politics and thought she preferred, which challenged people and thinking that are "gay." (Indicative of her gathering, the phrase "gay affirmative" meant for Eve the thinking now considered queer.)

Eve doesn't jettison. She carries what she weathers *on* her, in her, keeping her boldest, Gothic, some would say paranoid claims—her own queer pain and ours, to boot—as the atmospherics that surround her forecasts (her casting forward) for repair. She is never without (our) loss. In fact, she knows it as what cannot be lost, since it's more primal, more set in stone—itself more dramatic in large and small ways—than any Gothic politics. But it's the subtle regard she pays it that might make us think she's jettisoned views of homophobic, capitalist, racist damage, and despoilments amid her attention to breathing and breath. We could surely miss Eve's reaching for the fibers of our stony loss. Stony fibers? Stony loss as a type of weather? (In a moment, I'll defend these rather mixed metaphors.)

Eve was clearly bold. That is everywhere evident here. She concretized what otherwise would float as complexities too diffuse to state—and showed it wasn't paranoid to see the concrete force of paranoia working all around us. Her Gothic tableau—man chasing man on the Arctic floes—crystallized the pathos of homophobic panic. A triangle—simple geometric arrangement—added "women" to these stark relations that, at their heart, starkly excluded the women they admitted. She lit up in neon, Bruce Nauman–like, "Hetero/ Homo," making us attend to its spare division of sexual life in all its permutations. "One man, one woman"—the sleek bigoted marriage formulation, which quite campily made the specter of "homo" relations the frightful center of straight definition in its cherished core—confirmed Eve's status as Gothic prophet. She cut glass, moreover, with her pointed titles: "Jane Austen and the Masturbating Girls"; "How to Bring Your Kids Up Gay"; *Gary in Your Pocket.*

On the point of Gary, one perceives her daring. The young Gary Fisher, whose life and writing were lost to AIDS, even as both his living and writing were vibrant to Eve and preserved as such, occupied something like a crossroads-cliff edge, in all its contours. A place where paths converge at a ledge. Here Fisher skirted the edges, drops, and elations of where the block-iest concepts ("black," "gay," "male," "slave," to name just a few) met and crossed each other, often for Fisher with laughter, entertainment, momentary insights, and welcome danger. Eve, as his editor, attended to these crossings in all their micro-details (in all their stony fibers, I will suggest). As a result, implicit in her work, if not worked out, are materials for a *theory* of the incommensurate: a sense of where and how the frequently hardening, titanic terms of "black" and "queer" (among any number of large, nonequivalent, fateful terms) might intersect, lending not just denotative meanings to each other, in a Gothic drama, but far-reaching, highly textured, historically accretive connotations, subtle and telling if one feels for them. Eve's intermittent use of "switchpoint," often just in passing, holds tremendous promise for crafting finer theories, which I and others have tried to release—are releasing still.

I suppose in a weird way Eve is Basil Wotton, a crucial combination of Basil Hallward and Lord Henry Wotton—proto-gay men, nicely enough—from Wilde's *The Picture of Dorian Gray.* In her persona, Eve, like Basil, enters the paranoid Gothic she describes, realizing, powerfully, that to sketch its shape is to dirty one's hands with it, do battle with it, risk its knife plunged into one's ear, even risk the irony of sounding non-ironic in calling attention to its melodramas. All while enjoying, like Lord Henry, the epigrammatic embrace of nuance that laughs it off, steps to its side, slips on a different genre of response (as one would don a condom), juggles it, inverts it—no one dies. (Shades of Gary Fisher while he was alive.)

Indeed, the weather in Wilde intrudes, subtly siding with sensation and decay—the *enjoyment* of loss—as if to suggest that something fleeting in the air and on the ground is always cutting through our scenes of struggle and might be worthy of remark, or bliss. "The wind shook some blossoms from the trees, and the heavy lilac-blooms, with their clustering stars, moved to and fro in the languid air"; "the blue cloud-shadows chased themselves across the grass like swallows"; "the sunlight slipped over the polished leaves." Nietzsche writes of fleetingness as what we fail to grasp, to finger with our minds: "A tree is a new thing at every instant; we affirm the *form* because we do not seize the subtlety of an absolute moment." To which Barthes replies: "We are scientific because we lack subtlety."[1] Eve was expert in Gothic form, almost scientific in her diagnoses. She could account for the Tree of Fear, discern the forms of widespread panic that still govern much of current life. Where would our thinking be had she not? But can we be surprised that she cared to realize subtleties that constitute our pleasures, shot through with pain, fleeting beauty, decay, and sharp desire?

We are back to stony fibers, cubist climatology, stony loss. Eve did not canyoneer that I know of—part of her charm. Eve on a rock, with a helmet and a rope, is very hard to conjure. Yet her mysticism of materiality flowers out on ledges. What you realize there, standing on a cliff, in a slot of stone, about to descend, is the weather *in* the rock. Standing on stone, you are standing on weather: the current congealment, the absolute archive, of the effects of water, wind, and time, of erosive loss, where the climate's cubed.

The rock you see is the shape of loss in stone. It, the rock, is a Derrida-style, thus Eve-style, manifest density, a materiality that *shows* you what Derridean, Sedgwickian theory looks like and feels like underfoot. Yet, you'd be forgiven for feeling it as form more than an ever fleeting subtlety changing slowly under your feet. In fact, rappel it, tethered to a rope, and its Gothic features loom quite large. It's titanic; it could kill you; it makes you paranoid. You face your paranoia—and if you descend, you decide against it, or work intriguingly in and around it. Perversely, you give yourself to the rock, the Gothic form, you so fear. You let it receive you. As Eve (and Gary Fisher) would appreciate, you let it let itself be used by you. Your back to the void, your feet *on* the weather, on these stony fibers, you give yourself to air. The feeling is bold; the movements subtle, micro-textured. You control the speed at which the air can take you, if all goes well. A beautiful terror.

This is what I've learned from the weather in Eve.

NOTE

Epigraphs: Langston Hughes, "Strange Hurt," *PoetryNook.com*, accessed February 12, 2019, https://www.poetrynook.com/poem/strange-hurt; Nietzsche qtd. in Roland Barthes, *The Pleasure of the Text*, trans. Richard Miller (New York: Hill and Wang, 1975), 61.

1 The Nietzsche quotation and the Barthes quotation are from Barthes, *The Pleasure of the Text*, 61.

Acknowledgments

In addition to expressing my gratitude to these authors, I would like to acknowledge a few people whose energy over the years kept this project afloat. Michael O'Rourke was its genius inventor. Denis Flannery, Jason Edwards, Jonathan Goldberg, and Hal Sedgwick have all pushed to see this through to its original intention. Lee Edelman performed some crack reading and brainstorming, as usual. I also warmly thank Ramzi Fawaz for leading the parade—a pride parade but also a critically enthusiastic, caring, and critical one—into the present of the future. Robyn Taylor-Neu was a brilliant and attentive reader, constantly editing, reformatting, and attending to details this tired editor missed. Thanks also very much to Carmen Merport Quiñones and Rivky Mondal for organizing the final manuscript. Collaboration is not just at the heart of production: it is its heart. I thank you all.

Bibliography

Anderson, Benedict. *Mythology and the Tolerance of the Javanese*. Jakarta: Equinox, [1965] 2009.

Armantrout, Rae. *Versed*. Middletown, CT: Wesleyan University Press, 2010.

Barber, Stephen M., and David L. Clark. "Queer Moments: The Performative Temporalities of Eve Sedgwick." In *Regarding Sedgwick: Essays on Queer Culture and Critical Theory*, edited by Stephen M. Barber and David L. Clark, 1–54. New York: Routledge, 2002.

Barthes, Roland. *The Pleasure of the Text*, translated by Richard Miller. New York: Hill and Wang, 1975.

Berlant, Lauren. *Cruel Optimism*. Durham, NC: Duke University Press, 2011.

Berlant, Lauren, and Michael Warner. "Sex in Public." *Critical Inquiry* 24, no. 2 (1998): 547–66.

Berlant, Lauren, and Michael Warner. "What Does Queer Theory Teach Us about X?" *PMLA* 110, no. 3 (May 1995): 343–49.

Bersani, Leo. "'Ardent Masturbation' (Descartes, Freud, and Others)." *Critical Inquiry* 38 (Autumn 2011): 1–16.

Bersani, Leo. "Is the Rectum a Grave?" In *AIDS: Cultural Analysis/Cultural Criticism*, edited by Douglas Crimp, 197–222. Cambridge, MA: MIT Press, 1988.

Best, Stephen, and Sharon Marcus. "Surface Reading: An Introduction." *Representations* 108, no. 1 (Fall 2009): 1–21.

Birasri, Silpa. *Thai Buddhist Sculpture*. Bangkok: National Culture Institute, 1956.

Bishop, Elizabeth. "The Sandpiper." *New Yorker*, July 21, 1962, 30.

Blofeld, John. *Bodhisattva of Compassion: The Mystical Tradition of Kuan Yin*. Boston: Shambala, 2009.

Bond Stockton, Kathryn. "Eve's Queer Child." In *Regarding Sedgwick: Essays on Queer Culture and Critical Theory*, edited by Stephen M. Barber and David L. Clark, 181–200. New York: Routledge, 2002.

Boucher, Sandy. *Discovering Kwan Yin: Buddhist Goddess of Compassion: A Woman's Book of Ruminations, Meditations, Prayers, and Chants*. Boston: Beacon, 1999.

Bradway, Tyler. "Bad Reading: The Affective Relations of Queer Experimental Literature after AIDS." *GLQ* 24, nos. 2–3 (2018): 189–212.

Braidotti, Rosi. *Metamorphoses: Towards a Materialist Theory of Becoming*. Cambridge: Polity, 2002.

Brown, Angus Connell. "Look with Your Hands." In *Bathroom Songs: Eve Kosofsky Sedgwick as a Poet*, edited by Jason Edwards, 75–84. New York: Punctum, 2017.

Burke, Edmund. *A Philosophical Inquiry into the Origin of Our Ideas of the Sublime and Beautiful*. Oxford: Oxford University Press, [1757] 1990.

Butler, Judith. "Capacity." In *Regarding Sedgwick: Essays on Queer Culture and Critical Theory*, edited by Stephen M. Barber and David L. Clark, 109–19. New York: Routledge, 2002.

Butler, Judith. "The Force of Fantasy: Feminism, Mapplethorpe and Discursive Excess." In *The Judith Butler Reader*, edited by Sarah Salih, 183–203. Oxford: Blackwell, 2004.

Butler, Judith. *Frames of War: When Is Life Grievable?* London: Verso, 2009.

Butler, Judith. *Gender Trouble: Feminism and the Subversion of Identity*. New York: Routledge, 1990.

Butler, Judith. *Gender Trouble: Feminism and the Subversion of Identity*. New York: Routledge, 1999.

Butler, Judith. *Giving an Account of Oneself*. New York: Fordham University Press, 2005.

Butler, Judith. "Imitation and Gender Subordination." In *Inside/Out: Lesbian Theories, Gay Theories*, edited by Diana Fuss, 13–31. New York: Routledge, 1991.

Butler, Judith. "Is Kinship Always Already Heterosexual?" *Differences* 13, no. 1 (2002): 14–44.

Butler, Judith. "Values of Difficulty." In *Just Being Difficult: Academic Writing in the Public Arena*, edited by Jonathan D. Culler and Kevin Lamb, 199–216. Stanford, CA: Stanford University Press, 2003.

Cameron, Sharon. *Beautiful Work*. Durham, NC: Duke University Press, 2000.

Castle, Terry. *The Apparitional Lesbian: Female Homosexuality and Modern Culture*. New York: Columbia University Press, 1993.

Cavafy, Constantine. "Pictured." In *C. P. Cavafy: Collected Poems*, revised edition, translated by Edmund Keeley and Philip Sherrard, edited by George Savidis, 59. Princeton, NJ: Princeton University Press, 1992.

Chambers, Anne. *Suminagashi: The Japanese Art of Marbling—A Practical Guide*. London: Thames and Hudson, 1991.

Charon, Rita. *Narrative Medicine: Honoring the Stories of Illness*. Oxford: Oxford University Press, 2006.

Cohen, Cathy J. "Punks, Bulldaggers, and Welfare Queens: The Radical Potential of Queer Politics?" GLQ 3, no. 4 (1997): 437–65.

Crompton, Andrew. "How to Look at a Reading Font." *Word and Image* 30, no. 2 (2014): 79–89.

Culler, Jonathan. "Lyric Continuities: Speaker and Consciousness." *Neohelicon* 13, no. 1 (1986): 105–23.

Culler, Jonathan. "Reading Lyric." *Yale French Studies* 69 (1985): 98–106. doi:10.2307/2929927.

Culler, Jonathan, and Kevin Lamb. "Introduction." In *Just Being Difficult? Academic Writing in the Public Arena,* edited by Jonathan Culler and Kevin Lamb, 1–12. Stanford, CA: Stanford University Press, 2003.

Damisch, Hubert. *A Theory of Cloud: Toward a History of Painting.* Stanford, CA: Stanford University Press, 2002.

Dean, Tim. *Unlimited Intimacy: Reflections on the Subculture of Barebacking.* Chicago: University of Chicago Press, 2009.

de Certeau, Michel. *The Practice of Everyday Life.* Translated by Steven Rendall. Berkeley: University of California Press, 1984.

DeLauretis, Teresa, ed. *The Practice of Love: Lesbian Sexuality and Perverse Desire.* Bloomington: Indiana University Press, 1994.

DeLauretis, Teresa, ed. "Queer Theory: Lesbian and Gay Sexualities." *Differences* 3, no. 2 (1991): iii–xviii.

de l'Isle-Adam, Villiers. *Tomorrow's Eve (L'Eve future).* Translated by Robert Martin Adams. Carbondale: University of Illinois Press, 2000.

de Man, Paul. *Blindness and Insight: Essays in the Rhetoric of Contemporary Criticism.* London: Routledge, 1989.

Derrida, Jacques. "A Silkworm of One's Own (Points of View Stitched on the Other Veil)." *Oxford Literary Review* 18, no. 1 (1996): 3–66.

Dickens, Charles. *The Haunted House.* London: Oneworld Classics, [1862] 2009.

Dickinson, Emily. "Poem 587." In *The Complete Poems of Emily Dickinson,* edited by Thomas H. Johnson, 287. Boston: Little, Brown and Company, 1960.

Didi-Huberman, Georges. "The Art of Not Describing: Vermeer—The Detail and the Patch." *History of the Human Sciences* 2, no. 2 (1989): 135–69.

Duggan, Lisa. "The New Homonormativity: The Sexual Politics of Neoliberalism." In *Materializing Democracy: Toward a Revitalized Cultural Politics,* edited by Russ Castronovo and Dana D. Nelson, 175–94. Durham, NC: Duke University Press, 2002.

Dumm, Thomas. *Loneliness as a Way of Life.* Cambridge, MA: Harvard University Press, 2008.

Edelman, Lee. *No Future: Queer Theory and the Death Drive.* Durham, NC: Duke University Press, 2004.

Edwards, Jason. "Bathroom Songs: Eve Kosofsky Sedgwick as a Poet." In *Bathroom Songs: Eve Kosofsky Sedgwick as a Poet,* edited by Jason Edwards, 29–35. New York: Punctum, 2017.

Edwards, Jason. *Eve Kosofsky Sedgwick.* Abingdon, UK: Routledge, 2009.

Emerson, Ralph Waldo. *Essays and Lectures.* New York: Library of America, 1983.

Eng, David. *The Feeling of Kinship: Queer Liberalism and the Racialization of Intimacy.* Durham, NC: Duke University Press, 2010.

Fawaz, Ramzi. "How to Make a Queer Scene, or Notes toward a Practice of Affective Curation." *Feminist Studies* 42, no. 3 (2016): 757–68. doi:10.15767/feministstudies.42.3.0757.

Fawaz, Ramzi. *The New Mutants: Superheroes and the Radical Imagination of American Comics*. New York: New York University Press, 2016.

Felski, Rita. *Beyond Feminist Aesthetics*. London: Hutchinson Radius, 1989.

Ferenczi, Sándor. "Confusion of Tongues between Adults and the Child." *Contemporary Psychoanalysis* 24, no. 2 (2013): 196–206. doi:10.1080/00107530.1988.10746234.

Fickle, Dorothy H. *Images of the Buddha in Thailand*. Oxford: Oxford University Press, 1989.

Fiedler, Leslie. *Love and Death in the American Novel*. New York: Stein and Day, 1960.

Firestone, Shulamith. *The Dialectic of Sex: The Case for Feminist Revolution*. New York: William Morrow, 1970.

Fisher, Gary. *Gary in Your Pocket: Stories and Notebooks of Gary Fisher*, edited by Eve Kosofsky Sedgwick. Durham, NC: Duke University Press, 1996.

Flatley, Jonathan. "Like: Collecting and Collectivity." *October* 132 (Spring 2010): 71–98.

Foucault, Michel. *The Hermeneutics of the Subject: Lectures at the Collège de France, 1981–1982*. New York: Palgrave Macmillan, 2005.

Foucault, Michel. *The History of Sexuality, Volume 1: An Introduction*. Translated by Robert Hurley. New York: Random House, 1978.

Fried, Michael. *Absorption and Theatricality: Painting and Beholder in the Age of Diderot*. Chicago: University of Chicago Press, 1980.

Fried, Michael. *Realism, Writing, and Disfiguration: On Thomas Eakins and Stephen Crane*. Chicago: University of Chicago Press, 1987.

Gallop, Jane. *The Deaths of the Author*. Durham, NC: Duke University Press, 2011.

Gallop, Jane. "The Ethics of Reading: Close Encounters." *Journal of Curriculum Theorizing* 16, no. 3 (2000): 7–17.

Gallop, Jane. *Feminist Accused of Sexual Harassment*. Durham, NC: Duke University Press, 1997.

Gallop, Jane. "The Queer Temporality of Writing." In *Queer Times, Queer Becomings*, edited by Ellen McCallum and Mikko Tukhanen, 47–74. Buffalo: State University of New York Press, 2011.

Gallop, Jane. "The Teacher's Breasts." *Discourse* 17, no. 1 (Fall 1994): 3–15.

Gamson, Joshua. "Must Identity Movements Self-Destruct? A Queer Dilemma." *Social Problems* 42, no. 3 (1995): 390–407.

Gilbert, Sandra M., and Susan Gubar. *The Madwoman in the Attic: The Woman Writer and the Nineteenth-Century Literary Imagination*. New Haven, CT: Yale University Press, 1979.

Glück, Louise. "The Garment." In *Poems, 1962–2012*, 382. New York: Farrar, Straus, and Giroux, 2012.

Halberstam, Judith [Jack]. "The Anti-Social Turn in Queer Studies." *Graduate Journal of Social Science* 5, no. 2 (2008): 140–56.

Halberstam, Judith [Jack]. *In a Queer Time and Place*. New York: New York University Press, 2005.

Halberstam, Judith [Jack]. "Shame and White Gay Masculinity." *Social Text* 84–85 (Fall–Winter 2005): 219–34.

Hall, Donald E., and Annamarie Jagose, eds. *The Routledge Queer Studies Reader*. New York: Routledge, 2013.

Halperin, David M. "The Normalization of Queer Theory." *Journal of Homosexuality* 45, nos. 2–4 (2003): 339–43.

Halperin, David M. *Saint Foucault: Towards a Gay Hagiography*. New York: Oxford University Press, 1995.

Hanson, Ellis. "The Future's Eve: Reparative Reading after Sedgwick." *South Atlantic Quarterly* 110, no. 1 (Winter 2011): 101–19.

Haraway, Donna. "A Cyborg Manifesto: Science, Technology, and Socialist-Feminism in the Late Twentieth Century." In *Simians, Cyborgs and Women: The Reinvention of Nature*, 149–81. New York: Routledge, [1985] 1991.

Hardt, Michael. "The Common in Communism." In *The Idea of Communism*, edited by Costas Douzinas and Slavoj Žižek, 131–44. London: Verso, 2010.

Hertz, Neil. "Medusa's Head: Male Hysteria under Political Pressure." *Representations* 4 (1983): 27–54.

Hoffmann, Yoel, ed. *Japanese Death Poems Written by Zen Monks and Haiku Poets on the Verge of Death*. Boston: Tuttle, 1986.

Hong, Grace Kyungwon, and Roderick A. Ferguson, eds. *Strange Affinities: The Gender and Sexual Politics of Comparative Racialization*. Durham, NC: Duke University Press, 2011.

Huffer, Lynne. *Are the Lips a Grave? A Queer Feminist on the Ethics of Sex*. New York: Columbia University Press, 2013.

Huffer, Lynne. *Mad for Foucault: Rethinking the Foundations of Queer Theory*. New York: Columbia University Press, 2010.

Hughes, Langston. "Strange Hurt." *PoetryNook.com*. Accessed February 12, 2019. https://www.poetrynook.com/poem/strange-hurt.

Irigaray, Luce. "When the Goods Get Together." Translated by Claudia Reeder. In *New French Feminisms: An Anthology*, edited by Elaine Marks and Isabelle de Courtivron, 107–10. New York: Schocken, 1981.

Jagose, Annamarie. "Counterfeit Pleasures: Fake Orgasm and Queer Agency." *Textual Practice* 24, no. 3 (2010): 517–39.

Jagose, Annamarie. "Eve Kosofsky Sedgwick." In *Key Contemporary Social Theorists*, edited by Anthony Elliott and Larry Lay, 239–45. Malden, MA: Blackwell, 2003.

Jagose, Annamarie. "Feminism's Queer Theory." *Feminism and Psychology* 19, no. 2 (2009): 157–74.

Jagose, Annamarie. *Orgasmology*. Durham, NC: Duke University Press, 2013.

Jagose, Annamarie. "Thinkiest." *PMLA* 125, no. 2 (April 2010): 378–81.

Jakobsen, Janet. "Queer Is? Queer Does? Normativity and the Problem of Resistance." *GLQ* 4, no. 4 (1998): 551–36.

James, Henry. *The Art of the Novel*. Chicago: University of Chicago Press, 2011.

James, Henry. *Complete Stories: 1898–1910*. New York: Library of America, 1996.

James, Henry. *The Europeans*. New York: Penguin Classics, 2008.

James, Henry. *The Golden Bowl*. New York: Penguin Classics, 1987.

James, Henry. *The Notebooks of Henry James*. Edited by F. O. Matthiessen and Kenneth B. Murdock. New York: Oxford University Press, 1947.

James, Henry. *A Small Boy and Others: A Critical Edition*. Edited by Peter Collister. Charlottesville: University of Virginia Press, 2011.

James, Henry. *Washington Square*. New York: Oxford World's Classics, 2010.

James, Henry. *The Wings of the Dove*. Edited by Donald Crowley and Richard A. Hocks. New York: W. W. Norton, 2003.

James, William. "A World of Pure Experience." *Journal of Philosophy, Psychology, and Scientific Methods* 1, no. 20 (1904): 533–43.

Johnson, Barbara. *A Life with Mary Shelley*. Stanford, CA: Stanford University Press, 2014.

Johnson, Barbara. "Melville's Fist: The Execution of Billy Budd." In *The Critical Difference: Essays in the Contemporary Rhetoric of Reading*, 79–109. Baltimore: Johns Hopkins University Press, 1981.

Johnson, Barbara. *Mother Tongues: Sexuality, Trials, Motherhood, Translation*. Cambridge, MA: Harvard University Press, 2003.

Johnson, Barbara. "My Monster/My Self." *Diacritics* 12, no. 2 (1982): 2–10.

Johnson, Barbara. *Persons and Things*. Cambridge, MA: Harvard University Press, 2008.

Johnson, Barbara. "Using People: Kant with Winnicott." In *The Turn to Ethics*, edited by Marjorie Garber, Beatrice Hanssen, and Rebecca L. Walkowitz, 47–64. New York: Routledge, 2000.

Johnson, Barbara. "Using People: Kant with Winnicott." In *Persons and Things*, by Barbara Johnson, 94–108. Cambridge, MA: Harvard University Press, 2008.

Kaplan, Fred. *Henry James: The Imagination of Genius: A Biography*. London: Hodder and Stoughton, 1992.

Karcher, Stephen. *The Kuan Yin Oracle: The Voice of the Goddess of Compassion*. London: Piatkus, 2001.

Kerr, Mark, and Kristen O'Rourke. "Sedgwick Sense and Sensibility: An Interview with Eve Kosofsky Sedgwick." *Thresholds: Viewing Culture* 9 (1994). http://nideffer.net/proj/Tvc/interviews/20.Tvc.v9.intrvws.Sedg.html.

Kurnick, David. "What Does Late Jamesian Style Want?" *The Henry James Review* 28, no. 1 (2007): 213–22.

Lacan, Jacques. *The Ethics of Psychoanalysis 1959–1960: The Seminar of Jacques Lacan*, vol. 7. Edited by Jacques-Alain Miller. Translated by Dennis Porter. New York: W. W. Norton, 1997.

Lacan, Jacques. *The Psychoses 1955–1956: The Seminar of Jacques Lacan*, vol. 3. Edited by Jacques-Alain Miller. Translated by Russell Grigg. New York: W. W. Norton, 1997.

La Fountain-Stokes, Lawrence. "Gay Shame, Latino/a Style: A Critique of White Queer Performativity." In *Gay Male Latino Studies: A Critical Reader*, edited by Michael Hames-García and Ernesto J. Martínez, 55–80. Durham, NC: Duke University Press, 2011.

Litvak, Joseph. "Review of *The Weather in Proust*." *Modernism/Modernity* 19, no. 4 (November 2012): 805–7.

Litvak, Joseph. *Strange Gourmet: Sophistication, Theory, and the Novel*. Durham, NC: Duke University Press, 1997.

Lochrie, Karma. *Heterosyncrasies: Female Sexuality When Normal Wasn't*. Minneapolis: University of Minnesota Press, 2005.

Mackenzie, John M. *Orientalism: History, Theory and the Arts*. Manchester: Manchester University Press, 1995.

Marcus, Sharon. *Between Women: Friendship, Desire and Marriage in Victorian England*. Princeton, NJ: Princeton University Press, 2007.

Marcus, Sharon. "Gen/Ten: Eve Kosofsky Sedgwick's Between Men at 30." Columbia University Academic Commons, 2015. Accessed February 10, 2019. doi:10.7916/D8BZ65M6.

Martin, Biddy. "Extraordinary Homosexuals and the Fear of Being Ordinary." *Differences* 6, nos. 2–3 (1994): 100–25.

Martin, Biddy. "Sexualities without Genders and Other Utopias." *Diacritics* 24, nos. 2–3 (Summer–Autumn 1994): 104–21.

Martin, Randy. *Financialization of Daily Life*. Philadelphia, PA: Temple University Press, 2002.

Marvell, Andrew. "To His Coy Mistress." In *The Norton Anthology of Poetry*, edited by Margaret Ferguson, Tim Kendall, and Mary Jo Slater, 511. New York: W. W. Norton, 2018.

McBride, Dwight A. *Why I Hate Abercrombie and Fitch: Essays on Race and Sexuality*. New York: New York University Press, 2005.

McLuhan, Marshall. *The Mechanical Bride*. London: Routledge and Kegan Paul, [1951] 1967.

Melville, Herman. *Billy Budd and Other Stories*. New York: Penguin Classics, 1986.

Menon, Madhavi. *Indifference to Difference: On Queer Universalism*. Minneapolis: University of Minnesota Press, 2015.

Merck, Mandy, and Stella Sanford, eds. *Further Adventures of the Dialectic of Sex: Critical Essays on Shulamith Firestone*. New York: Palgrave Macmillan, 2010.

Merrill, James. "Carp." In *Collected Poems*, edited by J. D. McClatchy and Stephen Yenser, 531. New York: Alfred A. Knopf, 2002.

Michelson, Annette. "On the Eve of the Future: The Reasonable Facsimile and the Philosophical Toy." *October* 29 (Summer 1984): 3–20.

Muñoz, José Esteban. *Cruising Utopia: The Then and There of Queer Futurity*. New York: New York University Press, 2009.

Muñoz, José Esteban. "Race, Sex and the Incommensurate: Gary Fisher with Eve Kosofsky Sedgwick." In *Queer Futures: Reconsidering Ethics, Activism, and the Political*, edited by Elahe Yekani, Eveline Killian, and Beatrice Michaelis, 103–15. Aldershot, UK: Ashgate, 2013.

Murphy, Erin, and J. Keith Vincent, eds. "Honoring Eve" (special issue). *Criticism* 52, no. 2 (Spring 2010).

Murphy, Erin, and J. Keith Vincent. "Introduction." *Criticism* 52, no. 2 (2010): 159–76.

Namaste, Ki. "'Tragic Misreadings': Queer Theory's Erasure of Transgender Subjectivity." In *Queer Studies: A Lesbian, Gay, Bisexual, and Transgender Anthology*, edited by Brett Beemyn and Mickey Eliason, 183–203. New York: New York University Press, 1996.

Nancy, Jean-Luc. *Being Singular Plural*. Stanford, CA: Stanford University Press, 2000.

Nancy, Jean-Luc. "Communism, the Word." In *The Idea of Communism*, edited by Costas Douzinas and Slavoj Žižek, 145–53. London: Verso, 2010.

Nancy, Jean-Luc. *Hegel: The Restlessness of the Negative*. Minneapolis: University of Minnesota Press, 2002.

Nancy, Jean-Luc. *The Truth of Democracy*. Translated by Pascale-Anne Brault and Michael Naas. New York: Fordham University Press, 2010.

Nichols, Ben. "Reductive: John Rechy, Queer Theory, and the Idea of Limitation." *GLQ* 22, no. 3 (June 2016): 409–35.

Ohi, Kevin. *Dead Letters Sent: Queer Literary Transmission*. Minneapolis: University of Minnesota Press, 2015.

Palmer, Martin, and Jay Ramsay, with Man-Ho Kwok. *The Kuan Yin Chronicles: The Myths and Prophecies of the Chinese Goddess of Compassion*. Charlottesville, VA: Hampton Roads, [1995] 2009.

Parker, Andrew. *The Theorist's Mother*. Durham, NC: Duke University Press, 2012.

Patton, Cindy. "Love without the Obligation to Love." *Criticism* 52, no. 2 (2010): 215–24.

Perez, Hiram. "You Can Have My Brown Body and Eat it, Too!" *Social Text* 84–85 (Fall–Winter 2005): 171–91.

Prettejohn, Elizabeth. *Art for Art's Sake: Aestheticism in Victorian Painting*. New Haven, CT: Yale University Press, 2007.

Prettejohn, Elizabeth. *Beauty and Art, 1750–2000*. Oxford: Oxford University Press, 2005.

Prosser, Jay. *Second Skins: The Body Narratives of Transsexuality*. New York: Columbia University Press, 1998.

Proust, Marcel. *Remembrance of Things Past: Swann's Way and Within a Budding Grove*. Translated by C. K. Scott Moncrieff and Terence Kilmartin. New York: Random House, 1982.

Proust, Marcel. *The Guermantes Way*. Translated by C. K. Scott Moncrieff and Terence Kilmartin. New York: Random House, 1981.

Puar, Jasbir. "Mapping U.S. Homonormativities." *Gender, Place and Culture* 13, no. 1 (February 2001): 67–88.

Puar, Jasbir. *Terrorist Assemblages: Homonationalism in Queer Times*. Durham, NC: Duke University Press, 2007.

Quinn, Vincent. "Loose Reading: Sedgwick, Austen, Critical Practice." *Textual Practice* 14, no. 2 (2000): 305–26.

Quintilian. *The Institution Oratoria of Quintilian*, vol. 3. Translated by H. E. Butler. New York: G. P. Putnam's Sons, 1922.

Raitt, A. W. *The Life of Villiers de l'Isle-Adam*. New York: Oxford University Press, 1981.

Rankine, Claudia. *Don't Let Me Be Lonely: An American Lyric*. Minneapolis: Greywolf, 2004.

Reid-Pharr, Robert F. *Black Gay Man: Essays*. New York: New York University Press, 2001.

Rimbaud, Arthur. *Selected Poems and Letters*. Translated by Jeremy Harding. London: Penguin, 2004.

Rosenberg, Jordana. "The Molecularization of Sexuality: On Some Primitivisms of the Present." *Theory and Event* 17, no. 2 (2014). Accessed February 12, 2019. https://muse.jhu.edu/article/546470.

Ross, Marlon B. "Beyond the Closet as Raceless Paradigm." In *Black Queer Studies: A Critical Anthology*, edited by E. Patrick Johnson and Mae Henderson, 161–89. Durham, NC: Duke University Press, 2005.

Rubin, Gayle. "The Traffic in Women: Notes on the 'Political Economy' of Sex." In *Toward an Anthropology of Women*, edited by Rayne R. Reiter, 157–210. New York: Monthly Review, 1975.

Russ, Joanna. "Pornography by Women, for Women, with Love." In *Magic Mommas, Trembling Sisters, Puritans, and Perverts: Feminist Essays* by Joanna Russ, 79–99. Trumansburg, NY: Crossing, 1985.

Said, Edward W. *Orientalism*. London: Penguin, [1978] 2003.

St. Armand, Barton Levi. "Veiled Ladies: Dickinson, Bettine, and Transcendental Mediumship." In *Studies in the American Renaissance*, edited by Joel Myerson, 1–51. Charlottesville: University Press of Virginia, 1987.

Salamon, Gayle. *Assuming a Body: Transgender and the Rhetorics of Materiality*. New York: Columbia University Press, 2010.

Scarry, Elaine. *Dreaming by the Book*. New York: Farrar, Straus and Giroux, 1999.

Scholock, Adele. "Queer Theory in the First Person: Academic Autobiography and the Authoritative Contingencies of Visibility." *Cultural Critique* 66 (2007): 127–59.

Schor, Naomi. "Female Paranoia: The Case for Psychoanalytic Feminist Criticism." *Yale French Studies* 62 (1981): 204–19.

Sedgwick, Eve Kosofsky. *Between Men: English Literature and Male Homosocial Desire*. New York: Columbia University Press, 1985.

Sedgwick, Eve Kosofsky. *Between Men: English Literature and Male Homosocial Desire*. New York: Columbia University Press, 1993.

Sedgwick, Eve Kosofsky. *The Coherence of Gothic Conventions*. New York: Arno, 1976.

Sedgwick, Eve Kosofsky. *The Coherence of Gothic Conventions*. London: Methuen, 1985.

Sedgwick, Eve Kosofsky. *A Dialogue on Love*. Boston: Beacon, 2000.

Sedgwick, Eve Kosofsky. *Epistemology of the Closet*. London: Harvester, 1991.

Sedgwick, Eve Kosofsky. *Epistemology of the Closet*. Berkeley: University of California Press, 1991.

Sedgwick, Eve Kosofsky. *Epistemology of the Closet*. Berkeley: University of California Press, 2008.

Sedgwick, Eve Kosofsky. *Fat Art, Thin Art*. Durham, NC: Duke University Press, 1994.

Sedgwick, Eve Kosofsky. "How to Bring Your Kids Up Gay." *Social Text*, no. 29 (1991): 18–27. doi:10.2307/466296.

Sedgwick, Eve Kosofsky. "The L Word: Novelty in Normalcy." *Chronicle of Higher Education*, January 16, 2004, B10–11.

Sedgwick, Eve Kosofsky. "Melanie Klein and the Difference Affect Makes." *South Atlantic Quarterly* 106, no. 3 (Summer 2007): 624–42.

Sedgwick, Eve Kosofsky, ed. *Novel Gazing: Queer Readings in Fiction*. Durham, NC: Duke University Press, 1997.

Sedgwick, Eve Kosofsky. "The 1001 Seances." *GLQ* 17, no. 4 (2001): 457–517.

Sedgwick, Eve Kosofsky. "Paranoid Reading and Reparative Reading; or, You're So Paranoid, You Probably Think This Introduction Is about You." In *Novel Gazing: Queer Readings in Fiction*, edited by Eve Kosofsky Sedgwick, 1–37. Durham, NC: Duke University Press, 1997.

Sedgwick, Eve Kosofsky. "A Poem Is Being Written." *Representations* 17 (Winter 1987): 110–42.

Sedgwick, Eve Kosofsky. "Privilege of Unknowing." *Genders* 1 (Spring 1988): 102–24.

Sedgwick, Eve Kosofsky. "Queer Performativity: Henry James's *The Art of the Novel*." *GLQ* 1 (1993): 1–16.

Sedgwick, Eve Kosofsky. "Socratic Raptures, Socratic Ruptures: Notes toward Queer Performativity." In *English Inside and Out*, edited by Susan Gubar and Jonathan Kamholtz, 122–36. New York: Routledge, 1993.

Sedgwick, Eve Kosofsky. "Teaching/Depression." *Scholar and Feminist Online* 4, no. 2 (Spring 2006). Accessed February 12, 2019. http://www.barnard.columbia.edu/sfonline/heilbrun/conference.htm.

Sedgwick, Eve Kosofsky. *Tendencies*. Durham, NC: Duke University Press, 1993.

Sedgwick, Eve Kosofsky. "This Piercing Bouquet." In *Regarding Sedgwick*, edited by Stephen M. Barber and David L. Clark, 246. New York: Routledge, 2002.

Sedgwick, Eve Kosofsky. "Tide and Trust." *Critical Inquiry* 15, no. 4 (Summer 1989): 745–57.

Sedgwick, Eve Kosofsky. *Touching Feeling: Affect, Pedagogy, Performativity*. Durham, NC: Duke University Press, 2003.

Sedgwick, Eve Kosofsky. "Trace at 46." *Diacritics* 10, no. 1 (1980): 3–20.

Sedgwick, Eve Kosofsky. *The Weather in Proust*, edited by Jonathan Goldberg. Durham, NC: Duke University Press, 2011.

Sedgwick, Eve Kosofsky, and Adam Frank, eds. *Shame and Its Sisters*. Durham, NC: Duke University Press, 1995.

Sedgwick, Eve Kosofsky, and Adam Frank. "Shame in the Cybernetic Fold: Reading Silvan Tomkins." *Critical Inquiry* 21, no. 2 (Winter 1995): 496–522.

Sedgwick, Eve Kosofsky, and Michael Moon. "Confusion of Tongues." In *Breaking Bounds: Whitman and American Cultural Studies*, edited by Betsy Erkkila and Jay Grossman, 23–29. New York: Oxford University Press, 1996.

Sedgwick, Eve Kosofsky, and Michael Moon. "Divinity: A Dossier, a Performance Piece, a Little-Understood Emotion." *Discourse* 13, no. 1 (Fall–Winter 1990–91): 12–39.

Sedgwick, Eve Kosofsky, Michael Moon, Benjamin Gianni, and Scott Weir. "Queers in (Single Family) Space." *Assemblage* 24 (August 1994): 30–37.

Sedgwick, Eve Kosofsky, Michael Moon, Benjamin Gianni, and Scott Weir. "Queers in (Single Family) Space." In *The Design Culture Reader*, edited by Ben Highmore, 40–49. New York: Routledge, 2009.

Sedgwick, Eve Kosofsky, and Andrew Parker, eds. *Performativity and Performance*. London: Routledge, 1995.

Sedgwick, Eve Kosofsky, and Michael D. Snediker. "Queer Little Gods: A Conversation." *Massachusetts Review* 49, nos. 1–2 (2008): 194–218. http://www.jstor.org/stable/25091298.

Sellberg, Karin, and Lena Wånggren. "Intersectionality and Dissensus: A Negotiation of the Feminist Classroom." *Equality, Diversity and Inclusion* 31, nos. 5–6 (2012): 542–55.

Seltzer, Mark. *Serial Killers: Death and Life in America's Wound Culture*. New York: Routledge, 1998.

Selznick, Brian. *The Invention of Hugo Cabret*. New York: Scholastic, 2007.

Shelley, Mary. *Frankenstein; or, The Modern Prometheus*. Rev. ed. Edited by Maurice Hindle. London: Penguin, 1992.

Sherman, William H. "Toward a History of the Manicule." Accessed July 13, 2006. www.livesandletters.ac.uk/papers/FOR_2005_04_001.pdf.

Snediker, Michael D. *Contingent Figure: Aesthetic Duress from Ralph Waldo Emerson to Eve Kosofsky Sedgwick*. Minneapolis: University of Minnesota Press, forthcoming Fall 2020.

Solomon, Melissa. "Flaming Iguanas, Dalai Pandas, and Other Lesbian Bardos (A Few Perimeter Points)." In *Regarding Sedgwick: Essays on Queer Culture and Critical Theory*, edited by Stephen M. Barber and David L. Clark, 201–16. New York: Routledge, 2002.

Somerville, Siobhan B. "Feminism, Queer Theory, and the Racial Closet." *Criticism* 52, no. 2 (Spring 2010): 191–200.

Spillers, Hortense. "Mama's Baby, Papa's Maybe: An American Grammar Book." *Diacritics* 17, no. 2 (Summer 1987): 64–81.

Stein, Gertrude. *The Making of Americans.* Normal, IL: Dalkey Archive, 1995.

Stein, Gertrude. "What Are Master-Pieces and Why Are There So Few of Them." In *Writings and Lectures, 1909–1945,* edited by Patricia Meyerowitz, 153. Baltimore: Penguin, 1971.

Stephens, Elizabeth. "Queer Memoir: Public Confession and/as Sexual Practice in Eve Kosofsky Sedgwick's *A Dialogue on Love.*" *Australian Humanities Review* 48 (2010). http://press-files.anu.edu.au/downloads/press/p41611/html/04.xhtml?referer=1295&page=5.

Sullivan, Nikki. *A Critical Introduction to Queer Theory.* Edinburgh: Edinburgh University Press, 2003.

Sullivan, Nikki. "Being, Thinking, Writing With." *Cultural Studies Review* 9, no. 1 (2003): 51–59.

Swensen, Cole. *Noise That Stays Noise: Essays.* Ann Arbor: University of Michigan Press, 2011.

Tiffany, Daniel. *My Silver Planet.* Baltimore: Johns Hopkins University Press, 2014.

Updike, John. "The Rumor." In *The Afterlife and Other Stories,* by John Updike, 200–214. London: Penguin, 1995.

Valocchi, Stephen. "Not Yet Queer Enough: The Lessons of Queer Theory for the Sociology of Gender and Sexuality." *Gender and Society* 19, no. 6 (2005): 750–70.

van Dijck, Jose. *The Transparent Body: A Cultural Analysis of Medical Imaging.* Seattle: University of Washington Press, 2005.

Vermeule, Blakey. "Is There a Sedgwick School for Girls?" *Qui Parle* 5, no. 1 (Fall–Winter 1991): 53–72.

Wada, Yoshiko Iwamoto. *Memory on Cloth: Shibori Now.* Tokyo: Kodansha, 2002.

Wada, Yoshiko Iwamoto, Mary Kellogg Rice, and Jane Barton. *Shibori: The Inventive Art of Japanese Shaped Resist Dyeing.* Tokyo: Kodansha, [1983] 1999.

Warner, Michael, ed. *Fear of a Queer Planet: Queer Politics and Social Theory.* Minneapolis: University of Minnesota Press, 1993.

Warner, Michael. "Introduction: Fear of a Queer Planet." *Social Text* 29 (1991): 3–17.

Warner, Michael. "Queer and Then?" *Chronicle of Higher Education,* January 1, 2012. http://chronicle.com/section/The-Chronicle-Review/41.

Warner, Michael. *The Trouble with Normal: Sex, Politics and the Ethics of Queer Life.* New York: Free Press, 1999.

Weiss, Allen S. "Narcissistic Machines and Erotic Prostheses." In *Camera Obscura, Camera Lucida: Essays in Honor of Annette Michelson,* edited by Richard Allen and Malcolm Turvey, 55–74. Amsterdam: Amsterdam University Press, 2003.

Whitman, Walt. *Leaves of Grass: The First (1855) Edition.* Edited by Malcolm Cowley. New York: Penguin, 1986.

Wiegman, Robyn. *American Anatomies: Theorizing Race and Gender*. Durham, NC: Duke University Press, 1995.

Wiegman, Robyn. "Sex and Negativity; or, What Queer Theory Has for You." *Cultural Critique* 95 (Winter 2017): 219–43.

Wiegman, Robyn. "'The Times We're In': Queer Feminist Criticism and the Reparative 'Turn.'" *Feminist Theory* 15, no. 1 (April 2014): 1–24.

Wiegman, Robyn. "The Vertigo of Critique: Rethinking Heteronormativity." In *Object Lessons* by Robyn Wiegman, 301–43. Durham, NC: Duke University Press, 2012.

Wiegman, Robyn, and Elizabeth A. Wilson. *Queer Theory without Antinormativity*. Durham, NC: Duke University Press, 2015.

Wilner, Josh. Personal communication with H.A. Sedgwick. Originally published in "Eve's First Publication?," *Eve Kosofsky Sedgwick* (blog). December 22, 2012. Accessed February 12, 2019, http://evekosofskysedgwick.net/blog/page5/.

Yingling, Tom. AIDS *and the National Body*. Durham, NC: Duke University Press, 1997.

Yu, Chun-Fang. *Kuan-yin: The Chinese Transformation of Avalokitesvara*. New York: Columbia University Press, 2001.

Contributors

LAUREN BERLANT teaches English at the University of Chicago. Recent books include *Cruel Optimism* (Duke University Press, 2011), addressing precarious publics and the aesthetics of affective adjustment in the contemporary US and Europe; *Desire/Love* (2012), an introduction to concepts of attachment; and, with Lee Edelman, *Sex, or the Unbearable* (Duke University Press, 2014), a dialogue/argument about what can be done with self-disturbance and repair. Her latest experiment on the poetics of attention, encounter, and worlding, written with Kathleen Stewart, is called *The Hundreds* (Duke University Press, 2019).

KATHRYN BOND STOCKTON is the Distinguished Professor of English, Associate Vice-President for Equity and Diversity, and inaugural Dean of the School for Cultural and Social Transformation at the University of Utah. She is the author of *The Queer Child, or Growing Sideways in the Twentieth Century* (Duke University Press, 2009) and is writing the theatrical memoir *Making Out, Queerly: Kissing, Reading, Sex with Ideas* (forthcoming).

JUDITH BUTLER is Maxine Elliot Professor in the Department of Comparative Literature and the Program of Critical Theory at the University of California, Berkeley. She is the author of a large number of highly influential texts in social theory, from *Gender Trouble* (1990) to *Notes toward a Performative Theory of Assembly* (2016). She has received numerous awards, including the Adorno Prize from the City of Frankfurt in honor of her contributions to feminist and moral philosophy and the diploma of Chevalier of the Order of Arts and Letters from the French Cultural Ministry.

LEE EDELMAN is the Fletcher Professor of English Literature at Tufts University. His work brings together Lacanian analysis, rhetorical criticism, and the politics of social and cultural representation. His most recent books are *No Future: Queer Theory and the Death Drive* (Duke University Press, 2004) and, with Lauren Berlant, *Sex, or the Unbearable* (Duke University Press, 2014), both of which engage what many now call "the antisocial turn" in queer theory. His current project, *Bad Education*, thinks about queerness, the negation of value, and the ideology of the aesthetic.

JASON EDWARDS is a Professor of Art History at the University of York. He is the author of the Routledge "Critical Thinkers" volume on Sedgwick and the editor of *Bathroom Songs: Eve Kosofsky Sedgwick as a Poet* (2017), which includes Sedgwick's uncollected poetry. He is currently completing a monograph on Sedgwick's fiber art.

RAMZI FAWAZ is an Associate Professor of English at the University of Wisconsin, Madison. He is the author of *The New Mutants: Superheroes and the Radical Imagination of American Comics* (2016). His work has been published in numerous journals, including *American Literature*, GLQ, *Feminist Studies*, *Callaloo*, and *Feminist Review*. His new book, *Queer Forms*, explores the relationship between feminist and queer politics and formal innovation in the art and culture of movements for women's and gay liberation.

DENIS FLANNERY is an Associate Professor of American and English Literature at the University of Leeds. His published works include his first monograph, *Henry James: A Certain Illusion* (2000), and *On Sibling Love, Queer Attachment and American Writing* (2007). His most recent book (co-edited with Michèle Mendelssohn) is the collection *Alan Hollinghurst: Writing under the Influence* (2016). Current projects include a book on the Dutch theater company Toneelgroep Amsterdam; the completion of a collaborative memoir begun with his father, Denis Kevin Flannery (1919–2009); and *Tearful Light*, on Henry James.

JANE GALLOP is a Distinguished Professor of English at the University of Wisconsin, Milwaukee. She is the author of a number of books, including *The Deaths of the Author: Reading and Writing in Time* (2011). She recently completed a book titled *Sexuality, Disability, and Aging: Queer Temporalities of the Phallus* (Duke University Press, 2019).

JONATHAN GOLDBERG is Arts and Sciences Distinguished Professor Emeritus at Emory University. His recent publications include *This Distracted Globe: World-Making in Early Modern Literature* (2016, co-edited with Marcie Frank and Karen Newman), *Melodrama: An Aesthetics of Impossibility* (Duke University Press, 2016), *Saint Marks: Words, Images, and What Persists* (2018), and *Sappho:]fragments* (2018).

MERIDITH KRUSE is a Lecturer in the Writing Program at the University of Southern California.

MICHAEL MOON is the author of *Disseminating Whitman* (1991), *A Small Boy and Others: Imitation and Initiation in American Culture from Henry James to Andy Warhol* (Duke University Press, 1998), *Darger's Resources* (Duke University Press, 2012), and, most recently, *Arabian Nights: A Queer Film Classic* (2017). He is also the editor of the revised Norton critical edition of Walt Whitman's poetry.

JOSÉ ESTEBAN MUÑOZ (1967–2013) was Professor and Chair of Performance Studies at New York University. He was the author of the forthcoming *The Sense of Brown*, as well as *Disidentifications: Queers of Color and the Performance of Politics* (1999) and *Cruising Utopia: The Then and There of Queer Futurity* (2009). With Jonathan Flatley and Jennifer Doyle, he co-edited *Pop Out: Queer Warhol* (1996) and, with Celeste Fraser Delgado, *Everynight Life: Culture and Dance in Latin/o America* (1997).

CHRIS NEALON is a Professor of English at Johns Hopkins University. He is the author of two books of criticism, *Foundlings: Lesbian and Gay Historical Emotion before Stonewall* (Duke University Press, 2001) and *The Matter of Capital: Poetry and Crisis in The American Century* (2011), and three books of poetry: *The Joyous Age* (2004), *Plummet* (2009), and *Heteronomy* (2014). He is currently at work on a study of academic antihumanism.

ANDREW PARKER is a Professor of French and the Chair of Comparative Literature at Rutgers University. He is the author most recently of *The Theorist's Mother* (Duke University Press, 2012), which follows traces of the maternal in the lives and works of canonical male theorists from Karl Marx and Sigmund Freud to Jacques Lacan and Jacques Derrida. He is also the editor and translator of Jacques Rancière's *The Philosopher and His Poor* (Duke University Press, 2004) and co-editor (with Eve Kosofsky Sedgwick) of *Performativity and Performance* (1995), (with Janet Halley) of *After Sex?* (Duke University Press, 2007), and of three other essay collections. A book on Marx and figurations of theater and a collaborative multilingual online edition of Julio Cortázar's novel *Rayuela/Hopscotch* are in progress.

H. A. SEDGWICK, EVE SEDGWICK'S partner, is currently working, with lots of help, on the development and preservation of her archive, as well as on the creation of a website and a small foundation in her name.

KARIN SELLBERG is a Lecturer in Humanities in the School of Historical and Philosophical Inquiry at the University of Queensland, Australia. She has published extensively in the fields of gender studies, medical humanities, and critical theory. She is the editor of the *Cengage Interdisciplinary Handbook on Gender: Time* (2018), co-editor (with Lena Wånggren and Kamillea Aghtan) of *Corporeality and Culture* (2015), and co-editor of special journal issues for, among others, *Australian Feminist Studies, Rhizomes: Cultural Studies in Emerging Knowledge, InterAlia: A Journal of Queer Studies*, and *Somatechnics*.

MICHAEL D. SNEDIKER is an Associate Professor of American Literature and Poetics at the University of Houston. He is the author of *Queer Optimism: Lyric Personhood and Other Felicitous Persuasions* (2008) and is writing a book of essays about chronic pain titled *Contingent Figure: Aesthetic Duress from Ralph Waldo Emerson to Eve Kosofsky Sedgwick* (forthcoming 2020). His essays have appeared in journals including *Qui Parle, Henry James Review, Modernism/modernity*, and *J19*. He has also written two books of poems, *The Apartment of Tragic Appliances* (2013) and *The New York Editions* (2017).

MELISSA SOLOMON is an independent scholar of queer studies. Her published work includes, among many other essays, "The Female World of Exorcism and Displacement: Or, Relations between Women in Henry James's Nineteenth-Century *The Portrait of a Lady*," included in Eve Kosofsky Sedgwick's *Novel Gazing: Queer Readings in Fiction* (Duke University Press, 1997), and "Flaming Iguanas, Dalai Pandas, and Other Lesbian Bardos," included in Stephen M. Barber and David L. Clark's *Regarding Sedgwick: Essays on Queer Culture and Critical Theory* (2013).

ROBYN WIEGMAN is a Professor of Literature at Duke University and the former director of women's studies at Duke and the University of California, Irvine. She is the author of *Object Lessons* (Duke University Press, 2012) and *American Anatomies: Theorizing Race and Gender* (Duke University Press, 2002) and a co-editor of numerous anthologies on topics in American studies, feminist studies, and queer theory.

Index

Banville, John, 94, 95
Barale, Michele, 2
Barber, Stephen, 113, 194, 236; Sedgwick's
    interview with, 114, 127
Barrett, Lindon, 163
Barthes, Roland, 277
Basil Hallward, in *The Picture of Dorian Gray*
    (Wilde), 276
*Bathroom Songs: Eve Kosofsky Sedgwick as a
    Poet* (Edwards, ed.), 35
Baudelaire, Charles, 147
Beatrix Protheroe, in *The Warm Decembers*
    (Sedgwick), 73, 84, 212
beauty, 84, 94, 156, 194, 211, 277; of Sedgwick,
    238
becoming, 48, 51, 174, 230; Sedgwick and,
    176, 196–98
Belton, Don, 163
Berlant, Lauren, 2, 47, 61, 137, 167, 273n89; on
    affect, 39–42; on failure, 37–38; on fantasy,
    54–56; on loss, 49–50
Bersani, Leo, 108, 206; "Is the Rectum a
    Grave?," 97, 109
Best, Stephen, 101
*Between Men: English Literature and Male
    Homosocial Desire* (Sedgwick), 119, 147, 167,
    182, 189, 245, 254, 255, 268n43; feminist
    theory and, 270–71n57, 271n62; introduc-
    tion to, 251, 268n44; methodology of, 123;
    new preface to, 114, 115–16, 117, 118, 253; as
    Sedgwick's first book, 251; significance of,
    114, 253; triangular desire in, 122, 251–52;
    Whitman in, 214; Wiegman and, 250
Billy Budd (Melville), Sedgwick on, 11–12,
    169
binary, binarism, 29, 30; gender, 184, 186;
    hetero-homo, 169, 172
blacks: blackness and, 256; feminism of, 28;
    as gay men, 158, 256; literary tradition of,
    154; white liberals and, 4. *See also* African
    Americans
blindness, 73, 133
"Bodhisattva Fractal World" exhibition
    (Sedgwick), 72, 75–77, 83–85
bodhisattva imagery, 75–77, 85
body, embodiment, 56, 96, 119, 130, 190,
    221; breathing and, 69; coming-to-, 186;
    differences in, 7, 11, 28; in *Frankenstein*

(Shelley), 183, 185; identity and, 7; James
    and, 105; queer, 198; relationship to, 56;
    Sedgwick on, 56, 74, 137, 168, 220;
    Sedgwick's, 8, 18, 189, 197, 198–99, 257,
    265n32; Western, 198
Bohm, David, 129
boldness, Sedgwick's, 275
Bolger, Dermot, 94, 95
Bollas, Christopher, 49
Boston University, Sedgwick Lecture, 178
bourgeoisie, 143, 146, 267n42. *See also* middle
    class
Bowers v. Hardwick, 3
Bradway, Tyler, 29
Braidotti, Rosi, 198
Bray, Alan, 116
breath, breathing, 64, 69, 70, 129;
    Sedgwick and, 65, 275
Brontë, Emily, *Wuthering Heights*, 76
Bronzino (Agnolo di Cosimo), 72
Brown, Ken, 72
Browning, Elizabeth Barrett, 187n10
Buckley, William F., 184, 186
Buddha, Buddhism, 8, 10, 46, 64, 69, 75–76,
    84, 166, 171, 176; Freud and, 70; reality
    and, 82; Sedgwick and, 128, 247, 248;
    Sedgwick on, 68–69
Burke, Edmund, 86
Butler, Judith, 11, 130, 199, 204–5, 249–50,
    266n35, 267n40, 269n51; on Proust
    and Sedgwick, 63–70
Byron, Lord, 181

Caleb Williams (Godwin), 182
Cameron, Julia Margaret, 72, 73
Cameron, Sharon, 130
cancer, Sedgwick's, 25, 37, 117, 128, 217–18, 219,
    240, 256, 259, 261n5, 265n32
canon: Asian, 73; gay studies and, 264n24;
    Sedgwick and, 8; Western, 73, 251
capitalism, 146, 172, 173, 174, 180
Carceri d'invenzione (Piranesi), 167
Cartesian logic, 133, 134
Cartesian moment, 203
categories, 122, 123; of identity, 190, 246,
    259
Cather, Willa, 8, 137; "Paul's Case" (1905),
    137; Sedgwick on, 124–25

detachment, space of, 51
detective novels, Sedgwick and, 145
Dialogue on Love, A (Sedgwick), 41, 51–52, 56, 167, 182, 211–12; close reading of, 176; dread in, 59; Gothic writing practice in, 175; love in, 199; queer patience of, 198; Sedgwick in, 197; as semiconfessional memoir, 196–98; therapy in, 221
Dickens, Charles, 253; *The Haunted House*, 95; Little Dorrit and, 238
Dickinson, Emily, 98, 216, 236
difference, differences, 13, 16, 84, 133, 137; identity and, 7, 18; narcissism of small, 28; ungraspable, 122; women of color feminism and, 28
digital practice, 44
disability studies, 28, 29
discourse, discourses: of affect management, 59–60; of identification, 190, 191–92
disrepair, 4, 42. *See also* reparative, reparativity
disruption, 70, 168, 169, 196, 256. *See also* rupture, ruptures
domination, 154, 158, 159, 160, 161
drama, dramatics, 58; Edelman on, 50–54, 57; of heterosexual transgression, 172; as linear narrative, 52; of negativity, 56; of omnipotence, 64; of queer politics, 171; of recognition, 118; of Sedgwick reading herself, 120; self's, 54; of substance and abstraction, 168
dread, 47, 48; abandonment and, 42; failure of knowledge and, 59; queerness and, 40–41; Sedgwick and, 54; Sedgwick on, 50, 53, 64; space free of, 51
drives, theory of, 64
dualism, 44, 123, 227
Dublin, 92–93; Sedgwick in, 34
Duke University Press, 35, 127
Dumm, Tom, 39–40
Durham, N.C., Sedgwick's house in, 148
Dutton, Dennis, 210
Dylan, Bob, 102

Edelman, Lee, 2, 37, 56–61, 265n33; on drama, 50–54; on failure, 38–39; on loss, 47–49; on reparativity, 43–47
Edison, Thomas, 143–44, 146, 147

editor, Sedgwick as, 2, 276
Edwards, Jason, 101; on Sedgwick, 189, 191, 200n8; Sedgwick's poetry and, 35, 96–97
Eliot, George, 253; *Adam Bede*, 172, 180; *Daniel Deronda*, 238
Elizabeth, in *Frankenstein* (Shelley), 181, 182
embodiment. *See* body, embodiment
Emerson, Ralph Waldo, 39, 204, 205, 214, 215, 217, 225; *Nature* (1836), 203, 207–8
Emory University, 121
empiricism, radical, 203, 206
enjambent, 74, 159, 212, 220, 229
epistemology, 46, 73, 79; affect and, 53, 54
Epistemology of the Closet (Sedgwick), 118, 167–70, 182, 183, 186, 189–90, 206, 209, 245, 247, 258–59, 268n43, 273n87; axioms in, 246, 254, 264n24; binarisms deconstructed in, 30; challenge to leftist criticism in, 258; final chapter of, 109n1; Flannery and, 93; homophobia and paranoia in, 179; introduction to, 14, 17–18, 21, 121–22, 129, 142, 169, 210, 226, 255; motivation for writing, 157–58; opening line of, 13–14; reissue of, 124; strategic stance of, 123
equivalence, 80, 153, 163; calculus of, 157; non-, 153, 154, 155, 204, 232n15; politics of, 154, 156, 161; refusal of, 161
erotic, erotics: ethics of, 132–39; of racial humiliation, 153
eroticism, 83, 161, 238
erotic triangles, 122–23, 267n41, 269n51, 270n56; in *Between Men* (Sedgwick), 252
Eve of the Future, The (Villiers de l'Isle-Adam), 142–45
everyday living, 171, 174
exhibitions of Sedgwick's fiber and book art, 72, 80, 97
"Experimental Critical Writing" class (Sedgwick's), 240

fabric, 78, 150; Sedgwick and, 79, 84, 129, 147, 167, 214, 218–20, 229; social, 215–16. *See also* fiber arts, Sedgwick and; textile arts; textiles
failure, 37–39; defeat and, 44; of knowing, 59

fainting, 56, 272n74; Sedgwick's, 256–58, 272n74

Fairer, David, 94

family: Oedipal, 180, 183; Sedgwick on, 17; Sedgwick's friends as, 238

fantasm, fantasmatic (phantasmatic), 27, 58, 102, 147, 186. *See also* fantasy, fantasies

fantasy, fantasies, 41, 42, 51, 54, 55, 103, 147, 184; of James, 103, 104; of omnipotence, 128; Sedgwick and, 52, 192; Sedgwick on, 40, 125, 158; of sexual submission, 83, 155, 175

Fat Art, Thin Art (Sedgwick), 35, 73, 75, 190, 199, 215

father, 58; Flannery's, 92, 93

fatness, 79–80; of Sedgwick's textiles, 78, 80; social implications of Sedgwick's, 192

Fawaz, Ramzi, 2

feedback loops, 44, 79

feelings, 10, 23, 25, 26, 27, 133, 136, 141

Felski, Rita, 198–99

femaleness, Sedgwick on, 126

feminism, feminists, 9, 142, 186, 264n24; academic, 170; anti-, 3; black, 28, 250; cultural production of, 29, 253; patriarchy reconsidered by, 253; post-, 239; queer, 133–34; queer men and, 158; Sedgwick and, 126, 250, 251; shifts in, 172

feminist criticism: of Gothic novels, 185; Sedgwick and, 245

feminist theory, 123, 268n43

Ferenczi, Sándor, 146, 178

Ferguson, Roderick, 28

fetishism, fetish, 31, 55, 150, 161, 246; racial, 159, 160–61, 165

Feuillade, Louis, 147

fiber arts, Sedgwick and, 72–86, 129, 217–18

ficto-criticism, Sedgwick's, 54

figuration, figures, 124, 152, 168, 169, 171; Sedgwick on, 125

Firestone, Shulamith, 186, 188n26

Fisher, Gary, 76, 277; "Arabesque," 158–59, 160–61; *Gary in Your Pocket* (1996), 152–56, 160–61, 163–64, 243, 276; Sedgwick and, 152–64, 243, 276; Sedgwick's reading of, 155–56

Flaubert, Gustav, 210

food, Sedgwick and, 237

Foucault, Michel, 134, 138–39, 168, 198, 205, 266n35; *The History of Sexuality, Volume 1*, 246; Sedgwick and, 9

fractals, 228; Sedgwick and, 215, 232n19

Frank, Adam, 78

Frankenstein (Shelley), 179, 180, 182, 183, 185, 187n10; Sedgwick's reading of, 180–81

Frankenstein, Age of, 182, 183, 186; in Sedgwick's periodization, 179

Frankenstein's monster, 180, 181, 182, 185

French language, 175, 216

Freud, Sigmund, 57, 60, 69, 70, 118, 144, 186, 187n10; "A Child Is Being Beaten," 219; Dr. Schreber case and, 180, 182; Sedgwick and, 9. *See also* uncanny (*unheimlich*)

Fried, Michael, 73

Friel, Brian, 94

friends: of Sedgwick, 34, 37, 152, 155, 178, 178, 193, 218, 237, 256; Sedgwick as, 196, 237

Gallop, Jane, 25, 132–35

Gamson, Joshua, 191

Gary in Your Pocket (Fisher; Sedgwick, ed.), 152–56, 160–61, 163–64, 243, 276

Gaskell, Elizabeth, 95

gay liberation, 31, 243

gay men: allies of, 169; creativity of, 115, 120; culture of, 25; Sedgwick cross-identified with, 8, 18, 25, 249, 250 253, 265n32

gay politics, 153, 171, 174–75, 243

gays and lesbians, 13, 154; activism of, 275; classic writers as, 21; of color, 163, 165n21; identification and identity of, 125, 138, 264n24; as scholars, 116; Sedgwick on, 12–13; social eradication of, 134; society's view of, 23; as victims, 190. *See also* "lesbian" *main entries*

gay studies, 13, 114, 117

gender, genders, 6, 63, 204, 258; asymmetry of, 124; binarism of, 186; calculus of power and, 252; as category, 123; Cather and, 124; class and, 122, 253; differences of, 178; Gothic and, 117–18; identity and, 7, 191, 201n11; inequalities of, 270n56; liminality of, 137–38; non-normative, 4; reification of, 239; separatism of, 138; sex and, 125; study of, 264n24; transitivity of, 28, 264n28; in *The Wings of Doves* (James), 99, 100

and, 13, 190–93; Sedgwick and, 190, 191, 192, 195, 200, 249, 253. *See also* identification, identifications

imitation ballad, 205

"in," 94, 99; Flannery on, 92–109; in James's works, 95, 101–5; rectums and, 97–98; in Sedgwick's works, 96–109; Updike's use of, 93, 99

incommensurability, 152–64

incompletion, 39

Independent Colleges, Dublin, Sedgwick memorial seminar at, 34

Industrial Revolution, 180

injunction theory, 18, 135, 196

interiority, 94, 96, 98, 104, 199

intersubjectivity, 179, 180

"In the Bardo" (Sedgwick exhibit, CUNY, SUNY), 72, 80, 97

Ireland, 34, 94

Irigaray, Luce, 134, 270n54

"I" voice of Sedgwick, 197

Jagose, Annamarie, 193, 244, 265n28, 273n89

Jakobsen, Janet, 263–64n19

James, Henry, 8, 11, 77, 85, 94–95, 101–2, 150, 167, 182, 187n10, 207, 210–12, 216, 221; fisting and, 102–5; *The Lesson of the Master*, 224; *A Little Tour in France*, 95; *Roderick Hudson*, 215–16; Sedgwick on, 93, 96–109, 201n11, 211, 215–16, 223–24; *The Spoils of Poynton*, 223–24; "The Beast in the Jungle," 96, 170, 215, 221, 224, 229; "The Turn of the Screw," 95; *Washington Square*, 130; *The Wings of the Dove*, 93, 97–100, 106–8, 223

James, William, 203, 204

Jarrell, Randell, 272n73; "Hope," 256, 258, 272n74

jealousy, 66, 67

Jewett, Sarah Orne, *The Country of the Pointed Firs*, 238

Johns Hopkins University, Sedgwick's exhibition at, 72

Johnson, Barbara, 64–66, 92–94, 99, 102, 185, 186, 188n17, 227; Sedgwick and, 9, 63, 65, 70

juncture, 124–25, 245, 271n61

karma, 46–47, 52, 58

Kate Croy, in *The Wings of the Dove* (James), 98, 99, 100, 106–8, 110n14, 223

kimono patchworks of Sedgwick, 74, 75, 79, 218

kitsch, 205, 206, 210

Klein, Melanie, 4, 43, 47–50, 65, 79, 84; on reparative impulse, 135–36, 159; Sedgwick and, 9, 52, 60, 150, 185

knowing, knowingness, 6, 50, 54, 58, 59, 127, 157; Sedgwick and, 23–24, 27–28. *See also* knowledge

knowledge, 25, 26, 40, 59, 138–39, 150, 195, 251

Kosofsky, Rita Goldstein (Sedgwick's mother), 35, 239–40

Kruse, Meridith, 132

K/S (Kirk and Spock) slash fiction, 145, 151n4

Kurnick, David, 97, 107–8

Lacan, Jacques, 203, 208–9, 213

Lauper, Cyndi, 221

Lawrence v. Texas (2003), 3

Leeds College, 97

Lefebvre, Henri, 174

leftists, 23, 168

legacies of Sedgwick, 4–5, 22, 24, 141, 144, 146; construction of a way of knowing, 27–28; intellectual, 10–11; theoretical, 9

lesbian feminists, 250, 268n48

lesbianism, lesbians, 3, 169, 190, 200n8, 251, 256, 264n24, 268n44; studies, 260n2, 268n48; politics of, 171, 174–75; Sedgwick and, 242, 245, 246, 249, 262n9. *See also* gays and lesbians

Lévi-Strauss, Claude, 168

LGBT, 153, 175; LGBTQ+ and, 138

liberalism, 146, 261n7; queer, 243

libido, 64, 65, 69

Lionel Croy, in *The Wings of the Dove* (James), 96, 97, 98, 107, 108; Sedgwick on, 99, 100, 105

listing, in Sedgwick's work, 16–18

literature and literary studies, 29, 30, 94, 132, 267n41; post-Romantic, 178; queer theory and, 14; Sedgwick and, 19, 21, 169, 187, 192, 251, 254; students and scholars of, 94, 152, 154. *See also* canon; Gothic

movement politics, Sedgwick and, 170

multiplicity, 19, 31; Sedgwick and, 10, 14–18, 27, 29

Muñoz, José Esteban, 152, 162

Murphy, Erin, 189

mutiny of resistance, Sedgwick's, 227

mysticism: of Proust, 53, 129, 130; of Sedgwick, 277; Sedgwick and, 48, 52, 82

myth of Sedgwick, 274–75

Nancy, Jean-Luc, 153, 156, 157, 159, 162, 194

narcissism, 28, 95, 137, 211, 216

narrative, narratives, 13, 182, 191, 193, 197; Sedgwick's, 191, 192

narrative exposure, 193–95

narrative medicine, 197–98

narrator, in *Remembrance of Things Past* (Proust), 63–64, 66–68, 70

national allegory, in *Frankenstein* (Shelley), 181

nature, 203, 205, 264n24

Nauman, Bruce, 275

needles, 83

negativity, 4, 38, 44, 45, 46, 56, 59, 60–61; Sedgwick and, 57

Negri, Antonio, 176

neoconservatives, 3

neoliberalism, 30

neo-Nazis, Trump and, 4

Neoplatonism, 127, 128

New Criticism, 132, 136

Nichols, Beverly, 173

Nietzsche, Friedrich, 179, 180, 182, 187n5, 276–77

"no": in Buddhist thought, 46; place of the, 38, 44, 46, 48; rupture of, 57; saying, 44

nonequivalence, 153, 204

non-necessity, 55

nonself pedagogy of Buddhism, 46

normalization of AIDS, 242, 243

normativity, 15, 248, 250, 259; Sedgwick and, 249

novel, novels, 9, 95, 167, 253; Gothic, 96, 168, 173, 179, 180–85; James's, 85, 96–100, 106–8, 223, 224; Sedgwick's love for, 51; Sedgwick's reading of, 120, 184–86; Villiers's, 142–47

Novel Gazing: Queer Readings in Fiction (Sedgwick), 43, 182

nurture, 22, 27, 43, 136, 199, 264n24

Obama, Barack, 3, 128

object, objects, 27, 65, 72, 203, 204, 205, 207; Fisher as self-abjected black, 158; of love, 69; queer studies and, 204; racialized sexual, 155

object choice, 155, 252; gender of, 6, 246; same-sex, 247, 264n28

object-oriented ontology (ooo), 206

obsession, 26; Sedgwick on, 25

O'Connell, Mark, 94

Oedipus, Oedipal scenario, 46, 64, 68, 269n52

Ohi, Kevin, 222

Oliver, Mary, 238

omnipotence, 64, 65, 66

ontology and ontological turn, 92, 204, 206, 227

optical illusion, 80

optimism, 37, 42

"or," 45, 60, 61

Orientalism, 86

O'Rourke, Michael, 1, 2, 34

Orphic chant, 207

otherness, other, 6, 134, 156, 157, 192

out-of-syncness, 56

pain, 130, 199, 204; chronic, 208–9; queer and, 199, 275; as quilting point, 218; Sedgwick's, 219

paranoid, paranoia, 27, 41, 44, 46, 58, 60, 172, 277; female, 184–85; Gothic and, 119–20, 179, 182; reparativity and, 29, 45, 57, 101, 127, 185; Sedgwick on, 43, 179

paresthesia, Sedgwick's, 83

Parker, Andrew, 178

particularlist, Sedgwick as, 11–14

passivity, of patient, 197

patient, Sedgwick as, 196, 218

patriarchy, 251, 253, 267n41, 270n54, 271n57

Patton, Cindy, 25, 195

pedagogy, 82, 132, 133, 164n21, 171, 195; queer, 25, 86; Sedgwick and, 25, 86, 217, 240–41, 245, 255

261–62n7; development of, 14, 174, 175, 186, 190; Sedgwick and, 72, 114, 128, 198, 203, 219, 231, 243–44; Segdwick and, 206. *See also* queer inquiry and critique; queer scholars

quilting point, 213, 218

Quintilian, 210–11

race and racism, 4, 7, 31, 122, 123, 161, 250, 258, 268n43; sex and, 152–64; study of, 28, 152, 163

Rancière, Jacques, 175, 196

Rankine, Claudia, 39, 40

readers, 245, 273n89; of Sedgwick, 193, 197, 199, 209, 253, 255

Reagan, Ronald, 216; culture war of, 3, 4

realism, reality, 40, 60, 108, 204; as flowerlike, 80–83

rectum, 97–98. *See also* sex: anal

Reid-Pharr, Robert, 152, 154, 163

reincarnation, Sedgwick and, 48, 52

relationality, 16, 19, 38, 39, 69, 125, 154, 274; loss and, 48, 49; Sedgwick and, 47, 196

relationships, 7; Sedgwick's love, 8

repair, reparation, 38, 41, 42, 54, 185; Sedgwick and, 199. *See also* reparative, reparativity

reparative, reparativity, 4, 37, 48, 60, 61, 160, 273n87; Edelman on, 43–47; paranoia and, 29, 45, 57, 127; reading and, 101, 136; Sedgwick and, 4, 43, 159

reparative impulse, 23, 29; Sedgwick on, 26–27

repetition, 38, 59

resistance, 134, 226, 227, 228

Rich, Adrienne, 268n48

Riggs, Marlon, *Tongues Untied* (film), 256

Rolling Stone magazine, 114

Romantics, 179; post-, 178

Rorschach techniques, 80

Rosenberg, Jordana, 204–5, 206

Rossetti, Dante Gabriel, 72

Rouault, George, 72

Rubens, Peter Paul, 72

Rubin, Gayle, 37, 123, 172, 269–70n54

rupture, ruptures, 46, 57; failure and, 38, 39

Ruskin, John, 72

Safie, in *Frankenstein* (Shelley), 181

St. Anthony, 106, 108

same-sex desire, 8, 9, 264n28

San Francisco, 158

scarf, Sedgwick's mid-1990s, 74–75

Scarry, Elaine, 96, 204

scars, scarification, 199

Schiele, Egon, 72

Schor, Naomi, 185

Schreber, Doctor, 180, 182, 183, 186

science culture, 146

science fiction, 146

Scott, Judith, 72, 129–30

scouring, 130, 211, 212, 213

sculpture, 130; Sedgwick and, 73

Sedgwick, Eve, 127; archives of, 35, 36; birth and birthday of, 51, 237; cancer of, 25, 37, 117, 128, 217–19, 240, 256, 259, 261n5, 265n32; colleagues and friends of, 34, 37, 152, 155, 178, 178, 193, 218, 237, 256; conceptual tools of, 23, 28, 54, 134; death of, 3, 35, 37, 92, 128, 142, 178; as editor, 2, 152; as fiber artist, 72–86, 128–29, 147; as inexhaustible, 166–76; legacies of, 4–5, 9, 10–11, 22, 24, 27–28, 141, 144, 146; love for, 193; as patient, 197; pedagogy of, 24–25, 86, 217, 240–41, 245, 255; poems of, 35, 75, 96–97, 175, 194, 199; protests North Carolina PBS, 256; Proust and, 63–70; as teacher, 187n10, 195–96, 200n8; writings of, 9, 24; writings of, early, 6–7, 35, 36, 68, 118, 126, 128, 142, 168, 178, 204; writings of, later, 26, 35, 128, 147, 195, 228–29; young, 115–17, 192, 194, 219, 239–40

Sedgwick, Eve, books by, 73, 77, 113; *Between Men: English Literature and Male Homosocial Desire*, 3, 9, 35, 114, 118, 119, 122, 147, 167, 172, 182, 189, 214, 245, 250–55; *The Coherence of Gothic Conventions*, 96, 117–20, 167, 170, 175, 183–85; *A Dialogue on Love*, 41, 46–47, 51–52, 56, 59, 167, 176, 182, 196–98, 211–12, 221; *Epistemology of the Closet*, 3, 6–7, 9, 13–14, 21, 30, 36, 93, 109n1, 118, 121–24, 129, 142, 157–58, 167–72, 179, 182, 186, 189, 206, 209, 240, 245, 255, 258–59; *Fat Art, Thin Art*, 35, 73, 75, 199, 215; *Novel Gazing: Queer Readings in Fiction*, 2, 4, 43, 182;

solipsism, 179, 180, 183
Solomon, Melissa, 35–36
Somerville, Siobhan, 268n43
space: anti-, 198; for communication, 197;
    free of dread, 51; inner, 150; of narrative
    practice, 198; of no karma, 52; queer as,
    189, 191; self and, 196; social, 194; universe
    as livable, 58
specificity, 122; of texts, 133, 139
spectacle, 49, 50, 150, 173
Spinoza, Baruch, 204
spiritualism, 147–50
Stockton, Kathryn Bond, 194
Stant, Charlotte, 209
Star Trek, K/S/ slash fiction and, 145
State University of New York, Sedgwick's
    exhibition at, 72
statistics, Sedgwick's use of, 23
Stein, Gertrude, 145, 150–51n3, 150n2
Stephens, Elizabeth, 197
Sterne, Laurence, 253
Stewart, Susan, 205
stone as archive, 277
straight queer, 191
strategy and methodology, 122
structuralism, structuralists, 10, 168, 170, 171,
    174; Sedgwick and, 166, 173
student, students: of Sedgwick, 195–96, 218,
    240; Sedgwick as, 196
style, Sedgwick's critical, 212–13
stylist, Sedgwick as prose, 16, 20–24, 80, 141,
    206
subject, subjectivity, 18, 44, 61, 65
sublime, Sedgwick and, 73
submission, 159, 163
suicides, 184
Sullivan, Nikki, 194
suminagashi, Sedgwick's practice of, 227
survival, 39, 59, 64, 69, 134; of object, 65, 66

taboo, 103
tact, Sedgwick's, 239
taste, Sedgwick's, 238
teacher, Sedgwick as, 195, 196, 240–41,
    254–55
teaching, Sedgwick on, 217. See also pedagogy:
    Sedgwick and
temporality, Sedgwick and, 113, 114, 116, 118

Tendencies (Sedgwick), 117, 125, 182, 206; "A
    Poem Is Being Written" reprinted in, 192;
    Christmas effect in, 124; "Divinity" in, 192;
    foreword to, 113, 114; images in, 73; intro-
    duction to, 245, 260n2; "Jane Austen and
    the Masturbating Girls" in, 205–6; Kruse
    on, 134–37; mesh metaphor in, 74; preface
    to, 220; queer patience of, 198; queer
    space in, 191; readers of, 253; Sedgwick's
    personal experiences in, 190
tending, tendencies, Sedgwick and, 7, 8, 9
Tennyson, Alfred Lord, 187n10
textile arts, Sedgwick and, 128, 129, 147,
    206–7, 225, 228
textiles, 216; Sedgwick's love for, 213,
    217–19
texts, 8, 10, 98, 100, 133, 195, 197, 213;
    mutability of, 78, 192; queer and, 132, 134;
    Sedgwick's, 58, 80, 198, 245; textiles and,
    74, 77
texture, textures, 73, 77, 166, 168–71, 208, 212,
    225, 230
Thackeray, William Makepeace, *Henry
    Esmond*, 172
theorist, theorists, 210; Sedgwick as, 196,
    207
theory: nature and, 203, 205; Sedgwick and,
    9, 10
therapist, Sedgwick's, 47, 229. *See also* Van
    Wey, Shannon
thick description, 124, 171
Ticknor, Caroline, 148
Tiffany, Daniel, 205
Tomkins, Silvan, 4, 8, 86; affect system of,
    10, 26, 28–29, 171, 196; Sedgwick and, 9,
    145–46
tone shifts, in Sedgwick's writings, 21
touching, Sedgwick's textiles and, 78
*Touching Feeling: Affect, Pedagogy, Performa-
    tivity* (Sedgwick), 76, 78, 84, 127, 134, 167,
    171, 182, 190; "Around the Performative"
    in, 97; chapter openings of, 76; as collec-
    tion, 26; "Interlude, Pedagogic" in, 256;
    introduction to, 22; manicules in, 76, 78;
    "Paranoid Reading and Reparative," 43;
    pedagogy in, 195; queer patience of, 198;
    reparative impulse in, 135–36
tragedy, 64